HISTORY

OF THE

FANNING FAMILY

A GENEALOGICAL RECORD TO 1900 OF THE DESCENDANTS OF EDMUND FANNING,

The Emigrant Ancestor in America, who settled in Connecticut in 1653

To which is prefixed
A General Account of the FANNING FAMILY in Europe
From Norman times, 1197, to the Cromwellian Confiscations, 1652–3

BY WALTER FREDERIC BROOKS

Illustrated with Plates and Maps

In Two Volumes
VOL. II

WORCESTER, MASSACHUSETTS
PRIVATELY PRINTED FOR THE COMPILER
1905

EDMUND FANNING ESQ.R L.L.D.

Lieutenant Governor of his Majesty's Province

OF NOVA SCOTIA,

and late Colonel of the Kings American Regiment of Fo

Reproduced from an Old Miniature

394. **DIANTHUS O ⁷ FANNING**, b. 1812, (*Amos*[6], *Elisha*[5], *David*[4], *Jonathan*[3], *Edmund*[2], *Edmund*[1]) m. at

Lydia Carroll King, dau. of Joshua Carroll (?) and ( ) King, and b. at Westfield, Mass.,

Dr. Dianthus O Fanning, son of Amos and Sarah (Hazen) Fanning, was born at West Springfield, Mass., 19 Nov., 1812. Res. Baltimore, Md., New York City and Brooklyn. His name appears in the New York City Directories, 1847 to 1855–6, but about that time went to South America as a physician, and soon afterward died at Virgin Bay, Central America (it is said — others say Africa) of cholera. His family removed to Brooklyn, where his widow died 14 April, 1896.

Issue:

+766. I. CHARLES[8], b. at

767. II. HENRY[8], b. at . He never married. Relatives state was in the Civil War, and d. in the War. Others say was an assistant paymaster in U.S. Navy, stationed at Brooklyn. The Bureau of Navigation, Navy Dept., Washington, D.C., has no record of a Henry Fanning who ever served as an officer in the Navy.

768. III. FRANCES IDA[8], b. at Baltimore, Md., 18 Feb., 1845; m. at Brooklyn, N.Y. in 1861, John Jay Rennie, a furniture dealer and auctioneer. Res. Detroit, Mich. It is said his grandfather was Sir John Rennie who built the London Bridge. He d. at Brooklyn, N.Y., 13 Aug., 1890. She d. at Brooklyn about 1896.

Issue:

I. WALTER OGDEN HENRY RENNIE, b. 12 May, 1868; m. in 1893 and has issue two ch.

II. FRANCIS JAY RENNIE, b. 23 Dec., 1876; m. Miss Engeman. He d. at Los Angeles, Cal., 21 March, 1904. No issue.

[Other children died in infancy.]

397. **SIDNEY[7] FANNING**, b. 1820, (*Amos[6], Elisha[5], David[4], Jonathan[3], Edmund[2], Edmund[1]*)

m. at Hempstead, N.Y., 12 Oct., 1843,

Phebe Ann Bedell,

dau. of Hiram Kilby and Hannah (De Mott) Bedell, and b. at Hempstead, N.Y., 1 April, 1824.

Sidney Fanning was born at Albany, N.Y., 10 May, 1820. He was a dry goods merchant in New York City, and resided there and at Hempstead, N.Y., where he d. 24 June, 1875. His will dated 11 June, 1875, probated same month, mentions wife Phebe Ann; children, John Bedell, Edward Thompson, Cornelia and Fanny A. Fanning, and Harriet A., wife of Edgar Tappen. Widow res. at Arlington, N.J.

Issue:

769. I. CHARLES SIDNEY[8], b. at Hempstead, N.Y., 14 April, 1845; d. 16 March, 1847.

770. II. HARRIET ADALINE[8], b. at Hempstead, N.Y., 18 Aug., 1848; m. at Hempstead, N.Y., 18 Aug., 1868, Edgar Tappen. Res. East Williston, N.Y. Issue: Frederick Fanning, d. infancy, Minnie, Sidney Fanning, and Willett Underhill Tappen.

771. III. HIRAM HAZEN[8], b. at Hempstead, N.Y., 18 July, 1850; d. 7 June, 1851.

772. IV. FANNY AMELIA[8], b. at New York, N.Y., 6 Jan., 1854; m. at Hempstead, N.Y., 17 Oct., 1877, Frederick William Rouse, merchant. Res. Jersey City. She d. 12 Feb., 1885. Issue: Herbert Edwin Rouse.

+773. V. JOHN BEDELL[8], b. at New York, N.Y., 1 Aug., 1858.

774. VI. RICHARD BOLLES[8], b. at New York, N.Y., 3 July, 1860; d. 13 May, 1861.

+775. VII. EDWARD THOMPSON[8], b. at New York, N.Y., 27 June, 1862.

776. VIII. CORNELIA[8], b. at Hempstead, N.Y., 14 Feb., 1864; m. 1st, Willet McCann, and divorced; m. 2d, a Randel, and res. 23 Madison Ave., Jersey City, N.J.

399. **FREDERIC HAZEN[7] FANNING**, b. 1824, (*Amos*[6], *Elisha*[5], *David*[4], *Jonathan*[3], *Edmund*[2], *Edmund*[1])
m. at

Josephine Carroll,
dau. of John William Henry and Emeline (Mott) Carroll, and b. at

Frederic Hazen Fanning, son of Amos and (Hazen) Fanning, was born at Albany, N.Y., 17 Dec., 1824. He resided in New York City, except between the years 1859 and 1876, when he lived in Utica, N.Y. He was engaged in clerical work most of his life. He was a member of Engine Co. No. 41 of the old New York Volunteer Fire Department.

He d. at St. Luke's Hospital, New York City, 25 March, 1894.

Widow d. at New York City 28 Aug., 1903, and was bur. in Woodlawn Cemetery.

Issue:

+777. I. FREDERICK ANGELO[8], b. at New York, N.Y., 1 Jan., 1853.

+778. II. HENRY CARROLL[8], b. at New York, N.Y., 11 Oct., 1859.

779. III. (Son)[8], b. at ; d. young.

780. IV. (Son)[8], b. at ; d. young.

781. V. (Son)[8], b. at ; d. young.

408. **CHARLES HIRAM[7] FANNING**, b. 1837, (*Hiram*[6], *Elisha*[5], *David*[4], *Jonathan*[3], *Edmund*[2], *Edmund*[1])
m. at Albany, N.Y., in Feb., 1861,
Charlotte Louise McDonald,
dau. of Thomas Charles and Sarah Jane (Lay) McDonald, and b. at Albany, N.Y., 10 May, 1842.

Charles Hiram Fanning, son of Hiram and Mary Ann (Mayell) Fanning, was born at Albany, N.Y., 22 Aug., 1837. He is an editor and publisher, and resides at 131 West 98th St., New York, N.Y.

Issue:

782. I. CORA ESTELLE[8], b. at Albany, N.Y., 19 Dec., 1863; m. at Greenbush, Rensselaer Co., N.Y., 14 May, 1884, Marvin Clark Pinckney. Res. Greenbush, N.Y. He was a railroad conductor, and killed in a railroad wreck near Pittsfield, Mass., in May, 1898. Issue: Frederick Pinckney, b. at Greenbush, N.Y., in 1886.

+783. II. ALBERT BARRINGER[8], b. at Albany, N.Y., 23 July, 1866.

+784. III. EDWARD LAY[8], b. at Albany, N.Y., 10 Aug., 1868.

785. IV. AIMEE BEATRICE[8], b. at Rensselaer, N.Y., 29 Jan., 1870; unm.

786. V. RALPH MAYELL[8], b. at Rensselaer, N.Y., 3 June, 1879; unm., and res. New York, N.Y.

412. JAMES MATTHEW[7] FANNING, b. 1802, (*James*[6], *James*[5], *James*[4], *James*[3], *Thomas*[2], *Edmund*[1])
m. at Moriches, L.I., 15 May, 1839,
Glorianna Smith,
dau. of Josiah and Sally (Brewster) Smith,
and b. at East Moriches, L.I., 7 Sept., 1806.

James Matthew Fanning, son of James and Mary (Howell) Fanning, was born at Aquebogue, L.I., 27 Dec., 1802. He settled at Moriches, L.I., 3 Nov., 1814, at the time his father removed there from Riverhead. At age of seventeen he taught school and then took up surveying. Was commissioned 15 March, 1827, postmaster of Moriches, succeeding his father, who was appointed 19 June, 1815. He continued postmaster fifty years, or until 23 March, 1877, when his nephew, Edmund Hallock, was appointed, and is still filling that position in 1904.

James M. Fanning built a store in 1837 and commenced mercantile business, in which he continued until 1868. He inherited by will from his father in 1848 all his land in Brookhaven, Southampton, and Riverhead.

He d. at Moriches, L.I., 21 April, 1878.

Widow d. at Moriches, 24 Jan., 1880. Both bur. Moriches.

Issue:

787. i. MARY[8], b. at Moriches, L.I., 9 June, 1841; d. 14 April, 1856, in her 15th year.

419. **NATHANIEL[7] FANNING**, b. 1807, (*Nathaniel[6], James[5], James[4], James[3], Thomas[2], Edmund[1]*)
m. at Flanders, L.I., 8 March, 1827,
Abigail Goodale,
dau. of David and Harriet (Fordham) Goodale,
and b. at Flanders, L.I., 18 Nov., 1813.

Nathaniel Fanning was born at Flanders, L.I., 7 March, 1807; was a seaman and farmer; res. Flanders and Southampton, where his wife d. 22 May, 1891; he d. 6 Apr., 1893.

Issue:

788. I. HARRIET LUCRETIA[8], b. at Flanders, L.I., 24 March, 1830; m. 1 Dec., 1844, Daniel Shepard Havens. Res. Flanders and Southampton. She d. 12 Oct., 1868. Issue: Daniel W., Walter W., Anna L., Ullman R., Edward S., and Annie H.

789. II. ABIGAIL MATILDA[8], b. at Flanders, L.I., 24 June, 1832; m. 5 May, 1850, William Jagger. Res. Southampton. Issue: James M., Annetta L., Florence E., William H., Ada M., and Hubert A.

+790. III. JAMES HORACE[8], b. at Flanders, L.I., 9 Dec., 1833.

791. IV. BETSEY[8], b. at Flanders, L.I., 23 May, 1836; d. 1851.

792. V. MARY FRANCES[8], b. at Flanders, L.I., 27 May, 1838; m. 6 Jan., 1857, Thomas Archibald. Res. Southampton. She d. 8 Oct., 1858. He d. 6 Aug., 1878.

793. VI. CHARLOTTE ANN[8], b. at Flanders, L.I., 28 Aug., 1840; m. at New York, N.Y., 18 May, 1858, George Henry Post. Issue: Letitia A. and George L.

+794. VII. NATHANIEL EDMUND[8], b. at Flanders, L.I., 29 Oct., 1842.

+795. VIII. GILBERT[8], b. at Southampton, L.I., 30 June, 1846.

796. IX. EMMA JANE[8], b. at Southampton, L.I., 17 June, 1849; m. 17 Jan., 1883, Daniel Shepard Havens. No issue.

797. X. NANCY ROSALIE[8], b. at Southampton, L.I., 3 Jan., 1851; m. at Smithtown, L.I., 1 Sept., 1869, Daniel Shepard Havens. She d. 10 July, 1881. Issue: Lillian B.

+798. XI. FREDERICK ERNEST[8], b. at Southampton, L.I., 22 June, 1853.

422. **GAMALIEL[7] FANNING**, b. 1813, (*Nathaniel*[6], *James*[5], *James*[4], *James*[3], *Thomas*[2], *Edmund*[1])
m. at Southold, L.I., 14 June, 1834,
Jane Louisa Reeve,
dau. of Silas and Martha (Handy) Reeve,
and b. in Southold Town, L.I., 1 Sept., 1812.

Gamaliel Fanning, son of Nathaniel and Abigail (Terry) Fanning, was born at Flanders, L.I., 21 Jan., 1813; was a farmer, and resided in Branch Co., Mich., where he located in 1840. He was murdered 30 Oct., 1848, by a horse thief while he was in company with an officer and a posse of men, attempting his capture, in Fawn River Town, St. Joseph Co., Mich. The men followed the thief to a piece of woods where he was in hiding. Gamaliel came upon him lying upon the ground by the side of a large log. The thief arose and stabbed Gamaliel; the wounds were fatal, and he died in a few hours. The thief was caught, tried, and imprisoned, but died in prison.

Widow m. 2d, in 1850, David F. Gates, and res. in Bronson, Branch Co., Mich.

Issue:

799. I. BENJAMIN KING[8], b. at East Quogue, L.I., 20 Jan., 1837; d. 30 Jan., 1839.

425. **EDWARD KING CONKLIN[7] FANNING,** b. 1820, (*Nathaniel*[6], *James*[5], *James*[4], *James*[3], *Thomas*[2], *Edmund*[1])

m. 1st, at Baiting Hollow, L.I., 3 April, 1844,
Mary Benjamin,
dau. of Nathan and Elizabeth (Warner) Benjamin,
and b. at Baiting Hollow, L.I., 17 Feb., 1824.

She d. at Flanders, L.I., 24 May, 1850, bur. at Riverhead, L.I.

He m. 2d, at Northville, L.I., 24 March, 1851,
Rachel Ann Luce,
dau. of John and Mary Benjamin (Tuthill) Luce,
and b. at Northville, L.I., 25 Sept., 1833.

Rev. Edward King Conklin Fanning, was born at Flanders, L.I., 30 June, 1820; is a Methodist clergyman, and resides at Lawrence, L.I. Previous to 1853 he resided at or near Flanders, and after that date and until 1885, at the appointments of the Methodist Conference, at various places. Rev. Mr. Fanning is a man of strong character and positive convictions, and his ministry has been characterized by tireless activity, great earnestness of purpose and faithfulness in the discharge of the duties of his pastorate.

Issue by wife Mary:

800. I. MARY ADELINE[8], b. at Flanders, L.I., 4 Sept., 1845; d. 8 Jan., 1846.

801. II. ROSALINE[8], b. at Flanders, L.I., 9 Dec., 1846; d. 5 March, 1847; bur. Riverhead, L.I.

Issue by wife Rachel:

+802. III. EDWARD OLIN[8], b. at Flanders, L.I., 15 Sept., 1852.

803. IV. DAVID ELIAS[8], b. at Cold Spring Harbor, L.I., 15 March 1857; d. 5 Sept., 1857; bur. Riverhead, L.I.

804. v. RACHEL EMMA[8], b. at Cold Spring Harbor, L.I., 15 March, 1857; m. at Brooklyn, N.Y., 5 Nov., 1874, William Sands Stratton Powell, b. at Brooklyn, N.Y., 29 Oct., 1849. Occupation farmer. Res. Springfield, L.I., until 1893. She now res. Lawrence, L.I.

Issue born Springfield, L.I.:

i. MARY EMMA POWELL, b. 27 April, 1877; m. Gilbert Howson Thurston.

ii. ANNE ESTELLE POWELL, b. 1 June, 1883.

iii. ESTHER STRATTON POWELL, b. 2 June, 1890.

805. vi. ANNIE MARETTA[8], b. at Smithtown, L.I., 17 Oct., 1863; m. at Lawrence, L.I., 11 March, 1890, Rev. Samuel Gurney, b. at Long Branch, N.J., 3 Sept., 1860, a Methodist Episcopal clergyman, and res. at Bridgeport, Conn. They res. for a time at Long Island City, N.Y., Parkville, N.Y., and Long Hill, Conn. She d. at New York, N.Y. (in French Hospital), 13 June, 1894, and was bur. at Riverhead, L.I. No issue.

806. vii. HENRIETTA ESTELLE[8], b. at Smithtown, L.I., 29 June, 1865; d. 5 Oct., 1865, a. 3 mos., 6 ds. Bur. Riverhead, L.I.

426. **HARVEY LESTER[7] FANNING**, b. 1822, (*Nathaniel*[6], *James*[5], *James*[4], *James*[3], *Thomas*[2], *Edmund*[1])
m. at Northville, L.I., 29 Oct., 1846,
Mary Anne Tuthill,
dau. of Jehial and Joanna (Hallock) Tuthill,
and b. at Northville, L.I., 28 June, 1828.

Harvey Lester Fanning was born at Flanders, L.I., 13 June, 1822, was a farmer, and resided at Flanders, where he died 1 Dec., 1889. Widow resides Northville, L.I.

Issue:

807. I. JANE LOUISE[8], b. at Flanders, L.I., 23 March, 1849; m. at Mattituck, L.I., 9 March, 1869, John Edward Gildersleeve. Res. Mattituck, where she d. 28 Sept., 1888.

Issue:

I. FANNIE LOUISE GILDERSLEEVE, b. Oct., 1874.
II. JENNIE MAY GILDERSLEEVE, b. deceased.
III. JOHN ANDREW GILDERSLEEVE, b. 2 Feb., 1884.
IV. MARIAN KICKUP GILDERSLEEVE, b. Sept., 1888.

+808. II. HARVEY PIERSON[8], b. at Flanders, L.I., 25 April, 1852.

809. III. MARY ELLA[8], b. at Flanders, L.I., 20 Feb., 1855; m. at Good Ground, L.I., 9 March, 1873, Lewis E. Downs. Res. Atlanticville, L.I. She d. Southold, 14 Dec., 1886.

810. IV. EMILY ANN[8], b. at Flanders, L.I., 9 May, 1859; d. 11 Aug., 1863.

811. V. CARRIE MADISON[8], b. at Flanders, L.I., 3 Jan., 1863; m. at Northville, L.I., 11 Feb., 1890, John Henry Carleton. Res. Riverhead, L.I.

Issue:

I. WILLIAM MARTIN CARLETON, b. 20 Jan., 1892.
II. GEORGE HAVERLAND CARLETON, b. 28 Aug., 1894.
III. MARGRETTA HENDERSON CARLETON, b. 8 July, 1897.

812. VI. ADELINE WOODHULL[8], b. at Flanders, L.I., 26 Feb., 1866; d. 19 Jan., 1877.

+813. VII. JOSHUA TERRY[8], b. at Flanders, L.I., 2 Feb., 1869.

427. **FRANKLIN TERRY[7] FANNING,** b. 1825, (*Nathaniel[6], James[5], James[4], James[3], Thomas[2], Edmund[1]*) m. at Northville, L.I., 17 Dec., 1848,

Sarah Janette Luce,

dau. of George Orrin and Charity Wells (Hallock) Luce, and b. at Northville, L.I., 19 June, 1832.

Dea. Franklin Terry Fanning was born at Flanders, L.I., 14 Feb., 1825, is a farmer, and resides at Centreville, Riverhead Town, L.I. Has been deacon of Congregational Church there since 1875.

Issue:

814. i. ROSALIA JANETTE[8], b. at Southampton, L.I., 7 Nov., 1849; d. 9 Jan., 1850.

+815. ii. GEORGE TERRY[8], b. at Southampton, L.I., 20 March, 1851.

816. iii. HENRIETTA JANETTE[8], b. at Southampton, L.I., 10 July, 1853; m. at Riverhead, L.I., 23 Nov., 1875, Oliver Francis Wells, a farmer, and res. Northville, L.I.

Issue:

i. LELIA ELIZABETH WELLS, b. 2 Dec., 1876.
ii. BLANCHE ETTA WELLS, b. 6 Aug., 1884.
iii. FLORENCE WELLS, b. 15 Dec., 1891.
iv. OLIVER FRANCIS WELLS, b. 5 Jan., 1893.

817. iv. CHARRY EUGENIA[8], b. at Southampton, L.I., 17 July, 1855; d. 25 Oct., 1870.

818. v. CHAUNCEY FRANKLIN[8], b. at Southampton, L.I., 16 Aug., 1857; d. 6 April, 1862.

819. vi. ANNIE LUCE[8], b. at Southampton, L.I., 12 Aug., 1859; d. 13 Sept., 1863.

820. vii. WILLIAM[8], b. at Southampton, L.I., 16 Oct., 1862; d. 19 Oct., 1862.

821. viii. LUCY EMMA[8], b. at Southampton, L.I., 27 June, 1864; d. 11 Oct., 1870.

822. ix. HATTIE LOUISE[8], b. at Riverhead, L.I., 25 June, 1868; unm.

429. **JAMES[7] FANNING**, b. 1815, (*Israel*[6], *James*[5], *James*[4], *James*[3], *Thomas*[2], *Edmund*[1])

m. at New York, N.Y., 29 July, 1848,

Phebe Jenner,

dau. of Solomon and Elizabeth (Hauxhurst) Jenner, and b. at New York, N.Y.

James Fanning, son of Israel and Clarissa (Skidmore) Fanning, was born at Aquebogue, L.I., 28 Oct., 1815. He was for a number of years principal of a collegiate academy in New York City, was very successful, and accumulated quite a property.

He d. in New York, N.Y., 9 March, 1863, and was bur. at Franklinville, L.I. Widow res. in Florida with her third husband.

Issue:

823. I. CLARA LESLIE[8], b. at New York, N.Y., 16 Nov., 1849; d. 13 May, 1854, a. 4 yrs., 10 mos., 15 ds.

824. II. MARY ELIZABETH[8], b. at New York, N.Y., 1 Nov., 1851; m. at , Wallace W. Sharp.

Issue:

I. ETHEL SHARP, b. at

825. III. FANNIE[8], b. at New York, N.Y., ; d.

826. IV. LILLIE SKIDMORE[8], b. at New York, N.Y., 11 Sept., 1855; d. 11 Nov., 1858, a. 2 yrs., 8 mos.

827. V. JAMES ISRAEL[8], b. at New York, N.Y., 12 Aug., 1860; d. 16 Aug., 1862, a. 2 yrs.

To all and Singular *to whom these Presents shall come*
I Sir Arthur Edward Vicars F.S.A.
Ulster King of Arms and Principal Herald of All Ireland, Registrar and Knight Attendant of the Most Illustrious Order of Saint Patrick Do hereby **Certify** and Declare that the **Armorial Bearings** above depicted, that is to say:– Or, a Chevron gules, between three doves proper, for **Crest**, on a wreath of the Colours a Cherub proper, and for **Motto** *In Deo Spes Mea* do of right belong and appertain unto the Descendants of **John Fanning** of Ballingarry in the County of Tipperary, Esquire, with their due and proper differences according to the laws of Arms.

As witness my hand and Seal this *Twentieth* day of *May* in the Sixty first year of the Reign of Our Sovereign Lady Victoria by the Grace of God of the United Kingdom of Great Britain and Ireland, Queen, Defender of the Faith and so forth, and in the year of Our Lord One thousand eight hundred and ninety eight.

Arthur E. Vicars Ulster [redacted] King of Arms of All Ireland

Certificate of Arms registered for James Fanning of Stonehouse, Co. Waterford, Ireland, in 1775, lineally descended from John Fanning of Ballingarry, in 14th century.

431. **EDWARD[7] FANNING**, b. 1820, (*Israel*[6], *James*[5], *James*[4], *James*[3], *Thomas*[2], *Edmund*[1])
m. at Aquebogue, L.I., 24 Dec., 1850,
Alma Elizabeth Wells,
dau. of Daniel Terry and Harriet (Homan) Wells,
and b. at Aquebogue, L.I., 10 Sept., 1829.

Edward Fanning, son of Israel and Clarissa (Skidmore) Fanning, was born at Aquebogue, L.I., 15 Feb., 1820, was a farmer, and res. at Franklinville, L.I., on land inherited from his father Israel, by will in 1874, which he was occupying at that time.

His wife d. at Franklinville, now Laurel, L.I., 3 Oct., 1879.

He d. at Franklinville, L.I., 13 Sept., 1894.

Issue:

828. i. WILLIS IRVING[8], b. at Franklinville, L.I., 1 Feb., 1853; d. 17 April, 1857.

829. ii. MARY CATHERINE[8], b. at Franklinville, L.I., 1 June, 1855; d. 17 April, 1857.

+830. iii. WILLIS NEWTON[8], b. at Franklinville, L.I., 15 July, 1858.

831. iv. HARRIET LINWOOD[8], b. at Franklinville, L.I., 20 May, 1864; unm. in 1904.

832. v. FRANCES PURE[8], b. at Franklinville, L.I., 8 Oct., 1868; unm. in 1904.

833. vi. FLORENCE MARIA[8], b. at Franklinville, L.I., 2 Feb., 1876; unm. in 1904.

434. **SIMEON BENJAMIN[7] FANNING**, b. 1827, (*Israel*[6], *James*[5], *James*[4], *James*[3], *Thomas*[2], *Edmund*[1])
m. at Franklinville (now Laurel), L.I., 11 June, 1856,

Eleanor Emanuel Sayre,

dau. of John Nathan and Charlotte Jane (Emanuel) Sayre, and b. at New York City, 13 March, 1835.

Simeon Benjamin Fanning, son of Israel and Clarissa (Skidmore) Fanning, was born at Franklinville, L.I., 31 Dec., 1827 (also given 1828), was a farmer, and resided on the old homestead at Franklinville, L.I. (now Laurel), that his father came into possession of in 1826. The farm contains about 580 acres extending from Long Island Sound to the Great Peconic Bay, and is 3½ miles in length and 80 rods in width.

He d. at Laurel, L.I., 26 March, 1900, in his 72d year. Widow res. at Laurel.

Issue:

834. I. CHARLOTTE EMANUEL[8], b. at Franklinville, L.I., 5 March, 1860; m. at Franklinville, L.I., in 1881, Albert Etheridge Hawkins of Jamesport, L.I. He is a farmer. They res. at Jamesport, and have

Issue:

I. HARRY FANNING HAWKINS, b. at Franklinville, L.I., 1 June, 1882.

II. ELEANOR EMANUEL HAWKINS, b. at Jamesport, L.I., 1 March, 1885.

835. II. CLARA AUGUSTA[8], b. at Franklinville, L.I., 8 April, 1863; unm.

836. III. ISRAEL SAYRE[8], b. at Franklinville, L.I., 24 March, 1874.

436. **JOSEPH ADDISON**[7] **FANNING**, b. 1822, (*Joshua*[6], *James*[5], *James*[4], *James*[3], *Thomas*[2], *Edmund*[1])
m. at Philadelphia, Penn., 19 Aug., 1851,
Elizabeth Jane Tuthill,
dau. of James and Polly (Youngs) Tuthill,
and b. at Aquebogue, L.I., 7 Aug., 1827.

Joseph Addison Fanning, son of Dr. Joshua and Elma (Tuthill) Fanning, was born at Sag Harbor, L.I., 22 Aug., 1822. He fitted for college at Franklinville Academy, L.I., and entered Yale University, class of 1841, but left in his sophomore year. He then accepted a clerical position in Greenport, L.I., and afterward in New York City, and in 1844 removed to Augusta, Ga. He later engaged in mercantile business in Nashville, Tenn., St. Louis, Mo., and New Orleans, La. In 1873 he removed to Planchville, La. Feb. 2, 1875, he lost everything by a terrible hurricane, he and his wife barely escaping with their lives. He was assistant postmaster at Planchville, and his wife postmistress for several years. His wife taught private school in Planchville for over 20 years.

He d. at his residence in Planchville, La., 13 March, 1894, and his body brought to Jamesport, L.I., for interment.

Issue:

837. I. Mary Elma[8], b. at Philadelphia, Penn., 28 Sept., 1854; d. at St. Louis, Mo., 8 Nov., 1861.

441. **JOHN[7] FANNING**, b. 1811, (*John*[6], *John*[5], *James*[4], *James*[3], *Thomas*[2], *Edmund*[1])

m. at Baiting Hollow, L.I., 14 Sept., 1833,

Jemima Ann Benjamin,

dau. of John and Hannah (Benjamin) Benjamin, and b. at Baiting Hollow, L.I., 28 Feb., 1817.

Hannah Benjamin is said to have been daughter of Richard and Nancy (Fanning) Benjamin (?).

John Fanning was born at Flanders, L.I., 28 Feb., 1811, was a farmer, and res. at Middle Road, L.I., where he died 19 Nov., 1875, aged 64 years.

Widow d. at Southampton, L.I., 25 Sept., 1893, a. 76 yrs. Both bur. at Aquebogue, L.I.

Issue:

+838. I. JOHN WARREN[8], b. at Middle Road, L.I., 30 Aug., 1841.

839. II. ELMA ANNA[8], b. at Middle Road, L.I., in April, 1844; d. 23 Feb., 1857, a. 12 yrs. Bur. Aquebogue.

+840. III. EUGENE BOGART[8], b. at Middle Road, L.I., 26 Sept., 1846.

841. IV. HANNAH ELIZABETH[8], b. at Middle Road, L.I., 8 June, 1850; m. at Middle Road, 28 Nov., 1868, John Henry Enstine, a farmer, and res. Southampton, L.I.

Issue born Southampton:

I. THOMAS REEVES ENSTINE, b. 24 Dec., 1873.

II. BLANCHE ENSTINE, b. 14 July, 1879.

III. ORA ANNA ENSTINE, b. 1 Dec., 1883.

IV. JOHN HENRY ENSTINE, b. 10 March, 1886.

V. SIMON MILTON PERICO ENSTINE, b. 26 Nov., 1888.

VI. ROSE MYRTLE ENSTINE, b. 18 Feb., 1891.

VII. RALPH FANNING ENSTINE, b. 27 July, 1893.

(Three ch. d. young.)

+842. V. WILLIAM RICHARD[8], b. at Middle Road, L.I., 22 July, 1858.

446. **MOSES^{7} FANNING,** b. 1819, (*John^{6}, John^{5}, James^{4}, James^{3}, Thomas^{2}, Edmund^{1}*)
m. at Northville, L.I., 12 March, 1846,
Hannah Catharine Reeve,
dau. of Nathan and Abigail (Wells) Reeve,
and b. at Northville, L.I., 26 March, 1828.

Moses Fanning, son of John and Hannah (Sayre) Fanning, was born at Flanders, L.I., 5 Nov., 1819, was a farmer, and resided at Middle Road, Riverhead town, L.I., where his wife died 17 July, 1872.

He d. at Middle Road, L.I., 13 June, 1900. Bur. at Riverhead, L.I.

Issue:

843. I. HANNAH JANE^{8}, b. at Flanders, L.I., 25 April, 1847; d. at Riverhead, 12 May, 1857.

844. II. (Infant^{8}), b. at Flanders, L.I., 5 June, 1849.

+845. III. MOSES EUGENE^{8}, b. at Flanders, L.I., 9 Feb., 1851.

846. IV. JOHN LOCKWOOD^{8}, b. at Middle Road, L.I., 11 Sept., 1853; d. at Middle Road, 26 April, 1857.

847. V. (Infant^{8}), b. at Middle Road, L.I., about 1855; d. y'ng.

848. VI. KATHARINE JANE^{8}, b. at Middle Road, L.I., 1 Dec., 1857; m. at Middle Road, 31 Dec., 1878, Henry Howell, a farmer. Res. Middle Road, where she d. 13 March, 1897. Issue: Arthur Josiah, b. 25 Sept., 1884, and Alice Louise Howell, b. 10 April, 1893.

+849. VII. JOHN REEVE^{8}, b. at Middle Road, L.I., 25 June, 1860.

850. VIII. LOUISA MARY,^{8} b. at Middle Road, L.I., 1 March, 1862; m. at Middle Road, L.I., 10 April, 1889, Ira Amasa Gordon, a farmer. Res. Middle Road. No issue.

851. IX. (Infant^{8}), b. at Middle Road, L.I., about 1865. } twins;
852. X. (Infant^{8}), b. at Middle Road, L.I., about 1865. } d. y'ng.

455. **PETER WELLS[7] FANNING**, b. 1820, (*Peter*[6], *John*[5], *James*[4], *James*[3], *Thomas*[2], *Edmund*[1])
m. at Good Ground, L.I., 9 April, 1845,
Emeline Squires,
dau. of Nicholas and Sally (Smith) Squires,
and b. at Good Ground, L.I., 18 April, 1825.

Capt. Peter Wells Fanning, known as "Wells" Fanning, son of Peter and Mercy (Bishop) Fanning, was born at Flanders, L.I., 2 April, 1820, was a sailor, and resided at Flanders, where he died, 23 July, 1852; buried at Flanders, L.I. (g.s.). After his death his widow married, 14 Oct., 1864, Rev. Sylvester Downs, and resided at East Quogue, L.I. He died, and Emeline married 3d, 12 March, 1890, Lorenzo Dow Bellows, and resided at Good Ground, L.I., where she died 29 Jan., 1899. Buried at Flanders, L.I. (g.s.).

Issue:

853. I. EMMA JANE[8], b. at Flanders, L.I., 4 Feb., 1846; m. at Southampton, L.I., 30 Nov., 1866, William Foster Halsey, and res. at Quogue, L.I.

Issue:

I. WILLIAM FANNING HALSEY, b. at East Quogue, L.I., 29 Sept., 1878.

854. II. ALETHIA MARIA[8], b. at Flanders, L.I., 8 Aug., 1849; m. at Flanders, L.I., 20 Oct., 1866, Orange Terry[7] Fanning (No. 484), and res. at East Quogue, L.I., where she d. 3 March, 1872. Issue: one ch. who d. in infancy. (See data under Orange Terry[7] Fanning, No. 484.)

456. **FOSTER ROE[7] FANNING**, b. 1828, (*Peter*[6], *John*[5], *James*[4], *James*[3], *Thomas*[2], *Edmund*[1])
m. at Bethany, Wayne Co., Penn., 17 March, 1851,
Eunice Kimball Davison,
dau. of John Kimball and Mary Gaylord (Burr) Davison, and b. at Dyberry, Wayne Co., Penn., 3 Jan., 1835.

Foster Roe Fanning was born at Flanders, L.I., 5 Oct., 1828, was a farmer, and resided at New Suffolk, L.I., where he died 19 Dec., 1896.

Issue:

855. I. MARY FOSTER[8], b. at New Suffolk, L.I., 21 March, 1852; d. 9 Dec., 1860, a. 8 yrs.

856. II. ELIZABETH BURR[8], b. at New Suffolk, L.I., 27 Oct., 1854; d. 11 Nov., 1860, a. 6 yrs.

857. III. HARRIET ROE[8], b. at New Suffolk, L.I., 17 April, 1857; m. at New Suffolk, L.I., in April, 1889, Benjamin Rutherford Fitz, an artist, and res. in N.Y. He was educated in his art at Munich, Germany. D. at Peconic, L.I., 27 Dec., 1891. Bur. at Southold, L.I. Widow res. New Suffolk.

858. IV. MARY BURR[8], b. at New Suffolk, L.I., 17 Jan., 1862; m. at New Suffolk, L.I., 6 Nov., 1889, William Hallock Corwin, b. 20 March, 1865, a carpenter, and res. at New Suffolk, L.I. Issue: Henry Foster Corwin, b. at New Suffolk, L.I., 16 Nov., 1891.

+859. V. PETER WELLS[8], b. at New Suffolk, L.I., 17 Aug., 1864.

+860. VI. JOHN FOSTER[8], b. at New Suffolk, L.I., 11 Sept., 1866.

+861. VII. STUART LINCOLN[8], b. at New Suffolk, L.I., 5 Oct., 1869.

862. VIII. MABEL WEST[8], b. at New Suffolk, L.I., 9 March, 1874, unm. 1904.

863. IX. ELIZABETH WOOLEY[8], b. at New Suffolk, L.I., 19 Aug., 1876; unm. 1904.

458. **DANIEL WARNER⁷ FANNING**, b. 1821, (*James*[6], *John*[5], *James*[4], *James*[3], *Thomas*[2], *Edmund*[1])
m. at Riverhead, L.I., 19 Sept., 1845,
Emily Jane Robinson,
dau. of Samuel and Jane (Hildreth) Robinson,
and b. at Red Creek, Suffolk Co., L.I., 3 Nov., 1823.

Daniel Warner Fanning, son of James and Clarissa (Fournier) Fanning, was born at Flanders, L.I., 4 Dec., 1821, and resides at Good Ground, Suffolk Co., L.I. He is engaged in farming and fishing at the present time. In his younger days he followed the sea in the whaling business.

Issue:

864. I. Henry Martin[8], b. at Good Ground, L.I., 8 Nov., 1849; d. 15 April, 1852.

+865. II. Oliver[8], b. at Good Ground, L.I., 1 Aug., 1851.

+866. III. Benjamin Luther[8], b. at Good Ground, L.I., 28 Nov., 1856.

+867. IV. Daniel[8], b. at Good Ground, L.I., 8 May, 1861.

+868. V. Samuel Edmund[8], b. at Good Ground, L.I., 15 June, 1863.

869. VI. (Son)[8], not named, b. at Good Ground, L.I., 15 March, 1865; d. same day.

462. **HARLAN PAGE[7] FANNING**, b. 1837, (*James*[6], *John*[5], *James*[4], *James*[3], *Thomas*[2], *Edmund*[1])
m. at Good Ground, L.I., 31 Dec., 1868,
Lucretia Conklin,
dau. of Ira Watson and Lucretia Jane (Corwin) Conklin, and b. at Setauket, L.I., 7 Feb., 1850.

Harlan Page Fanning was born at Good Ground, L.I., 19 Oct., 1837, was a fruit and vegetable raiser, and resided at Good Ground.

She d. at Middletown, N.Y., 28 April, 1888, bur. at Good Ground.

He d. at Good Ground, L.I., 22 May, 1900.

Issue:

870. I. NELLIE MATILDA[8], b. at Good Ground, L.I., 30 March, 1870; m. at Good Ground, 15 March, 1889, Edward Francis Filer, a house builder, and res. at East Hampton, L.I.

Issue:

I. ALICE FILER, b. 12 March, 1890.
II. HARLAN FRANCIS FILER, b. 27 March, 1894.

871. II. WILLIAM PAGE[8], b. at Good Ground, L.I., 31 Oct., 1872. He served in the Spanish-American War, enlisting in May, 1898, at Newport News, Va., in Company D, 4th Virginia Regt.; was in Gen. Lee's Corps, and participated in raising the flag over Morro Castle, Havana, Cuba, 1 Jan., 1899. Unm.

872. III. LINA ARLETTA[8], b. at Good Ground, L.I., 26 Nov., 1875; m. at Good Ground, 16 Dec., 1894, Whitman Vail Randall. Res. East Moriches, L.I.

Issue:

I. CARLTON EARL RANDALL, b. 18 Oct., 1895.
II. NOUNA FANNING RANDALL, b. 8 Dec., 1896.
III. IDA ARLETTA RANDALL, b. 12 Jan., 1899.

873. IV. HARLAN ELWOOD[8], b. at Good Ground, L.I., 29 Jan., 1884.

465. **SAMUEL[7] FANNING**, b. 1818, (*Samuel*[6], *John*[5], *James*[4], *James*[3], *Thomas*[2], *Edmund*[1])
m. at New York, N.Y., in Dec., 1843,
Arletta Jane Terry,
dau. of William and Keturah (Corwin) Terry,
and b. at Aquebogue, L.I., 7 April, 1823.

Samuel Fanning was born at Aquebogue, L.I., in June, 1818. He kept a general store at Jamesport, L.I., where he resided and where he died 16 April, 1857.

Widow d. at Bridgeport, Conn., 30 March, 1892. Both bur. Jamesport.

Issue:

874. I. SAMUEL DE FOREST[8], b. at Jamesport, L.I., 23 Jan., 1845; d. 4 Sept., 1865, a. 20 yrs., 8 mos.; unm.

875. II. CHARLOTTE[8], b. at Jamesport, L.I., 8 Sept., 1846; m. at Jamesport, 25 Dec., 1867, William Pearson Jessup, a carpenter and builder. He served in Civil War '62 to '65. Res. Bridgeport, Conn., where she d. 12 April, 1899.

Issue born at Bridgeport, Conn.:

I. EVERETT ELWOOD JESSUP, b. 15 Feb., 1877.
II. INEZ ISADORE JESSUP, b. 3 Dec., 1880.
III. EDITH MITCHELL JESSUP, b. 7 Oct., 1882.
IV. GILBERT HARVEY JESSUP, b. 26 Nov., 1890.
(Three ch. d. in infancy.)

+876. III. CHARLES GRAHAM[8], b. at Jamesport, L.I., 17 April, 1848.

877. IV. INEZ[8], b. at Jamesport, L.I., 1 April, 1850; m. at Riverhead, L.I., 8 Aug., 1871, Frederick Bridges Smith. Res. Newark, N.J., where he d. 8 Feb., 1895.

Issue:

I. CHARLOTTE FANNING SMITH, b. 6 May, 1872.
II. ELIZABETH LAWRENCE SMITH, b. 26 May, 1882.
(Two ch. d. in infancy.)

466. GILBERT DENNISTON[7] FANNING, b. 1824,
(*Samuel[6], John[5], James[4], James[3], Thomas[2], Edmund[1]*)
m. at Cutchogue, L.I., 25 Jan., 1853,
Rebecca Jane Tuthill,
dau. of Captain Silas and Rebecca (Wells) Tuthill,
and b. at Cutchogue, L.I., 17 Jan., 1831.

Gilbert Denniston Fanning (named after a Methodist minister, Rev. Mr. Denniston) was born at Jamesport, L.I., 24 Feb., 1824. Graduate Franklinville Academy. Was a mariner, and resided with his brother Samuel at Jamesport several years. Mate on sloop "Suffolk" sailing between New York and New Suffolk, under Capt. Silas Tuthill (his grandfather). Settled at New Suffolk about 1851–2, where he died 5 Nov., 1858. Bur. at Cutchogue. His will, dated 15 Oct., 1858, proved 4 Jan., 1859, recorded at Riverhead, mentions dau. Georgiana Wells, dau. Lydia Rebecca Gilbert, and wife Rebecca Jane Fanning.

Widow res. at Mattituck, L.I., with her dau. Lydia.

Issue:

878. I. George Wells[8], b. at New Suffolk, L.I., 16 Nov., 1853; d. 21 Sept., 1855.

879. II. Georgiana Wells[8], b. at New Suffolk, L.I., 24 Dec., 1855; d. at Brooklyn, L.I., 2 May, 1875. Bur. at Cutchogue, L.I.

880. III. Lydia Gilbert[8], b. at New Suffolk, L.I., 15 June, 1855; m. at Mattituck, L.I., 20 April, 1881, William S. Du Bois. Res. at Mattituck, L.I.

Issue:

I. George Smith Fanning Du Bois, b. at Mattituck, L.I., 21 March, 1883.

468. **CHARLES WESLEY[7] FANNING**, b. 1829, (*Samuel*[6], *John*[5], *James*[4], *James*[3], *Thomas*[2], *Edmund*[1])
m. at Cutchogue, L.I., 11 Jan., 1851,
Miriam Aldrich,
dau. of Hiram and Miriam (Brown) Aldrich,
and b. at Jamesport, L.I., 11 April, 1833.

Charles Wesley Fanning was born at Jamesport, L.I., 8 March, 1829, graduated at Franklinville Academy, and became a mariner and captain of a schooner. Resided at New Suffolk, L.I., where he died 11 April, 1868. Bur. at Jamesport.

Issue:

881. I. CHARLES[8], b. at New Suffolk, L.I., 1 Feb., 1852; d. unm. at Jamesport, L.I., 1 Feb., 1880.

882. II. IDA[8], b. at New Suffolk, L.I., 28 Dec., 1854; m. at , Parker Moore. Res. Greenport, L.I. (No record obtainable.)

883. III. ALICE[8], b. at New Suffolk, L.I., 2 June, 1857; m. at , Eugene Wells. Res. Oakland, Cal. (No record obtainable.)

884. IV. MINNIE[8], b. at New Suffolk, L.I., 5 April, 1860; m. at Cutchogue, L.I., 28 July, 1886, Frank Hallock. Res. South Jamesport, L.I. Issue: Lucy Fanning, Edith Grant, and Vera Hallock.

885. V. JENNIE BLANCHE[8], b. at New Suffolk, L.I., 11 July, 1862; d. at Jamesport, L.I., 26 Jan., 1867.

886. VI. LUCY[8], b. at New Suffolk, L.I., 1 Aug., 1864; m. at New Suffolk, 30 July, 1887, Andrew Jackson Case, á grocer. Res. Peconic, L.I. Issue, all b. at Peconic: S. Spencer, Minnie Fanning, Leslie Benjamin, and Walter Curtis Case.

475. **EDGAR BENJAMIN[7] FANNING**, b. 1838, (*Abraham*[6], *John*[5], *James*[4], *James*[3], *Thomas*[2], *Edmund*[1])
m. at Riverhead, L.I., 26 Dec., 1865,
Mary Adelia Robinson,
dau. of Richard Davison and Polly (Sweezy) Robinson, and b. at Middle Road, L.I., 21 Oct., 1840.

Edgar Benjamin Fanning was born at Aquebogue, L.I., 19 April, 1838, is a farmer, and resides at Aquebogue, L.I.

Issue:

887. I. ELECTA ADELIA[8], b. at Middle Road, L.I., 9 or 10 Jan., 1867; m. at Middle Road, L.I., 12 May, 1888, Benjamin Ellsworth Goodale, and res. at Sound Ave., Riverhead, L. I. He is engaged in farming.

Issue:

I. CONSTANCE ELIZABETH GOODALE, b. 20 June, 1889.
II. ROSWELL FANNING GOODALE, b. 29 Aug., 1891.
III. ROBINSON JESSE GOODALE, b. 9 Jan., 1894.
IV. BENJAMIN WARREN GOODALE, b. 14 Feb., 1896; died June, 1899.
V. EDGAR CLEMENT GOODALE, b. 12 Jan., 1898.

888. II. ANNIE HALLOCK[8], b. at Middle Road, L.I., 1 Dec., 1875; m. at Middle Road, L.I., 24 Oct., 1894, Clarence Everett Salmon, b. 4 April, 1870. They res. at Aquebogue, L.I., where he is engaged in farming.

Issue:

I. EVELYN ADELIA SALMON, b. 22 Oct., 1895.
II. EMMA JERUSHA SALMON, b. 18 Jan., 1898.
III. GLADYS ENID SALMON, b. 21 June, 1900.

476. **ELBERT ALONZO[7] FANNING**, b. 1840, (*Abraham[6], John[5], James[4], James[3], Thomas[2], Edmund[1]*)
m. at Aquebogue, L.I., 2 March, 1875,
Sarah Jane Tuthill,
dau. of Nathan King and Jane Marilla (Salmon) Tuthill, and b. at Orient, L.I., 16 March, 1848.

Elbert Alonzo Fanning, son of Abraham and Martha Hallock (Luce) Fanning, and in the seventh generation in direct line from Edmund Fanning, the ancestor in America who settled in Conn. about the year 1653, was born at Northville, L.I., 14 Jan., 1840. He is a great-great-grandson of Capt. James and Hannah (Smith) Fanning, the first of the name on Long Island, and from whom nearly, if not all, the Fannings on Long Island are descended. He is a carpenter, contractor, and builder, and res. at Sound Ave. (formerly called Northville), Riverhead, L.I. His farm is known as Cliff Lee Farm.

Issue:

889. I. EDITH BERNICE[8], b. at Northville (now called Sound Ave.), Riverhead Town, L.I., 29 May, 1876.
890. II. IRWIN CLIFTON[8], b. at Northville, L.I., 25 March, 1880.
891. III. L LEON[8], b. at Northville, L.I., 22 Feb., 1887.
892. IV. VERA VIVIAN[8], b. at Northville, L.I., 25 March, 1891.

482. **WESLEY^7 FANNING**, b. 1839, (*Jacob^6, John^5, James^4, James^3, Thomas^2, Edmund^1*)

m. 1st at Manistee, Mich., 31 July, 1870,

Mrs. Mary Jane (Powell) Hammond,

dau. of David and Lydia (Montgomery) Powell, and wid. of John Hammond, and b. in Jefferson Co., N.Y., 24 Sept., 1834. She was a wid. with three ch.: Lulu C., Albert J., and Cora G. Hammond. She d. at San Jose, Cal., 25 Jan., 1886.

He m. 2d at Chicago, Ill., 4 Feb., 1889,

May Hess,

dau. of Charles and Eliza (Canfield) Hess, and b. at Clinton, Clinton Co., Ia., 28 March, 1851.

Wesley Fanning was born at East Quogue, L.I., 8 March 1839. Early in life followed farming and fishing; when of age he left home for New York City, where he embarked on board the bark "William Wilson," bound for Mexico. After following a sailor's life for a year or two, he enlisted as a volunteer in the 8th N.Y. Heavy Artillery in the last years of the Civil War. Honorably discharged at close of war he went to Wisconsin about 1867, then Michigan, and engaged in mechanical and milling business, where he married his 1st wife. After several years he went to Salina, Cal., and then to San Jose, Santa Clara Co., Cal. He came East in 1889 to visit his brother and three sisters on Long Island, and on his return West married in Chicago his 2d wife. He then returned to San Jose, Cal. He later bought 600 acres of land in Santa Cruz Co., near Ben Lomond; then lived four years in the city of Santa Cruz and improved his mountain farm, and then moved on to it, where he was residing in 1901, engaged in farming and milling.

Issue:

893. I. ROSENA EMILY^8, b. at Manistee, Mich., 15 Feb., 1871; d. 8 June, 1874.

894. II. MARY ALETHIA^8, b. at Manistee, Mich., 13 April, 1873; d. 18 Aug., 1873.

484. **ORANGE TERRY[7] FANNING,** b. 1844, (*Jacob*[6], *John*[5], *James*[4], *James*[3], *Thomas*[2], *Edmund*[1])
m. 1st at Flanders, L.I., 20 Oct., 1866,
Alethia Maria Fanning,
(No. 854), dau. of Peter Wells[7] and Emeline (Squires) Fanning,
and b. at Flanders, L.I., 8 Aug., 1849.
She d. at East Quogue, L.I., 3 March, 1872, a. 22 yrs.
He m. 2d at Port Jefferson, L.I., 28 Oct., 1880,
Mary Jennett Ritch,
dau. of Thomas Jefferson and Mary (Davis) Ritch,
and b. at Port Jefferson, L.I., 21 Jan., 1853.

Orange Terry Fanning was born at East Quogue, L.I., 9 Oct., 1844. He is a descendant of a Fanning on both his father's and mother's side. Paternally he is in the seventh generation, maternally the eighth. His mother was daughter of Nathaniel and Abigail (Terry) Fanning (see No.419). Nathaniel was own cousin to his father, Jacob Fanning.

Mr. Fanning farmed it at East Quogue until 1870, then removed to Michigan. Being discontented, he returned East, and relocated at Port Jefferson, L.I., in 1873, and started a general store, first as Overton & Fanning, then Fanning & Brewster, and in 1888, O. T. Fanning & Co., the present firm.

Mr. Fanning is prominent in town affairs, was trustee and overseer of poor, 1886–7; town collector, 1888; county clerk of Suffolk County 6 years, 1888 to 1894; now president of Peconic Bay Steamboat Co., president First National Bank, Port Jefferson, etc. Res. Port Jefferson, L.I.

Issue by wife Alethia Maria:

895. I. (Child)[8], b.; d. in infancy.

Issue by wife Mary Jennett:

896. II. Martin Ritch[8], b. at Port Jefferson, L.I., 18 March, 1884; d. 16 Dec., 1886.

897. III. Thomas Ritch[8], b. at Port Jefferson, L.I., 17 Mar., 1888.

493. **WILLIAM AUGUSTUS[7] FANNING**, b. 1810,
(*William*[6], *Phineas*[5], *Phineas*[4], *James*[3], *Thomas*[2], *Edmund*[1])
m. 1st at Sandy Hill, Washington Co., N.Y.,
Mary Danvers,
dau. of Matthew and Mary (Steele) Danvers,
and b. at Sandy Hill, N.Y.
She d. at Poughkeepsie, N.Y., in 1834.
He m. 2d at Poughkeepsie, N.Y., 23 July, 1837,
Kezia Coffin[7] Fanning,
dau. of Robert Barclay[6] (No. 234) and Phebe (Swain) Fanning, and b. at Poughkeepsie, N.Y., 26 Oct., 1819.

William Augustus Fanning was born at Brooklyn, N.Y., 21 March, 1810, was a rope manufacturer, and resided at Poughkeepsie, N.Y. Was county clerk of Dutchess Co., N.Y., two terms. He died at Poughkeepsie, N.Y., 14 Jan., 1887. Widow died at Poughkeepsie, 7 Aug., 1895.

Issue by wife Mary:

898. I. ISABELLA[8], b. at Sandy Hill, N.Y., 8 Dec., 1832; d. at Poughkeepsie, N.Y., 10 April, 1876, a. 42; unm.

Issue by wife Kezia:

899. II. EMILIE WOOD[8], b. at Poughkeepsie, N.Y., 14 May, 1838; m. at Poughkeepsie, 1 Oct., 1866, Henry Roland Howard. Res. Poughkeepsie.

Issue:

1. FRANK BARNARD HOWARD, b. 9 Dec., 1871.
(One ch. d. in infancy.)

900. III. WILLIAM SCHENCK[8], b. at Poughkeepsie, N.Y., in Sept., 1839; d. 6 March, 1844.

901. IV. ROBERT BARCLAY[8], b. at Poughkeepsie, N.Y., 23 Dec., 1840; d. 18 Nov., 1862; unm.; a promising lawyer.

+902. V. AUGUSTUS SCHENCK[8], b. at Poughkeepsie, N.Y., 26 Nov., 1844.

903. VI. EDMUND[8], b. at Poughkeepsie, N.Y., 15 Aug., 1848; d. unm.

904. VII. WALTER[8], b. at Poughkeepsie, N.Y., 9 Oct., 1854; d. '68.

905. VIII. PERRY[8], b. at Poughkeepsie, N.Y., in 1858; d. unm.

496. **THOMAS CHAPMAN[7] FANNING**, b. 1818, (*William*[6], *Phineas*[5], *Phineas*[4], *James*[3], *Thomas*[2], *Edmund*[1])
m. at New Paltz, Ulster Co., N.Y., 10 Oct., 1839,
Elizabeth Lee,
dau. of Samuel and Beulah (Harrison) Lee,
and b. at Poughkeepsie, N.Y., 5 July, 1820.

Thomas Chapman Fanning was born at Brooklyn, N.Y., 19 Dec., 1818, and like his father was engaged for many years in rope manufacturing, and resided at Poughkeepsie, N.Y. He afterward was a hotel keeper in the South, and a professor of dancing for 40 years, being a charter member of the Society of American Professors of Dancing, the first organization of the kind.

He d. in New York City, 26 June, 1897, and is bur. at Poughkeepsie, N.Y. Widow res. New Paltz, N.Y.

Issue:

906. I. WILLIAM AUGUSTUS[8], b. at Newburgh, N.Y., in 1841; d. a. 1 yr.

907. II. JOSEPHINE[8], b. at Newburgh, N.Y., 23 Sept., 1842; m. at Poughkeepsie, N.Y., 10 Sept., 1868, Rev. Joseph Emmanuel Lindholm, a Protestant Episcopal clergyman, b. Gottenburg, Sweden, 6 March, 1843. Res. New Paltz, N.Y. He is deceased.

Issue:

I. CARRIE LOUISE LINDHOLM, b. 5 July, 1869; m. 12 Feb., 1896, James J. Fitzgerald, a lawyer. Mem. State Legis. 1900–1–2. Res. New York, N.Y.

II. ANNA CHANDLER LINDHOLM, b. 19 Nov., 1870; m. 19 Jan., 1892, Elijah Selden Wightman. Res. Norwich, Conn.

III. HERBERT ALFRED LINDHOLM, b. 9 Nov., 1874.

IV. MARY FAY LINDHOLM, b. 12 April, 1883.

505. **JAMES NATHANIEL[7] FANNING**, b. 1819, (*Barclay P.*[6], *Nathaniel*[5], *Phineas*[4], *James*[3], *Thomas*[2], *Edmund*[1])

m. at Aquebogue, L.I., 10 Feb., 1842,

Mary Corwin Wells,

dau. of Eurystheus Howell and Mary (Corwin) Wells, and b. at Aquebogue, L.I., 25 Jan., 1824.

James Nathaniel Fanning was born in New York, N.Y., 26 Jan., 1819. He resided at New York and at Aquebogue, L.I.

He d. at New York, N.Y., 26 Feb., 1854. Bur. Evergreen Cemetery, L.I.

She d. at New York, N.Y., 10 April, 1894. Bur. Aquebogue, L.I.

Issue:

908. I. MARY CELESTE[8], b. at Aquebogue, L.I., 21 Sept., 1843 m. at Aquebogue, L.I., 3 June, 1869, Robert Joseph Black of New York and born there 2 Dec., 1838. Supt. of Dodd's Express Company. Res. at 1461 Washington Ave., N.Y.

Issue:

I. FLORENCE ESTELLE BLACK, b. 27 Jan., 1874.

909. II. ANNA ROSALIA[8], b. at Aquebogue, L.I., 31 Oct., 1846; m. at Aquebogue, L.I., 22 Nov., 1866, Henry Achilles Elliott, a printer, b. in New York, N.Y., in 1840. He d. in New York, 27 March, 1878, and is bur. at Clinton, Conn. She d. at New York, 2 April, 1881, and is bur. at Aquebogue, L.I.

Issue:

I. HARRY CLINTON ELLIOTT, b. at New York, N.Y., 6 June, 1869; m. at New York, 17 Dec., 1890, Ella May McCord. Res. Brooklyn, N.Y., and has issue, two sons.

511. **PHINEAS[7] FANNING**, b. 1818, (*Daniel Wells[6], Nathaniel[5], Phineas[4], James[3], Thomas[2], Edmund[1]*)
m. at Southold, L.I., 5 Nov., 1843,
Christiana Wines,
dau. of William and Bethia (Howell) Wines,
and b. at Mattituck, L.I., 26 Feb., 1813.

Phineas Fanning was born at Aquebogue, L.I., 14 March, 1818. He learned the trade of a shoemaker. The last forty years of his life he followed farming, and for over fifty years resided in Southold, L.I. He was in the Insane Hospital at Flatbush, L.I., for some time previous to his death, which occurred 22 May, 1899. Bur. at Southold.

She d. at Greenport, L.I., 17 Feb., 1899, and is bur. at Southold, L.I., in the cemetery of the Presbyterian Church.

Issue:

910. I. CARRIE[8], b. at Southold, L.I., 9 April, 1845; m. at Southold, 23 Dec., 1875, Louis Philip Bersenger, b. at Peconic, L.I., 9 Nov., 1847. Res. at Greenport, L.I. He was a carriage maker, and died 16 April, 1902.

Issue:

I. AMELIA WINES BERSENGER, b. at Greenport, L.I., 31 Dec., 1876.

II. FRANK LEROY BERSENGER, b. at Southold, L.I., 30 Dec., 1878.

+911. II. FRANK SIDNEY[8], b. at Southold, Suffolk Co., L.I., 25 Feb., 1847.

+912. III. CHARLES LEROY[8], b. at Southold, L.I., 2 May, 1851.

514. **DANIEL WELLS[7] FANNING**, b. 1823, (*Daniel Wells[6], Nathaniel[5], Phineas[4], James[3], Thomas[2], Edmund[1]*)
m. at Stockton, Cal., 12 Oct., 1861,
Sarah Ann Carvill,
dau. of Richard and Elizabeth (Ferron) Carvill,
and b. in County Lough, Ireland, 25 Dec., 1833.

Daniel Wells Fanning was born at Franklinville, L.I., 11 Aug., 1823. At breaking out of Mexican War he enlisted in 2d Dragoons, and was a farrier. Was under Generals Perry, Scott, and Taylor. Was in the battles of Palo Alto, Buena Vista, Cerro Gordo, Churubusco, Chepultepec, San Pasqual Tobasco, and Vera Cruz, from 1846 to 1848, and was wounded. In 1848 he settled in California, and was one of the original California '49-ers. Afterward carried on an extensive wheelwright and blacksmith business. Res. in Stockton, Cal., and later Bellota, Cal., where he died 15 June, 1898. Bur. Stockton. Widow resides Bellota.

Issue:

913. I. DANIEL WILLIAM[8], b. at Bellota, Cal., 3 Aug., 1862; d. 13 Aug., 1862.

914. II. FRANCIS HENRY[8], b. at Bellota, Cal., 24 June, 1864; is a blacksmith, and res. at Bellota, unm.

+915. III. WILLIAM JAMES[8], b. at Bellota, Cal., 17 Aug., 1866.

916. IV. CAROLINE ELIZABETH[8], b. at Bellota, Cal., 10 Nov., 1868; m. at Bellota, 5 Oct., 1896, Frank Aloyouis Creary. Res. New Hope, San Joaquin Co., Cal.

Issue:

I. GEORGE FANNING CREARY, b. 25 Sept., 1897.

II. DANIEL WELLS CREARY, b. 25 Dec., 1898.

917. V. ANNIE MEHITABLE[8], b. at Bellota, Cal., 6 Aug., 1870; m. at Bellota, 12 Oct., 1897, Joseph Theodore Lusignan. Res. Stockton, Cal.

918. VI. MARY SARAH[8], b. at Bellota, Cal., 21 June, 1873.

519. **JAMES BARCLAY[7] FANNING**, b. 1836, (*Daniel Wells[6], Nathaniel[5], Phineas[4], James[3], Thomas[2], Edmund[1]*)
m. at Mattituck, L.I., 16 Dec., 1868,
Eleanor Anna Aldrich,
dau. of John Youngs and Eleanor (Wells) Aldrich,
and b. at Mattituck, L.I., 21 Feb., 1848.

James Barclay Fanning, son of Daniel Wells and Frances (Woodhull) Fanning, was born at Mattituck, L.I., 6 Feb., 1836; is a merchant, and res. at Southold, L.I. He was postmaster at Peconic, L.I., from 1864 to 1874.

Issue:

919. I. John Aldrich[8], b. at Peconic, L.I., 3 Dec., 1869; d. 16 May, 1872.

920. II. Desiah Perkins[8], b. at Southold, L.I., 24 Nov., 1874; m. at Southold, L.I., 8 Dec., 1897, Silas Edgar Tuthill, a carpenter, and res. at Peconic, L.I.

Issue:

1. Burnett Fanning Tuthill, b. 25 Nov., 1898.

921. III. Warren Aldrich[8], b. at Southold, L.I., 8 Feb., 1881; d. 14 May, 1883.

922. IV. James Irving[8], b. at Southold, L.I., 29 Feb., 1884.

520. **CHARLES[7] FANNING**, b. , (*Solomon*[6], *Nathaniel*[5], *Phineas*[4], *James*[3], *Thomas*[2], *Edmund*[1])
m. at
Elizabeth Hart,
dau. of
and b. at

Charles Fanning, son of Solomon and ( ) Fanning, was born at New York, N.Y. (it is supposed), about 1815 to 1820. Was a dealer in metals, iron, and britannia ware, etc.,at Nos. 4 and 6 Burling Slip,New York, in which city he resided. His name is found in the city "Directory" there, in the years 1856–7, and thereafter to 1870 and later, but the date of his decease or that of his wife is not learned, after careful research. It is said he had one child only. No further record of the family, however, is obtainable, nor is it known whether the child grew up to maturity to marry and have family or not.

Issue:

923. 1. (Child)[8], b. at

526. **EDMUND FREDERICK AUGUSTUS[7] FANNING**, b. 1808, (*Edmund*[6], *Barclay*[5], *Phineas*[4], *James*[3], *Thomas*[2], *Edmund*[1])

m. at Nantucket, Mass., 19 Feb., 1829,

Sophia A Hodges,

dau. of Capt. Isaac and Lydia (Crocker) Hodges, and b. at Nantucket, Mass., about 1810.

Edmund Frederick Augustus Fanning was born at Nantucket, Mass., 28 Dec., 1808, where he resided and followed the sea. Named after Gen. Edmund Fanning and his son, of Nova Scotia, and thereby received an inheritance in the General's will. Removed to Nova Scotia in 1845 in order to obtain the inherited property, and died at Oak or Fanning's Island, Nova Scotia, 1 Jan., 1848. Widow died in Richmond, Ind., 7 Dec., 1870.

Issue:

924. I. MARY ABBY[8], b. at Nantucket, Mass., 30 June, 1830; m. at Davenport, Ia., 25 Dec., 1868, William Brown Barnes, a widower, whose dau. m. William Wallace Fanning (No. 928). Was a fruit raiser, and res. Davenport, Ia., where he d. 6 March, 1887. Wid. res. Los Angeles, Cal., 1898. Issue: Roy Edmund Fanning Barnes, b. 2 Sept., 1870.

925. II. EDMUND FREDERICK AUGUSTUS[8], b. at Nantucket, Mass., 19 March, 1832; d. 29 April, 1834.

926. III. EDMUND FREDERICK AUGUSTUS[8], b. at Nantucket, Mass., 3 June, 1840; d. 9 Sept., 1841.

927. IV. JOHN BARCLAY[8], b. at Nantucket, Mass., 14 Jan., 1842; d. at Richmond, Ind., 20 Nov., 1872, unm.

+928. V. WILLIAM WALLACE[8], b. at Nantucket, Mass., 23 Nov., 1843.

929. VI. SYLVESTER HODGES[8], b. at Oak or Fanning's Island, N.S., 16 July, 1846. He is a farmer. Res. Lincolnville, Wabash Co., Ind.; unm.

+930. VII. EDMUND FREDERICK AUGUSTUS[8], b. at Oak or Fanning's Island, N.S., 11 Sept., 1848.

527. **BARCLAY[7] FANNING**, b. 1814, (*Edmund[6], Barclay[5], Phineas[4], James[3], Thomas[2], Edmund[1]*)
m. at Nantucket, Mass., 10 March, 1840,
Sarah Allen Ellis,
dau. of Jesse and Lydia (Gardner) Ellis,
and b. at Nantucket, Mass., 15 Oct., 1821. After her husband's death she married 2d, 20 March, 1859, Jethro Barrett of Nantucket, and had issue, Sarah Elizabeth Barrett.

Barclay Fanning was born at Nantucket, Mass., 28 Sept., 1814, was a ship carpenter and builder, and resided at Nantucket, where he died 2 June, 1849. Widow resided afterwards at Campello, Mass., and died at Nantucket 11 Aug., 1898. Both bur. Nantucket.

Issue:

931. I. CAROLINE HENSON[8], b. at Nantucket, Mass., 28 Aug., 1841; m. at Nantucket, in 1860, William Henry Gruber, a sailor. He served two years in navy during Civil War, then enlisted in 2d Mass. Cavalry, confined in Andersonville prison in '64, and d. from effects of incarceration, 8 Feb., 1865.

Issue born at Nantucket:

I. CAROLINE AUGUSTA GRUBER, b. 21 Sept., 1860; m. 26 Jan., 1881, Frank Norris Haven, res. Campello.

II. WILLIAM EDMUND GRUBER, b. 17 July, 1864; m. at Brockton, Mass., 10 Sept., 1881, Margaret McDonough. Res. Brockton, Mass.

+932. II. EDMUND BARCLAY[8], b. at Nantucket, Mass., 29 Aug., 1843.

+933. III. ALEXANDER "CAMMY"* WILDER[8], b. at Nantucket, Mass., 8 Dec., 1845.

934. IV. LUCY STURTEVANT[8], b. at Nantucket, Mass., in spring of 1848, d. at Nantucket in Feb., 1850.

* "Campbell" probably, and no doubt named after Alexander Campbell Wilder Fanning (No. 249).

534. **FREDERICK[7] FANNING**, b. 1838, (*Frederick Deveau*[6], *Henry*[5], *Gilbert*[4], *James*[3], *Thomas*[2], *Edmund*[1])
m. at Charleston, S.C., 21 April, 1858,
Harriet Eugenia Chambers,
dau. of James Smith and Mary Erwin (Wilson) Chambers, and b. at Ebenezer, S.C., 16 March, 1838.

Frederick Fanning was born at Charleston, S.C., 6 May, 1838. Was a merchant, and resided at Charleston. Was in South Carolina Light Inft., C. S. A.,and on duty at Charleston two and a half years, during Civil War. In 1872 removed to Charlotte, N.C., where was deacon of Presbyterian Church, and then to Durham, N.C., where he died 18 March, 1883. Bur. Charleston. Widow resides Durham.

Issue (of whom four died in infancy) :

935. I. MARY WILSON[8], b. at Charleston, S.C.,29 March,1860.

+936. II. FREDERICK DEVEAU[8], b. at Charleston, S.C., 28 April, 1861.

937. III. ELIZABETH FULLERTON[8], b. at Spartanburg, S.C., 15 Jan.,1863; m. at Durham, N.C., Dr. Hamilton Moore Weedon, physician and druggist. Was surgeon C.S. A., Army Tenn., 1862 to '65. Res. Eufaula, Ala. Issue: Fanning Weedon, b. 16 Oct., 1896.

938. IV. THEODORA WAGNER[8], b. at Columbia, S.C., 23 Oct., 1864; m. 7 April, 1886, Edwin Adolphus Heartt. Res. Durham, N.C., where he d. No issue. Wid. m. 2d, 23 Nov., 1897, William Montague Jones, a lawyer. Res. Spartanburg, S.C.

939. V. EUGENIA[8], b. at Charleston, S.C., 19 Sept., 1866.

940. VI. HENRIETTA MARION[8],b. at Charleston, S.C.,24 March, 1868; m. 23 June, 1892, Edwin Crawford Murray. Res. Durham, N.C. Issue: Eugenia Fanning Murray, b. 10 Sept., 1894.

941. VII. FRANCES ROBERTSON[8], b. at Charleston, S.C., 5 Sept., 1869.

942. VIII. MARY GILLESPIE[8], b. at Charleston, S.C.

541. **ANDREW MURDOCK[7] FANNING,** b. 1834, (*Thomas Coit*[6], *Thomas*[5], *Thomas*[4], *Richard*[3], *Thomas*[2], *Edmund*[1])

m. at Brooklyn, N.Y., 8 Nov., 1859,

Mary Augusta Earl,

dau. of John and Amanda Augusta (Smith) Earl, and b. at New York, N.Y., 17 Aug., 1837.

Andrew Murdock Fanning, son of Thomas Coit and Cornelia (Shepard) Fanning, was born at Albion, N.Y., 1 April, 1834. He was a commission merchant in New York City, and resided in Brooklyn, where he died 6 Aug., 1887. Buried in Greenwood Cemetery.

Issue:

943. I. THOMAS COIT[8], b. at Brooklyn, N.Y., 11 Oct., 1863; d. 14 Nov., 1864.

944. II. MABEL SHEPARD[8], b. at Brooklyn, N.Y., 31 March, 1865; d. 13 Dec., 1865.

945. III. MAUD SHEPARD[8], b. at Brooklyn, N.Y., 5 Nov., 1866. Res. Brooklyn.

946. IV. MARY BEEBE[8], b. at Brooklyn, N.Y., 31 Aug., 1868; m. at Brooklyn, 21 Oct., 1891, Frank West Conkling, b. at Hudson, N.Y., 19 Jan., 1868. He is a reporter, and res. in Brooklyn, N.Y.

Issue:

I. ELLIOTT GARDINER CONKLING, b. at Brooklyn, N.Y., 1 Sept., 1892.

+947. V. HENRY SWEETSER[8], b. at Brooklyn, N.Y., 11 May, 1871.

948. VI. LEE WOOSTER[8], b. at Brooklyn, N.Y., 18 July, 1875. Connected with a wholesale lace house in New York City, and res. at Brooklyn; unm.

542. **DAVID GREENE[7] FANNING**, b. 1836, (*Thomas Coit*[6], *Thomas*[5], *Thomas*[4], *Richard*[3], *Thomas*[2], *Edmund*[1]) m. at Brooklyn, N.Y., 22 Dec., 1859,

Elizabeth Buckingham Lane,

dau. of Anthony and Elizabeth Stanton (Willcox) Lane, and b. at New York, N.Y., 19 May, 1834.

David Greene Fanning was born at Albion, N.Y., 30 Sept., 1836, graduated at the college of the City of New York in 1857, and taught school at Bloomfield, N.J., and Brooklyn, N.Y. Then connected himself with the 4th National Bank, New York City, where he was 36 or 37 years. He was a student and great reader. Was dignified and courtly, and made many friends. In height was 6 feet, 2 inches, and weighed about 200 lbs. He died at Flushing, L.I., 31 Dec., 1901. She died at Flushing, L.I., 9 Jan., 1902. Both cremated at Fresh Pond, L.I.

Issue:

949. I. EDITH HUBBARD[8], b. at Brooklyn, N.Y., 8 Sept., 1861; d. 19 Feb., 1863.

+950. II. ARTHUR LANE[8], b. at Brooklyn, N.Y., 20 Sept., 1863.

951. III. CARRA LOUISE[8], b. at Brooklyn, N.Y., 11 Oct., 1865; m. at Flushing, N.Y., 8 Oct., 1898, William Willits Seaman, and res. in New York City. No issue.

952. IV. MARIE AUGUSTA[8], b. at Brooklyn, N.Y., 7 June, 1868; d. at Tarrytown, N.Y., 21 Aug., 1869.

+953. V. WINTHROP SALTONSTALL[8], b. at Brooklyn, N.Y., 26 Nov., 1870.

954. VI. MARION STANTON[8], b. at Brooklyn, N.Y., 12 Nov., 18 d. at Brooklyn, 17 Nov., 1875.

544. **THOMAS COIT[7] FANNING**, b. 1840, (*Thomas Coit[6], Thomas[5], Thomas[4], Richard[3], Thomas[2], Edmund[1]*)
m. at Brooklyn, N.Y., 28 Oct., 1862,
Cornelia Lane,
dau. of Anthony and Elizabeth Stanton (Willcox) Lane, and b. at New York, N.Y., 1 Aug., 1838.

Dr. Thomas Coit Fanning was born at Albion, N.Y., 5 June, 1840. He removed with his parents in 1849 to Brooklyn, N.Y.; entered New York University, Department of Arts and Letters, in 1855, Department of Medicine in 1858, graduated in 1861, and went to Tarrytown, N.Y., to practise. Was in the U.S. Army as surgeon at Georgetown, D.C., in summer of 1862. Went to Fishkill Landing, 1862. Returned to Tarrytown in 1864, and practised there till 1894. Was village trustee and water commissioner of Tarrytown, N.Y., for several years. Removed to Walters Park, Penn., in 1898, where he is now located as a practising physician.

Issue:

+955. I. LOUIS MARTINE[8], b. at Tarrytown, N.Y., 12 May, 1866.

956. II. GRACE MERRITT[8] WINTHROP, b. at Tarrytown, N.Y., 9 Nov., 1867. Graduate of Wellesley College, Mass., in 1891. Studied two years in Sage School of Philosophy at Cornell University, Ithaca, N.Y. Since 1896, teacher in manual training, High School, Brooklyn, N.Y.; unm.

550. **JOHN THOMAS[7] FANNING**, b. 1837, (*John Howard*[6], *John*[5], *Thomas*[4], *Richard*[3], *Thomas*[2], *Edmund*[1])
m. at Norwich, Conn., 11 June, 1865,
Maria Louise Bensley,
dau. of James and Maria (Walker) Bensley,
and b. at Pawtucket, R.I., 10 Jan., 1845.

John Thomas Fanning was born at Norwich, Conn., 31 Dec., 1837, and was educated for the profession of architecture and civil engineering. Served in the 3d Regt., Conn. Vols. during the Rebellion, and later was field officer in the 3d Regt., Conn. Militia. He began his professional practice in Norwich, Conn., in 1862, and was 8 years acting city engineer there, and planned the city's water supply, cemetery, etc. He constructed Manchester, N.H.'s, water supply and many important buildings there and elsewhere in New England, and later was chief and consulting engineer in planning water powers and water supplies in not less than two-thirds of the United States. He is a fellow of the American Association for Advancement of Science, ex-director of the American Society of Civil Engineers, ex-pres. of the Am. Water Works Asso., etc. Author of many works on subject of water supplies and engineering topics. Has resided in Minneapolis, Minn., since 1886.

Issue:

957. I. JENNIE LOUISE[8], b. at Norwich, Conn., 2 Oct., 1866; m. at Minneapolis, Minn., 22 Aug., 1900, Thomas Alexander Jamieson, an investment broker, and res. at Minneapolis, Minn.

958. II. RENNIE BENSLEY[8], b. at Norwich, Conn., 21 Sept., 1868, a civil engineer, and res. in Minneapolis, Minn.; unm.

959. III. CLARA ELIZABETH[8], b. at Manchester, N.H., 11 Oct., 1878. Graduate of the University of Minnesota in 1901.

565. **HOWARD MALCOLM[7] FANNING,** b. 1826,
(*Richard*[6], *Asa*[5], *Richard*[4], *Richard*[3], *Thomas*[2], *Edmund*[1])
m. at Staten Island, N.Y., 4 Oct., 1848,
Laura Louise Butts,
dau. of William and Laura (Johnson) Butts,
and b. at Davenport, Delaware Co., N.Y., 25 June, 1829.

Howard Malcolm Fanning, son of Richard and Ann Eliza (Smith) Fanning, was born at Troy, N. Y., 3 June, 1826, is a farmer, and resides at Stockton, Cal. In 1846 he removed from Troy, N.Y., to Jersey City, N.J., where he resided about eight months. He then returned to Troy, and resided for a year, and then lived in Brandon, Vt., a year. In July, 1850, he left the East and went to California, where he has since resided. He was an alderman of Stockton in the years 1866 and 1867, and supervisor, 1867–73. He is President of the San Joaquin Society of California Pioneers.

Issue:

960. I. CLARA LOUISE[8], b. at Stockton, Cal., 21 Oct., 1852; m. at Stockton, Cal., 29 Dec., 1880, Frank Bugbee, a painter, b. at Little Rock, Ark., 29 May, 1853. He d. 14 Jan., 1896. Wid. res. Oakland, Cal. No issue.

961. II. DELIA JANE[8], b. at Stockton, Cal., 14 Feb., 1861; unm., and res. at Stockton, Cal.

+962. III. HARRY HOWARD[8], b. at Stockton, Cal., 15 Nov., 1863.

566. **OMAR ERASTUS[7] FANNING**, b. 1829, (*Asa*[6], *Asa*[5], *Richard*[4], *Richard*[3], *Thomas*[2], *Edmund*[1])
m. 1st at Round Grove, Whiteside Co., Ill., in March, 1855,

Louisa Simonson,

dau. of Frederick and Sabrina (Harvey) Simonson, and b. at Richford, Tioga Co., N.Y., 3 March, 1833.

She d. at Emerson, Ill., 7 Nov., 1868.

He m. 2d at Emerson, Ill., 22 Nov., 1870,

Mary Jenks Lefferts,

dau. of John and Mary Ann (Stackhouse) Lefferts, and b. at Newtown, Bucks Co., Penn., 20 Aug., 1840.

Omar Erastus Fanning was born at Oxford, N.Y., 2 Feb., 1829, from whence his parents removed to Union, Broome Co., N.Y., when he was about one year old. He resided there until Aug., 1851. He then removed to Emerson, Hopkins Township, Whiteside Co., Ill., where he resided until 1897, when he removed to Sterling, Ill., where he lived until his decease 11 May, 1902. He was a farmer.

Issue by wife Mary:

963. I. PHEBE[8], b. at Emerson, Ill., 4 Sept., 1871; m. at Sterling, Ill., 28 Dec., 1899, Charles Herrmann, a teacher, and res. at Streator, Ill.

Issue:

I. JOSEPHINE WILHELMA HERRMANN, b. at Sterling, Ill., 18 Nov., 1901.

964. II. FRANK CHARLES[8], b. at Emerson, Ill., 4 Nov., 1872. Res. Round Grove, Ill.; unm.

965. III. JESSIE[8], b. at Emerson, Ill., 15 June, 1874; umn.

966. IV. OMAR ASA[8], b. at Emerson, Ill., 18 June, 1876; unm.

567. **FRANKLIN[7] FANNING**, b. 1832, (*Asa*[6], *Asa*[5], *Richard*[4], *Richard*[3], *Thomas*[2], *Edmund*[1])
m. at Athens, Penn., 14 Sept., 1854,
Sarah Louise Scott,
dau. of William and Sarah (Bertram) Scott,
and b. at Athens, Penn., 4 Dec., 1836.

Franklin Fanning (known as "Frank" Fanning) was born at Union, Broome Co., N.Y., 13 July, 1832. He was a prominent civil engineer and surveyor, and resided at St. Joseph, Mo. The greater part of his life was spent in engineering and constructing railroads in the West. He was one of the pioneer railroad constructors in the United States, and served as chief and assistant engineer on many of the roads throughout the country. In 1874 he settled in St. Joseph, Mo. Was appointed city engineer of St. Joseph in 1882 and served for three years. The town of "Fanning," Doniphan Co., Kan., was named after him.

He d. at St. Joseph, Mo., 16 March, 1903.

Issue:

967. I. JULIA ALICE[8], b. at Sterling, Ill., 18 Jan., 1857; d. at Fulton, Ill., 30 Aug., 1858.

968. II. FRANKIE[8], b. at Athens, Penn., 14 June, 1859; m. at St. Joseph, Mo., 17 Nov., 1880, John Irving McDonald. He grad. Yale College, 1878, is a merchant, and res. at St. Joseph, Mo. She grad. Monticello Seminary, Ill.

Issue born at St. Joseph, Mo.:

I. IRVING McDONALD, b. 5 Nov., 1881.
II. LOUISE McDONALD, b. 9 March, 1884.
III. RUFUS LEE McDONALD, b. 20 July, 1888.

969. III. GERTRUDE[8], b. at Atchison, Kan., 12 Dec., 1869; d. at St. Joseph, Mo., 9 June, 1887.

570. **NEUVILLE DeROSTUS^7 FANNING**, b. 1838, (*Amasa Standish^6, Henry^5, Richard^4, Richard^3, Thomas^2, Edmund^1*)

m. 1st at Meadville, Penn., 4 July, 1855,
Lorinda Henderson,
dau. of
and b. at
She d. at Meadville, Penn., in Oct., 1857.
He m. 2d at California, Penn., 21 March, 1858,
Sarah Frances Underwood,
dau. of James Alexander and Lydia (Bright) Underwood, and b. at Elizabeth, Penn., 31 March, 1840.

Neuville DeRostus Fanning was born at Freedom, O., 6 Dec., 1838, graduated from Meadville College, Penn., and entered ministry, during which studied law, and was admitted to the bar by Supreme Court, Ill., 1862. Preached twenty years at Aurora, St. Charles, and Marengo, in Ill., ten years in Presbyterian Church, Jamestown, No. Dak. Then settled over Oak Park Cong. Church, Minneapolis, Minn., his last charge, where he died 1 Feb., 1891. Widow res. New York City.

Issue by wife Lorinda:

970. I. FLORENCE VIRGINIA^8, b. at Meadville, Penn., about 1857; m. at Marengo, Ill., Nov., 1876, John Marshall Wheelon. Res. Marengo and Livingston, Mont., where she d. 10 July, 1890. Issue: Neuville F., George B., Albert W. (Three ch. d. in infancy.)

Issue by wife Sarah:

971. II. IDA LILLIAN^8, b. at Brownsville, Penn., 29 April, 1859; m. at Jamestown, No. Dak., 7 Oct., 1888, Jeremiah Daniel Powell. Res. Lily Lake, Ill. Issue: Neuville Fanning Powell, b. 28 Sept., 1892.

+972. III. NEUVILLE OSGOOD^8, b. at St. Charles, Ill., 17 Mar., 1865.

973. IV. FRANK BAKER^8, b. at Marengo, Ill., 6 Dec., 1871. Grad. Minnesota State Univ. A journalist. Res. New York.

571. **ELIHU HAKES[7] FANNING**, b. 1830, (*Henry J[6], Henry[5], Richard[4], Richard[3], Thomas[2], Edmund[1]*)
m. at Worcester, Mass., 7 Sept., 1851,
Laura Annie May,
dau. of Schuyler and Betsey (Holman) May,
and b. at Sturbridge, Mass., 5 March, 1832.

Elihu Hakes Fanning, son of Henry J and Annie (Hakes) Fanning, was born at Norwich, Conn., 11 March, 1830. He learned the machinist trade in Providence, R.I., and located in Worcester, Mass., about 1850, where he soon entered the employ of the Worcester & Nashua R.R. Co., as locomotive engineer, and was in that capacity thirty-seven years, being one of the oldest locomotive engineers in point of service in New England.

He d. at Worcester, Mass., 6 Aug., 1891. Bur. in Hope Cemetery.

Widow res. at No. 2 Jacques Ave., Worcester.

Issue:

974. I. LAURETTA[8], b. at Worcester, Mass., 25 May, 1852; d. 28 April, 1858.

975. II. ANNIE MARY[8], b. at Nashua, N.H., 6 Feb., 1854; m. at Worcester, Mass., 25 Dec., 1886, Daniel Thorndike Felton, son of Daniel and Lydia Felton, and b. at Shrewsbury, Mass., 11 Feb., 1847, a carpenter. They res. at Worcester, Mass. No issue.

976. III. ELIHU CLINTON[8], b. at Worcester, Mass., 15 Sept., 1856; d. 5 May, 1858.

575. **JOHN NEWTON[7] FANNING,** b. 1839, (*Alexander Newton[6], Henry[5], Richard[4], Richard[3], Thomas[2], Edmund[1]*)
m. at Bellevue, Ia., 24 Sept., 1862,

Mary Stuart,

dau. of John and Eliza Jane (Glover) Stuart,
and b. at Lebanon, Ill., 10 Aug., 1843.

John Newton Fanning, son of Alexander Newton and Elizabeth Ann (Bagby) Fanning, was born at St. Charles, Mo., 5 Sept., 1839.

The first five years of his life were passed at St. Charles. In 1844 he removed with his parents to Galena, Ill., where he resided until 1851, in which latter year his folks located in Bellevue, Iowa. He lived in Bellevue many years, and married there in 1862, Mary Stuart, dau. of John and Eliza Jane (Glover) Stuart.

He learned the trade of a cooper in early life, and follows that occupation, and resides at 1040 Overton St., Los Angeles, Cal.

Issue:

977. I. EVA[8], b. at Bellevue, Ia., 11 July, 1863; d. 19 Aug., 1863.
+978. II. FRANK STUART[8], b. at Bellevue, Ia., 2 Oct., 1864.
+979. III. ALEXANDER NEWTON[8], b. at Bellevue, Ia., 17 May, 1867.
980. IV. JOHN PERCY[8], b. at Bellevue, Ia., 18 Nov., 1870. res. Los Agcles Cal.; unm.
981. V. MARY ELIZA[8], b. at Belevue, Ia., 31 Dec., 1876; unm.

577. **AMASA STANDISH⁷ FANNING**, b. 1845, (*Alexander Newton*[6], *Henry*[5], *Richard*[4], *Richard*[3], *Thomas*[2], *Edmund*[1])

m. at Jerseyville, Jersey Co., Ill., 23 Feb., 1880,
Martha Ellen Leonard,
dau. of Hiram and Amanda (Powell) Leonard,
and b. at Jerseyville, Ill., 21 April, 1857.

Amasa Standish Fanning was born at Galena, Ill., 1 Aug., 1845. At age of sixteen years, enlisted 31 March, 1862, in Company H, 5th Ia. Cav., in the Union Army. This company went to Benton Barracks, St. Louis, Mo., then to Fort Donaldson, under Grant, to Murfreesboro and Stone River, Chattanooga, Atlanta, Nashville, and back to Tennessee River, then on the famous Wilson Raid through Ala., Ga., and Tenn., and was discharged 11 Aug., 1865, at close of war. Was with company from day he enlisted until discharged, and was sick and off duty but one day. Was in battles of Fort Donaldson, Stone River, Lookout Mountain, Champion Hill, Kenesaw Mountain, Big Shanty, Dalton, Marietta; in all the Atlanta Campaign, Columbia, Tennessee, Franklin, Selma, Ala., Gerard, Columbus, Ga., Ebnezer Church, Ala., Corinth, Iuka, Peach Tree Creek; on the Raid through Georgia in 1864, Wilson Raid through Ala. and Ga., 1865, etc. Was with the company at Atlanta when it lost twenty-two men out of thirty-two in twenty minutes. Was slightly wounded twice His brother, Henry Weston Fanning (No. 575), served in the same company as Amasa; enlisted at the same time, and was discharged at same time. Amasa is a United States pensioner on account of service in the war and for disabilities received and resulting from it; was recently in Soldiers' Home at Santa Monica, Cal. Resides Los Angeles, Cal.

Issue:

982. I. WALTER LEONARD[8], b. at Bellevue, Ia., 23 Nov., 1880, res. at Los Angeles, Cal.

578. **ASA STANDISH^{7} FANNING,** b. 1845, (*Alexander Newton^{6}, Henry^{5}, Richard^{4}, Richard^{3}, Thomas^{2}, Edmund^{1}*)
m. at Winona, Winona Co., Minn., 24 May, 1887,
Rosa Mabel Markham,
dau. of Almyron and Eliza (Smith) Markham,
and b. at Beaver Dam, Dodge Co., Wis., 29 Jan., 1868.

Asa Standish Fanning, son of Alexander Newton and Elizabeth Ann (Bagby) Fanning, was born at Galena, Ill., 1 Aug., 1845. He was named after his maternal grandparent, Lovina Standish. She was dau. of Amasa and Zerviah (Smith) Standish, and a direct descendant of Capt. Myles Standish of Plymouth. When he was six years old his parents settled at Bellevue, Ia., removing there from Galena, Ill. He married late in life, 24 May, 1887, Rosa Mabel Markham. He has resided at Bellevue many years, and follows his occupation, that of a miller. No issue.

579. **ALEXANDER BAGBY[7] FANNING**, b. 1847, (*Alexander Newton*[6], *Henry*[5], *Richard*[4], *Richard*[3], *Thomas*[2], *Edmund*[1])

m. at Vinton, Ia., 4 Nov., 1873,

Sadie Alida Place,

dau. of Martin W. and Sadie (Mills) Place,
and b. at Jamesville, Wis., 4 Nov., 1857.

Alexander Bagby Fanning, son of Alexander Newton and Elizabeth Ann (Bagby) Fanning, was born at Galena, Ill., 23 May, 1847. He graduated at Bellevue College, Bellevue, Ia., in 1867, and soon after began to learn the printers' trade, which occupation he has followed since. He was residing at last accounts at San Francisco, Cal.

Issue:

983. I. BERTIE ALEXANDER[8], b. at Cedar Rapids, Ia., 1 Oct., 1874.
984. II. CLAUDIA ELIZABETH[8], b. at Belle Plaine, Ia., 16 July, 1877.
985. III. ROBERT MILLS[8], b. at Freeport, Ill., 8 Feb., 1880.
986. IV. CHARLES NEWTON[8], b. at Rock Island, Ill., 15 Dec., 1882.

(All unm. in 1899.)

580. **CHARLES GRANDSON[7] FANNING**, b. 1829,
(*Luther[6], Charles[5], Richard[4], Richard[3], Thomas[2], Edmund[1]*)
m. at Angelica, N.Y., 28 Oct., 1851,
Julia Roana Renwick,
dau. of John and Ruth (Gillette) Renwick,
and b. at Angelica, N.Y., 8 Feb., 1833.

Charles Grandson Fanning, son of Luther and Maria Caroline (Horton) Fanning, was born at Perry, N.Y., 10 May, 1829.

He was a cabinet maker, and res. at Cuba, N.Y.

He d. at Cuba, N.Y., 30 March, 1897, and was bur. there.

Widow res. at Andover, Allegany Co., N.Y.

Issue:

+987. I. CHARLES ADELBERT[8], b. at Angelica, Allegany Co., N.Y., 15 Feb., 1855.

988. II. ALICE[8], b. at Angelica, N.Y., 22 Jan., 1853; m. at Hinsdale, N.Y., 2 June, 1872, David E. Randolph, b. at Cuba, N.Y., 16 Aug., 1852, and res. at Andover, Allegany Co., N.Y.

Issue, born at Cuba, N.Y.:

I. RUTH INEZ RANDOLPH, b. 2 Dec., 1873.
II. LOTTA MABEL RANDOLPH, b. 22 June, 1884.

581. **WILLIAM HENRY**[7] **FANNING**, b.1831, (*Luther*[6], *Charles*[5], *Richard*[4], *Richard*[3], *Thomas*[2], *Edmund*[1])
m. 1st at Hornellsville, N.Y.,
Sarah Jane Francis,
dau. of
and b. at

She d. at Hornellsville, N.Y.,
He m. 2d at
Catharine Marvin,
dau. of
and b. at

William Henry Fanning, son of Luther and Maria Caroline (Horton) Fanning, was born at Perry, N.Y., 25 Dec., 1831. He was a railway employee, and resided at St. Louis, Mo., at the time of his death.

He d. at South St. Louis, Mo., 7 Dec., 1880, and was bur. at Decatur, Ill.

Widow married again about 1881 a Mr. Kirkpatrick, and removed to Binghamton, N.Y. No issue by either marriage.

588. **EDWIN PALMER[7] FANNING**, b. 1835, (*Calvin*[6], *Charles*[5], *Richard*[4], *Richard*[3], *Thomas*[2], *Edmund*[1])
m. at Perry, Wyoming Co., N.Y., 24 Aug., 1865,
Theodotia Locenia Barnard,
dau. of Barzile and Rebecca Maria (Nobles) Barnard, and b. at Perry Centre, Wyoming Co., N.Y., 1 June, 1846.

Edwin Palmer Fanning was born at Avon, N.Y., 18. April, 1835, was a baggageman, and resided at Perry, N.Y. His name is recorded simply "Edwin," and he added the "Palmer" in later years. In early life he learned the cooperage trade of his father, and worked at it for his brother Charles ten years. He accepted a position as baggageman on the Silver Lake R.R., which he held over fifteen years. He was in the Civil War, and enlisted 1 May, 1861, and served until close of war. Was in the First New York Dragoons, Co. D, from 1 Aug., 1862. He was in 44 engagements, and present at Lee's surrender at Appomattox 9 April, 1865. His wife d. at Perry, N.Y., 1 June, 1897. He died at Perry, N.Y., 9 Jan., 1903. Both bur. at Perry.

Issue:

989. I. IDA BELL[8], b. at Warsaw, Wyoming Co., N.Y., 19 Aug., 1866; d. 17 Feb., 1867.

+990. II. SANFORD CALVIN[8], b. at Perry, Wyoming Co., N.Y., 3 Jan., 1870.

991. III. LELA MATTIE[8], b. at Perry, Wyoming Co., N.Y., 20 April, 1877; m. at Perry, N.Y., 10 Oct., 1894, Clarence V. Bennett, b. 21 Sept., 1871. They res. at Perry, N.Y. He is baggage master on Silver Lake R.R. No issue.

589. **CHARLES ADDISON[7] FANNING**, b. 1837, (*Calvin*[6], *Charles*[5], *Richard*[4], *Richard*[3], *Thomas*[2], *Edmund*[1])
m. at Dalton, N.Y., 17 April, 1864,
Almira Doane,
dau. of Samuel Mills and Elizabeth (Van Antwerp) Doane, and b. at Portage, N.Y., 25 Aug., 1844.

Charles Addison Fanning, son of Calvin and Hannah Matilda (Lacey) Fanning, was born at Avon, N.Y., 8 May, 1837. In early life he learned the cooperage trade of his father, and started a factory in Perry, N.Y., in 1870, his brother Edwin working for him the first ten years. In 1884 he added the coal business to the cooperage, both of which, together with the retail ice business of the town, were run under his name until his death. In 1894, owing to failing health, he relinquished the active care of the business to his son Fred Doane Fanning, who took charge and complete management of it. After his decease his son succeeded to the business under the name of F. D. Fanning & Co.

He d. at Perry, N.Y., 16 Nov., 1898.

Issue:

+992. I. Fred Doane[8], b. at Perry, N.Y., 19 Dec., 1870.

593. **ASA[7] FANNING,** b. 1844, (*Palmer*[6], *Charles*[5], *Richard*[4], *Richard*[3], *Thomas*[2], *Edmund*[1])
m. at Fredonia, Mich., 22 Oct., 1872,
Anzoleta Swartwout,
dau. of William and Marie (Morse) Swartwout,
and b. at Half Moon, Saratoga Co., N.Y., 1 Oct., 1846.

Asa Fanning, son of Palmer and Clarissa Ann (Converse) Fanning, was born at Sweden, Monroe Co., N.Y., 11 Sept., 1844. When he was nine years of age, his father removed to the township of Newton, Calhoun Co., Mich., and there Asa grew up and has resided since. He has followed farming all his life.

Issue:

993. I. ZELLA MARY[8], b. at Newton, Calhoun Co.,Mich.,7 Feb., 1874.

994. II. CLAUDE WILLIAM[8], b. at Newton, Calhoun Co., Mich., 17 Sept., 1875.

995. III. RAY WALLACE[8], b. at Newton, Calhoun Co., Mich., 12 April, 1881.
(All unm. in 1899.)

597. **JAMES EDWARD[7] FANNING**, b. 1839, (*Silas[6], Charles[5], Richard[4], Richard[3], Thomas[2], Edmund[1]*)
m. at Lakeville, Livingston Co., N. Y., 24 March, 1860,
Elvira Elizabeth Cleveland,
dau. of Calvin and Mary Priscilla (Smith) Cleveland, and b. at Rochester, N.Y., 14 Sept., 1837.

James Edward Fanning, son of Silas and Charlotte (Bridges) Fanning, was born at Avon, Livingston Co., N.Y., 15 Sept., 1839. He resided at Avon, where he was employed in the steam saw mills. He enlisted 5 Aug., 1861, in the 136th N.Y. Vol. Regt., and served through the war of the Rebellion, and was discharged 6 July, 1865, from St. Marie's Hospital, Rochester, N.Y.

He d. at Avon, N.Y., 30 May, 1884 — was killed by the cars on Decoration Day.

Widow res. at Avon.

Issue:

+996. I. James Edwin[8], b. at Avon, N.Y., 17 June, 1860.

997. II. Clarence Calvin[8], b. at Avon, N.Y., 4 May, 1874. He is a cigar maker; res. Avon, N.Y.; unm. in 1897.

599. **HENRY LUTHER[7] FANNING,** b. 1843, (*Silas[6] Charles[5], Richard[4], Richard[3], Thomas[2], Edmund[1]*)
m. at South Haven, Mich., 24 Nov., 1867,
Sarah Adell Nichols,
dau. of Harlow K. and Eveline (Russell) Nichols,
and b. at South Butler, Wayne Co., N.Y., 27 Nov., 1853.

Henry Luther Fanning, son of Silas and Charlotte (Bridges) Fanning, was born at Avon, Livingston Co., N.Y., 29 March, 1843; went west with his parents, and settled at Bangor, Van Buren Co., Mich., where he has since resided. He was in the War of the Rebellion, enlisting in the Union Army 25 Sept., 1862, in Co. G, 136th N.Y. Vol. Inf., and was discharged 13 June, 1865, at close of war.

Issue:

+998. I. A J[8], b. at Bangor, Van Buren Co., Mich., 17 Sept., 1869.

999. II. Bertha May[8], b. at Bangor, Van Buren Co., Mich., 29 Feb., 1880.

601. **WILLIAM[7] FANNING**, b. 1848, (*Silas*[6], *Charles*[5], *Richard*[4], *Richard*[3], *Thomas*[2], *Edmund*[1])

m. at Columbia, Mich., 25 Dec., 1885,

Sarah Artemisia Hunt,

dau. of Theodore and Clo (Travis) Hunt,
and b. at Arlington, Mich., 12 Nov., 1855.

William Fanning, son of Silas and Charlotte (Bridges) Fanning, was born at Avon, Livingston Co., N.Y., 26 Aug., 1848.

He is a carpenter, and resides at Bangor, Van Buren Co., Mich.

Issue:

1000. I. EDWARD[8], b. at Arlington, Mich., 13 July, 1887; d. at age of 8 mos.

603. **GEORGE ALBERT[7] FANNING,** b. 1856, (*Silas[6] Charles[5], Richard[4], Richard[3], Thomas[2], Edmund[1]*)
m. at Geneseo, Livingston Co., N.Y., 18 March, 1883,

Catharine Dale,

dau. of George and Catharine (Huff) Dale,
and b. at Geneseo, Livingston Co., N.Y., 17 March, 1851.

George Albert Fanning, son of Silas and Charlotte (Bridges) Fanning, was born at Caledonia, Livingston Co., N.Y., 9 Oct., 1856. He removed to Michigan when he was ten years of age, but returned about 1881, and located in Geneseo, N.Y., where he has since resided. For ten years after his return he clerked it for a grocery firm. He and his wife are both members of the Methodist Episcopal Church.

Issue:

1001. I. BELLE[8], b. at Geneseo, N.Y., 20 Dec., 1883; d. 11 Aug., 1884.
1002. II. ALBERT[8], b. at Geneseo, N.Y., 9 April, 1886.

604. **CHARLES^7 FANNING**, b. 1861, (*Silas*^{6}, *Charles*^{5}, *Richard*^{4}, *Richard*^{3}, *Thomas*^{2}, *Edmund*^{1})

m. at Bangor, Van Buren Co., Mich., 30 Jan., 1882,

Elizabeth Haner,

dau. of Calvin and Ellen (Carter) Haner,
and b. at Bangor, Van Buren Co., Mich., 28 March, 1861.

Charles Fanning, son of Silas and Charlotte (Bridges) Fanning, was born at West Avon, Livingston Co., N.Y., 13 March, 1861. Early in life he went West and located. Resides at the present time at Shelby, Oceana Co., Mich. He is an engineer. No issue.

608. **JAMES ALONZO^7 FANNING,** b. 1825, (*Erastus^6, John^5, James^4, Richard^3, Thomas^2, Edmund^1*)
m. at Stockbridge, Mass., 13 Oct., 1847,
Harriet J Barton,
dau. of Joshua Allen and Relief (Vinton) Barton,
and b. at Stockbridge, Mass., 8 April, 1825.

James Alonzo Fanning, son of Erastus and Emeline (Beebe) Fanning, was born at Canaan, Conn.,9 June, 1825. He was a cotton-carder,and resided at New Hartford,Conn.

His wife d. at New Hartford, Conn., in Feb., 1873. Bur. at Stockbridge, Mass.

He d. at New Hartford, Conn., 28 Oct., 1876.

Issue:

+1003. I. GEORGE ALLEN^8, b. at

1004. II. HARRIET DELPHINE^8, b. at New Hartford, Conn., 14 Oct., 1852; m. at New Hartford, Conn.,13 Sept.,1876, Frank Hill, and res. at Burwell, Garfield Co., Neb. No issue.

1005. III. HELEN JANE^8, b. at , 1858; d. in 1860, a. 2 yrs., 3 mos.

+1006. IV. CHARLES MORTIMER^8, b. at Cold Spring, Mass., 26 Aug., 1861.

609. **GROVE[7] FANNING,** b. 1828, (*Erastus*[6], *John*[5], *James*[4], *Richard*[3], *Thomas*[2], *Edmund*[1])

m. at Guilford, Ulster Co., N.Y., 16 July, 1848,

Sarah Elizabeth Hooks,

dau. of John and Sarah (Morris) Hooks,
and b. at Marbletown, Ulster Co., N.Y., 19 Feb., 1829.
She d. at New Hartford, Conn., 12 April, 1869.
He m. 2d, at Harwinton, Conn., 24 Sept., 1878,

Mary Ann Johnson,

dau. of Jerome Bonaparte and Alvira (Mather) Johnson, and b. at Harwinton, Conn., 24 April, 1843.

Grove Fanning was born at Canaan, Conn., 29 Oct., 1828, and resides at Pleasant Valley, Conn. He was overseer spinning dept. in mills of the Greenwoods Co., many years at New Hartford, Conn. Past Commander of Edwin R. Lee Post G.A.R., No. 78. Was in the War of the Rebellion three years — enlisted 18 July, 1862, Co. I, 16th Regt. Conn. Vols. Afterwards transferred to Co. F. 3d Regt. V. R. C., and served till close of war. Discharged 6 July, 1865, serving as corporal at that time. Was wounded and is a United States pensioner.

Issue by wife Sarah:

1007. I. CAROLINE ELIZABETH[8], b. at New Hartford, Conn., 1 Oct., 1851; m. at New Hartford, 1 July, 1872, William Haines, a painter, b. at Preston Hollow, N.Y., 9 Sept., 1847. He went West about 1880, and is supposed to have been killed.

Issue:

I. GROVE EUGENE HAINES, b. at Catskill, N.Y., 22 April, 1874.

II. WALTER FANNING HAINES, b. at Durham, N.Y., 3 March, 1876, killed 12 Oct., 1898.

1008. II. IDA JANE[8], b. at New Hartford, Conn., 9 Aug., 1853; m. at New Hartford, Conn., 6 May, 1896, Albert Wells Hosmer. Res. Hartford, Conn. No issue.

611. **LUCIUS MORTIMER[7] FANNING**, b. 1835, (*Erastus*[6], *John*[5], *James*[4], *Richard*[3], *Thomas*[2], *Edmund*[1])
m. at Hartford, Conn., 25 Jan., 1868,
Annie Jane Morfey,
dau. of John and Jane (Boddington) Morfey,
and b. at Manchester, Eng., 16 April, 1846.

Lucius Mortimer Fanning was born at Barrington, Mass., 29 Sept., 1835; is a cotton spinner, and resides at Westport, Conn. He res. for several years at New Hartford, Conn., He enlisted 22 May, 1861, as musician in Co. B, 1st Conn. Heavy Artillery, and served three years and was honorably discharged 24 May, 1864. Was not wounded or taken prisoner. Is a United States pensioner. He was actively engaged in some of the fiercest battles of the Rebellion, *viz.*: Two battles of Chancellorsville, Va.; battle of the Wilderness, Rapidan, Bailey's Cross Roads, seven days' fight at Malvern Hill, Fair Oaks, Fredericksburg, at Golden's Farm, White Oak Swamp, Antietam, Petersburg, and closing battle of Gettysburg, Penn., etc.

Issue:

+1009. I. Grove Adelbert[8], b. at West Hartford, Conn., 30 May, 1869.

+1010. II. Frederic George[8], b. at South Manchester, Conn., 7 July, 1870.

1011. III. Joseph Alonzo[8], b. at South Manchester, Conn., 12 March, 1872. Res. Westport, Conn.; unm., 1904.

+1012. IV. Lucius Barzillai[8], b. at New Hartford, Conn., 27 Nov., 1873.

1013. V. Ernest Mortimer[8], b. at New Hartford, Conn., 7 May, 1877; d. and bur. there 30 July, 1881.

614. **JOHN ASAPH[7] FANNING**, b. 1839, (*John James*[6], *John*[5], *James*[4], *Richard*[3], *Thomas*[2], *Edmund*[1])
m. at Winchester Centre, Conn., 24 May, 1873,
Katherine McLean,
dau. of John and Dianna (Walton) McLean,
and b. at Newark, N.J., 14 Feb., 1850.

John Asaph Fanning (named after his grandfather Asaph Brooks), son of John James and Rachel (Brooks) Fanning, was born at Winchester, Conn., 10 March, 1839, and resides at Winchester Centre, Conn. He is at present engaged in teaming.

Issue:

1014. I. EDWARD JAMES[8], b. at Winsted, Conn., 23 Jan., 1878; d. 29 March, 1896.

1015. II. LAURA GRACE[8], b. at Winsted, Conn., 27 Sept., 1883; d. 22 March, 1884.

1016. III. CLARA MAY[8], b. at Winsted, Conn., 28 Feb., 1885.

618. **BURTON PHELPS[7] FANNING**, b. 1855, (*Edward*[6], *John*[5], *James*[4], *Richard*[3], *Thomas*[2], *Edmund*[1])
m. at Huntington, Mass., 17 Oct., 1883,
Estella Marion Cone,
dau. of Charles and Martha (Bronson) Cone,
and b. at Russell, Mass., 23 April, 1859.

Burton Phelps Fanning, son of Edward and Mary (Dean) Fanning, was born at Sandisfield, Mass., 3 June, 1855. He is a butcher, and resides at Westfield, Mass., 27 Orange St.

Issue:

1017. I. ROSA ESTELLA[8], b. at Granville, Mass., 25 Sept., 1884.
1018. II. BERTHA MARION[8], b. at Westfield, Mass., 14 March, 1887.
1019. III. EVA LILLIAN[8], b. at Westfield, Mass., 11 Jan., 1891.
1020. IV. LEON BURTON[8], b. at Westfield, Mass., 9 May, 1894.

620. **ELISHA KIMBALL[7] FANNING**, b. 1819, (*Chester Griswold[6], Oramel[5], James[4], Richard[3], Thomas[2], Edmund[1]*)
m. at Erie, Penn., 19 Oct., 1853,

Helen Myers,

dau. of Peter and ( ) Myers,
and b. at Orleans, Jefferson Co., N.Y., 1 Jan., 1836.

Elisha Kimball Fanning was born at Scipio, Cayuga Co., N.Y., 19 June, 1819. He was passenger conductor on the Lake Shore & Michigan Southern R.R., also freight agent of the Rome, Watertown, & Ogdensburg R.R. Co. at Watertown, N.Y., and was in the employ of that company as shipping clerk at Rome at the time of his death.

He d. at Rome, N.Y., 22 Nov., 1857.

After his death his wid. m. 2d, at Sackett's Harbor, N.Y. 27 Nov., 1861, William Howard, a hardware merchant of Watertown, N.Y. He was b. at Springfield, Mass., 16 Oct., 1826. Mrs. Howard d. at Watertown, N.Y., 29 Sept., 1883, having issue by Mr. Howard as follows: Charles W. Howard, b. 20 Nov., 1863; Frankie M. Howard, b. 24 Feb., 1870, d. 26 April, 1876.

Issue:

1021. I. CHARLES ORAMEL[8], b. at Watertown, Jefferson Co., N.Y., 28 Dec., 1854; d. at Auburn, Cayuga Co., N.Y., 4 July, 1859.

621. **CHARLES ORAMEL[7] FANNING**, b. 1821, (*Chester Griswold*[6], *Oramel*[5], *James*[4], *Richard*[3], *Thomas*[2], *Edmund*[1])
m. near Pendleton, Ore., about 1870,
Mary Reith,
dau. of
and b. at

Charles Oramel Fanning, son of Chester Griswold and Lucy Geer (Kimball) Fanning, was born at Scipio, N.Y., 30 Oct., 1821. He is said to be a well-to-do farmer, residing at Pendleton, Ore., where he owns a ranch of 500 acres about two miles out from Pendleton. No record, however, is obtainable. No issue.

623. **GEORGE WASHINGTON[7] FANNING**, b. 1826, (*Chester Griswold*[6], *Oramel*[5], *James*[4], *Richard*[3], *Thomas*[2], *Edmund*[1])

m. at Ira, Cayuga Co., N.Y., 12 Dec., 1854,

Kate Wilson,

dau. of John and Margaret (Mills) Wilson, and b. at Lowell, Mass., 28 Nov., 1831.

George Washington Fanning, son of Chester Griswold and Lucy Geer (Kimball) Fanning, was born at Jerusalem, Yates Co.,N.Y.,29 March, 1826; is a carpenter, and resides at Auburn, N.Y.

Issue:

1022. I. SARAH ELIZA[8], b. at Port Hope, Ontario, Canada, 6 March, 1858; m. at Skaneateles, Onondaga Co., N.Y., 20 Sept., 1886, James Gardiner.

He d. at Skaneateles, N.Y., 20 July, 1889, and wid. m.2d,26 Nov.,1895, Lorenzo W. Warner of Syracuse, N.Y.

Issue by her Gardiner marriage:

I. LUCY GRACE GARDINER, b. 5 Sept., 1887.

1023. II. SUSIE WILSON[8], b. at Auburn, N.Y., 14 March, 1866; m. at Auburn, N.Y., 18 Nov., 1895, George Ross Ostrander, and res. at Sennett, Cayuga Co., N.Y.

Issue:

I. ANNA KATE OSTRANDER, b. 21 Aug., 1896.

II. ETHEL ROSS OSTRANDER, b. 1 Nov., 1897.

624. **JAMES McKNIGHT^7 FANNING**, b. 1828, (*Chester Griswold^6, Oramel^5, James^4, Richard^3, Thomas^2, Edmund^1*)
m. at Phelps, Ontario Co., N.Y., 3 May, 1861.
Sarah Maria Burt,
dau. of Jonathan and Mary Ann (Harris) Burt,
and b. at Phelps, Ontario Co., N.Y., 17 June, 1842.

James McKnight Fanning, son of Chester Griswold and Lucy Geer (Kimball) Fanning, was born at Auburn, Cayuga Co., N.Y., 21 Dec., 1828. He is a brewer, and maltster and res. at Auburn, N.Y., having followed that occupation for twenty-five years. Previously he had been a carpenter and a cabinet maker and also a railroad man. He was drafted during the Civil War, but discharged by the examining physician.

Issue:

+1024. I. GEORGE BURT^8, b. at Palmyra, N.Y., 4 Sept., 1868.
1025. II. CHARLES HENRY^8, b. at Auburn, N.Y., 12 Nov., 1881; d. 26 April, 1883.

626. **CHESTER FREDERICK[7] FANNING**, b. 1834, (*Chester Griswold[6], Oramel[5], James[4], Richard[3], Thomas[2], Edmund[1]*)

m. at Clyde, Wayne Co., N.Y., 23 Sept., 1863,

Ellen Kirvan,

dau. of *

and b. at Montreal, Quebec., about 1848–49.

Chester Frederick Fanning, son of Chester Griswold and Lucy Geer (Kimball) Fanning, was born at Auburn, Cayuga Co., N.Y., 20 May, 1834. He learned the trade of a tinsmith when a young man, and in 1868 went West and settled at Big Rapids, Mecosta Co., Mich., and worked there at his trade for several years. He then located at Coldwater, Branch Co., Mich., where he resided until his decease, 2 Sept., 1890. He was buried at Coldwater.

His wid. m. at Big Rapids, Mich., 15 Jan., 1896, Philip M. Stevens of that city, where she now res. No issue by either m.

* Her parents died when she was about five or six years old, leaving her homeless and without relatives. Consequently, she is unable to give the exact date of her birth or the given names of her parents. She further states that in Dec., 1899, her house was burned with all its contents, and she lost all her books and papers, together with her marriage certificate and other documents.

627. **GURDON SATTERLEE[7] FANNING,** b. 1838, (*Chester Griswold*[6], *Oramel*[5], *James*[4], *Richard*[3], *Thomas*[2], *Edmund*[1])

m. at Fayette, Seneca Co., N.Y., 7 Oct., 1874,

Caroline Adelia Yeo,

dau. of Thomas Bruin and Clarissa (Ryan) Yeo, and b. at Waterloo, Seneca Co., N.Y., 21 March, 1840.*

Gurdon Satterlee Fanning was born at Auburn, N.Y., 6 Feb., 1838; is a brewer and maltster, and resides at Auburn. Is a successful business man, was supervisor, 1868–69. After graduating at Auburn Academy, he was for six years baggageman and freight master on N.Y. C. & H.R. R.R. From 1861 to 1864, was buying and shipping grain, and in latter year in employ of government, shipping oats to the army. Was drafted for the war at end of Rebellion, but was only five days in service, owing to close of war. 8 Aug., 1865, he purchased and built the brewery and malt house which has since been his business for over thirty years and has enlarged it from time to time as needs required. No issue.

---

* Thomas Bruin Yeo was said to be son of James Yeo of Newark, N.J., who was a nephew of Sir James Yeo a British Admiral in service on Lake Ontario in War of 1812, and was named after him. Sir James is said to have been brother-in-law to one of the Generals Clinton.

Cornelia Fanning Gay
1874 — 1900
From a bust by French

630. **CHARLES EDWIN[7] FANNING**, b. 1835,(*Charles Oramel*[6], *Oramel*[5], *James*[4], *Richard*[3], *Thomas*[2], *Edmund*[1])
m. at Cottage Grove, Minn., in Nov., 1872,
Georgina Frances Walker,
dau. of Francis and Caroline (McAllister) Walker,
and b. at Liverpool, Eng., 17 Dec., 1854.

Charles Edwin Fanning, son of Charles Oramel and Fidelia (Holbrook) Fanning, was born at Sand Bank,N.Y., 12 July, 1835; was a merchant, and resided at St. Paul, Minn., where he died 12 June, 1889. Buried at Cottage Grove, Minn. His widow survives.

Issue:

1026. i. CORNELIA SPALDING[8], b. at Cottage Grove, Minn., 7 March, 1874; m. at Boston, Mass., 15 Dec., 1898, Eben Howard Gay, a banker of Boston, and res. at 169 Beacon St.,that city,where she d. 20 Nov.,1900. Inter. in the Hingham,Mass.,Cemetery. (See Photogravure.)

1027. ii. ISABELLE[8], b. at Cottage Grove, Minn., 18 Dec., 1877. She was completing her education at Barnard Annex, Columbia College, New York City, in Class of 1897, when she d. suddenly within a few months of finishing her course, 17 March, 1897, and while on a brief visit to St. Paul. She is bur. in the family lot at Cottage Grove, Minn.

644. **NELSON[7] FANNING**, b. 1808, (*Benjamin*[6], *Walter*[5], *Thomas*[4], *John*[3], *John*[2], *Edmund*[1])
m. at Bristol, N.Y., 15 June, 1835, his cousin,
Anna Howell Hoy,
(called "Nancy") dau. of Richard and Sarah (Fanning) Hoy,
and b. at Albany, N.Y., 1 Oct., 1814.

Dr. Nelson Fanning was born at Bristol, N.Y., 14 Feb., 1808, was a physician and surgeon, and resided at Gilboa and afterwards Catskill, N.Y. Educated at a private academy at Jefferson in his native county, he studied medicine and graduated at the Berkshire Medical College in 1830 and commenced practice at Broome and then Gilboa. In 1862 he joined the Union Army as surgeon to the 134th N.Y. Vol. Inf., serving a year and a half, but was compelled to resign on account of poor health. He retired to Catskill, where he resided until his death. He was one of the oldest practicing physicians in the United States, being engaged in practice over sixty-seven years.

His wife d. at Catskill, N.Y., 24 Jan., 1893.

He d. at Catskill, N.Y., 28 Feb., 1896, a. 88 yrs. 14 ds.

Issue:

1028. I. MARY[8], b. at Strykersville, N.Y., 4 May, 1836; d. 11 May, 1836.

+1029. II. BENJAMIN[8], b. at Strykersville, N.Y., 12 April, 1837.

+1030. III. NELSON[8], b. at Strykersville, N.Y., 19 March, 1839.

1031. IV. WALTER DIES[8], b. at Gilboa, N.Y., 17 Oct., 1841; d. 1 Nov., 1846.

1032. V. JOHN TUTTLE[8], b. at Gilboa, N.Y., 1 Jan., 1844; d. 14 Feb., 1859.

1033. VI. HARRIET CLARKE[8], b. at Gilboa, N.Y., 29 Jan., 1846. Res. Catskill, N.Y.; unm.

1034. VII. SARAH ELIZABETH[8], b. at Gilboa, N.Y., 7 Oct., 1847. Res. Catskill, N.Y.; unm.

Nelson Fanning, M.D.
of Catskill, N.Y.
1803 – 1896

647. **CHARLES[7] FANNING,** b. 1807, (*Thomas[6], Walter[5], Thomas[4], John[3], John[2], Edmund[1]*)
m. at Prattsville, Green Co., N.Y., 4 March, 1831,
Elizabeth Robertson,*
dau. of Lovell Wood and ( ) Robertson, and b. at Claremont, Sullivan Co., N.H., 15 April, 1815. Lovell Wood Robertson was son of Eliphalet Jr., and Betsy (Wood) Robertson, and b. 16 Oct., 1790.

Charles Fanning was born at Blenheim, Schoharie Co., N.Y., 7 Dec., 1807. He was a wheelwright, and resided at Prattsville, Greene Co., N.Y., where he died 16 Oct., 1842.

Wid. d. at Deposit, Broome Co., N.Y., 13 Feb., 1895.

Issue:

+1035. I. JAMES MONROE[8], b. at Prattsville, Greene Co., N.Y., 21 Jan., 1832.

1036. II. AGNES SMEDBERGH[8], b. at Prattsville, Greene Co., N.Y., 15 Sept., 1835; m. at Gilboa, N.Y., 18 Sept., 1854, Lewis B. Hallock, a butcher. Res. East Durham, N.Y.

Issue born at Gilboa, N.Y.:

I. LIZZIE M. HALLOCK, b. 27 Oct., 1855.

II. G. FORD HALLOCK, b. 4 Nov., 1857; m. at East Durham, N.Y., 24 Dec., 1878, Martha Smith. He is a farmer.

III. J. FANNING HALLOCK, b. 4 Nov., 1857; m. 10 Feb., 1883, Mary E. Goff. He is a butcher.

+1037. III. GEORGE WASHINGTON FORD[8], b. at Prattsville, N.Y., 10 March, 1839.

1038. IV. CHARLES W [8], b. at Prattsville, N.Y., 30 Oct., 1842; d. 10 June, 1849.

---

* James M. Fanning of East Durham, N.Y., says his mother's maiden name was always spelled Robinson in his part of the country. Her father's name is recorded, however, at Claremont, N.H., where Elizabeth was born, as "*Lovell Wood Robertson.*"

648. **BOTTSFORD[7] FANNING**, b. about 1809, (*Thomas*[6], *Walter*[5], *Thomas*[4], *John*[3], *John*[2], *Edmund*[1])

m. at about 1836,

Eliza Morris,

dau. of

and b. at

She was from Jefferson, Schoharie Co., N.Y.

Bottsford Fanning, son of Thomas and (Bottsford) Fanning, was born at Blenheim, Schoharie Co., N.Y., about 1809. He was residing at Broome, Schoharie Co., in 1830. Soon afterward, however, he disappeared when still a young man, and it is said by some of his father's descendants he went West and became a missionary, and was killed by the Indians. Whether or not he had issue is not known. After careful research and extended inquiry among the relatives, no further information or record is obtainable.

650. **ASA[7] FANNING**, b. 1812, (*Thomas*[6], *Walter*[5], *Thomas*[4], *John*[3], *John*[2], *Edmund*[1])

m. at South Worcester, Otsego Co., N.Y., 1840,

Emeline Seeley,

dau. of Samuel and Huldah (Green) Seeley,
and b. at Delhi, Delaware Co., N.Y., 5 April, 1820.

Asa Fanning was born at Esperance, Schoharie Co., N.Y., 28 Jan., 1812. He was a millwright, and resided at South Worcester, Otsego Co., N.Y. He left a property in South Worcester when he died, which is now owned by his son, Nelson Charles Fanning.

He d. at South Worcester, N.Y., 17 April, 1892.

Wid. d. at South Worcester, N.Y., 10 Oct., 1892, and both bur. there.

Issue:

+1039. I. NELSON CHARLES[8], b. at Delhi, Delaware Co., N.Y., 26 Feb., 1842.

1040. II. BENJAMIN[8], b. at Delhi, Delaware Co., N.Y., 19 Jan., 1844. He never m. He was in the War of the Rebellion, and enlisted at Worcester, N.Y., in the 121st. N.Y., G. V., and d. at the Battle of Chancellorsville, 4 May, 1863.

+1041. III. SAMUEL[8], b. at Davenport, Delaware Co., N.Y., 7 April, 1851.

1042. IV. JAMES[8], b. at Davenport, N.Y., 3 Jan., 1853; d. same yr.

1043. V. MARTHA HULDAH[8], b. at Davenport, N.Y., 6 March, 1855; m. at South Worcester, Otsego Co., N.Y., 3 Oct., 1886, John Smith Adee, a painter and paper hanger. Res. South Worcester, N.Y. Issue: Oscar James Adee, b. 30 Nov., 1890.

1044. VI. ASA E   [8], b. and d. same year.

652. **HORACE[7] FANNING,** b. 1815, (*John*[6], *Walter*[5], *Thomas*[4], *John*[3], *John*[2], *Edmund*[1])
m. at Blenheim, Schoharie Co., N.Y., 25 June, 1843,
Mary Anna Dorman,
dau. of Moses and Phœbe (Badgley) Dorman,
and b. at Blenheim, N.Y., 26 April, 1819.

Horace Fanning, son of John and Experience (Hall) Fanning, was born at Schoharie, N.Y., 29 May, 1815. He was a shoemaker in early life, and afterward followed farming, and resided at Schoharie.

His wife d. at Schoharie, N.Y., 6 Feb., 1896, and is bur. there. He d. at Schoharie, N.Y., 16 April, 1897, a. 81 yrs., 10 mos., 18 ds.

Issue:

1045. I. EMMA GRACE[8], b. at Schoharie, N.Y., 30 Sept., 1853; m. at Schoharie, N.Y., 3 April, 1897, Charles Lawyer, and res. in Schoharie, N.Y. He is a farmer, son of George and Catharine (Vroman) Lawyer, and was b. at Schoharie, 2 May, 1842.

656. **EDWIN[7] FANNING**, b. 1824*, (*John[6], Walter[5] Thomas[4], John[3], John[2], Edmund[1]*)

m. at East Berne, Albany Co., N.Y., 19 March, 1849,

Elizabeth Pears,

dau. of Jacob and Nancy (Seaverson) Pears, and b. at East Berne, Albany Co., N.Y., 28 July, 1818.

Edwin Fanning, son of John and Experience (Hall) Fanning, was born at Schoharie, N.Y.; was a farmer, and resided at Howe's Cave, Schoharie Co., N.Y., where he died 20 June, 1895. Bur. at Barnerville, Schoharie Co., N.Y. Wid. res. at Howe's Cave.

Issue:

+1046. I. JACOB HENRY[8], b. at Schoharie, N.Y., 4 May, 1851.

* The record in his family Bible reads 5 August, 1820. An older family Bible, however, of Horace Fanning at Schoharie, reads 5 Aug., 1824.

660. BENJAMIN[7] FANNING, b. 1833, (*John[6], Walter[5], Thomas[4], John[3], John[2], Edmund[1]*)

m. at Schoharie, N.Y., 23 Dec., 1862,

Elmira Garner,

dau. of Frederick and Betsey (Worick) Garner,
and b. at Schoharie, N.Y., 30 April, 1841.

Benjamin Fanning, son of John and Experience (Hall) Fanning, was born at Schoharie, N.Y., 5 Feb., 1833; is a farmer and resides at Fultonham, Schoharie Co., N.Y. Previous to 1896 he resided for 26 years at Seward, N.Y.

Issue:

1047. I. John[8], b. at Seward, N.Y., 26 Nov., 1864; d. 14 May, 1866.

+1048. II. Jesse Smith[8], b. at Seward, N.Y., 8 April, 1868.

663. **HENRY[7] FANNING**, b. 1812, (*Frederick*[6], *Walter*[5], *Thomas*[4], *John*[3], *John*[2], *Edmund*[1])

m. at Belleville, Ontario, Canada, 7 Nov., 1834,

Miriam Young,

dau. of Oliver and Mary (Lawrence) Young, and b. at Second Concession of Sidney, Ont., Can., March, 1812.

Henry Fanning, son of Frederick and Hannah (Davis) Fanning, was born at Wolf Island, near Kingston, Ont., Can., 14 Feb., 1812. He was a farmer, and later a hotel keeper. He owned a farm at Sidney, two miles from Frankfort and twelve from Belleville, which he sold and thereupon removed to Belleville, where he resided until his decease.

He d. at Belleville, 20 March, 1866.

Wid. d. at Belleville, 24 March, 1869. Both bur. in Belleville Cemetery.

Issue:

+1049. I. FREDERICK[8], b. at Fourth Concession of Sidney, Ontario, Canada, 7 Sept., 1835.

1050. II. MARY MATILDA[8], b. at Fourth Concession of Sidney, Ontario, Canada, 2 May, 1837; m. 1st at Belleville, Ontario, Canada, 14 May, 1856, William Henry Bonter. He d. at Halifax, N.S., 7 April, 1863. Wid. m. 2d at Belleville, Ontario, Canada, 14 June, 1869, James Panton Hopkins, a merchant, b. in Dorset, Eng. Res. Little Rock, Ark.

Issue by Bonter marriage:

I. OSCAR WASHINGTON BONTER, b. 26 Feb., 1857.

Issue by Hopkins marriage:

II. ELIZABETH ISABELLA HOPKINS, b. 23 July, 1870.

III. HENRY PANTON HOPKINS, b. 13 Oct., 1871.

IV. JAMES HERBERT HOPKINS, b. 27 July, 1876.

1051. III. MARGARET JANE[8], b. at Fourth Conces. of Sidney, Ont., Can., 29 Jan., 1839; m. at Belleville, Ont., Can., in 1860, Donaldson A. Bogart, a dentist. Res. Hamilton, Ont., where he d. in 1886. Wid. res. Little Rock, Ark. Is a music teacher.

Issue born at Hamilton, Ont.:

I. MARY ISABELLE BOGART, b. in Feb., 1864; m. Charles H. Haile. Res. N.Y.

II. HARRY LAZIER BOGART, b. 28 Nov., 1869.

III. WALTER SCOTT BOGART, b. in June, 1872; d. in Jan., 1876.

+1052. IV. GEORGE WALTER[8], b. at Fourth Conces. of Sidney, Ont., Can., 13 May, 1841.

1053. V. HANNAH ALZINA[8], b. at Fourth Conces. of Sidney, Ont., Can., 24 Aug., 1842; a music teacher. Res. Little Rock, Ark.; unm.

1054. VI. HIRAM WESLEY[8], b. at Fourth Conces. of Sidney, Ont., Can., in Aug., 1844. Never m. Studied medicine, but d. in 1870 before receiving his diploma.

1055. VII. NANNIE ARVILLA[8], b. at Fifth Conces. of Sidney Ont., Can., 29 Dec., 1848; m. at Hamilton, Ont., Can., 5 April, 1883, Joseph Charlton, a glassblower. Res. No. Hamilton, Ont., Can. No issue.

1056. VIII. MIRIAM EMILY[8], b. at Fifth Conces. of Sidney, Ont., Can., in 1848; d. 1849.

1057. IX. MARTHA AGNES[8], b. at Belleville, Ont., Can., 4 May, 1850; d. 1854.

1058. X. MARKLIN HENRY[8], b. at Belleville, Ont., Can., in 1852; d. in 1854.

664. **GEORGE[7] FANNING**, b. 1814, (*Frederick[6], Walter[5], Thomas[4], John[3], John[2], Edmund[1]*)

m. 1st, in Township of Sidney, Ont., Can., 25 Feb., 1836.

Sarah Ostrom,

dau. of Gilbert and Hannah (Burleigh) Ostrom, and b. at Wolf Island, Ont., Can., 15 Feb., 1814.

She d. at Chebanse, Ill., 8 March, 1874.

He m. 2d, at Kankakee, Ill., 21 Sept., 1874,

Eliza Ann Gilbert,

dau. of Caleb and Sarah (Ross) Gilbert, and b. in Hastings Co., Can., 8 May, 1844.

George Fanning was born at Wolf Island near Kingston, Ont., Can., 10 Oct., 1814. Settled in Second Conces. of Sidney, where he engaged in tannery business until 1865, when he removed to Chebanse, Ill., where he farmed it a part of the time and where he resided until his decease.

His wife d. at Chebanse, Ill., 8 July, 1890.

He d. at Chebanse, Ill., 22 March, 1897, a. 82 yrs.

Issue by wife Sarah :

1059. I. HANNAH ELLEN[8], b. at Sidney, Can., 29 Nov., 1836 m. at Sidney, 28 Feb., 1855, Jacob Henry Hogle, a farmer. Res. Orillia, Ont., Can. Issue: Ida Hogle, b. at Sidney, 15 March, 1856; m. at Orillia, Arthur H. Wainwright.

1060. II. HARRIETT MATILDA[8], b. at Sidney, Can., 2 March, 1838; m. 31 July, 1862, Bowen A. Lucas, a farmer. Res. Wallbridge, Ont., Can. No issue.

1061. III. SARAH ELIVA[8], b. at Sidney, Can., 27 Feb., 1840; m. at Chebanse, Ill., 20 March, 1866, Thomas Millburn. Res. Beatrice, Neb.

Issue (one ch. d. in infancy):

I. ELLA MATILDA MILLBURN, b. 2 March, 1868.

II. GEORGE H. MILLBURN, b. 2 April, 1871.

III. ALBERT L. MILLBURN, b. 22 March, 1874.

+1062. IV. FREDERICK WALTER[8], b. in Township of Thurlow, District of Hastings, Ont., Can., 6 Oct., 1841.

+1063. V. RICHARD GILBERT[8], b. at Sidney, Can., 14 June, 1845.

+1064. VI. GEORGE BALDWIN[8], b. at Sidney, Can., 17 April, 1848.

+1065. VII. JOHN NELSON[8], b. at Sidney, Can., 24 June, 1850.

1066. VIII. AURELIA AGNES[8], b. at Sidney, Can., 25 May, 1854; m. 1st, at Chebanse, Ill., 26 Feb., 1872, George Francis Grosse, a merchant. Res. Chebanse, where he d. 23 July, 1885. Wid. m. 2d, 30 March, 1887, Benjamin James Wynneparry, a mfg. chemist. Res. Detroit, Mich.

Issue by Grosse marriage:

I. RILLA ESTELLE GROSSE, b. 12 Dec., 1873.

II. FRANCIS MURIEL GROSSE, b. 30 Sept., 1883. (Three ch. d. young.)

Issue by Wynneparry marriage:

III. GEORGE DURWARD WYNNEPARRY, b. 18 Oct., 1888.

Issue by wife Eliza:

1067. IX. JAMES J[8], b. at Chebanse, Ill., 3 Aug., 1875; d. 27 Nov., 1884.

1068. X. MARY MAUDE[8], b. at Chebanse, Ill., 29 April, 1879; m. at Kankakee, Ill., 5 April, 1899, Dr. Isaac Benson Ennis, of Martinton, Ill., where they reside.

1069. XI. MYRTLE KERR[8], b. at Chebanse, Ill., 12 Nov., 1882; d. 26 March, 1884.

1070. XII. MAY GEW[8], b. at Chebanse, Ill., 12 Nov., 1882; d. 28 Aug., 1883.

667. **JOHN BENJAMIN[7] FANNING**, b. 1821, (*Frederick*[6], *Walter*[5], *Thomas*[4], *John*[3], *John*[2], *Edmund*[1])
m. in Sidney, Ont., Can., 1 Dec., 1848,
Susan Orr,
dau. of John and Catharine (Bleecker) Orr,
and b. in Sidney, Ont., Can., 30 Sept., 1826.

John Benjamin Fanning was born at Wolf Island, near Kingston, Ont., Can., 14 March, 1821; is a farmer, and resides in Sterling, Ont., Can.

His wife d. at Sterling, Ont., 21 March, 1900.

Issue:

+1071. I. JOHN ROWE[8], b. at Rawdon, Ont., Can., 30 Sept., 1849.

+1072. II. FREDERICK BENJAMIN[8], b. at Rawdon, Ont., Can., 12 April, 1851.

+1073. III. WILLIAM HENRY[8], b. at Rawdon, Ont., Can., 18 July, 1853.

+1074. IV. GEORGE BLEECKER[8], b. at Rawdon, Ont., Can., 19 March, 1855.

1075. V. OWEN MYERS[8], b. at Rawdon, Ont., Can., 14 Oct., 1857; d., 8 Aug., 1898; unm.

+1076. VI. ELLIS BURRELL[8], b. at Rawdon, Ont., Can., 26 March, 1861.

1077. VII. GATREY EMMA[8], b. at Rawdon, Ont., Can., 22 April, 1862; m. at Rawdon, Ont., Can., 5 Sept., 1888, Alexander Moore, a farmer. Res. Thurlow township, Dist. of Hastings, Ont., Can., where she had

Issue:

I. GATREY KETHIA MOORE, b. 13 Sept., 1890.
II. JULIAN ALEXANDER MOORE, b. 8 Aug., 1892.
III. BURLEY CAMPBELL MOORE, b. 8 Nov., 1894.
IV. BERTHIA FANNING MOORE, b. 28 Jan., 1898.

1078. VIII. CYNTHIA JANE[8], b. at Rawdon, Ont., Can., 17 Jan., 1865; m. at Colborne, Ont., Can., 23 Sept., 1890, William Denton Rowley. Res. Owosso, Mich.

Issue:

I. BEATRICE ARMILA ROWLEY, b. 23 April, 1893.

668. **ISAAC[7] FANNING,** b. 1823, (*Frederick*[6], *Walter*[5], *Thomas*[4], *John*[3], *John*[2], *Edmund*[1])
m. at Consecon, Ont., Can., 12 Sept., 1846,
Sarah Ann Gilbert,
dau. of Samuel and (White) Gilbert,
and b. in Sidney Township, Dist. of Hastings, Ont., Can., in May, 1825.

Isaac Fanning was born in the township of Sidney, Dist. of Hastings, Ont., Can., 26 Oct., 1823. He resided in the town of Trenton, Ont., Can., where he kept a hotel many years.

His wife d. at Belleville, Ont., Can.

He d. at Trenton, Ont., Can., 21 April, 1893.

Issue:

1079. I. CLARISSA[8], b. at Belleville, Ont., Can., 24 July, 1847; m. at Hamilton, Ont., Can., , Dr. Dennis, and res. at Hamilton, where she d. He res. at Georgetown, Ont., Can., where he has one ch. living.

1080. II. JOHN LEE[8], b. at Belleville, Ont., Can., ; unm.

1081. III. LOUISA[8], b. at Belleville, Ont., Can., in Jan., 1851; d. at Sidney, Ont., Can., in early life; unm.

669. **DAVID FREDERICK[7] FANNING**, b. 1823, (*Frederick*[6], *Walter*[5], *Thomas*[4], *John*[3], *John*,[2], *Edmund*[1])
m. at Chatham, Ont., Can., 14 Sept., 1847,
Louisa Miller,
dau. of Peter and Catharine (Brundige) Miller,
and b. at Chatham, Ont., 26 June, 1830.

David Frederick Fanning was born at Sidney, Ont. Can., 26 Oct., 1823. He went West about 1866 or 1867, and bought a farm at Primghar, O'Brien Co., Ia., where he located and followed farming.

He d. at Independence, Ia., 28 March, 1898. Bur. at Primghar.

Wid. res. Chatham, Ont., Can.

Issue:

1082. I. CATHARINE[8], b. at Chatham, Ont., 18 Aug., 1851; m. at Chatham, Ont., 24 Oct., 1873, Theodore Charles Holmes, a machinist. Res. Walkerville, Ont.

Issue born at Chatham:

I. GERTRUDE HOLMES, b. 13 Feb., 1877.

II. ROY HOLMES, b. 31 Jan., 1880.

+1083. II. JOHN FREDERICK[8], b. at Charing Cross, Ont., 21 Nov., 1852.

+1084. III. ANDREW CONRAD[8], b. at Chatham, Ont., 21 Oct., 1857.

1085. IV. EMMA[8], b. at Chatham, Ont., ; m. at Chatham. Ont., , Fred Goodland, a butcher. Res. Chatham. (No record obtainable.)

1086. V. SARAH[8], b. at Newbury, Ont., 29 Oct., 1861 ; m. at Chatham, Ont., 25 Nov., 1884, William Ball, a tinsmith. Res. Nelson, B.C.

Issue:

I. WILLIAM RAY BALL, b. 1 Feb., 1886.

II. ARTHUR SUTHERLAND BALL, b. 14 March, 1890; d. 28 Nov., 1892.

671. **SYLVESTER[7] FANNING**, b. 1828, (*Frederick[6], Walter[5], Thomas[4], John[3], John[2], Edmund[1]*)
m. at Belleville, Ont., Can., 25 Nov., 1849,
Eliza Orr,
dau. of John and Catharine (Bleecker) Orr,
and b. in the Township of Sidney, Dist. of Hastings, Ont., Can., 1 April, 1829.

Sylvester Fanning was born at Sidney, Ont.,Can.,4 Nov., 1828; is a farmer, and resides at Havelock, Ont., Can.

Issue :

+1087. I. GEORGE HENRY[8], b. at Rawdon, Ont., Can., 20 Nov., 1851.

1088. II. SARAH ANN[8], b. at Rawdon, Ont., Can., 12 May, 1855; m. at Toronto, Can., 24 June, 1891, Edward Irwin, a conductor on the Can. Pac. R.R. Res. Havelock, Ont.

Issue born at Havelock :

I. PEARL IRWIN, b. 5 April, 1892.
II. ROBERT ATHO IRWIN, b. 2 July, 1893.
III. FRANK ATHO IRWIN, b. 28 Oct., 1895.

+1089. III. CHARLES BIRDSLEY[8], b. at Rawdon, Ont., Can., 3 Feb., 1857.

+1090. IV. WESLEY ARDEN[8], b.at Belmont, Ont., Can., 12 Aug., 1859.

1091. V. JENNIE MAY[8], b. at Sidney, Ont., Can., 3 May, 1861; m. at Campbellford, Ont., 1 July, 1882, John Maidens, a merchant. Res. Havelock, Ont.

Issue :

I. GEORGE ARTHUR MAIDENS, b. 8 Dec., 1883.
II. DELLA MAY MAIDENS, b. 21 March, 1885.
III. LEAH FERNA MAIDENS, b. 12 July, 1887.
IV. JOHN EARL MAIDENS, b. 1 June, 1891.
V. GRACE WINNIFRED MAIDENS, b. 30 Jan., 1894.
VI. BLEECKER FOY MAIDENS, b. 11 Sept., 1896.

+1092. VI. WALTER BLAKE[8], b. at Belmont, Ont., Can., 20 Sept., 1871.

681. **ROBERT STARK[7] FANNING**, b. 1835, (*Patrick*[6], *Charles*[5], *Thomas*[4], *John*[3], *John*[2], *Edmund*[1])

m. 1st, at Brooklyn, N.Y., 9 Oct., 1861,

Elizabeth Dwight Paddock,

dau. of Rev. Seth B. and Emily (Flagg) Paddock, and b. at Norwich, Conn., 31 March, 1838.

She d. at Detroit, Mich., 4 July, 1866. Bur. Astoria, L.I.

He m. 2d, at Astoria, L.I., 6 Oct., 1868,

Ellen Wikoff Mulligan,

dau. of William and Ellen (Wikoff) Mulligan, and b. at Astoria, L.I., 1 May, 1849.

Robert Stark Fanning was born at Norwich, Conn., 22 April, 1835. He early settled in New York City, where he became a merchant, and achieved for himself an honorable standing among the merchants of that city, and gained the esteem of all who were brought into contact with him. He resided at Astoria, L.I., where he died 4 Feb., 1876, at the early age of 40.

Widow res. at Astoria. His will, dated 3 Feb., 1876, probated 28 Feb., 1876, at Jamaica, L.I., mentions wife Ellen W. Fanning and three ch.: Lizzie F., Ellen W., and Julia M. Fanning, all under 14 yrs. of age. S. J. Coggswell of Jamaica was appointed special guardian of the ch. on that date. Letters of guardianship were given Ellen W. Fanning of L.I. City, for Lizzie F. Fanning, a minor, under 14, 10 March, 1876.

Issue by wife Elizabeth :

1093. I. ELIZABETH FLAGG[8], b. at Astoria, L.I., 24 Sept., 1863.

Issue by wife Ellen :

1094. II. ELLEN WIKOFF[8], b. at Astoria, L.I., 30 Dec., 1870.

1095. III. JULIA MULLIGAN[8], b. at Astoria, L.I., 17 Feb., 1875.

684. **CHARLES[7] FANNING**, b. 1830, (*John Watson*[6], *Charles*[5], *Thomas*[4], *John*[3], *John*[2], *Edmund*[1])
m. at Jewett City, Conn., 20 May, 1861,
Helen Marr Thompson,
dau. of Asa and Betsey (Vaughan) Thompson,
and b. at Norwich, Conn., 17 July, 1837.

Charles Fanning, son of John Watson and Mary (Wilson) Fanning, was born at Jewett City, Conn., 20 March, 1830, where he resided most of his life. In 1896 or 1897 removed to Preston, Conn., where he now resides. Is retired from business.

Issue recorded at Jewett City, Conn.:

1096. I. KATIE THOMPSON[8], b. at Jewett City, Conn., 15 Sept., 1865; d. 20 Nov., 1870, a. 5 yrs., 2 mos. (g.s.). Bur. Jewett City.

1097. II. BESSIE VAUGHAN[8], b. at Jewett City, Conn., 22 Dec., 1873; m. at Jewett City, Conn., 28 Oct., 1896, Donald Mackintosh Foster, a pharmacist, and res. at Swampscott, Mass.

Issue:

I. CHARLES REGINALD FOSTER, b. 28 Oct., 1902.

685. **FREDERICK HUDSON[7] FANNING**, b. 1832, (*John Watson[6], Charles[5], Thomas[4], John[3], John[2], Edmund[1]*)
m. at Jewett City, Conn., 3 Dec., 1855,
Ellen Amelia Pellet,
dau. of Amassa and Lydia (Bingham) Pellet,
and b. at Canterbury, Conn., 31 Aug., 1838.

Frederick Hudson Fanning was born at Jewett City, Conn., 24 Oct., 1832. (Named after one James Hudson.) He learned the trade of a mechanic, and has followed it many years at Jewett City, where he has resided all his life. He served in the War of the Rebellion, enlisting in May, 1861, in a battery of light artillery, but was transferred to the 5th Conn. Inf. He went to the front 1 July, 1861, and was in nearly all the engagements that the regiment was in. Was a prisoner at Belle Isle for about four months. Was not wounded while in service, but contracted rheumatism, and is a United States pensioner therefrom. He was representative in the Conn. Legislature in 1880 and selectman of Griswold in 1895, 1896, 1897, and 1898.

Issue:

1098. I. FREDERICK WILSON[8], b. at Jewett City, Conn., 17 Aug., 1858; d. 30 Aug., 1858.

1099. II. MARY LUCINDA[8], b. at Putnam, Conn., 25 July, 1860; m. at Jewett City 3 Oct., 1895, Frank Everett Olds. He is a dealer in cotton and wool waste, and res. at Jewett City, Conn. She d. 27 March, 1901.

+1100. III. FREDERICK HUDSON[8], b. at Jewett City, Conn., 30 Oct., 1864.

689. **CHARLES HENRY[7] FANNING**, b. 1812, (*Henry Willson[6], Thomas[5], Thomas[4], John[3], John[2], Edmund[1]*)
m. at Jewett City, Conn., 9 March, 1834, by Rev. George Perkins,

Julia Ann Cole,

dau. of Capt. Samuel and Permelia (Streeter) Cole of Jewett City, Conn. and b. at Smithfield, RI., 4 Aug., 1811.

Capt. Samuel Cole was born in Mass. in 1789, d. in Jewett City, Conn., 6 Aug., 1860.

Permelia (Streeter) Cole was b. in Smithfield, R.I., in 1789; d. in Jewett City, Conn., 27 Oct., 1869.

Charles Henry Fanning, son of Henry Willson and Sarah (Hale) Fanning, was born at Marlborough, Conn., 2 Oct., 1812. Removed with his parents to Norwich and then Jewett City, Conn., where when he grew up became overseer in Slater's Cotton Mills. Resided after marriage at Bozrahville, Greenville, Jewett City, Conn., Lonsdale, R.I., and Providence, R.I., where he was overseer of weaving in the "Steam Mill" on Eddy St. He went West for his health, but returned home and died at Providence, R.I., 2 May, 1856. Bur. Jewett City.

His wid. m. 2d, at Jewett City, 23 May, 1864, Eben H. Clark, a hotel keeper, and res. in Penn. 15 yrs. Mr. Clark d. at Cherry Ridge, Penn., 15 April, 1879. Wid. d. at Worcester, Mass., 24 April, 1891. Bur. Jewett City.

Issue:

+1101. i. Charles Henry[8], b. at Bozrahville, Conn., 13 Feb., 1835.

+1102. ii. Alfred Hale[8], b. at Bozrahville, Conn., 25 Jan., 1837.

+1103. iii. William Barnard[8], b. at Lonsdale, R.I., 5 Sept., 1843.

+1104. iv. Augustus Foster[8], b. at Lonsdale, R.I., 23 Aug., 1845.

1105. v. Julia Permelia[8], b. at Lonsdale, R.I., 9 Feb., 1847; d. 14 Aug., 1847.

1106. vi. Juliette Willard[8], b. at Providence, R.I., 31 Oct., 1852; d. 22 Feb., 1854.

691. **HENRY WILLIAMS[7] FANNING**, b. 1816, (*Henry Willson[6], Thomas[5], Thomas[4], John[3], John[2], Edmund[1]*)
m. at Norwich, Conn., 29 Oct., 1839,
Mary Ann Whaley,
dau. of Levi and Lovinda (Gardner) Whaley,
and b. at Norwich, Conn., 22 Aug., 1818.

Levi Whaley was b. 14 July, 1787. Lovinda Gardner was b. 15 Jan., 1790, and was sister to Sidney Gardner, who m. Fanny Maria Fanning (No. 352).

Henry Williams* Fanning, son of Henry Willson and Sarah (Hale) Fanning, was born at Marlborough, Conn., 23 May, 1816. When a few weeks old his parents removed to Norwich, and soon to Jewett City. His first employment was in Slater's Cotton Mills there. He then kept a country store for a few years, built a small mill for the manufacture of twine and cotton batting a mile from the village, and named the place Dorrville after Gov. Dorr of R.I. After four or five years the mill burned down. About 1853 he removed to Newton Upper Falls, Mass., where he resided until his death, and where he carried on the grocery business for thirty years. He ran a farm also the greater part of the time. Later in life he retired from business, having by thriftiness and hard work accumulated a good competency. Was lieutenant in local militia.

His wife d. at Newton Upper Falls, Mass., 25 May, 1877.

He d. at Newton Upper Falls, Mass., 5 Aug., 1900.

Issue:

+1107. I. EUGENE[8], b. at Jewett City, Conn., 17 March, 1842.
+1108. II. HENRY HALE[8], b. at Woonsocket, R.I., 10 June, 1851.
+1109. III. FRANK[8], b. at Newton Upper Falls, Mass., 13 April, 1854.

---

* Named after one Henry Williams of Glastonbury, Conn. He was to have received a red shirt and a red cap for his name, but Mr. Williams failed to keep his part of the contract. Either he lost his possessions, or the lad was unworthy the rich gifts.

695. **GEORGE FAULKNER[7] FANNING**, b. 1825 (*Henry Willson[6], Thomas[5], Thomas[4], John[3], John[2], Edmund[1]*)
m. at Cincinnati, O., 29 Sept., 1850.
Catherine Payne,
dau. of Daniel and Rebecca (Test) Payne,
and b. at Redding, O., 1 May, 1826. Rebecca Test was b. in Germany.

George Faulkner Fanning, son of Henry Willson and Sarah (Hale) Fanning, was born at Jewett City, Conn., 4 Sept., 1825. He early learned the trade of carriage making at Norwich, and worked at it at New Haven a year or two, and at Greenville, So. Car., and Amesbury, Mass. When the California gold fever broke out, he was one of the original "49-ers" and sailed from Boston for San Francisco, *via* Cape Horn. After residing in Cal. a year he returned East and lived at Cincinnati, O., and Covington, Ky., fifteen years, following his trade. In 1866 or 1867 he returned to California, and has resided there since at San Francisco, Petaluma, and San Rafael with his daughters. Is now (1904) residing at 3777 23d St., San Francisco, with his dau. Carrie.

His wife d. at Petaluma, Cal., 2 Oct., 1892. Bur. at San Rafael.

Issue:

1110. I. SARAH[8], b. at Cincinnati, O., 7 Aug., 1851; d. 9 Aug., 1851.

1111. II. FRANK[8], b. at Cincinnati, O., 10 Dec., 1852; d. 11 Jan., 1853.

1112. III. KATE MAY[8], b. at Covington, Ky., 9 May, 1854; m. at Honolulu, H.I., 26 July, 1883, David MacCartney, b. at Pittsburg, Penn., 21 May, 1856, a druggist. Res. Honolulu, H.I., where he d. 2 Sept., 1884.

Issue:

I. VIDA MAY MACCARTNEY, b. at Petaluma, Cal., 14 Dec., 1884.

1113. IV. EMMA[8], b. at Covington, Ky., 9 Sept., 1856; m. at San Francisco, Cal., 13 May, 1896, Charles Samuel Barney, a widower with one son, Charles Royce Barney, by a previous marriage. Res. San Rafael, Cal. He is a real estate and insurance man, and was b. at Frederick City, Md., 2 May, 1841. No issue.

1114. V. CARRIE[8], b. at Covington, Ky., 31 July, 1859; m. at Honolulu, H.I., 18 July, 1883, Joshua Daniel Tucker, b. at Sacramento, Cal., 10 June, 1859. Res. at Honolulu, H.I., Petaluma, Cal., and San Francisco, Cal.

Issue born at Honolulu:

I. HENRIETTA TUCKER, b. 24 Jan., 1885.

II. HARRISON MORTON TUCKER, b. 1 May, 1889.

III. KATHRYN TUCKER, b. 8 Oct., 1891.

1115. VI. MURIEL BIRCH[8], b. at Covington, Ky., 26 Feb., 1863. Res. San Francisco, Cal.; unm. 1904.

1116. VII. MARIA LULU[8], b. at Covington, Ky., 20 Nov., 1865. m. 1st, at San Francisco, Cal., 4 Feb., 1891, Walter Minton Heywood, b. at Berkley, Cal. Res. San Francisco, Cal., where he d. Wid. m. 2d, at San Rafael, Cal., in July, 1896, James Linton Torbert. Res. Honolulu, H.I.

Issue by her Heywood marriage:

I. ZUMRI HEYWOOD, b. at San Francisco, Cal., in 1892; d., a. 3 mos.

II. GEORGE MINTON HEYWOOD, b. at San Rafael, Cal., 7 Feb., 1894.

Issue by her Torbert marriage:

III. JAMES TORBERT, b. at Honolulu, H.I., 26 Oct., 1897.

697. **DAVID HALE[7] FANNING**, b. 1830, (*Henry Willson[6], Thomas[5], Thomas[4], John[3], John[2], Edmund[1]*)
m. at Worcester, Mass., 28 Sept., 1859,
Rosamond Hopkins Dawless,
dau. of Young Simmons and Adaline Fidelia (Willard) Dawless,
and b. at Sterling, Mass., 6 May, 1837.

David Hale Fanning, son of Henry Willson and Sarah (Hale) Fanning, was born at Jewett City, Conn., 4 Aug., 1830. He resides in Worcester, Mass., and is a prominent manufacturer of corsets in that city, — president of the Royal Worcester Corset Co.

His wife d. at Worcester, Mass., 14 Dec., 1901. Bur. in the family lot in Rural Cemetery.

(For complete sketch of David Hale Fanning, see Biographical part of this volume.)

Issue:

1117. I. AGNES MARIA[8], b. at Worcester, Mass., 29 Sept., 1864; m. at Worcester, Mass., 6 April, 1892, John Edward Lancaster, of that city, b. in New York, N.Y., 1 Dec., 1863. He is a corset manufacturer. Res. Worcester, Mass. She was educated at Mt. Holyoke and Lasell seminaries, Mass.

Issue born at Worcester:

I. JOHN EDWARD LANCASTER, b. 27 Feb., 1893.
II. ROBERT ALLAN LANCASTER, b. 9 Sept., 1895.
III. ROSAMOND LANCASTER, b. 19 April, 1897.

1118. II. FRANK EVERETT[8], b. at Worcester, Mass., 20 March, 1869; d. 21 Aug., 1869.

1119. III. HELEN JOSEPHINE[8], b. at Worcester, Mass., 10 June, 1870. Graduate of Mt. Holyoke Seminary and College, Class of 1891. Res. Worcester; unm.

699. **GEORGE WASHINGTON[7] FANNING**, b. 1818,
(*John Faulkner[6], Thomas[5], Thomas[4], John[3], John[2], Edmund[1]*)

m. at Norwich, Conn., 1 Sept., 1846,

Martha Maria Martin,

dau. of Anson and Betsey (Lawton) Martin,
and b. at Kingston, Penn., 6 Feb., 1820.

George Washington Fanning, son of John Faulkner and Betsey (Gates) Fanning, was born at Preston, Conn., 8 March, 1818; was a millwright by trade and after his marriage settled in Greenville, Conn., then a suburb but now a part of Norwich. He enlisted in the 18th Regt. Conn. Vols. 29 July, 1862, and served until 26 March, 1864. Was taken prisoner and confined in Libby Prison, and later Belle Isle. After the war be returned to his old trade, that of mill business, and resided at Greenville until his death.

His wife d. at Greenville, Conn., 1 Aug., 1887, a. 67 yrs. 5 mos., 25 ds.

He d. at Greenville, Conn., 10 Nov., 1887, a. 69 yrs., 8 mos., 2 ds. Both bur. in Yantic Cemetery, Norwich.

Issue:

1120. i. NOYES HAMILTON[8], b. at Greenville, Conn., 8 July, 1847. He never m. Res. at Greenville, Conn., where had store at one time. Served as paymaster's assistant under his uncle, George Martin, on S.S. "Mendota" in Civil War.

1121. ii. FRANCES HENRIETTA[8], b. at Greenville, Conn., 7 Aug., 1854; d. 6 April, 1855.

1122. iii. LAURA BETSEY[8], b. at Greenville, Conn., 2 Sept., 1856; d. 19 Jan., 1863.

+1123. iv. JOHN EARLE[8], b. at Greenville, Conn., 27 May, 1859.

EIGHTH GENERATION

701. **GEORGE[8] FANNING**, b. 1837, (*William*[7], *James*[6], *George*[5], *William*[4], *Edmund*[3], *Edmund*[2], *Edmund*[1]) m. at Ledyard, Conn., 16 April, 1862,

Mary Abbie Spicer,

dau. of Edmund and Bethiah Williams (Avery) Spicer, and b. at Ledyard, Conn., 23 Sept., 1837.

George Fanning was born at Ledyard, Conn., 4 Oct., 1837. He is a farmer, residing at Ledyard, and cultivates one of the best farms in the State. He has held many positions of trust and honor. Was elected School Visitor in Oct., 1859, and served as acting school visitor and Secretary of the Board for several years. In Oct., 1895, was again re-elected for a term of three years. In Nov., 1880, he was elected Judge of Probate, defeating Col. William T. Cook. Was defeated by James A. Billings in Nov., 1884. In Nov., 1888, was re-elected again, and retired Jan. 9, 1895, succeeded by Russell Gallup. In office ten years.

Issue:

1124. I. MARY BETHIAH[9], b. at Ledyard, Conn., 19 March, 1863; m. at Ledyard, 11 July, 1894, Walter Abbott Waterman of Griswold, Conn., b. at Providence, R.I., 2 June, 1870. He graduated at Yale College, Class of 1894; res. Mt. Vernon, N.Y. Issue: Hilda Fanning Waterman, b. at Mt. Vernon, N.Y., 5 Feb., 1898.

1125. II. FANNIE ELIZABETH[9], b. at Ledyard, Conn., 19 Nov., 1864. Res. Hartford, Conn.; unm.

1126. III. SUSAN ELIDA[9], b. at Ledyard, Conn., 21 Sept., 1866; m. at Ledyard, 21 Sept., 1886, Christopher Allyn Brown 2d, b. at Brooklyn, N.Y., 5 Sept., 1864. He was a merchant at Gales Ferry, where he d. 26 Feb., 1890. Wid. res. Ledyard.

Issue:

I. FANNIE ELIDA BROWN, b. 19 Aug., 1887.

II. CHRISTOPHER ALLYN BROWN, b. 14 June, 1890.

+1127. IV. WILLIAM EDMUND[9], b. at Ledyard, Conn., 27 June, 1870.

1128. V. HARRIET EUNICE[9], b. at Ledyard, Conn., 18 Dec., 1872; m. at Ledyard, Conn., 10 March, 1898, William Seabury Thomas, b. at Groton, Conn., 26 Aug., 1862. Res. Groton, where he follows farming.

706. **WILLIAM WILLIAMS[8] FANNING**, b. 1837, (*Rufus Leeds*[7], *Rufus*[6], *Asher*[5], *Jonathan*[4], *Jonathan*[3], *Edmund*[2], *Edmund*[1])

m. at Meriden, Conn., 23 March, 1863,

Sarah Maria Woodworth,

dau. of Lyman and Polly Ann (Gray) Woodworth, and b. at Norwalk, Conn., 15 Sept., 1844.

William Williams Fanning, son of Rufus Leeds and Mary Louisa (Williams) Fanning, was born at Norwich, Conn., 22 April, 1837; was a commercial traveller and resided at Hartford, Conn.

His wife d. at Hartford, 23 June, 1902.

He d. at Hartford, 11 May, 1904. No issue.

708. **ERASTUS WILLIAMS[8] FANNING**, b. 1846, (*Rufus Leeds*[7], *Rufus*[6], *Asher*[5], *Jonathan*[4], *Jonathan*[3], *Edmund*[2], *Edmund*[1])

m. at Erie, Penn., 17 Sept., 1872,

Margaret Lowry,

dau. of James and Eliza (Canaan) Lowry, and b. at Kingston, Ontario, Can., 4 Feb., 1846.

Erastus Williams Fanning was born at Norwich, Conn., 26 Jan., 1846. He removed to Pennsylvania in 1870, and resides at Erie in that State and is a railroad employee. He was in the War of the Rebellion and served in Company F, 1st Conn. Cavalry, enlisting 2 Aug., 1864.

Issue :

1129\. I. ESTELLE LOWRY[9], b. at Erie, Penn., 28 Aug., 1878.

1130\. II. HERBERT AMBROSE[9], b. at Erie, Penn., 11 June, 1875; d. 3 July, 1875.

710\. **EDWIN GIDEON[8] FANNING**, b. 1868, (*George Talcott[7], Rufus[6], Asher[5], Jonathan[4], Jonathan[3], Edmund[2], Edmund[1]*)

m. at Wallawalla, Washington, 6 May, 1894,

Mamie Jane Kelley,

dau. of William and Susan Elizabeth (Fee) Kelley, and b. at New York, N.Y., 6 Nov., 1872.

Edwin Gideon Fanning was born at Lawrence, Kansas, 6 Dec., 1868; is an engineer and machinist, and resides at at Boise, Idaho. No issue.

722\. **CHARLES EDWARD[8] FANNING**, b. 1846, (*Kinney Nathaniel[7], Jonathan[6], Asher[5], Jonathan[4], Jonathan[3], Edmund[2], Edmund[1]*)

m. at Coldwater, Mich., 22 Sept., 1869,

Sarah Catherine Hurlbut,

dau. of Aeneas and Lucretia (Smith) Hurlbut, and b. at Somerset, Niagara Co., N.Y., 28 July, 1849.

Charles Edward Fanning was born at Hopewell, Ontario Co., N.Y., 27 Aug., 1846; is an engineer and resides at Coldwater, Mich.

Issue :

1131\. I. ADA BELLE[9], b. at Coldwater, Mich., 11 Nov., 1870; m. at Coldwater, Mich., 20 Nov., 1890, Austin Holland, a painter. Res. Fenton, Mich.

Issue :

I. CATHERINE MARIE HOLLAND, b. 30 April, 1893.

II. EARL WILCOX HOLLAND, b. 9 Sept., 1895.

III. ROYCE EDWARD HOLLAND, b. 23 Sept., 1901.

+1132. II. CHARLES WESLEY[9], b. at Coldwater, Mich., 3 May, 1873.

1133. III. CAROLINE GERTRUDE[9], b. at Coldwater, Mich., 8 May, 1876; m. at Coldwater, Mich., 25 Dec., 1895, Clyde Roland Hilliar. Res. Coldwater, Mich.

Issue:

I. ROLAND EDWARD HILLIAR, b. 10 Aug., 1901.

+1134. IV. HERBERT KINNEY[9], b. at Coldwater, Mich., 7 July, 1878.

728. **ISAAC NEWTON[8] FANNING**, b. 1838, (*William Jane*[7], *Elisha*[6], *Elisha*[5], *David*[4], *Jonathan*[3], *Edmund*[2], *Edmund*[1])

m. at Leona, Bradford Co., Penn., 25 Feb., 1863,

Ruth Renelcia Woodworth,

dau. of Samuel B. and Elizabeth (Christman) Woodworth, and b. at Bainbridge, Chenango Co., N.Y., 29 Nov., 1842.

Isaac Newton Fanning was born at Leona, Penn., 4 July, 1838; was a farmer and resided at Leona, where he died 17 Oct., 1877. Buried at Leona.

Widow m. 2d, at Leona, in Jan., 1884, William Hurley McMahan, and res. at Leona.

Issue:

1135. I. ULYSSES WILLIAM[9], b. at Leona, Penn., 7 Sept., 1864.

1136. II. EDITH MAY[9], b. at Leona, Penn., 25 Aug., 1867.

Both unm. and res. with their mother, Ruth F. McMahan, on the farm their father left at Leona, Penn.

1137. III. BERTHA ADELIA[9], b. at Leona, Penn., 26 Aug., 1873; m. at Leona, Penn., 26 June, 1895, Ray Mattocks, and res. in Springfield, Bradford Co., Penn.

Issue:

I. RUTH ESTHER MATTOCKS, b. 13 April, 1896.

II. CLAY WALLACE MATTOCKS, b. 9 Sept., 1899.

733. **IRA SMITH[8] FANNING**, b. 1840, (*David Grace[7], Elisha[6], Elisha[5], David[4], Jonathan[3], Edmund[2], Edmund[1]*)
m. at Covington, Penn., 25 Feb., 1868,
Celestia Lucretia Welch,
dau. of James and Rozilla (Rich) Welch,
and b. at Sullivan, Tioga Co., Penn., 23 June, 1844.

Ira Smith Fanning was born at Springfield, Penn., 29 June, 1840. He is a farmer and resides at Wetona, Penn. He was in the Civil War, was enrolled 27 Nov., 1861, in Co. C, Seventh Penn. Cavalry, and served until his discharge at Louisville, Ky., 3 Nov., 1862, on account of sickness and disability.

Issue:

1138. I. ANTIS BELLE[9], b. at Wetona, Penn., 13 Jan., 1871; m. at Wetona, Penn., 25 Nov., 1891, Joseph Washington Campbell, and res. at Hoblet, Penn.

Issue:

I. DORA TEMPIE CAMPBELL, b. 25 Jan., 1896.
II. HELEN LUCRETIA CAMPBELL, b. 29 Jan., 1900.

+1139. II. HUGH JAMES[9], b. at Wetona, Penn., 17 May, 1877.

734. **MELVIN DAVID[8] FANNING**, b. 1842, (*David Grace[7], Elisha[6], Elisha[5], David[4], Jonathan[3], Edmund[2], Edmund[1]*)
m. 1st at Troy, Penn., 26 June, 1870,
Mary Emma Vankirk,
dau. of Joseph J. and Margaret (Jeroloman) Vankirk,
and b. at South Creek, Penn., 20 Sept., 1850.
She d. at Wetona, Penn., 3 June, 1888, and is bur. there.
He m. 2d, at Elmira, N.Y., 11 Sept., 1889,
Lizzie Hildreth,
dau. of Smith and Rachel (Gillett) Hildreth,
and b. at Wellsburg, N.Y., in 1861.

Melvin David Fanning was born at Springfield, Penn., 15 July, 1842. He is a farmer and resides at Wetona, Penn. He was in the Civil War. Was enrolled 27 Aug., 1864, in Co. C, 7th Reg. Penn. Cavalry, and served until discharged at Nashville, Tenn., 17 June, 1865.

Issue by wife Mary:

1140. I. (Dau.[9]), b. at Wetona, Penn., 12 Aug., 1871; d. 12 Aug., 1871.

1141. II. FLORENCE ANTIS[9], b. at Wetona, Penn., 16 July, 1872. Graduate of Mansfield, Penn., State Normal School and is a teacher.

1142. III. DAVID JOSEPH[9], b. at Wetona, Penn., 14 Feb., 1875. Graduate of Mansfield, Penn., State Normal School and Dickinson College, Carlisle, Penn.

1143. IV. LLOYD MELVIN[9], b. at Wetona, Penn., 20 Dec., 1879. A farmer.

Issue by wife Lizzie:

1144. V. CECIL EARL[9], b. at Wetona, Penn., 26 July, 1894.

735. **ADELBERT CANEDY[8] FANNING**, b. 1851, (*David Grace*[7], *Elisha*[6], *Elisha*[5], *David*[4], *Jonathan*[3], *Edmund*[2], *Edmund*[1])

m. at Troy, Penn., 16 April, 1885.

Jennie Eugenia Loomis,

dau. of Edwin Erastus and Louisa Maria (Ballard) Loomis, and b. at West Burlington, Penn., 18 Oct., 1858.

Judge Adelbert Canedy Fanning was born at Springfield, Penn., 25 July, 1851; is a lawyer and resides at Towanda, Penn. Graduate of Law Department of Michigan University, Ann Arbor, in 1874, where he received degree of LL.B. Was District Attorney of Bradford Co., Penn., 1881 to 1884. Was appointed in 1899 President Judge of the 42d Judicial District of Penn. (See sketch in Biographical Part.)

Issue:

1145. I. ADELBERT CARL[9], b. at Troy, Penn., 12 Aug., 1886.
1146. II. PAULINE FRANCES[9], b. at Troy, Penn., 15 Aug., 1890; d. 25 March, 1893, and bur. in Oak Hill Cemetery, Troy, Penn.

737. **ELISHA PHILANDER[8] FANNING**, b. 1841, (*Edwin*[7], *Elisha*[6], *Elisha*[5], *David*[4], *Jonathan*[3], *Edmund*[2], *Edmund*[1])

m. at Smithfield, Bradford Co., Penn., 29 Sept., 1867,

Mary Jane Mosher,

dau. of Giles W. and Mary Ann (Brown) Mosher, and b. at Venice, Cayuga Co., N.Y., 6 Aug., 1846.

Elisha Philander Fanning was born at Springfield, Penn. 16 Dec., 1841; is a farmer and resides in Fox Township, Penn.; Postoffice address, Shunk. He served in the Civil War, enlisting at Pine Creek, Penn., in April, 1861, in Co. B, 1st Penn. Rifles, and served in many of the hardest battles of the war. Was captured in the night attack upon Fort Johnson, 3 July, 1864, and confined in Libby and Salisbury prisons nine months. Was exchanged, returned to regiment and discharged at Harrisburg, 12 July, 1865.

Issue:

+1147. I. PERRY EUGENE[9], b. at Springfield, Penn., 19 Oct., 1870.
1148. II. BESSIE ANN[9], b. at Springfield, Penn., 1 June, 1876; m. 28 Jan., 1895, George Jackson Williams, a farmer, and res. at Shunk, Penn. No issue.
1149. III. CHARLOTTE MARGARET[9], b. in Fox Township, Penn., 4 Jan., 1886; m. 4 April, 1903, Calvin Chester Fleming, a farmer, and res. at Wellsboro, Tioga Co., Penn.

738. **WALLACE PHILANDER[8] FANNING**, b. 1843, (*Edwin[7], Elisha[6], Elisha[5], David[4], Jonathan[3], Edmund[2], Edmund[1]*)

m. 1st, at Le Roy, Bradford Co., Penn., 30 Sept., 1867.

Sallie Maria Hoagland,

dau. of Benjamin and Louisa (Tilliston) Hoagland, and b. at Le Roy, Penn., 11 April, 1845.

She d. at Shunk, Penn., 5 July, 1881, and was bur. at Fox Centre, Penn.

He m. 2d, at Springfield, Penn., 6 April, 1883,

Philinda Mosher,

dau. of Giles W. and Mary Ann (Brown) Mosher, and b. at Locke, Cayuga Co., N.Y., 27 Dec., 1853.

Wallace Philander Fanning, was born at Springfield, Penn., 2 March, 1843; is a farmer and resides at Grover, Bradford Co., Penn. Has been Town Commissioner. He was in the Civil War, enlisting 24 March, 1862, at Elmira, N.Y., in Co. B, 14th N.Y. Vols., and served through the war until discharged 17 Feb., 1865.

Issue:

1150. I. Marion[9], b. in Fox Township, Penn., 28 July, 1870.
1151. II. Fidelia[9], b. in Fox Township, Penn., 12 Sept., 1874; d. 21 March, 1889.

739. **SANDFORD RESCOM[8] FANNING**, b. 1845, (*Edwin[7], Elisha[6], Elisha[5], David[4], Jonathan[3], Edmund[2], Edmund[1]*)

m. at Canton, Bradford Co., Penn., 6 July, 1863,

Eveline Margaret Shattuck,

dau. of Evert and Amy (Porter) Shattuck, and b. at in 1840.

Sandford Rescom Fanning was born at Springfield, Penn., 24 Feb., 1845. He is a miller and resides in Fox Township, Sullivan Co., Penn. Has held offices of Commissioner, Town Clerk, School Director, and Overseer of Poor. Post-office address, Shunk, Sullivan Co., Penn.

He was in the Civil War, enlisting 8 Sept., 1864, at Troy, Bradford Co., Penn. Enrolled as private in Co. K, 11th Penn. Cavalry. Participated in the battles of Malvern Hill, Five Forks, Danville, and numerous minor engagements and skirmishes. Present at the surrender of Gen. Lee at Appomattox. Discharged at Richmond, Va., 16 May, 1865.

Issue:

1152. I. ELSWORTH ELISHA[9], b. in Fox Township, Penn., in May, 1864; d. in May, 1865, and bur. at Fox Centre, Penn.

1153. II. LEE SHATTUCK[9], b. in Fox Township, Penn., in May, 1866; d. in June, 1866, and bur. at Fox Centre, Penn.

1154. III. MATILDA ARAMENTA[9], b. in Fox Township, Penn., 23 March, 1867; m. in 1887 to Casius McKinster. Res. Grover, Penn.

+1155. IV. WARREN HAROLD[9], b. in Fox Township, Penn., 22 Aug., 1870.

1156. V. LEORA AMY[9], b. in Fox Township, Penn., 18 March, 1880; m. in 1902, to Frank Reedy. Res. Elmira, N.Y.

1157. VI. ALVAH CLEIGHTON[9], b. in Fox Township, Penn., 20 Oct., 1884.

744. **WILLIAM[8] FANNING**, b. 1858, (*Edwin*[7], *Elisha*[6], *Elisha*[5], *David*[4], *Jonathan*[3], *Edmund*[2], *Edmund*[1])
m. at Lake Run, Penn., 6 June, 1878,

Susan Van Buskirk,

dau. of John and Margaret Perlina (Larason) Buskirk, and b. in Lycoming Co., Penn., 17 Dec., 1856.

William Fanning, son of Edwin and Alvira Margaret (Hart) Fanning, was born in Fox Township, Penn., 20 May, 1858. He resides at Costello, Penn., and is employed in a tannery.

Issue:

1158. I. EDWIN^{9}, b. at Barbours Mills, Penn., 4 Jan., 1883.
+1159. II. PERRY^{9}, b. at Fall Brook, Penn., 21 Aug., 1885.

748. **WILLIAM LOUIS^{8} FANNING**, b. 1850, (*Elisha^{7}, Elisha^{6}, Elisha^{5}, David^{4}, Jonathan^{3}, Edmund^{2}, Edmund^{1}*)
m. at Terrytown, Penn., 22 Oct., 1873,

Percilla Adaline Horton,

dau. of Richard and Rhoda (Horton) Horton,
and b. at Sheshequin, Penn., 14 March, 1847.

William Louis Fanning, son of Elisha and Mary Cornelia (Ayres) Fanning, was born at Springfield, Penn., 5 Feb., 1850. He was a miller and resided at Terrytown, Penn., where he died 29 May, 1879. Buried at Hornbrook, Penn. About two years after his death his widow was married to David La Fayette Fell of Frenchtown, Penn. About five years later he went west and did not return, and after securing divorce, she married 18 Dec., 1895, Joseph Emory Smith of Berkshire, Tioga Co., N.Y., where they now reside. No issue by either marriage.

750. **JOHN RILEY^{8} FANNING**, b. 1854, (*Elisha^{7}, Elisha^{6}, Elisha^{5}, David^{4}, Jonathan^{3}, Edmund^{2}, Edmund^{1}*)
m. at Terrytown, Penn., 1 Jan., 1878,

Ida Lucinda Aloway,

dau. of John and Sarah (Horton) Aloway,
and b. at Towanda, Penn., 7 Aug., 1858.

John Riley Fanning, son of Elisha and Mary Cornelia (Ayers) Fanning, was born at Berrytown, Penn., 14 June, 1854; is a farmer and resides at Berrytown.

Issue:

1160. I. CHARLES ELISHA[9], b. at Berrytown, Penn., 8 Jan., 1879.
1161. II. CARRIE ETHEL[9], b. at Berrytown, Penn., 26 Jan., 1882; m. at Wellsburg, N.Y., 22 Oct., 1902, Fred Huntley. Res. Elmira, N.Y. No issue.
1162. III. ADDIE EVA[9], b. at Berrytown, Penn., 17 April, 1884.
1163. IV. JOHN MARTIN[9], b. at Berrytown, Penn., 5 Nov., 1892.
1164. V. HAROLD RAYMOND[9], b. at Berrytown, Penn., 14 March, 1900.

752. **GEORGE WESLEY[8] FANNING**, b. 1860, (*Elisha[7], Elisha[6], Elisha[5], David[4], Jonathan[3], Edmund[2], Edmund[1]*)
m. at Coleman, Mich., in 1882,

Ida Sumner,

dau. of and Lucy (Booth) Sumner,
and b. at

George Wesley Fanning, son of Elisha and Mary Cornelia (Ayers) Fanning, was born at Springfield, Penn., 23 Oct., 1860. He is a bill poster. He resided at Coleman, Mich., until the death of his wife. At last accounts he was residing at Detroit, Mich.

Issue:

1165. I. ATHEL[9] (son), b. at Coleman, Mich.; d. at age of 6 mos.
1166. II. EARL[9], b. at Coleman, Mich., about 1898.

759. **CLAYTON McKEAN[8] FANNING**, b. 1860, (*Luther Jones[7], Elisha[6], Elisha[5], David[4], Jonathan[3], Edmund[2], Edmund[1]*)
m. at Franklindale, Penn., 26 Oct., 1881,

Anna Delight Spalding,

dau. of Joseph and Louisa (Kelder) Spalding,
and b. at Franklindale, Bradford Co., Penn., 4 March, 1860.

View of Old Winthrop House, Fishers Island, 1902
Built in Seventeenth Century.

Clayton McKean Fanning was born at West Burlington, Penn., 17 June, 1860; is a farmer and local Methodist preacher, and resides at West Burlington, Penn.

Issue:

1167. I. Edna Louise[9], b. at West Burlington, Penn., 15 Jan., 1886.

1168. II. Orrill Beatrice[9], b. at West Burlington, Penn., 2 Sept., 1889.

1169. III. Ruth Hannah[9], b. at West Burlington, Penn., 5 April, 1892.

1170. IV. Luther Joseph[9], b. at Granville, Penn., 23 Oct., 1894.

764. **CHARLES EDWARD[8] FANNING**, b. 1853, (*William Harrison*[7], *John*[6], *Elisha*[5], *David*[4], *Jonathan*[3], *Edmund*[2], *Edmund*[1])

m. at Washington, D.C., 12 Nov., 1874,

Mary Ellen Gray,

dau. of Anthony and Alice (Callan) Gray,
and b. at Washington, D.C., 14 March, 1853.

Charles Edward Fanning, son of William Harrison and Willimmer (Warren) Fanning, was born at Washington, D.C., 27 Sept., 1853; is a contractor of public works, and resides at Omaha, Neb.

Issue:

1171. I. Alice Annetta[9], b. at Washington, D.C., 18 Oct., 1875; m. at Omaha, Neb., 20 April, 1898, Louis Borsheim, and has issue, Helen Fanning Borsheim.

1172. II. Margaret Mary[9], b. at Washington, D.C., 17 Nov., 1880.

766. **CHARLES[8] FANNING**, b. , (*Dianthus O——*[7], *Amos*[6], *Elisha*[5], *David*[4], *Jonathan*[3], *Edmund*[2], *Edmund*[1])

m. at

——— ———,

dau. of
and b. at

Charles Fanning, son of Dr. Dianthus O. and Lydia Carroll (King) Fanning, was born about the year 1840, but no record of him, however, is obtainable, except that he died at 55 Hicks Street, Brooklyn, N.Y., 19 Feb., 1871.

Issue:

1173. I. DESSIE[9], b. at ; m. at , and said to res. in Chicago, Ill.

773. **JOHN BEDELL[8] FANNING**, b. 1858, (*Sidney*[7], *Amos*[6], *Elisha*[5], *David*[4], *Jonathan*[3], *Edmund*[2], *Edmund*[1]) m. 1st, at Rockville Centre, L.I., 8 Oct., 1879,

Ida Jane DeMott,

dau. of Samuel and Drusilla (Langdon) De Mott, and b. at Rockville Centre, L.I., 11 Feb., 1859.

She d. at Brooklyn, N.Y., 1 Nov., 1887.

He m. 2d, at Brooklyn, N.Y., 10 April, 1890.

Eliza Jane Everist,

dau. of and b. at Baltimore, Md.

John Bedell Fanning, son of Sidney and Phebe Ann (Bedell) Fanning, was born at New York, N.Y., 1 Aug., 1858. He is a clerk, and connected with the Metropolitan Branch, Brooklyn Union Gas Co., and resides at 1021 Eighth Ave., Brooklyn, N.Y.

Issue by wife Ida Jane:

1174. I. LIDA EVERIST[9], b. at Rockville Centre, L.I., 2 Jan., 1881; m. at Brooklyn, N.Y., 15 April, 1903, Edward Francis Burling. Res. Brooklyn, N.Y., 20 Jackson Place.

Issue:

I. DALCEDIA FANNING BURLING, b. 25 Jan., 1904.

1175. II. SIDNEY BEDELL[9], b. at Brooklyn, N.Y., 3 Feb., 1882; d. 27 Dec., 1882.

1176. III. JOHN SAMUEL[9], b. at Brooklyn, N.Y., 10 Feb., 1886.

775. **EDWARD THOMPSON[8] FANNING**, b. 1862, (*Sidney*[7], *Amos*[6], *Elisha*[5], *David*[4], *Jonathan*[3], *Edmund*[2], *Edmund*[1])

m. at East Orange, N.J., 2 June, 1887,

Mary Hatt,

dau. of John Howard and Julia (Clarkson) Hatt, and b. at East Orange, N.J., 2 March, 1865.

Edward Thompson Fanning was born in New York City, 27 June, 1862. He is a clerk with Lesher, Whitman & Co., 670–674 Broadway, New York City, and resides at Arlington, N.J.

Issue:

1177. I. HOWARD SIDNEY[9], b. at East Orange, N.J., 11 May, 1888.

1178. II. EDWARD CHESTER[9], b. at Arlington, N.J., 21 Dec., 1895; d. 21 March, 1897.

777. **FREDERICK ANGELO[8] FANNING**, b. 1853, (*Frederic Hazen*[7], *Amos*[6], *Elisha*[5], *David*[4], *Jonathan*[3], *Edmund*[2], *Edmund*[1])

m. at

Mrs. Rhoda Ella McIntyre Brownell,

dau. of Ezra and Anna Maria (Davis) McIntyre, and b. at Binghampton, N.Y., 9 March, 1835.

She was wid. of William Henry Brownell.

* Frederick Angelo Fanning, son of Frederic Hazen and Josephine (Carroll) Fanning, was born at New York, N.Y., 1 Jan., 1853. He resides at St. Louis, Mo., and is a dealer in wall paper and window shades.

Issue:

+ 1179. I. WALTER[9], b. at Utica, N.Y., 17 Aug., 1875.

* The above data is obtained from relatives, and its correctness is not guaranteed, as Frederick Angelo Fanning declines to furnish any information about his family.

778. **HENRY CANOLL^{8} FANNING**, b. 1859, (*Frederic Hazen^{7}, Amos^{6}, Elisha^{5}, David^{4}, Jonathan^{3}, Edmund^{2}, Edmund^{1}*)

m. at New York, N.Y., 8 June, 1879,

Ellie Cecilia Reilly,

dau. of James Francis and Honora (Reilly) Reilly, and b. at Connaught, Ireland, 1 April, 1860.

Henry Canoll Fanning, son of Frederic Hazen and ( ) Fanning, was born in New York City, 11 Oct., 1859. He is an electrical engineer, and resides at New York City. He had an honorable discharge after ten years' service as First Sergeant of Company C., Ninth Regiment, N.Y.S.N.G.

Issue:

1180. I. JOSEPH FREDERICK^{9}; b. at New York, N.Y., 19 March, 1880. Res. New York City; unm.

1181. II. JAMES FRANCIS^{9}, b. at New York, N.Y., 18 May, 1882; d. at New York, N.Y., 6 June, 1886.

1182. III. JOSEPHINE CECILIA^{9}, b. at New York, N.Y., 8 Aug., 1884; d. at New York, N.Y., 11 July, 1886.

1183. IV. EMILY GRACE^{9}, b. at New York, N.Y., 13 Dec., 1888.

783. **ALBERT BARRINGER^{8} FANNING**, b. 1866, (*Charles Hiram^{7}, Hiram^{6}, Elisha^{5}, David^{4}, Jonathan^{3}, Edmund^{2}, Edmund^{1}*)

m. at in April, 1898,

——— ———,

dau. of

and b. at

Albert Barringer Fanning, son of Charles Hiram and Charlotte Louise (McDonald) Fanning, was born at Albany, N.Y., 23 July, 1866. He is a marine engineer and resided at Newark, N.J., in 1898. No issue.

784. **EDWARD LAY[8] FANNING**, b. 1868, (*Charles Hiram[7], Hiram[6], Elisha[5], David[4], Jonathan[3], Edmund[2], Edmund[1]*)

m. at , 8 Sept., 1888,

Elizabeth N Clark,

dau. of

and b. at

Edward Lay Fanning, son of Charles Hiram and Charlotte Louise (McDonald) Fanning, was born at Albany, N.Y., 10 Aug., 1868. He was recently in the advertising business at Albany. Afterward said to be residing in Chicago, Ill. No record obtainable.

Issue :

1184. I. EDNA MAY[9], b. at ; d. 1898.
1185. II. LAURA[9], b. at
1186. III. WALTER[9], b. at

790. **JAMES HORACE[8] FANNING**, b. 1833, (*Nathaniel[7], Nathaniel[6], James[5], James[4], James[3], Thomas[2], Edmund[1]*)

m. at Southampton, L.I., 19 August, 1862,

Betsey Jones Ludlow,

dau. of John and Harriet (Squires) Ludlow,
and b. at Southampton, L.I., 29 March, 1833.

James Horace Fanning, was born at Flanders, L.I., 9 Dec., 1833; is a farmer and resides at Southampton, L.I.

Issue :

1187. I. JAMES LESLIE[9], b. at Southampton, L.I., 13 Nov., 1863; d. 27 Nov., 1863.
1188. II. ADA MATILDA[9], b. at Southampton, L.I., 27 July, 1866; m. at Southampton, L.I., 4 October, 1883, Edward Ross Bishop, a painter. Res. at Southampton, L.I., but without issue.
+ 1189. III. ERNEST LINWOOD[9], b. at Southampton, L.I., 14 Dec., 1869.

794. **NATHANIEL EDMUND[8] FANNING,** b. 1842, (*Nathaniel[7], Nathaniel[6], James[5], James[4], James[3], Thomas[2], Edmund[1]*)

m. at Smithtown Branch, L.I., 20 Jan., 1864,

Phebe Reeve,

dau. of Hewlett and Maria (Reeve) Reeve, and b. at Aquebogue, L.I., 25 Dec., 1842.

Nathaniel Edmund Fanning was born at Flanders, L.I., 29 Oct., 1842. He resided at Southampton, L.I. Was in real estate business at one time.

His wife d. at Southampton, L.I., 3 Oct., 1897, and bur. there.

Issue:

1190. I. EDWARD[9], b. at Southampton, L.I., 9 Feb., 1866; d. same day.

+1191. II. EDWARD EMERSON[9], b. at Southampton, L.I., 10 Aug., 1867.

1192. III. WILMOT EVERETT[9], b. at Southampton, L.I., 1 Oct., 1869; unm. He is a druggist at 97 Seventh Ave., Brooklyn, N.Y.

1193. IV. BERTHA VIRGINIA[9], b. at Patchogue, L.I., 24 July, 1874; m. at Southampton, L.I., 23 Jan., 1896, William Lewis Donnelly, and res. at Southampton, L.I. No issue.

1194. V. GRACE HEYWOOD[9], b. at Patchogue, L.I., 14 July, 1877; unm., 1899.

795. **GILBERT[8] FANNING,** b. 1846, (*Nathaniel[7], Nathaniel[6], James[5], James[4], James[3], Thomas[2], Edmund[1]*)

m. at Greenport, L.I., 20 Jan., 1869,

Maria Louise Horton,

dau. of Silas Sutton and Catharine Matilda (Payne) Horton, and b. at Sag Harbor, L.I., 17 June, 1849.

Gilbert Fanning was born at Southampton, L.I., 30 June, 1846; is a carpenter, and resides at Greenport, L.I.

Issue :

1195. I. EFFIE LOUISE[9], b .at Southampton, L.I., 20 April, 1871,

1196. II. CLARENCE G[9]., b. at Greenport, L.I., 21 July, 1873; d. 23 July, 1876.

1197. III. CLARENCE VERNON[9], b. at Greenport, L.I., 9 Nov., 1877.

798. **FREDERICK ERNEST[8] FANNING**, b. 1853, (*Nathaniel[7], Nathaniel[6], James[5], James[4], James[3], Thomas[2], Edmund[1]*)

m. at Bridgehampton, L.I., 26 Oct., 1876,

Annie Edwards,

dau. of James and Anna Eliza (Thompson) Edwards, and b. at

Frederick Ernest Fanning was born at Southampton, L.I., 22 June, 1853, where he resides.

Issue :

1198. I. MAUD EDWARDS[9], b. at Southampton, L.I., 29 Nov., 1880; m. 20 June, 1900, to Nathan H. Sayre.

1199. II. MABEL ARRIETTA[9], b. at Southampton, L.I., 12 April, 1882.

1200. III. FRANK PLATT[9], b. at Southampton, L.I., 4 June, 1884.

802. **EDWARD OLIN[8] FANNING**, b. 1852, (*Edward King Conklin[7], Nathaniel[6], James[5], James[4], James[3], Thomas[2], Edmund[1]*)

m. at Brooklyn, N.Y., 4 July, 1875,

Ellen Gertrude Van Clief,

dau. of Jacob and Elizabeth (Kells) Van Clief, and b. at Greenville, N.J., 31 Jan., 1855.

She d. at , 2 June, 1876, aged 21 years, 4 mos., 2 days, and is buried at Riverhead, L.I.

He m. 2d, at Jersey City, N.J., in March, 1880,

Louise Frankohl,

dau. of Frederick and Marietta (Wilson) Frankohl, and b. at Brooklyn, N.Y., 3 Oct., 1861.

Edward Olin Fanning was born at Flanders, L.I., 15 Sept., 1852. He early began to follow the water, and served two years as mate with Captain William Taylor. He has now been a master and pilot for over twenty years, having received his license at the age of 23 years. He resides in Brooklyn, N.Y., at No. 161 55th St.

Issue by wife Ellen :

1201. I. EDWARD G[9], b. at Brooklyn, N.Y., 2 June, 1876; d. 22 July, 1876, aged 1 mo., 20 days; bur. at Riverhead, L.I.

Issue by wife Louise :

1202. II. ETTIE LOUISE[9], b. at Brooklyn, N.Y., 18 July, 1881.

1203. III. ELLEN GERTRUDE[9], b. at Brooklyn, N.Y., 5 Oct.,1884.

1204. IV. EDWARD HARRIGAN[9], b. at Brooklyn, N.Y., 28 March, 1886.

1205. V. ANNIE FRANKOHL[9], b. at Brooklyn, N.Y., 16 March, 1889.

808. HARVEY PIERSON[8] FANNING, b. 1852, (*Harvey Lester[7], Nathaniel[6], James[5], James[4], James[3], Thomas[2], Edmund[1]*)

m. at Flanders, L.I., 31 Dec., 1876,

Zola May Goodale,

dau. of Oscar and Betsey (Davis) Goodale,
and b. at Flanders, L.I., 24 Oct., 1858.

Harvey Pierson Fanning was born at Flanders, L,I.. 25 April, 1852. He resides at Flanders and keeps a summer boarding house. He followed coasting for several years, and was a sea captain and owner and master of his own vessel.

Issue :

1206. I. ADDIE LOUISE[9], b. at Flanders, L.I., 23 March, 1878; d. 1 March, 1879.

1207. II. OSCAR FORD[9], b. at Flanders, L.I., 18 May, 1880.

1208. III. CORA MAY[9], b. at Flanders, L.I., 6 Jan., 1882; d. 6 Sept., 1882.

1209. IV. MAY[9], b. at Flanders, L.I., 27 Feb., 1886.

813. **JOSHUA TERRY[8] FANNING**, b. 1869, (*Harvey Lester*[7], *Nathaniel*[6], *James*[5], *James*[4], *James*[3], *Thomas*[2], *Edmund*[1])

m. at Mattituck, L.I., 8 March, 1887,

Mamie Florence Benjamin,

dau. of Simeon Oscar and Adelia (Hallock) Benjamin, and b. at Northville, L.I., 29 Feb., 1868.

Joshua Terry Fanning was born at Flanders, L.I., 2 Feb., 1869; is a farmer, and resides at Northville, L.I.

Issue :

1210. I. MARJORIE MAY[9], b. at Northville, L.I., 30 July, 1888.

1211. II. FLORENCE ADELIA[9], b. at Northville, L.I., 15 Feb., 1893.

815. **GEORGE TERRY[8] FANNING**, b. 1851, (*Franklin Terry*[7], *Nathaniel*[6], *James*[5], *James*[4], *James*[3], *Thomas*[2], *Edmund*[1])

m. at Stony Brook, N.Y., 1 Sept., 1881,

Ella Maria Gould,

dau. of James Nelson and Clarissa (Williamson) Gould, and b. at Stony Brook, N.Y., 15 Feb., 1852.

Dr. George Terry Fanning was born at Southampton, L.I., 20 March, 1851; is a physician, and resides at Smithtown Branch, L.I. He studied medicine at the University of Michigan and at Bellevue Hospital Medical College,

New York, graduating from the latter in 1877, and immediately commenced the practice of his profession at Stony Brook and Smithtown Branch, L.I.

Issue:

1212. I. GEORGE HAROLD⁹, b. at Stony Brook, N.Y., 2 April, 1884.

830. **WILLIS NEWTON⁸ FANNING**, b. 1858, (*Edward⁷, Israel⁶, James⁵, James⁴, James³, Thomas², Edmund¹*) m. at Lake Grove, L.I., 28 Feb., 1895,

Elvina Overton Hallock,

dau. of John Willis and Annie Douglas (Newton) Hallock, and b. at Lake Grove, L.I., 10 April, 1863.

Willis Newton Fanning was born at Franklinville, L.I., 15 July, 1858; is a farmer, and resides at Laurel, L.I.

Issue:

1213. I. LELAND EDWARD⁹, b. at Franklinville, L.I., 20 Feb., 1896.

838. **JOHN WARREN⁸ FANNING**, b. 1841, (*John⁷, John⁶, John⁵, James⁴, James³, Thomas², Edmund¹*) m. at Northville, L.I., 25 March, 1861,

Mary Ann Reeve,

dau. of Nathan and Abigail (Wells) Reeve, and b. at Northville, L.I., 3 July, 1842.

John Warren Fanning was born at Middle Road, L.I., 30 Aug., 1841; is a farmer, and resides at Baiting Hollow, L.I. His wife d. at Baiting Hollow, L.I., 10 Nov., 1903.

Issue:

1214. I. JOHN TERRY⁹, b. at Northville, L.I., 13 Feb., 1863; d. 4 Feb., 1878.

1215. II. FRANKIE WARREN⁹, b. at Baiting Hollow, L.I., 29 Oct., 1870; d. 5 Feb., 1875.

1216. III. Jessie Blanche⁹, b. at Bating Hollow, L.I., 3 Oct., 1877; m. at Bating Hollow, L.,I., 29 Jan., 1902, John Alonzo Hulse, a farmer, and res. at Wading River, L.I. No issue.

1217. IV. John Warren⁹, b. at Baiting Hollow, L.I., 4 Ma'y 1885.

840. EUGENE BOGART⁸ FANNING, b. 1846, (*John⁷, John⁶, John⁵, James⁴, James³, Thomas², Edmund¹*) m. at Baiting Hollow, L.I., 12 Feb., 1874,

Encie Sophia Young,

dau. of Benjamin Franklin and Mary (Corwin) Young, and b. at Baiting Hollow, L.I., 1 Aug., 1853.

Eugene Bogart Fanning was born at Middle Road, 26 Sept., 1846; is a farmer and resides at Middle Road, L.I., (Riverhead Town).

Issue:

1218. I. Grace Anna⁹, b. at Middle Road, L.I., 22 March, 1875; m. at Riverhead, L.I., 30 Dec., 1903, Oliver Francis Downs.

1219. II. Florence May⁹, b. at Middle Road, L.I., 12 Oct., 1876.

1220. III. John Leslie⁹, b. at Middle Road, L.I., 2 March, 1878.

1221. IV. Harold Young⁹, b. at Middle Road, L.I., 8 Feb., 1883.

1222. V. Benjamin Eugene⁹, b. at Middle Road, L.I., 25 March, 1885.

1223. VI. Walter Franklin⁹, b. at Middle Road, L.I., 8 July, 1890.

1224. VII. Isabel Skidmore⁹, b. at Middle Road, L.I., 12 Nov., 1894.

842. **WILLIAM RICHARD^{8} FANNING**, b. 1858, (*John^{7} John^{6}, John^{5}, James^{4}, James^{3}, Thomas^{2}, Edmund^{1}*)
m. at Wading River, L.I., 31 March, 1880,

Ella Jane Hulse,

dau. of John and Kate (Hulse) Hulse,
and b. at Baiting Hollow, L.I., 21 Aug., 1860.

William Richard Fanning was born at Middle Road L.I., 22 July, 1858, where he resides and follows farming.

Issue:

1225. I. JOHN HULSE^{9}, b. at Riverhead, L.I., 22 Aug., 1881.
1226. II. MARY ELLA^{9}, b. at Riverhead, L.I., 27 Sept., 1885.
1227. III. RALPH STANLEY^{9}, b. at Riverhead, L.I., 29 Nov., 1889.

845. **MOSES EUGENE^{8} FANNING**, b. 1851, (*Moses^{7} John^{6}, John^{5}, James^{4}, James^{3}, Thomas^{2}, Edmund^{1}*)
m. at Baiting Hollow, L.I., 18 June, 1881,

Lillie Idell Edwards,

dau. of Spofford and Mary Sophia (Raynor) Edwards,
and b. at Baiting Hollow, L.I., 1 Dec., 1860.

Moses Eugene Fanning, son of Moses and Hannah Catharine (Reeve) Fanning, was born at Flanders, L.I., 9 Feb., 1851; is a farmer, and resides at Middle Road, Riverhead Town, L.I. No issue.

849. **JOHN REEVE^{8} FANNING**, b. 1860, (*Moses^{7}, John^{6}, John^{5}, James^{4}, James^{3}, Thomas^{2}, Edmund^{1}*)
m. at Baiting Hollow, L.I., 15 May, 1885,

Ida Frances Wells,

dau. of Rienzi Lawrence and Lucetta (Raynor) Wells,
and b. at

John Reeve Fanning, son of Moses and Hannah Catharine (Reeve) Fanning, was born at Middle Road, L.I., 25 June, 1860; is a farmer, and resides at Middle Road, L.I.

Issue:

1228. I. Amy Lucetta[9], b. at Middle Road, L.I., 27 Sept., 1890.

1229. II. Stella Catharine[9], b. at Middle Road, L.I., 21 June, 1892.

1230. III. Marian Reeve[9], b. at Middle Road, L.I., 9 Jan., 1900.

859. **PETER WELLS[8] FANNING,** b. 1864, (*Foster Roe*[7], *Peter*[6], *John*[5], *James*[4], *James*[3], *Thomas*[2], *Edmund*[1])
m. at New York, N.Y., 5 Nov., 1887,
Minnie Vandervoort,
dau. of Charles M. and Deborah (Horton) Vandervoort, and b. at New York, N.Y., 3 Dec., 1863.

Peter Wells Fanning, was born at New Suffolk, L.I., 17 Aug., 1864; is a tinsmith, and resides at Southampton, L.I.

Issue:

1231. I. Foster Roe[9], b. at Bridgehampton, L.I., 10 Jan., 1889.

1232. II. Florence Davison[9], b. at Bridgehampton, L.I., 11 April, 1891.

1233. III. Ruth Edna[9], b. at Mattituck, L.I., 20 July, 1892.

860. **JOHN FOSTER[8] FANNING,** b. 1866, (*Foster Roe*[7], *Peter*[6], *John*[5], *James*[4], *James*[3], *Thomas*[2], *Edmund*[1])
m. at Cutchogue, L.I., 6 Dec., 1888,
Carrie Eloise Moore,
dau. of Ira B. and Rhoda A. (Tuthill) Moore, and b. at Cutchogue, L.I., 31 March, 1868.

John Foster Fanning was born at New Suffolk, L.I., 11 Sept., 1866, where he resides and follows farming.

Issue:

1234. I. Russell Moore[9], b. at New Suffolk, L.I., 11 May, 1890.

1235. II. Marjorie Kimball[9], b. at New Suffolk, L.I., 17 June, 1896.

1236. III. Laura Hoagland[9], b. at New Suffolk, L.I., 17 Feb., 1898.

861. **STUART LINCOLN[8] FANNING**, b. 1869, (*Foster Roe[7], Peter[6], John[5], James[4], James[3], Thomas[2], Edmund[1]*)
m. at Laurel, L.I., 28 Dec., 1899,

Blanche Seeley,

dau. of Rev. William Henry and Caroline (Nelson) Seeley, and b. at Sag Harbor, L.I., 7 Nov., 1871.

Stuart Lincoln Fanning, son of Foster Roe and Eunice Kimball (Davison) Fanning, was born at New Suffolk, L.I., 5 Oct., 1869. He is a mason and contractor, and resides at New Suffolk, L.I.

Issue :

1237. I. KATHERINE SEELEY[9], b. at New Suffolk, L.I., 21 Dec. 1900.

1238. II. HILDA[9], b. at New Suffolk, L.I., 20 Feb., 1902.

865. **OLIVER[8] FANNING**, b. 1851, (*Daniel Warner[7], James[6], John[5], James[4], James[3], Thomas[2], Edmund[1]*)
m. at Good Ground, L.I., 11 April, 1873,

Rhoda Elizabeth Raynor,

dau. of Carrington and Mary Elizabeth (Brooks) Raynor, and b. at Good Ground, L.I., 24 Dec., 1855.

Oliver Fanning was born at Good Ground, L.I., 1 Aug., 1851; is a farmer, and bayman, and resides at Good Ground. He is constable and deputy sheriff in town of Southampton, L.I., which office he has held since 1 April, 1886.

Issue :

1239. I. ADDIE LINWOOD[9], b. at Good Ground, L.I., 11 June, 1876; m. at Good Ground, L.I., 26 Jan., 1896, William Tedeman. He is a farmer, and res. at Good Ground, L.I., and has issue:

I. HENRY OLIVER TEDEMAN, b. 14 April, 1899.

1240. II. NESSIE ELIZA[9], b. at Good Ground, L.I., 4 Oct., 1889.

1241. III. CHARLOTTE ELIZABETH[9], b. at Good Ground, L.I., 5 April, 1896.

866. **BENJAMIN LUTHER[8] FANNING**, b. 1856, (*Daniel Warner*[7], *James*[6], *John*[5], *James*[4], *James*[3], *Thomas*[2], *Edmund*[1])

m. at Northville, L.I., 16 Sept., 1885,

Carrie Luella Downs,

dau. of Manley Wells and Augusta Emily (Smith) Downs, and b. at Northville, L.I., 14 Oct., 1858.

Benjamin Luther Fanning was born at Good Ground, L.I., 28 Nov., 1856, and resides there. He is engaged in trucking at the present time.

Issue:

1242. I. EMILY DOWNS[9], b. at Good Ground, L.I., 9 June, 1886.
1243. II. WALTER BENJAMIN[9], b. at Good Ground, L.I., 16 Feb., 1890.
1244. III. ROSS MONTROSE[9], b. at Good Ground, L.I., 26 Sept., 1892.

867. **DANIEL[8] FANNING**, b. 1861, (*Daniel Warner*[7], *James*[6], *John*[5], *James*[4], *James*[3], *Thomas*[2], *Edmund*[1])

m. at Eastport, L.I., 18 Sept., 1881,

Ida Belle Warner,

dau. of William Wallis and Julia Ann (Skidmore) Warner, and b. at Good Ground, L.I.

Daniel Fanning was born at Good Ground, L.I., 8 May, 1861, and resides there. He is a farmer, and engaged in fishing.

Issue:

1245. I. LEVERETT EUGENE[9], b. at Good Ground, L.I., 17 Nov., 1882.
1246. II. JAMES HENRY[9], b. at Good Ground, L.I., 18 Feb., 1884.
1247. III. EDMUND WILLIAM[9], b. at Good Ground, L.I., 25 Sept., 1885.
1248. IV. SAMUEL HARRISON[9], b. at Good Ground, L.I., 17 May, 1889; d. 23 May, 1891.

868. **SAMUEL EDMUND[8] FANNING**, b. 1863, (*Daniel Warner*[7], *James*[6], *John*[5], *James*[4], *James*[3], *Thomas*[2], *Edmund*[1])

m. at Good Ground, L.I., 30 Nov., 1887,

Annie Alfretta Fournier,

dau. of Isaiah and Annie (Ketcham) Fournier,
and b. at Sea, 15 Oct., 1865.

Samuel Edmund Fanning was born at Good Ground, L.I., 15 June, 1863; is a bayman and resides at Good Ground.

Issue:

1249. I. LULU BLANCHE[9], b. at Good Ground, L.I., 24 Jan., 1889.

1250. II. ANNIE ALFRETTA[9], b. at Good Ground, L.I., 21 Oct., 1894.

876. **CHARLES GRAHAM[8] FANNING**, b. 1848, (*Samuel*[7], *Samuel*[6], *John*[5], *James*[4], *James*[3], *Thomas*[2], *Edmund*[1])

m. at Bridgeport, Conn., 22 Feb., 1882,

Matilda Wellington,

dau. of William and Mary (Radcliffe) Wellington,
and b. at Great Neck, L.I., 9 Oct., 1859.

Charles Graham Fanning was born at Jamesport, L.I., 17 April, 1848, is a carpenter, and resides at Bridgeport, Conn.

Issue:

1251. I. SAMUEL VERNON[9], b. at Bridgeport, Conn., 26 Oct., 1884.

902. **AUGUSTUS SCHENCK[8] FANNING**, b. 1844, (*William Augustus*[7], *William*[6], *Phineas*[5], *Phineas*[4], *James*[3], *Thomas*[2], *Edmund*[1])

m. at Poughkeepsie, N.Y., 28 May, 1884,

Mary Ellen Morgan,

dau. of William and Catharine (Rifenburg) Morgan, and b. at Rosendale, Ulster Co., N.Y., 13 Aug., 1853.

Augustus Schenck Fanning was born at Poughkeepsie, N.Y., 26 Nov., 1844, and has always resided there. He graduated at Eastman's Business College in 1861. Was in the county clerk's office as special deputy from 1877 to 1880. Is at present an advertising agent.

Issue:

1252. I. FRED[9], b. at Poughkeepsie, N.Y., 31 Dec., 1875.

911. **FRANK SIDNEY[8] FANNING**, b. 1847, (*Phineas*[7], *Daniel Wells*[6], *Nathaniel*[5], *Phineas*[4], *James*[3], *Thomas*[2], *Edmund*[1])

m. at Brooklyn, N.Y., 1 Sept., 1872, (Salmon Record),

Jennie Vandenberg,

dau. of Peter and Antoinette (Granby) Vandenberg, and b. at Athens, N.Y., 8 Aug., 1847.

Frank Sidney Fanning was born at Southold, L.I., 25 Feb., 1847; is a carpenter and builder, and resides at Brooklyn, N.Y., 266 Cleveland Street.

Issue:

1253. I. CARRIE ANTOINETTE[9], b. at Southold, L.I., 4 June, 1876.

1254. II. PHINEAS[9], b. at Brooklyn, N.Y., 28 Sept., 1881.

912. **CHARLES LEROY[8] FANNING**, b. 1851, (*Phineas*[7], *Daniel Wells*[6], *Nathaniel*[5], *Phineas*[4], *James*[3], *Thomas*[2], *Edmund*[1])

m. at Brooklyn, N.Y., 30 April, 1884,

Charlotte Elizabeth Thomas,

dau. of James Arnold and Adah (Ashald) Thomas, and b. at Brooklyn, N.Y., 19 April, 1855.

Charles LeRoy Fanning was born at Southold, N.Y., 2 May, 1851; is a buyer for a jewelry house in New York City and resides at Brooklyn, N.Y., 30 Schenck Avenue.

Issue:

1255. I. EDMUND LEROY^{9}, b. at Brooklyn, N.Y., 31 Jan., 1887; d. 8 Nov., 1894.

1256. II. WILLIAM HENRY^{9}, b. at Brooklyn, N.Y., 14 Oct., 1889.

1257. III. CLARENCE LESLIE^{9}, b. at Brooklyn, N.Y., 14 March, 1893; d. 10 Aug., 1893.

915. **WILLIAM JAMES^{8} FANNING**, b. 1866, (*Daniel Wells^{7}, Daniel Wells^{6}, Nathaniel^{5}, Phineas^{4}, James^{3}, Thomas^{2} Edmund^{1}*)

m. at Suisun City, Cal., 2 May, 1895,

Nellie Marion Peters,

dau. of John Henry and Alice Adelaide (Hitchens) Peters, and b. at Burson, Calaveras Co., Cal., 5 March, 1876.

William James Fanning was born at Bellota, Cal., 17 August, 1866; is a blacksmith and resides at Linden, San Joaquin Co., Cal.

Issue:

1258. I. JOHN LELAND^{9}, b. at Linden, San Joaquin Co., Cal., 25 May, 1896.

928. **WILLIAM WALLACE^{8} FANNING**, b. 1843, (*Edmund Frederick Augustus^{7}, Edmund^{6}, Barclay^{5}, Phineas^{4}, James^{3}, Thomas^{2}, Edmund^{1}*)

m. 1st, at Davenport, Ia., 8 Oct., 1871,

Mary Wall Barnes,

dau. of his sister's husband, William Brown Barnes, (see No. 924) by a first wife, Martha Wall of Richmond, Ind.

She d. in childbirth, 3 Feb., 1877.

He m. 2d, at Richmond, Ind., 12 Aug., 1879.

Mrs. Lettie Peck Johnson,

dau. of Dr. George and Angeline (Cropper) Peck, and b. at Cleveland, O., 9 Sept., 1850.

She was widow of John H. Johnson.

William Wallace Fanning was born at Nantucket, Mass., 23 Nov., 1843; is a cabinet-maker and workman in fine woods, furniture, etc., and resides at Richmond, Ind.

Issue by wife Mary:

1259. I. LOUIS CLIFFORD[9], b. at Richmond, Ind., 10 Nov., 1872.

1260. II. DAISY SOPHIA[9], b. at Richmond, Ind., 21 Sept., 1874. Resides Gilbert, Ia.

1261. III. CHARLES[9], b. at Richmond, Ind., 10 Jan., 1877, d. 25 June, 1877.

Issue by wife Lettie:

1262. IV. ANNA[9], b. at Richmond, Ind., 10 Sept., 1883.

930. **EDMUND FREDERICK AUGUSTUS[8] FANNING**, b. 1848, (*Edmund Frederick Augustus[7], Edmund[6], Barclay[5], Phineas[4], James[3], Thomas[2], Edmund[1]*)

m. at Lincolnville, Wabash Co., Ind., 20 Jan., 1869.

Mary Ann Havenridge,

dau. of John and Elizabeth (Charles) Havenridge, and b. at Lincolnville, Ind., 15 Nov., 1848.

She d. at Lincolnville, 4 Sept., 1871, aged 20 y., 2 mos., 5 days.

He m. 2d, at Lincolnville, Ind., 9 Oct., 1872,

Mary Anne Darrow,

dau. of John and Charity (Copeland) Darrow, and b. near Lincolnville, Ind., 21 Jan., 1851.

Edmund Frederick Augustus Fanning was born at Oak or Fanning's Island, N.S., 11 Sept., 1848; is a farmer and resides at Lincolnville, Wabash Co., Ind. He is known as "Fred" or "Frederick" Fanning.

Issue by wife Mary Anne Havenridge :

1263. I. LYCURGUS[9], b. at Lincolnville, Ind., 31 June, 1870; d. 8 Sept., 1870.

Issue by wife Mary Anne Darrow :

+1264. II. JOHN BARCLAY[9], b. at Lincolnville, Ind., 24 July, 1873.
1265. III. SOPHIA LOUISE[9], b. at Lincolnville, Ind., 22 Aug., 1877.

932. **EDMUND BARCLAY[8] FANNING**, b. 1843, (*Barclay[7], Edmund[6], Barclay[5], Phineas[4], James[3], Thomas[2], Edmund[1]*)

m. at Brockton, Mass., 8 April, 1866.

Martha Ann Lyon,

dau. of Vinal and Damaris Williams (Keith) Lyon, and b. at North Bridgewater, Mass., 10 Nov., 1842.

Edmund Barclay Fanning was born at Nantucket, Mass. 29 Aug., 1843; is foreman of sole leather department for Preston B. Keith at Brockton, Mass., where he has been for twenty-seven years. He resides at Brockton, Mass.

Issue :

+1266. I. EDMUND GRAY[9], b. at Brockton, Mass., 26 Aug., 1867.
+1267. II. CHARLES HENRY[9], b. at Brockton, Mass., 18 Sept., 1869.
1268. III. MATTIE SNYDER[9], b. at Brockton, Mass., 10 Feb., 1873.
1269. IV. ELLIS VINAL[9], b. at Brockton, Mass., 2 Aug., 1879.
1270. V. ELSIE KEITH[9], b. at Brockton, Mass., 19 Feb., 1885.

933. **ALEXANDER "CAMMY" WILDER^{8} FANNING**, b. 1845, (*Barclay^{7}, Edmund^{6}, Barclay^{5}, Phineas^{4}, James^{3}, Thomas^{2}, Edmund^{1}*)

m. at Campello, Mass., 16 May, 1877,

Rebecca Maria Jewett Davenport,

dau. of Nathaniel Marion, and Charlotte (French) Davenport,

and b. at East Bridgewater, Mass., 19 April, 1852.

Alexander "Cammy" Wilder Fanning was born at Nantucket, Mass., 8 Dec., 1845; is a shoemaker and resides at Campello, Mass. He is known simply as "Alexander Fanning." Was named after his great uncle, Col. A. C. W. Fanning (No. 249).

Issue:

1271. I. ARTHUR^{9}, b. at Campello, Mass., 26 Aug., 1880.

935. **FREDERICK DEVEAU^{8} FANNING**, b. 1861 (*Frederick^{7}, Frederick Deveau^{6}, Henry^{5}, Gilbert^{4}, James^{3}, Thomas^{2}, Edmund^{1}*)

m. at Durham, N.C., 18 Feb., 1902,

Annie Petway Rawls,

dau. of Isaiah and Annie Southerland (Petway) Rawls, and b. at Snow Hill, N.C., 25 Feb., 1873.

Frederick Deveau Fanning, son of Frederick and Harriet Eugenia (Chambers) Fanning, was born at Charleston, S.C., 28 April, 1861. He attended military school at Charlotte, N.C., and then entered mercantile life. Resides at Durham, N.C., and is a bookkeeper and connected with the Durham Hosiery Mills of that city.

Issue:

1272 I. FREDERICK DEVEAU^{9}, b. at Durham, N.C., 14 Nov., 1902.

947. **HENRY SWEETSER[8] FANNING**, b. 1871, (*Andrew Murdock[7], Thomas Coit[6], Thomas[5], Thomas[4], Richard[3], Thomas[2], Edmund[1]*)

m. at Brooklyn, N.Y., 27 Jan., 1888,

Mary Loretta King,

dau. of Thomas and Mary (Galliger) King,
and b. at Brooklyn, N.Y., in March, 1870.

Henry Sweetser Fanning was born at Brooklyn, N.Y., 11 May, 1871, where he resides and is a salesman for an importing house in New York City.

Issue:

1273. I. LESTER DAVID[9], b. at Brooklyn, N.Y., 1 March, 1889; d. 28 March, 1889.

1274. II. BLANCHE SHEPARD[9], b. at Brooklyn, N.Y., 18 July, 1890.

1275. III. FLORENCE LORETTA[9], b. at Brooklyn, N.Y., 1 Nov., 1892.

950. **ARTHUR LANE[8] FANNING**, b. 1863, (*David Greene[7], Thomas Coit[6], Thomas[5], Thomas[4], Richard[3], Thomas[2], Edmund[1]*)

m. at Chicago, Ill., 13 June, 1888,

Jennie Chapin Farr,

dau. of James and Laura Jennie (Chapin) Farr,
and b. at Chicago, Ill., 8 Jan., 1864.

Arthur Lane Fanning was born at Brooklyn, N.Y., 20 Sept., 1863. He is assistant sales agent, American Can Co., Chicago, Ill. Resides at Evanston, Ill., 1232 Hinman Avenue.

Issue:

1276. I. KATHARINE⁹, b. at Evanston, Ill., 4 April, 1889.
1277. II. ELIZABETH LANE⁹, b. at Evanston, Ill., 14 Oct., 1890.
1278. III. JANE CHAPIN⁹, b. at Evanston, Ill., 23 Aug., 1892.
1279. IV. RUTH NORTON⁹, b. at Evanston, Ill., 9 April, 1895.
1280. V. DAVID GREENE⁹, b. at Evanston, Ill., 11 July, 1902.

953. **WINTHROP SALTONSTALL⁸ FANNING,** b. 1870, (*David Greene⁷, Thomas Coit⁶, Thomas⁵, Thomas⁴, Richard³, Thomas², Edmund¹*)

m. at Brooklyn, N.Y., 2 Feb., 1897,

Marie Talbot Metcalfe,

dau. of George and Elizabeth Talbot (Root) Metcalfe, and b. at Brooklyn, N.Y., 16 Dec., 1867.

Winthrop Saltonstall Fanning was born at Brooklyn, N.Y., 26 Nov., 1870, and resides at Montclair, N.J. He is a mechanical engineer for E. K. Adams, New York City.

Issue:

1281. I. MARION TALBOT⁹, b. at Flushing, N.Y., 16 Jan., 1899.
1282. II. STANTON METCALFE⁹, b. at Flushing, N.Y., 30 July, 1901.

955. **LOUIS MARTINE⁸ FANNING,** b. 1866, (*Thomas Coit⁷, Thomas Coit⁶, Thomas⁵, Thomas⁴, Richard³, Thomas², Edmund¹*)

m. at Whitestone, L.I., 12 May, 1891,

Lillie Louise Tostevin,

dau. of Frederick N. and Harriet (Hawkridge) Tostevin, and b. at Brooklyn, N.Y., 23 May, 1869.

Louis Martine Fanning was born at Tarrytown, N.Y., 12 May, 1866; is clerk for the American Can Company, New York City, and resides at Whitestone, L.I.

Issue:

1283. I. EDITH DEAN⁹, b. at Whitestone, L.I., 23 March, 1893.
1284. II. WINTHROP COIT⁹, b. at Whitestone, L.I., 1 Aug., 1895.

962. **HARRY HOWARD[8] FANNING**, b. 1863, (*Howard Malcolm[7], Richard[6], Asa[5], Richard[4], Richard[3], Thomas[2], Edmund[1]*)

m. at Stockton, Cal., 28 Oct., 1888,

Catherine Ortman,

dau. of Henry Ernest and Frances (Hansel) Ortman, and b. at Stockton, Cal., 12 Dec., 1865.

Harry Howard Fanning was born at Stockton, Cal., 15 Nov., 1863; is a bookkeeper, and resides at 603 North Sutter St., Stockton, Cal.

Issue:

1285. I. LOUISE[9], b. at Stockton, Cal., 2 April, 1891.

972. **NEUVILLE OSGOOD[8] FANNING**, b. 1865, (*Neuville DeRostus[7], Amasa Standish[6], Henry[5], Richard[4], Richard[3], Thomas[2], Edmund[1]*)

m. at Lamoure, No. Dakota, 10 Aug., 1885,

Mildred Hill Mulliken,

dau. of Francis Granger and Victoria (Howse) Mulliken, and b. at Tuscola, Ill., 9 Feb., 1862.

Neuville Osgood Fanning was born at St. Charles, Ill., 17 March, 1865, and is a journalist. He engaged in newspaper work when he was sixteen and has followed it ever since. He started from the bottom of the ladder, with the mechanical part, and learned all the parts to the business, until at the age of nineteen he was the owner of a paper in Dakota. About 1896 he located in New York City and received by appointment from Tammany an important office in that city in 1897 — Deputy Commissioner in the Department of Correction, which office he held five years. He is now connected with the editorial department of the *Brooklyn Eagle*.

Issue :

1286. I. HAZEL CAROLINE[9], b. at Jamestown, North Dakota, 11 September, 1886.

1287. II. LEONARD MULLIKEN[9], b. at New Rockford, North Dakota, 4 July, 1888.

1288. III. NEUVILLE OSGOOD[9], b. at Minneapolis, Minnesota, 23 August, 1895.

978. **FRANK STUART[8] FANNING**, b. 1864, (*John Newton[7], Alexander Newton[6], Henry[5], Richard[4], Richard[3], Thomas[2], Edmund[1]*)

m. at Fair Play, Wisconsin, 2 Nov., 1890,

Georgia Melville Dorchester,

dau. of Andrew Jackson and Illinois (Carpenter) Dorchester, and b. at Galena, Ill., 22 Nov., 1864.

Frank Stuart Fanning was born at Bellevue, Ia., 2 Oct., 1864; is a tinner, and resides at Bellevue.

Issue :

1289. I. NINA LUELLA[9], b. at Bellevue, Ia., 4 June, 1891.

979. **ALEXANDER NEWTON[8] FANNING**, b. 1867, (*John Newton[7], Alexander Newton[6], Henry[5], Richard[4], Richard[3], Thomas[2], Edmund[1]*)

m. at Los Angeles, Cal., 19 Dec., 1888,

Lillie May Lyman,

dau. of Gaylord and Marinda (Conant) Lyman, and b. at Chariton, Ia., 7 June, 1870.

Alexander Newton Fanning was born at Bellevue, Iowa, 17 May, 1867, is a salesman and resides at Los Angeles, Cal. He lives at 832 West Eighteenth Street.

Issue :

1290. I. GAYLORD ALEXANDER[9], b. at Los Angeles, Cal., 16 Oct., 1897.

987. CHARLES ADELBERT[8] FANNING, b. 1855, (*Charles Grandson*[7], *Luther*[6], *Charles*[5], *Richard*[4], *Richard*[3], *Thomas*[2], *Edmund*[1])

m. at Trenton, Mich., 16 Aug., 1882,

Carrie Augusta Stokes,

dau. of John William and Ruth (Bothwell) Stokes, and b. at Amherstburg, Essex Co., Ontario, 24 June, 1858.

Charles Adelbert Fanning was born at Angelica, N.Y., 15 Feb., 1855; is a telegraph operator, and resides at Detroit, Mich. He was postmaster of Grasse Isle, Mich., 1882 and 1883.

Issue:

1291. I. GEORGE STOKES[9], b. at Detroit, Mich., 25 April, 1885.
1292. II. WILLIAM SANDERS[9], b. at Detroit, Mich., 10 May, 1887.
1293. III. CHARLES RENWICK[9], b. at Detroit, Mich., 13 July, 1891.

990. SANDFORD CALVIN[8] FANNING, b. 1870, (*Edwin Palmer*[7], *Calvin*[6], *Charles*[5], *Richard*[4], *Richard*[3], *Thomas*[2], *Edmund*[1])

m. at Perry, N.Y., 28 Jan., 1891,

Carrie Elizabeth Hack,

dau. of Adam Godfred and Mary Jane (Gruber) Hack, and b. at Titusville, Penn., 24 March, 1873.

Sandford Calvin Fanning was born at Perry, Wyoming Co., N.Y., 3 Jan., 1870; is a farmer and resided until recently at Perry Centre, N.Y.

Issue:

1294. I. RUTH ESTELLA[9], b. at Rochester, N.Y., 16 May, 18
1295. II. FLORENCE GRACE[9], b. at Perry, N.Y., 12 Aug., 1

992. **FRED DOANE^{8} FANNING**, b. 1870, (*Charles Addison^{7}, Calvin^{6}, Charles^{5}, Richard^{4}, Richard^{3}, Thomas^{2}, Edmund^{1}*)

m. at Perry, N.Y., 1 Aug., 1900,

Nellie Saxton Rudgers,

dau. of James Hiram and Emma (Saxton) Rudgers,
and b. at Perry, N.Y., 1 Sept., 1874.

Fred Doane Fanning, son of Charles Addison and Almira (Doane) Fanning, was born at Perry, N.Y., 19 Dec., 1870. He graduated at Eastman's College, Poughkeepsie, N.Y., in 1890, and then connected himself with his father in the coal and ice business at Perry, to which business he succeeded at the death of his father in 1898, under the name of F. D. Fanning & Co. No issue.

996. **JAMES EDWIN^{8} FANNING**, b. 1860, (*James Edward^{7}, Silas^{6}, Charles^{5}, Richard^{4}, Richard^{3}, Thomas^{2}, Edmund^{1}*)

m. at Avon, Livingstone Co., N.Y., 26 May, 1887,

Ida Jane Wills,

dau. of William Harden and Pheba (Melspaugh) Wills,
and b. at Rochester, N.Y., 26 Jan., 1865.

James Edwin Fanning was born at Avon, N.Y., 17 June, 1860, and is a brakeman on the Erie R.R. Resides at Avon. No issue.

998. **A J^{8} FANNING**, b. 1869, (*Henry Luther^{7}, Silas^{6}, Charles^{5}, Richard^{4}, Richard^{3}, Thomas^{2}, Edmund^{1}*)

m. at Grand Rapids, Mich., 13 May, 1895,

Maude Schultz,

dau. of John and Lida (Glyndon) Schultz (or Southworth),
and b. at New York, N.Y., 12 Jan., 1876.

A. J. Fanning was born at Bangor, Van Buren Co., Mich., 17 Sept., 1869; is a railroad brakeman, and resides at Grand Rapids, Mich. No issue.

1003. **GEORGE ALLEN[8] FANNING**, b. , (*James Alonzo*[7], *Erastus*[6], *John*[5], *James*[4], *Richard*[3], *Thomas*[2], *Edmund*[1])

m. at

——— ———,

dau. of
and b. at

No record is obtainable of George Allen Fanning, eldest son of James Alonzo and Harriet (Barton) Fanning.

1006. **CHARLES MORTIMER[8] FANNING**, b. 1861, (*James Alonzo*[7], *Erastus*[6], *John*[5], *James*[4], *Richard*[3], *Thomas*[2], *Edmund*[1])

m. at New Britain, Conn., 24 Dec., 1879,

Marion Sarah Atwood,

dau. of James David and Olive (Rust) Atwood,
and b. at New Britain, Conn., 14 Oct., 1862.

Charles Mortimer Fanning was born at Cold Spring, Mass., 26 Aug., 1861; is a conductor, and resides at New Britain, Conn., 29 South Burritt Street.

Issue:

1296. I. MATTIE MAY[9], b. at New Britain, Conn., 4 May, 1884.
1297. II. ADDIE ATWOOD[9], b. at New Britain, Conn., 24 Nov., 1886; d. at Birmingham, Conn., 30 July, 1891, and is bur. at New Britain, Conn.
1298. III. OLIVE HARRIETT[9], b. at New Britain, Conn., 28 Sept., 1889.
1299. IV. ALICE MARION[9], b. at Birmingham, Conn., 28 June, 1893.

1009. **GROVE ADELBERT[8] FANNING**, b. 1869, (*Lucius Mortimer[7], Erastus[6], John[5], James[4], Richard[3], Thomas[2], Edmund[1]*)

m. at Hartford, Conn., 11 May, 1892,

Mabel Abby Rose,

dau. of

and b. at Collinsville, Conn., 20 Oct., 1873.

Grove Adelbert Fanning was born at West Hartford, Conn., 30 May, 1869; was a grocery salesman, and resided at Bridgeport, Conn.

He d. at Westport, Conn., 26 March, 1898, and was bur. in New Hartford, Conn. Wid. res. in Hartford. No issue.

1010. **FREDERIC GEORGE[8] FANNING**, b. 1870, (*Lucius Mortimer[7], Erastus[6], John[5], James[4], Richard[3], Thomas[2], Edmund[1]*)

m. at Norwalk, Conn., 19 July, 1897,

Belle Beatrice Fancher,

dau. of John Wesley and Melissa Josephine (Ferris) Fancher, and b. at Westport, Conn., 10 June, 1881.

Frederic George Fanning, son of Lucius Mortimer and Annie Jane (Morfey) Fanning, was born at South Manchester, Conn., 7 July, 1870. He resides at New Haven, Conn. In State Militia, Co. D, South Norwalk, Conn. Foreman of the New Haven Truck and Storage Co.

Issue:

1300. I. (Son)[9], b. at New Haven, Conn., 22 Jan., 1901; d. 24 Dec., 1902.

1012. **LUCIUS BARZILLAI[8] FANNING**, b. 1873, (*Lucius Mortimer[7], Erastus[6], John[5], James[4], Richard[3], Thomas[2], Edmund[1]*)

m. at Port Chester, N.Y., 22 Oct., 1900,

Bertha Agnes Baker,

dau. of Charles Edward and Lydia Ann (Robertson) Baker, and b. at Westport, Conn., 26 Jan., 1881.

Lucius Barzillai Fanning, son of Lucius Mortimer and Annie Jane (Morfey) Fanning, was born at New Hartford, Conn., 27 Nov., 1873. He is a paper-maker, and resides at Westport, Conn.

Issue:

1301. I. CHESTER MORTIMER[9], b. at Westport, Conn., 15 April, 1902.

1024. **GEORGE BURT[8] FANNING**, b. 1868, (*James McKnight[7], Chester Griswold[6], Oramel[5], James[4], Richard[3], Thomas[2], Edmund[1]*)

m. at Auburn, N.Y., 25 Dec., 1894,

Grace Campbell,

dau. of Irvin and Harriet (Conklin) Campbell, and b. at Conquest, Cayuga Co., N.Y., 27 Feb., 1877.

George Burt Fanning was born at Palmyra, N.Y., 4 Sept., 1868; is a shoe cutter, and resides at Auburn, N.Y. No issue.

1029. **BENJAMIN[8] FANNING**, b. 1837, (*Nelson[7], Benjamin[6], Walter[5], Thomas[4], John[3], John[2], Edmund[1]*)

m. at Conesville, Schoharie Co., N.Y., 12 Feb., 1856,

Canilda Humphrey Phelps,

dau. of Rolla and Catharine (   ) Phelps, and b. at Conesville, N.Y., 11 June, 1835.

Dr. Benjamin Fanning was born at Strykersville, N.Y., 12 April, 1837; is a physician, and resides at Gilboa, N.Y.

He is not practicing, however, at present, but is Assistant Postmaster there. He followed farming until a year or two after marriage. He then studied medicine under the instruction of his father, Dr. Nelson Fanning, one of the leading physicians in the State. He was at Burlington, Vt., attending a course of lectures when the Civil War broke out; on returning home about 1 July, 1861, he enlisted as private in Company B, 4th New York Heavy Artillery, but being unable to endure the hardships of a soldier's life, was honorably discharged after a few months' service. He then resumed the study of medicine, and completed his course at the Berkshire Medical College, Pittsfield, Mass., in the Fall of 1863. He immediately commenced the practice of his profession at Gilboa, N.Y., afterwards removing to Conesville, where he continued to practice until 1892, when on account of poor health he gave up practicing entirely. In the Spring of 1893, he again moved back to Gilboa, and was appointed Assistant Postmaster.

Issue:

+1302. I. CHARLES BRECKENRIDGE[9], b. at Conesville, N.Y., 1 Feb., 1857.

1303. II. GRACE ELIZABETH[9], b. at Gilboa, N.Y., 8 May, 1868; m. at Conesville, N.Y., 31 Dec., 1890, Theodore Southard. He is a farmer. Res. Lexington, Dawson Co., Nebraska.

Issue:

I. ERNEST SOUTHARD, b. 21 Dec., 1892.
II. NANCY FANNING SOUTHARD, b. 11 April, 1896.
III. HARRIET SARAH SOUTHARD, b. 12 June, 1898.
IV. CHRISTINA DIES SOUTHARD, b. 14 Nov., 1899.

1030. **NELSON^{8} FANNING**, b. 1839, (*Nelson^{7}, Benjamin^{6} Walter^{5}, Thomas^{4}, John^{3}, John^{2}, Edmund^{1}*)
m. at Gilboa, N.Y., 19 March, 1861,
Julia Weismer,
dau. of Robert and Julia (Jay) Weismer,
and b. at Gilboa, N.Y., 20 April, 1840.

Dr. Nelson Fanning was born at Strykersville, N.Y., 19 March, 1839; was a physician and resided at Catskill, N.Y., where he died 17 May, 1904. He graduated at Albany Medical College, 27 Dec., 1859.

Issue:

1304. I. JULIA^{9}, b. at Gilboa, 29 July, 1863.

1035. **JAMES MONROE^{8} FANNING**, b. 1832, (*Charles^{7}, Thomas^{6}, Walter^{5}, Thomas^{4}, John^{3}, John^{2}, Edmund^{1}*)
m. at Albany, N.Y., 9 Jan., 1866,
Lucy Maria James,
dau. of Frederick Perkins and Delia (Sears) James,
and b. at Albany, N.Y., 18 June, 1835.

James Monroe Fanning was born at Prattsville, Greene Co., N.Y., 21 Jan., 1832; is a merchant and resides at East Durham, N.Y.

Issue:

1305. I. FRED JAMES^{9}, b. at Albany, N.Y., 23 Nov., 1866; d. at Ledgedale, Penn., 1 June, 1881.
1306. II. HARRY WINNIE^{9}, b. at Ledgedale, Penn., 7 Feb., 1874. Clerk in New York City.

1037. **GEORGE WASHINGTON FORD^{8} FANNING**, b. 1839, (*Charles^{7}, Thomas^{6}, Walter^{5}, Thomas^{4}, John^{3}, John^{2}, Edmund^{1}*)
m. at Limestone, Cattaraugus Co., N.Y., 15 Sept., 1864,
Harriet Melissa Filler,

dau. of Munroe and Livonia (Hull) Filler,
and b. in McKean Co., Penn., 21 Oct., 1849.

George Washington Ford Fanning (called "Ford") was born at Prattsville, N.Y., 10 March, 1839, and resides at Woodville, O. He was in the Civil War, serving two years in the Army of the Potomac. Was in Co. C, 27th N.Y.S.V. He enlisted in April, 1861, and served until expiration of time of enlistment, and was discharged 10 June, 1863.

Issue :

1307. I. ELIZABETH LIVONIA[9], b. at Limestone, N.Y., 17 Aug., 1865; m. in Clarion Co., Penn., 8 Dec., 1886, William Albert Alsbach.

Issue :

I. WALTER G. ALSBACH, b. 2 Nov., 1887.
II. CARL H. ALSBACH, b. 20 Feb., 1890.
III. ILMA IRENE ALSBACH, b. 21 March, 1894.

1308. II. ADA ESTELLE[9], b. at Limestone, N.Y., 3 Oct., 1867; m. at Obi, N.Y., 25 April, 1885, W. W. Henton.

Issue :

I. FORD C. HENTON, b. 3 Nov., 1887.
II. HAZEL L. HENTON, b. 4 April, 1891.
III. GUY N. HENTON, b. 11 Aug., 1893.

1309. III. CHARLES FORD[9], b. at Rochester, N.Y., 16 Dec., 1888; d. 9 May, 1889.

1039. **NELSON CHARLES[8] FANNING**, b. 1842, (*Asa*[7], *Thomas*[6], *Walter*[5], *Thomas*[4], *John*[3], *John*[2], *Edmund*[1]) m. at Fergusonville, Delaware Co., N.Y., 17 March, 1860,

Joanna O'Leary,

dau. of Daniel and Mary ( ) O'Leary,
and b. in County Cork, Ireland, 25 Feb., 1840.

Nelson Charles Fanning was born at Delhi, Delaware Co., N.Y., 26 Feb., 1842. He is a contractor and builder, and resides in Fergusonville, Delaware Co., N.Y. For fourteen years of his life after he became twenty-one, he was superintendent of a tanning company in Fergusonville. After the business gave out in that section, he resumed the trade of carpenter and builder, which he had previously learned.

Issue:

1310. I. MARY EMELINE[9], b. at Fergusonville, N.Y., 13 Feb., 1861; m. 12 Nov., 1877, Pommeroy F. Peters, a blacksmith, son of John and Rebecca Peters. He d. 20 Jan., 1881. She d. 12 May, 1888. He served three years in the Rebellion in the 144th Regiment, N.Y.S.V.

Issue:

I. LOUISA PETERS, b. 14 June, 1879.

1311. II. AGNES LOUISA[9], b. at Fergusonville, N.Y., 5 Dec., 1862; d. at Fergusonville, 4 Nov., 1888.

+1312. III. CHARLES STEWART[9], b. at Fergusonville, N.Y., 9 Nov., 1864.

1313. IV. BENJAMIN NELSON[9], b. at Fergusonville, N.Y., 1 Nov., 1868; d. at Fergusonville, 21 March, 1893.

1314. V. HATTIE AUGUSTA[9], b. at Fergusonville, N.Y., 7 Oct., 1872; m. 1 Aug., 1893, John J. McMorris, a farmer. Res. Fergusonville, N.Y.

Issue:

I. LULA VIVIENNE MCMORRIS, b. at Eminence, Schoharie Co., N.Y., 25 July, 1894 or 1895.

1315. VI. LULU MARGUERITE[9], b. at Fergusonville, N.Y., 20 June, 1879.

1316. VII. MAURICE HUMPHREY[9], b. at Fergusonville, N.Y., 12 Jan., 1881.

1317. VIII. ELIZABETH[9], b. at Fergusonville, N.Y., 9 Jan., 1870; d. 28 Jan., 1870.

1041. **SAMUEL⁸ FANNING,** b. 1851, (*Asa*[7], *Thomas*[6], *Walter*[5], *Thomas*[4], *John*[3], *John*[2], *Edmund*[1])
m. at Cohoes, N.Y.,

———— ————,

dau. of
and b. at

Samuel Fanning was born at Davenport, Delaware Co., N.Y., 7 April, 1851. He was a carpenter and resided at Cohoes, N.Y. His wife died soon after marriage. He died at Cohoes, N.Y., 12 July, 1890. No issue.

1046. **JACOB HENRY[8] FANNING,** b. 1851, (*Edwin*[7], *John*[6], *Walter*[5], *Thomas*[4], *John*[3], *John*[2], *Edmund*[1])
m. at Cobleskill, Schoharie Co., N.Y., 13 May, 1871,

Ella Walford,

dau. of Dow and Julia (Telepaugh) Walford,
and b. at Central Bridge, Schoharie Co., N.Y..

Jacob Henry Fanning was born at Schoharie, N.Y., 4 May, 1851; is a farmer and resided recently at Howes Cave, Schoharie Co., N.Y.

Issue:

1318. I. GRANT WELLINGTON[9], b. at Cobleskill, N.Y., 28 July, 1873.
1319. II. HOMER JAY[9], b. at Cobleskill, N.Y., 2 June, 1875.
1320. III. LENA MAY[9], b. at Cobleskill, N.Y., 13 Oct., 1878.

1048. **JESSE SMITH[8] FANNING,** b. 1868, (*Benjamin*[7], *John*[6], *Walter*[5], *Thomas*[4], *John*[3], *John*[2], *Edmund*[1])
m. at Schoharie, N.Y., 19 Nov., 1890,

Maggie Young,

dau. of Peter and Cornelia (Wood) Young,
and b. at Schoharie, N.Y., 2 Feb., 1861.

Jesse Smith Fanning was born at Seward, N.Y., 8 April, 1868. He is a butcher, and resides at Fultonham, Schoharie Co., N.Y.

Issue:

1321. I. ALMOND[9], b. at Seward, N.Y., 7 Feb., 1893; d. 12 Aug., 1893.

1049. **FREDERICK[8] FANNING,** b. 1835, (*Henry*[7], *Frederick*[6], *Walter*[5], *Thomas*[4], *John*[3], *John*[2], *Edmund*[1])
m. at Belleville, Ontario, Can., 20 Dec., 1871,
Anna Maud Beatrice Sicken,
dau. of Whitner and Lavina (Derby) Sicken,
and b. at Rochester, N.Y., 10 May, 1856.

Frederick Fanning was born in the Fourth Concession of Sidney, Ontario, Can., 7 Sept., 1835. When a young man he studied law for two or three years, but did not follow it. He afterward removed to the States and went West, and resided in Leadville, Colo. He has been for some time engaged in prospecting and mining.

His wife died at Morris, Ill., 11 July, 1888, and is bur. there.

Issue:

+1322. I. CHARLES WHITNEY[9], b. at Rochester, N.Y., 26 May, 1873.

1052. **GEORGE WALTER[8] FANNING,** b. 1841, (*Henry*[7], *Frederick*[6], *Walter*[5], *Thomas*[4], *John*[3], *John*[2], *Edmund*[1])
m. at Kingston, Ont., Can., 13 Nov., 1863,
Georgiana Marie George,
dau. of John Bigger and Lavina (Derby) George,
and b. at Morven, Ont., Can., 27 Feb., 1846.

George Walter Fanning was born in the Fourth Concession of Sidney, 13 May, 1841; is in the commission business, and resides at Belleville, Ont., Can. He attended Victoria Cobourg College for some time, and was two years studying in a French College at Terrebonne, a short distance from Montreal. Is a dentist by profession, but does not follow it. Is engaged in buying and shipping horses.

His wife died at Belleville, Ont., Can., in Dec., 1899.

Issue:

1323. I. LULA BEATRICE[9], b. at Belleville, Ont., Can., 24 Aug., 1867; m. at Pictou, Ont., Can., 9 Sept., 1888, Robert Stanley Conley, a mechanic. Res. Cleveland, O.

Issue:

I. HARRY FANNING CONLEY, b. 25 July, 1889.

II. EVA GEORGIE CONLEY, b. 12 July, 1895.

1324. II. EVA GEORGIE[9], b. at Belleville, Ont., Can., 13 April, 1869; m. at Belleville, Ont., Can., 2 April, 1890, James Steele Bonar, an engineer. Res. Cornwall, Ont., Can.

Issue:

I. BEEBY IRENE BONAR, b. 7 March, 1892.

II. GLADYS MARGRETT BONAR, b. 27 Aug., 1896.

III. JOHN DONALDSON BONAR, b. 6 Nov., 1898.

1325. III. CORA MAY[9], b. at Belleville, Ont., Can., 22 Jan., 1875; m. at Belleville, Ont., Can., 27 Dec., 1897, William Henry Meyers, a printer. Res. Niagara Falls, N.Y.

Issue:

I. MARION GERALDINE MEYERS, b. 15 Oct., 1898.

1326. IV. ETHEL PEARL[9], b. at Belleville, Ont., Can., 3 Oct., 1877.

1327. V. GEORGE WALTER[9], b. at Belleville, Ont., Can., 8 Nov., 1879.

1062. **FREDERICK WALTER[8] FANNING**, b. 1841, (*George[7], Frederick[6], Walter[5], Thomas[4], John[3], John[2], Edmund[1]*)

m. at Belleville, Ont., Can., 31 July, 1862,

Carrie M Meyers,

dau. of

and b. at Belleville, Ont., Can., 7 March, 1843.

Dr. Frederick Walter Fanning was born in the township of Thurlow, District of Hastings, Ont., Can.,6 Oct., 1841. He graduated at the University of Michigan in 1867; is a physician and surgeon and resides at Butler, Ind.

Issue :

+1328. I. CHARLES HERBERT[9], b. at Belleville, Ont., Can., 29 Feb., 1864.

1329. II. FRANK DU VERNAY[9], b. at Butler, Ind., 4 May, 1873.

1063. **RICHARD GILBERT[8] FANNING**, b. 1845, (*George*[7], *Frederick*[6], *Walter*[5], *Thomas*[4], *John*[3], *John*[2], *Edmund*[1])

m. at Kankakee, Ill., 6 Oct., 1869,

Mary Elizabeth Marine,

dau. of Jesse and Lydia (Henderson) Marine, and b. in St. Joseph Co., Ind., 11 May, 1851.

Richard Gilbert Fanning was born at Sidney, District of Hastings, Ont., Can., 14 June, 1845. He removed with his parents in March, 1865, to Iroquois Co., Ill., and in 1868 to Kankakee Co., Ill. In Sept., 1878, he moved to Riley Co., Kansas, and in Oct., 1891, to Leoti, Wichita Co., Kan., where he now resides. He is a farmer.

Issue :

1330. I. IRENE ALICE[9], b. in Kankakee Co., Ill., 20 Feb., 1872; m. near May Day, Riley Co., Kan., 19 Jan., 1898, David Marion Lemarr, a farmer. Res. near Lillivale, Kay Co., Oklahoma.

Issue :

I. MOLENE LUCILLE LEMARR, b. at Lillivale, Oklahoma, 7 Jan., 1899.

1331. II. EMMA ALVIRA[9], b. in Kankakee Co., Ill., 24 Dec., 1873; m. at Clay Centre, Clay Co., Kan., 19 Aug., 1891, Frank E. Sebring, a farmer. Res. near Antioch, Miami Co., Kan.

Issue:

I. MAUD I. SEBRING, b. 5 March, 1894.

II. BEULAH GLADYS SEBRING, b. 15 June, 1898.

1332. III. JESSE GILBERT[9], b. in Kankakee Co., Ill., 20 Dec., 1877.

1333. IV. BEN WYNNE[9], b. in Wichita Co., Kan., 10 Dec., 1891

1064. **GEORGE BALDWIN[8] FANNING**, b. 1848, (*George*,[7] *Frederick*[6], *Walter*[5], *Thomas*[4], *John*[3], *John*[2], *Edmund*[1])

m. at Waldron, Kankakee Co., Ill., 16 Oct., 1872,

Amanda Melvina Wood,

dau. of Daniel Harvey and Sarah Ann (Ranney) Wood, and b. at Springfield, Ill., 25 Sept., 1856.

George Baldwin Fanning was born at Sidney, District of Hastings, Ont., Can., 17 April, 1848. He is a farmer, and resides at Alta, Buena Vista Co., Ia.

Issue:

1334. I. GEORGE ROY[9], b. in Kankakee Co., Ill., 18 May, 1878.

1335. II. SARAH WINIFRED[9], b. at Alta, Ia., 9 April, 1882.

1336. III. GERTRUDE GRACE[9], b. at Alta, Ia., 25 April, 1885.

1337. IV. HARRY HARVEY[9], b. at Alta, Ia., 10 July, 1889.

1065. **JOHN NELSON[8] FANNING**, b. 1850, (*George*[7], *Frederick*[6], *Walter*[5], *Thomas*[4], *John*[3], *John*[2], *Edmund*[1])

m. at

——— ———,

dau. of

and b. at

John Nelson Fanning was born at Sidney, Can., 24 June, 1850. It is said he married and had issue one child. No record, however, is obtainable.

Issue:

1338. I. (Infant)[9], b. at

1071. **JOHN ROWE[8] FANNING**, b. 1849, (*John Benjamin[7], Frederick[6], Walter[5], Thomas[4], John[3], John[2], Edmund[1]*)

m. at , 1 May, 1877,

Annie Otto Shelton,

dau. of William John and Mary (Hough) Shelton, and b. at Bridgeport, Conn., 5 Jan., 1854.

John Rowe Fanning was born in Rawdon (township), County of Hastings, Ont., Can., 29 Sept., 1849. Received a public school and academic education, and graduated at the Government Military School at Toronto, in Spring of 1869, and during summer of same year was in charge of the U. S. Consul's Office at Kingston, Ont., and in spring of 1870 went to Rochester, N.Y., and entered the law office of Ripsom & Ferry where he remained one year and a half and then became managing clerk in the law office of Hon. Joseph A. Stull, where he continued till admitted to practice in 1873. Not being a citizen, a special act of the legislature of the State of New York was passed, allowing him to take the oath of office and practice, and became naturalized as soon as time of residence would permit. Began practice of law as soon as admitted. In Oct., 1875, entered into partnership for practice of law with Charles M. Williams, which still continues under firm name of Fanning & Williams. In politics has been a Democrat, and served as City Attorney of Rochester, N.Y., from 1881 to 1883. Received his party nomination for Special County Judge in fall of 1883, and again a nomination for the office of County Judge in fall of 1895, which nominations were wholly unsought.

He resides at Brighton, Monroe Co., N.Y. No issue.

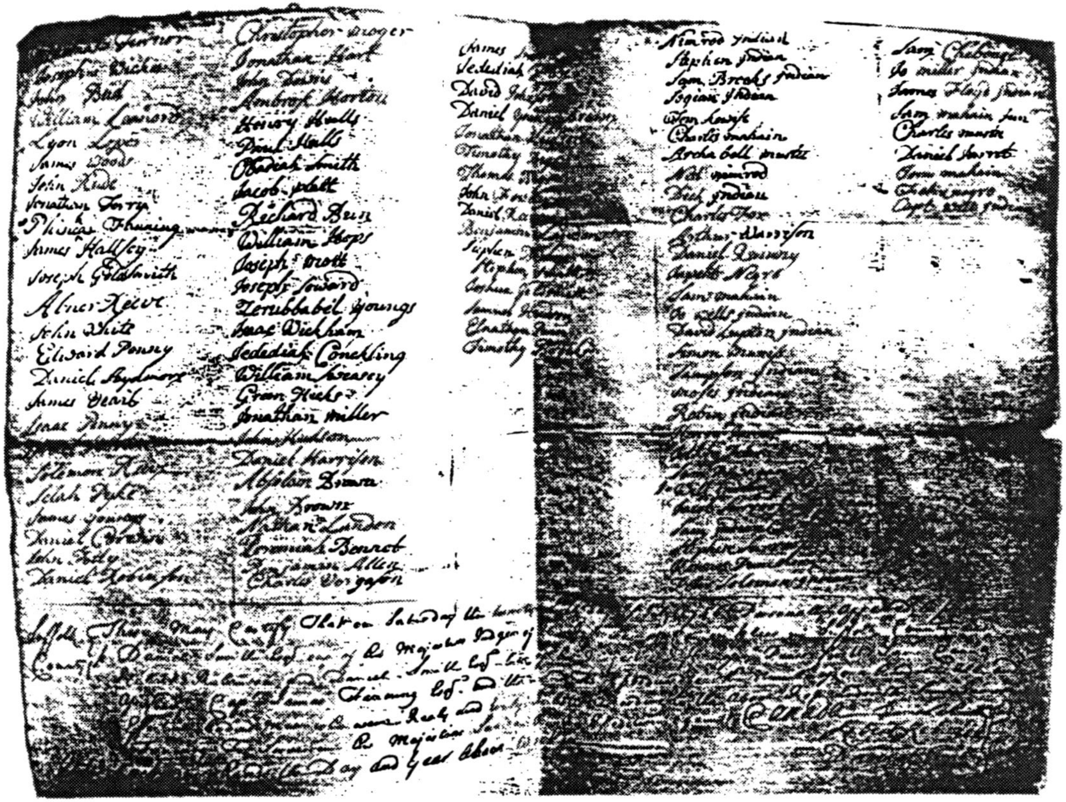

Roll of Capt. James Fanning's Company, July 26th 1746.
Enlisted to serve on an Expedition against Canada.

1072. **FREDERICK BENJAMIN[8] FANNING,** b. 1851, (*John Benjamin*[7], *Frederick*[6], *Walter*[5], *Thomas*[4], *John*[3], *John*[2], *Edmund*[1])

m. at Rawdon, Ont., Can., 5 Jan., 1876,

Emma Alwilda Hogle,

dau. of Joseph and Catherine (Maybee) Hogle, and b. at Rawdon, Ont., Can., 10 April, 1855.

Frederick Benjamin Fanning was born at Rawdon, Ont., Can., 12 April, 1851, where he resides and follows farming.

Issue:

1339. I. HARRY HOGLE[9], b. at Rawdon, Ont., Can., 5 Dec., 1876.
1340. II, BURRELL AUBREY[9], b. at Rawdon, Ont., Can., 17 Feb., 1879.

1073. **WILLIAM HENRY[8] FANNING,** b. 1853, (*John Benjamin*[7], *Frederick*[6], *Walter*[5], *Thomas*[4], *John*[3], *John*[2], *Edmund*[1])

m. at Rawdon, Ont., Can., 26 Oct., 1875,

Annie Catharine Green,

dau. of John and Amanda (McMullen) Green, and b. at Rawdon, Ont., Can., 14 April, 1853.

William Henry Fanning was born at Rawdon, Ont., Can., 18 July, 1853, where he resides and follows farming.

Issue:

1341. I. JOHN ROSWELL[9], b. at Rawdon, Ont., Can., 26 Oct., 1876.
1342. II. ELLA MOOERS[9], b. at Rawdon, Ont., Can., 21 Nov., 1878; m. at Rawdon, Ont., Can., 7 Sept., 1897, William E. Caverly, a farmer, and res. at Stirling, Ont., Can.
1343. III. GILBERT LORNE[9], b. at Rawdon, Ont., Can., 9 Feb., 1882; d. 24 Feb., 1883.

1074. **GEORGE BLEECKER[8] FANNING**, b. 1855, (*John Benjamin*[7], *Frederick*[6], *Walter*[5], *Thomas*[4], *John*[3], *John*[2], *Edmund*[1])

m. at

——— ———,

dau. of

and b. at

George Bleecker Fanning was born at Rawdon, Ont., Can., 19 March, 1855. (No further record, however, is obtainable from the family.)

1076. **ELLIS BURRELL[8] FANNING**, b. 1861, (*John Benjamin*[7], *Frederick*[6], *Walter*[5], *Thomas*[4], *John*[3], *John*[2], *Edmund*[1])

m. 1st, at Philadelphia, Penn., 18 March, 1885,

Mary Emma Kennard,

dau. of Joseph and Anna (Robinson) Kennard,
and b. in Centreville, Queen Anne Co., Md., 5 Nov., 1860.

She d. at Double Pipe Creek, Md., 31 Oct., 1891.

He m. 2d, at Trenton, N.J., 22 Jan., 1896,

Myra Pace Caplin,

dau. of John Arthur and Marie (Stanton) Caplin,
and b. at Syracuse, N.Y., 13 Sept., 1862.

Dr. Ellis Burrell Fanning was born at Rawdon, Ont., Can., 26 March, 1861. He graduated at the Hahnemann Medical College in 1885, is a physician, and resides in Philadelphia, Penn.

Issue by wife Mary:

1344. I. Burleigh Kennard[9], b. at Crumpton, Queen Anne Co., Md., 21 Sept., 1889.

1083. **JOHN FREDERICK⁸ FANNING**, b. 1852, (*David Frederick*[7], *Frederick*[6], *Walter*[5], *Thomas*[4], *John*[3], *John*[2], *Edmund*[1])

m. at Chatham, Ont., 13 Oct., 1881,

Emma Yott,

dau. of Joseph and Sarah Olive (Grimshaw) Yott, and b. at Wolf Island, near Kingston, Ont., Can., 15 Aug., 1862.

John Frederick Fanning was born at Charing Cross, Ont., Can., 21 Nov., 1852. Resides at Walkerville, Ont., Can. He is an engineer.

Issue:

1345. I. SARAH LOUISA[9], b. at Walkerville, Ont., Can., 6 Jan., 1883.

1346. II. HERBERT FREDERICK[9], b. at Walkerville, Ont., Can., 5 Jan., 1888.

1084. **ANDREW CONRAD[8] FANNING**, b. 1857, (*David Frederick*[7], *Frederick*[6], *Walter*[5], *Thomas*[4], *John*[3], *John*[2], *Edmund*[1])

m. at St. Paul, Minn., 13 Sept., 1887,

Mary Murphy,

dau. of James and Delia (Conway) Murphy, and b. at St. Paul, Minn., 8 May, 1865.

Andrew Conrad Fanning was born at Chatham, Ont., Can., 21 Oct., 1857; is a tinsmith, and resided at St. Paul, Minn., for some years. He now lives at Anaconda, Mont.

Issue:

1347. I. FLORENCE MARIE[9], b. at St. Paul, Minn., 27 June, 1888.

1087. **GEORGE HENRY[8] FANNING**, b. 1851, (*Sylvester*[7], *Frederick*[6], *Walter*[5], *Thomas*[4], *John*[3], *John*[2], *Edmund*[1])

m. at Blairton, County of Peterborough, Ont., Can., 16 April, 1878,

Nettie Wilde,

dau. of Jonathan and Ellen (Dafoe) Wilde, and b. at Richmond, Carleton Co., Ont., Can., 24 May, 1855.

George Henry Fanning was born at Rawdon, Ont., Can., 20 Nov., 1851. He is engaged in mining in the Rainy River District in the western part of Ontario, Can., and resides at Dinorwic.

Issue:

1348. I. LULU MAY[9], b. at Evart, Mich., 5 May, 1885.
1349. II. ELIZABETH ELENOR[9], b. in township of Dummer, County of Peterborough, Ont., Can., 17 March, 1887.
1350. III. CHARLES ROY[9], b. in township of Dummer, County of Peterborough, Ont., Can., 7 April, 1888.

1089. **CHARLES BIRDSLEY[8] FANNING**, b. 1857, (*Sylvester*,[7] *Frederick*[6], *Walter*[5], *Thomas*[4], *John*[3], *John*[2], *Edmund*[1])

m. at Belmont, Ont., Can., 28 March, 1883,

Emeline Eugenie Patterson,

dau. of William John and Mary (Garrett) Patterson, and b. at Rednersville, Prince Edward Co., Ont., Can., 6 July, 1856.

Charles Birdsley Fanning was born at Rawdon, Ont., Can., 3 Feb., 1857; is a car inspector, and resides at Havelock, Ont., Can. No issue.

1090. **WESLEY ARDEN[8] FANNING**, b. 1859, (*Sylvester[7], Frederick[6], Walter[5], Thomas[4], John[3], John[2], Edmund[1]*)

m. at Lindsay, Ont., Can., 1 Nov., 1882,

Annie Henry,

dau. of Samuel Wainwright and Rebecca (Milburn) Henry, and b. at Lindsay, Ont., Can., 9 Sept., 1864.

Wesley Arden Fanning was born at Belmont, Ont., Can. 12 Aug., 1859; is a harness maker, and resides at Cambray, Ont., Can.

Issue:

1351. I. ETHEL EARL[9], b. at Lindsay, Ont., Can., 4 Jan., 1884.
1352. II. BERTIE MAY[9], b. at Cambray, Ont., Can., 16 Feb., 1885.
1353. III. PEARL[9], b. at Cambray, Ont., Can., 23 Sept., 1888.
1354. IV. ORR[9], b. at Cambray, Ont., Can., 9 Dec., 1892.

1092. **WALTER BLAKE[8] FANNING**, b. 1871; (*Sylvester[7], Frederick[6], Walter[5], Thomas[4], John[3], John[2], Edmund[1]*)

m. in Town of Fenelon, Ont., Can., 2 Jan., 1895,

Agnes Rogers,

dau. of James and Mary (Moffat) Rogers, and b. in Fenelon, Ont., Can., 28 July, 1873.

Walter Blake Fanning was born at Belmont, Ont., Can., 20 Sept., 1871; is a brakeman on the Canadian Pacific R.R. and resides at Havelock, Ont., Can.

Issue:

1355. I. BURRELL MOORE[9], b. at Belmont, County Peterborough, Can., 18 April, 1896.

1100. **FREDERICK HUDSON[8] FANNING**, b. 1864, (*Frederick Hudson[7], John Watson[6], Charles[5], Thomas[4], John[3], John[2], Edmund[1]*)

m. at Jewett City, Conn., 28 Feb., 1888,

Mary Jessie Arnold,

dau. of Peleg Amos and Hannah (Buronay) Arnold, and b. at Exeter, R.I., 26 Feb., 1868.

Frederick Hudson Fanning was born at Jewett City, Conn., 30 Oct., 1864; is in the stable business, and resides at Jewett City. No issue.

1101. **CHARLES HENRY[8] FANNING**, b. 1835, (*Charles Henry[7], Henry Willson[6], Thomas[5], Thomas[4], John[3], John[2], Edmund[1]*)

m. at Providence, R.I., 17 Sept., 1857,

Sarah Eldridge Hamlin,

dau. of Nathan and Cynthia (Eldridge) Hamlin, and b. at Providence, R.I., 9 Sept., 1835.

Charles Henry Fanning was born at Bozrahville, Conn., 13 Feb., 1835. He is a jeweler at Providence, R.I. In October, 1849, he removed with his parents from Lonsdale to Providence, R.I., and went to learn the jewelry trade there in April, 1852, with Samuel Allen on Canal Street. He continued with him until the Fall of 1859, when he (Allen) failed and gave up business. In May, 1860, he went to work for Wilcox & Battell and has been connected with them ever since. The firm name having been changed to D. Wilcox & Co. They reside at Edgewood, Pawtucket, R.I. No issue.

1102. **ALFRED HALE[8] FANNING**, b. 1837, (*Charles Henry[7], Henry Willson[6], Thomas[5], Thomas[4], John[3], John[2], Edumnd[1]*)

m. at Newtonville, Mass., 15 Jan., 1862,

Louisa G Davey,

dau. of
and b. at Boston, Mass., 27 July, 1841.

She d. at Waltham, Mass., 8 March, 1868.

He m. 2d, at Providence, R.I., 11 Oct., 1875,

Alice Lillian Packard,

dau. of Henry Martin and Mary Elizabeth (Smith) Packard and b. at West Mansfield, Mass., 19 Oct., 1856.

He d. at North Attleboro, Mass., 8 Jan., 1881, and his wid. m. second at Providence, R.I., 28 Oct., 1888, James Clinton MacAdams, and res. at Providence.

Alfred Hale Fanning was born at Bozrahville, Conn., 25 Jan., 1837. When a young man he learned the jewelers' trade with his brother Charles. He did not follow his trade, however, but went out to White Plains, N.Y., where he kept a grocery store for two or three years. He then went to work for Holmes, Booth & Hayden in New York City, general jobbers, photograph supplies, silverware, etc., and was with them for a number of years. Later he removed to Waltham, Mass., and after that to Attleboro, where he worked at his trade until his decease in 1881.

Issue by wife Louisa :

1356. I. Louise Juliette[9], b. at White Plains, N.Y., 30 Dec., 1862; m. at Central Falls, R.I., 4 Nov., 1885, Charles Henry Scofield, b. at Danielson, Windham Co., Conn., 15 Aug., 1862, a compositor, son of Uri Bolivar and Abby Jane (Young) Scofield. They resided at Central Falls, R.I., where she d. 7 Dec., 1888. He res. in Boston, Mass.

Issue:

I. CHARLES ALFRED SCOFIELD, b. at Pawtucket, R.I., 19 Nov., 1886; d. at Danielson, Conn., 21 Feb., 1891.

II. ARTHUR FANNING SCOFIELD, b. at Central Falls, R.I., 3 Oct., 1888; d. at Central Falls, 23 Aug., 1889.

Issue by wife Alice:

1357. II. FRANK HENRY[9], b. at North Attleboro, Mass., 7 June, 1880.

1103. **WILLIAM BARNARD[8] FANNING**, b. 1843, (*Charles Henry[7], Henry Willson[6], Thomas[5], Thomas[4], John[3], John[2], Edmund[1]*)

m. at Spencer, Mass., 1 Jan., 1867,

Ida Adelaide Bemis,

dau. of Joshua E. and Lucelia (Seaver) Bemis, and b. at East Brookfield, Mass., 4 April, 1845.

William Barnard Fanning was born at Lonsdale, R.I., 5 Sept., 1843. He is a clerk in the employ of the State Mutual Life Assurance Company, Worcester, Mass., in which city he resides.

Issue:

1358. I. FLORENCE LOUISE[9], b. at Worcester, Mass., 5 Nov., 1870; m. at Worcester, Mass., 4 March, 1889, Harry Francis Estey, b. at Lancaster, Mass., 18 April, 1866, and son of Arba and Eliza (Bigelow) Estey. He is a telegraph clerk in the Banking House of Kinnicutt & DeWitt, Worcester. Res. Worcester.

Issue:

I. STUART BIGELOW ESTEY, b. 4 Oct., 1889.

1359. II. HOWARD CHANDLER BEMIS[9], b. at Worcester, Mass., 11 Jan., 1878.

1104. **AUGUSTUS FOSTER[8] FANNING**, b. 1845, (*Charles Henry[7], Henry Willson[6], Thomas[5], Thomas[4], John[3], John[2], Edmund[1]*)

m. at Providence, R.I., 28 Dec., 1871,

Phebe Eliza Morse,

dau. of Henry and Phebe (Ryan) Morse, and b. at Pontiac, R.I., 2 Sept., 1849.

Henry Morse, b. in Coventry, R.I., 3 July, 1805; d. at Pontiac, R.I., 3 June, 1850.

Phebe Ryan, b. in Pontiac, R.I., 2 Feb., 1813; d. at Providence, R.I., 29 March, 1873.

Henry Morse, m. to Phebe Ryan in Coventry, R.I., 9 Dec., 1827.

Augustus Foster Fanning was born at Lonsdale, R.I., 23 Aug., 1845. He, like his brother Charles, is a jeweler, and resides in Providence, R.I., and is connected with Messrs. D. Wilcox & Co., that city. He served in the United States Navy during the War of the Rebellion, and was located principally on the coast of Florida in the Gulf of Mexico. Enlisted at Providence, 4 Aug., 1864, discharged at Philadelphia, Penn., 29 June, 1865, at the close of the war.

Issue:

1360. I. BERTHA AUGUSTA[9], b. at Providence, R.I., 10 Dec., 1872.

1107. **EUGENE[8] FANNING**, b. 1842, (*Henry Williams[7], Henry Willson[6], Thomas[5], Thomas[4], John[3], John[2], Edmund[1]*)

m. at Newton Upper Falls, Mass., 5 Jan., 1871.,

Ann Maria Cargill,

dau. of William and Ann Mills (Story) Cargill, and b. at Needham, Mass., 16 Oct., 1843.

Eugene Fanning was born at Jewett City, Conn., 17 March, 1842, and removed with his parents about 1853 to Newton Upper Falls, Mass., where he has since resided. He is engaged in the general job printing business, with his two brothers. They are also manufacturers of folding paper boxes. The firm name is the Fanning Printing Co.

Issue:

1361. I. WILLIAM HENRY[9], b. at Newton Upper Falls, Mass., 11 June, 1872.

1108. **HENRY HALE[8] FANNING**, b. 1851, (*Henry Williams*[7], *Henry Willson*[6], *Thomas*[5], *Thomas*[4], *John*[3], *John*[2], *Edmund*[1])

m. at Dedham, Mass., 28 June, 1882,

Lizzie Adelaide Farrington,

dau. of Reuben and Emily (Alden) Farrington, and b. at Dedham, Mass., 10 Oct., 1851.

Henry Hale Fanning was born at Woonsocket, R.I., 10 June, 1851. When about a year and a half old his parents removed from Jewett City Conn., to Newton Upper Falls, Mass., where he now resides. He is in the printing business there with his two brothers under the name of the Fanning Printing Co., General Job Printers and manufacturers of folding paper boxes.

Issue:

1362. I. EMILY FARRINGTON[9], b. at Newton Upper Falls, Mass., 21 Aug., 1883.

1109. **FRANK**[8] **FANNING,** b. 1854, (*Henry Williams*[7], *Henry Willson*[6], *Thomas*[5], *Thomas*[4], *John*[3], *John*[2], *Edmund*[1])

m. at Monson, Mass., 5 Sept., 1877,

Mary Persis Guilford,

dau. of Reverend Earl and Lucy Maria (Bement) Guilford, and b. at North Reading, Mass., 25 May, 1852.

She is a direct descendant of John Alden.

John Alden and Priscilla Mullens were married in Feb., 1621. Eleven children were born to them. The youngest son, John Alden, married the eldest daughter (Rose) of Miles Standish, and had nine children, and it is from this union that Mary Persis Guilford Fanning is directly descended.

Rev. John Alden married Nancy Grey of Pelham, Mass., in 1771; they had fourteen children. Their ninth child, Minerva Alden, married Anson Bement. Their daughter, Lucy Maria Bement, married in Sept., 1840, Earl Guilford. Their fourth child was Mary Persis Guilford, who married Frank Fanning.

Frank Fanning was born at Newton Upper Falls, Mass., 13 April, 1854, and has always resided there. He is engaged with his brothers, Eugene and Henry, in the printing and paper box manufacturing business, under the name of the Fanning Printing Co.

1123. **JOHN EARLE**[8] **FANNING,** b. 1859, (*George Washington*[7], *John Faulkner*[6], *Thomas*[5], *Thomas*[4], *John*[3], *John*[2], *Edmund*[1])

m. at Delhi, Delaware Co., N.Y., 17 Aug., 1886,

Le Nettie Marie Bisbee,

dau. of Myron Curtis and Mary Jane (Pease) Bisbee, and b. at Delhi, N.Y., 12 March, 1863.

John Earle Fanning was born at Greenville, Conn., 27 May, 1859; was educated in the public schools in Norwich, and early in life settled down to mercantile pursuits. At first he occupied a position in a clothing house. In March, 1883, he entered the employ of N. S. Gilbert & Sons, Norwich, furniture dealers, and remained with them many years. He is now in the art and designing business at 31 Willow St., Norwich, under name of "The Fanning Studios." No issue.

NINTH GENERATION

1127. **WILLIAM EDMUND⁹ FANNING**, b. 1870, (*George*[8], *William*[7], *James*[6], *George*[5], *William*[4], *Edmund*[3], *Edmund*[2], *Edmund*[1])
m. at Norwich, Conn., 24 May, 1893,
Ada Marie Moxley,
dau. of Solon A. and Mary (Adams) Moxley,
and b. at Montville, Conn., 25 May, 1869.

William Edmund Fanning was born at Ledyard, Conn., 27 June, 1870. He graduated from Snell's Business College, Norwich, and located at Hartford, where he is proprietor of the Empire Steam Laundry.

Issue:

1363. I. RUTH EUGENIA[10], b. at Norwich, Conn., 28 Feb., 1894.
1364. II. ESTHER ADA[10], b. at Hartford, Conn., 23 May, 1896.
1365. III. GEORGE[10], b. at Hartford, Conn., 28 July 1897.

1132. **CHARLES WESLEY⁹ FANNING**, b. 1873, (*Charles Edward*[8], *Kinney Nathaniel*[7], *Jonathan*[6], *Asher*[5], *Jonathan*[4], *Jonathan*[3], *Edmund*[2], *Edmund*[1])
m. at Coldwater, Mich., 23 Feb., 1897,
Lulu Newton,
dau. of
and b. at

Charles Wesley Fanning was born at Coldwater, Mich., 3 May, 1873; is a barber, and resides at Youngstown, O. No issue.

1134. **HERBERT KINNEY[9] FANNING**, b. 1878, (*Charles Edward[8], Kinney Nathaniel[7], Jonathan[6], Asher[5], Jonathan[4], Jonathan[3], Edmund[2], Edmund[1]*)

m. at Coldwater, Mich., 1 May, 1902,

Helen De Voe Miner,

dau. of Cornelius Everett and Carrie (De Voe) Miner, and b. at Montgomery, Mich., 10 March, 1882.

Herbert Kinney Fanning was born at Coldwater, Mich., 7 July, 1878; is a machinist, and resides at Battle Creek, Mich.

Issue:

1366. I. HERBERT DE VOE[10], b. at Battle Creek, Mich., 10 April, 1903.

1139. **HUGH JAMES[9] FANNING**, b. 1877, (*Ira Smith[8], David Grace[7], Elisha[6], Elisha[5], David[4], Jonathan[3], Edmund[2], Edmund[1]*)

m. at Wetona, Penn., 29 Nov., 1900,

Agnes Eliza Bailey,

dau. of Richmond and Julietta (Phelps) Bailey, and b. at Wetona, Penn., 2 Dec., 1883.

Hugh James Fanning was born at Wetona, Penn., 17 May, 1877; is a farmer, and resides at Troy. No issue.

1147. **PERRY EUGENE[9] FANNING**, b. 1870, (*Elisha Philander[8], Edwin[7], Elisha[6], Elisha[5], David[4], Jonathan[3], Edmund[2], Edmund[1]*)

m. at Greenwood, Penn., 18 Dec., 1898,

Eudora Brown,

dau. of Reuben and Samantha (Morgan) Brown, and b. at Shunk, Penn., 20 June, 1876.

Perry Eugene Fanning, son of Elisha Philander and Mary (Mosher) Fanning, was born at Springfield, Penn., 19 Oct., 1870. He is a farmer, and resides in Fox Township, Penn., P. O. Address, Shunk, Penn.

Issue:

1367. I. EDGAR RAYMOND[10], b. in Fox Township, Penn., 29 Jan., 1900.

1368. II. AUDLEY HARLAND[10], b. in Fox Township, Penn., 24 May, 1902.

1155. **WARREN HAROLD[9] FANNING,** b. 1870, (*Sandford Rescom[8], Edwin[7], Elisha[6], Elisha[5], David[4], Jonathan[3], Edmund[2], Edmund[1]*)
m. at Wellsburg, N.Y., 15 April, 1891,

Emma Lillian Foster,

dau. of William R. and Sarah Ann (Cranmer) Foster, and b. at Le Roy, Penn., 3 April, 1870.

Warren Harold Fanning, son of Sandford Rescom and Eveline (Shattuck) Fanning, was born in Fox Township, Penn., 22 Aug., 1870; is a merchant and postmaster, and resides in Fox Township, Penn., P. O. Address, Shunk, Penn.

Issue:

1369. I. HAROLD ROYCE[10], b. at Shunk, Penn., 26 Jan., 1892.

1370. II. CHARLES CLAUDIUS[10], b. at Shunk, Penn., 27 April, 1894.

1159. **PERRY[9] FANNING,** b. 1885, (*William[8], Edwin[7], Elisha[6], Elisha[5], David[4], Jonathan[3], Edmund[2], Edmund[1]*)
m. at Costello, Penn., 31 March, 1903,

Carrie Rittburg,

dau. of George and Mary (Nesler) Rittburg, and b. at Costello, Penn., 22 Oct., 1882.

Perry Fanning, son of William and Susan (Van Buskirk) Fanning, was born at Fall Brook, Penn., 21 Aug., 1885, and resides at Costello, Penn., where he works in a tannery.

1179. **WALTER[9] FANNING,** b. 1875, (*Frederick Angelo[8], Frederic Hazen[7], Amos[6], Elisha[5], David[4], Jonathan[3], Edmund[2], Edmund[1]*)

m. at

———— ————,

dau. of

and b. at

Walter Fanning was born at Utica, N.Y., 17 Aug., 1875. (No further record, however, is obtainable from the family.)

1189. **ERNEST LINWOOD[9] FANNING,** b. 1869, (*James Horace[8], Nathaniel[7], Nathaniel[6], James[5], James[4], James[3], Thomas[2], Edmund[1]*)

m. at Southampton, L.I., 25 April, 1891,

Elvina Stansie Dickerson,

dau. of Townsend and Gertrude (Appleford) Dickerson, and b. at Wading River, L.I., 8 Jan., 1870.

Ernest Linwood Fanning was born at Southampton, L.I. 14 Dec., 1869; is a printer, and resides at Southampton, L.I.

Issue:

1371. I. EUNICE ESTELLE[10], b. at Southampton, L.I., 1 April, 1892.

1372. II. HOWARD LINWOOD[10], b. at Southampton, L.I., 24 March, 1896.

1191. **EDWARD EMERSON[9] FANNING,** b. 1867, (*Nathaniel Edmund[8], Nathaniel[7], Nathaniel[6], James[5], James[4], James[3], Thomas[2], Edmund[1]*)

m. at Bay Shore, L.I., 29 Dec., 1891,

Martha Mahala Thurber,

dau. of Francis Lawson and Mary Eliza (Bedell) Thurber, and b. at Bay Shore, L.I., 5 Aug., 1872.

Edward Emerson Fanning was born at Southampton, L.I., 10 Aug., 1867, where he resides. He is a butcher.

Issue:

1373. I. FRANK EMERSON[10], b. at Bay Shore, L.I., 15 Nov., 1892.

1265. **JOHN BARCLAY[9] FANNING,** b. 1873, (*Edmund Frederick Augustus*[8], *Edmund Frederick Augustus*[7], *Edmund*[6], *Barclay*[5], *Phineas*[4], *James*[3], *Thomas*[2], *Edmund*[1])

m. at Lincolnville, Ind., 24 Sept., 1893,

Gertrude Tyner,

dau. of David and Charlotte (Banister) Tyner, and b. near Lagro, Ind., 13 April, 1873.

Gertrude Tyner's parents died at her birth, and she was brought up by her maternal grandparents, the Banisters, who resided on a farm near Dora, Wabash Co., Ind.

John Barclay Fanning was born at Lincolnville, Wabash Co., Ind., 24 July, 1873. He was educated at Earlham College, near Richmond, Ind., an institute owned and controlled by Quakers, and of strict discipline. After graduating he returned to Lincolnville to live and bought out a drug store, in which business he is now engaged.

Issue:

1374. I. DONALD SYLVESTER[10], b. at Lincolnville, Ind., 1 Sept., 1894; d. 27 Oct., 1894.

1266. **EDMUND GRAY[9] FANNING,** b. 1867, (*Edmund Barclay*[8], *Barclay*[7], *Edmund*[6], *Barclay*[5], *Phineas*[4], *James*[3], *Thomas*[2], *Edmund*[1])

m. at Campello, Mass., 19 Nov., 1889,

Sarah Maria Lothrop,

dau. of Eugene Terry and Sarah (Southworth) Lothrop, and b. at Easton, Mass., 6 July, 1868.

Edmund Gray Fanning was born at Brockton, Mass., 26 Aug., 1867; is a bookkeeper, and resides at Campello, Mass.

Issue:

1375. I. DORA LOTHROP[10], b. at Campello, Mass., 14 June, 1892.

1376. II. MARJORIE LYON[10], b. at Campello, Mass., 2 Oct., 1894.

1267. **CHARLES HENRY⁹ FANNING**, b. 1869, (*Edmund Barclay*[8], *Barclay*[7], *Edmund*[6], *Barclay*[5], *Phineas*[4], *James*[3], *Thomas*[2], *Edmund*[1])

m. at Campello, Mass., 3 Feb., 1891,

Sarah Louise Lincoln,

dau. of Isaac Augustus and Helen (Thompson) Lincoln, and b. at North Bridgewater, now Brockton, Mass., 28 June, 1869.

Charles Henry Fanning was born at Brockton, Mass., 18 Sept., 1869; was a grocer at Campello, Mass., where he resided and where he died, 18 Feb., 1897. He is bur. at Brockton.

Wid. survives and res. at Campello. No issue.

1302. **CHARLES BRECKENRIDGE**[9] **FANNING**, b., 1857, (*Benjamin*[8], *Nelson*[7], *Benjamin*[6], *Walter*[5], *Thomas*[4] *John*[3], *John*[2], *Edmund*[1])

m. at Coxsackie, N.Y., 25 Dec., 1877,

Sarah Jane Egnor,

dau. of Charles and Mary (Anderson) Egnor, and b. at Catskill, N.Y., 19 May, 1858.

Charles Breckenridge Fanning was born at Conesville, N.Y., 1 Feb., 1857. He has been messenger for the American Express Co. for many years. Resides at Kingston, N.Y.

Issue:

+1377. I. WILLARD[10], b. at Catskill, N.Y., 12 Oct., 1878.

1378. II. BESSIE MAE[10], b. at Kingston, N.Y., 7 July, 1894.

1312. **CHARLES STEWART**[9] **FANNING**, b. 1864, (*Nelson Charles*[8], *Asa*[7], *Thomas*[6], *Walter*[5], *Thomas*[4], *John*[3], *Edmund*[1])

m. at Cannonsville, N.Y., 9 Nov., 1886,

Julia Ann Peet,

dau. of Franklin L. and Mary Ann (Cox) Peet,
and b. at Mount Upton, N.Y., 17 June, 1864.

Charles Stewart Fanning was born at Fergusonville, N.Y., 9 Nov., 1864; is a hardware merchant at Davenport, N.Y., and resides at Fergusonville.

Issue:

1379. I. CHARLES HAROLD[10], b. at Fergusonville, N.Y., 18 Jan., 1891.

1322. **CHARLES WHITNEY[9] FANNING**, b. 1873, (*Frederick[8], Henry[7], Frederick[6], Walter[5], Thomas[4], John[3], John[2], Edmund[1]*)

m. at Napanee, Ont., Can., 30 Sept., 1896,

Harriet Adelaide Hosey,

dau. of William Nelson and Clarinda Jane (Night) Hosey, and b. at Napanee, Ont., Can., 10 May, 1873.

Charles Whitney Fanning was born at Rochester, N.Y., 26 May, 1873; is an engineer, and resides at Olean, N.Y. No issue.

1328. **CHARLES HERBERT[9] FANNING**, b. 1864, (*Frederick Walter[8], George[7], Frederick[6], Walter[5], Thomas[4], John[3], John[2], Edmund[1]*)

m. at Waterloo, Ind., 11 June, 1885,

Rebecca Catharine Till,

dau. of Samuel and Sophia (Slaybough) Till,
and b. at Waterloo, Ind., 31 July, 1868.

Charles Herbert Fanning was born at Belleville, Ont., Can., 29 Feb., 1864. He is an engineer and resides at Butler, Ind.

TENTH GENERATION

1377. **WILLARD[10] FANNING,** b. 1878, (*Charles Breckenridge[9], Benjamin[8], Nelson[7], Benjamin[6], Walter[5], Thomas[4], John[3], John[2], Edmund[1]*)
m. at Kingston, N.Y., 24 Nov., 1898,
Estelle Saulpaugh,
dau. of George and Mary (Brown) Saulpaugh, and b. at Kingston, N.Y., 12 April, 1879.

Willard Fanning was born at Catskill, N.Y., 12 Oct., 1878; is a stenographer, and resides at Kingston, N.Y.

BIOGRAPHICAL

EDMUND FANNING², JUNIOR (No. 2).

(For his Genealogical data, see page 91.)

Edmund Fanning, eldest son of Edmund and Ellen (   ) Fanning, the American ancestors, was born in Ireland about 1651 and came to this country with his parents at the time of their settling in Connecticut. He was reared on his father's farm in Stonington, and resided there until he grew to manhood.

In 1678 he married at Stonington, Margaret, daughter of William and Mary Billings (spelled both Billing and Billings in the Connecticut Records). William Billings removed from Dorchester, Mass., the day of his marriage, 5 February, 1657–8, to what is now North Stonington, Conn., where he located and where he resided until his decease 16 March, 1712–13. His homestead farm, as granted and laid out to him, was on Cossaduck Hill, and contained about four hundred acres. His will, dated 3 October, 1712, proved 14 April, 1713, on file at New London, mentions wife Mary, sons William and Ebenezer, daughters Lydia, Margaret, Mary, Mercy, Abigail, Dorothy and Patience, granddaughter Mary and grandson Beriah Grant.

Previous to his father's death, Edmund Fanning had located on his Groton lands, on the west bank of the Upper Mystic, on the original grant of fifty acres to the elder Fanning in 1664. He resided on this farm until his decease about the year 1715. The farm appears to have been allotted to him during his father's lifetime and was confirmed to him at his death, when in the settlement of his estate the sons make acknowledgment in the Probate Court that they are satisfied with the portions that had been allotted to each of them during their father's lifetime.

It is to be regretted that the deeds (except the original grant of fifty acres to his father) are not on record showing the acquisition of Edmund Fanning, Junior's, farm. No record exists that can now be found showing purchases of additional land by either father or son. Whether they acquired it by grant or purchase is not clear. It may be that the original grant of fifty acres covered much more than that area, as was frequently the case in early grants. Certain it is, however, that in 1715 Edmund Fanning, Junior's, farm contained about four hundred acres. At his death the farm descended to his two sons Edmund and Jonathan, who, on the first day of July, 1715, agree upon a dividing line between their portions,[1] Jonathan taking the northern and Edmund the southern part of the farm. Edmund's share was triangular in shape, and bounded on the west by a brook running into Mystic River, on the east by Mystic River, and north by his brother Jonathan's land. Jonathan's share lay north of Edmund's and extended to Lantern ("Lanthorn") Hill Lower Pond and Lieut. Stanton's land, and was bounded on the west by William Williams' farm, and on the east by Mystic River. This four hundred acres was the homestead farm of Edmund Fanning, Junior, eldest son of Edmund the American ancestor. As already stated, it remained in this branch of the Fanning family nearly one hundred and fifty

[1] *Vide* Groton Deeds, Book 1, p. 286.

years, a portion of it being owned and occupied by Phineas Fanning, a descendant in the fifth generation, as late as 1799. In that year Phineas sold his remaining part of it, seventy acres, to Capt. John Holmes of Stonington.[1]

On this Groton farm is located the old Fanning burying-ground, about twenty rods west of Mystic Brook and about one hundred rods south of Alonzo Main's house.

The lands occupied by the remnant of the Pequot tribe of Indians at Noank[2] were early taken away from them (about 1667) and afterward were distributed to the inhabitants. (See map.) In the distribution of these "Noank Lots," so-called, in July, 1712, Edmund Fanning had laid out to him in Noank Neck Lot No. 24 in the first tier in the first division, which descended to his son Edmund, who sold it in turn to Samuel Burrows, 25 June, 1715.[3]

Edmund Fanning was given a grant of land of thirty acres by the town of Stonington on the east side of Pawcatuck River, 11 December, 1672, as appears from the following record on the Stonington books:

"The 11th of December: 1672, Thos. Brand Joshua Baker Emund faning Junior ——— These all are to be considered In the second place for to have theyr grants on the est side of poquatuck River when the former grants are layd out to the fore mentioned Inhabitants
Daniell Sha Deliveranse Blackeman These are to have Thirtie ackers apeece."[4]

And again the following record:[5]

---

[1] *Vide* Groton Deeds, Book 13, p. 126.

[2] Spelled variously in olden times, "Naiwayonk," "Naywank," "Nowayunk," etc

[3] *Vide* Groton Deeds, Book 1, p. 274.

[4] *Vide* Stonington Records, Book 1, p. 56.

[5] *Vide* Stonington Records, Book 1, p. 194.

"The names of those that had 30 acker grants on the est side of Poquatuck River and there Lots:
"Thos. Brand 12, Joshua baker 15, Edward ffaning 1, John Ascrat 14, Joshua Holmes 2, george Denison Junior 8, Tho. Renolds 16, Steeven Richardson 10, Robert Stanton 11, Tho. Edwards 9, William Jonson 13, Samuel Minor 5, Josia Osborne 4, Daniel Mason 6, Daniel Sha 7, Deliverance Blackman 3."

Edmund Fanning was one of the English volunteers in the Narragansett War,[1] and for his services therein received a grant of land in Voluntown, which was the ninety-seventh lot in number, and "ye 4th lot in ye 8th tier," and laid out to him in March, 1706, consisting of eighty-nine acres.[2] This lot descended to his son Jonathan, who sold it to John Butler of Voluntown 9 September, 1742.[3]

It is difficult to determine to a certainty in which of the three old houses on the Groton farm Edmund Fanning resided, but there is reason for believing it was the old house called the Barnes house (described in the article under Edmund Fanning No. 10, 3d generation, in the Biographical part of this volume). This house is first mentioned in 1769, when George Fanning sold thirty acres of the farm to Ezra Barnes,[4] in which deed he referred to the old house as the "mansion house." It was a very old house at that time and was soon after torn down to make room for a new structure, and in its stead the present Barnes house was erected near its site, which house is still standing. Whether the first of these houses was erected by Edmund Fanning, Junior, or his father is not known.

---

[1] *Vide* Note No. 4 on p. 76.
[2] *Vide* Voluntown Deeds, Book 1, p. 60.
[3] *Vide* Voluntown Deeds, Book 2, p. 278.
[4] *Vide* Groton Deeds, Book 8, p. 115.

No record of the settlement of Edmund Fanning's estate can be found either at New London, Groton, or Stonington,[1] nor the date of his death nor that of his wife. It is supposed his death occurred about 1715, for on July 1st of that year his two sons, Edmund and Jonathan, agree upon the dividing line of their farms, which they presumably had just inherited from their father.[2]

He and his wife were without doubt buried in the old Fanning family burying-ground on this farm, but with unmarked headstones.

---

[1] Doubtless these records were among those destroyed by Arnold when he burned New London, 6 Sept., 1781.

[2] Edmund[2] was living, 14 January, 1713–14, when his name appears as witness to a Deed at New London. *Vide* Book 6, p. 322. He was dead, however, before 25 June, 1715, which is proved by a Deed of that date from Edmund Fanning, 3d Generation, to Samuel Burrows. *Vide* Groton Deeds, Book 1. p. 274.

THOMAS[2] FANNING, (No. 4).

(For Genealogical data, see page 92.)

Thomas Fanning, second son of Edmund Fanning, Senior, the first of the name in Connecticut, was born, it is supposed on Fishers Island, N. Y., about 1655. No record of his birth however, is obtainable, and the date can only be approximated.

He resided with his parents on their Stonington, Conn., farm, until his father's decease in 1683, and after marrying in the following year, continued to reside there for a few years. At his father's death he inherited one-half of the homestead farm of 120 acres at Stonington, his brother James having the other half, the southern portion.[1]

He sold this 60 acres with the homestead buildings thereon in 1693 to Lieut. James Avery as appears by the following deed:

"Know all men by these Prefents that I Thomas faning of Stonington In the Collony of Conecticott have sold allieniated tranf-fered and made over I Doe by thefe prefents sell allienate Confirm and make over unto Leiut. James Averie of New London of the Collony aforesyd: the one half part of the Land which my father lived upon: the halfe part of the farm: Containing fixtie acres more or Lesf: Bounded to the South with my brother James fanings Land now in the poffesion of Leiu. James Averie on the North with Land belonging to Nathaniel Beby, on the Eaft with the fyd Bebees Land: on the weft with the frefh brooke that Runs into miftick River I fay all the fore mentioned Land, with the houfe that ftands thereon &c: all fencing with all other preveledges & appurtenances thereunto Belonging granted, or Intended to be granted to him the James averie his Heirs Executors administrators and affignes for Ever; and I the fyd Thomas faning Doe for myfelf my Heirs executors administrators Covenant promise Grant to and with the fyd avery his Heirs Executors and

[1] See map of the Stonington farm of Edmund Fanning, Senior, in this work.

adminiſtrators ſhall and may quiettly and peaceablely use poſſes or Diſpoſe or Injoye the ſyd Land houſing or fencing without any Lett, hindrance trouble molleſtation or objection of me the ſyd Thomas faning or of any of mine or from any other perſon or perſons whatſoever of the above named Thomas faning have ReCeived of the above named James Avery the ſum of ſixteen pounds in Caſh with which I acknowledge myſelf fully Sattiſfied, Content & payed for the Land and houſe abovementioned. In confirmation of the above premiſes and with the Latter Clauſe I Doe hereunto ſett my hand and seale this 18th: of DeCember 1693

witneſſed by us The O marke of
Samuell Avery Thomas faning a seale {SEAL}
John faning

DeCember the 18th: 1693: Thomas faning appeared and Did acknowledged this inſtrument to be hiz act & Deed before me James Avery. Commiho': Entered in Stonington Records this 26" of Janarie 169$\frac{3}{4}$ P me John stanton
Recorder."

Thomas Fanning's particular residence in Stonington after the year 1693 is not known. There are no deeds on record conveying property to or from him after this date. He was of Stonington, however, at the time of his decease in 1704, and his death is recorded in the Stonington Records of "Births, Marriages and Deaths," showing that he still resided in that town.

Thomas Fanning and his brother John, in the distribution of their father, Edmund's, estate in 1683, came into possession of a one hundred acre lot called the "Pukhunganuck Lot" near Pendleton Hill, North Stonington, which was an original grant to Edmund Fanning, Senior. This tract of land they sold 12 July, 1701, to William Billings of Preston.

Thomas Fanning had another Grant of land in New London:

"At a Town Meeting holden at New London on September the 1st 1686 Thomas ffaning hath given & granted to him thirty eacers of upland on the East side of the River foure mile frome the meeting house not hindering former Grants."

This Grant, however, was not laid out until ten years afterwards in 1696, and was sold on the 28 January of that year to William Williams, Junior, as appears by the Records at New London:

"Thomas ffanning having Given him thirty Acres of Land at A Town Meeting held at New London September 1, 1686 and having Sold Sayde Grant unto William Williams Junior wee have Layed out Sayde Grant: unto Sayde Williams as followeth: Beginning at a small white oake tree: marked on four Sides, Adjoining to Land in the possession of Richard Williams on the north Side and So Running west and by north neerest Seaventy poles to a Red oake tree by a Small Runn of water frome thense South and by west to A Greate Walnut tree marked on ffoure sides being allso Seaventy Rods: from thense Easte & by South to Land in the possession of William Williams Senor and bounded upon his Land Seaventy Rod Then north and by Easte to the first boundary: highways "Excepted" & allowed ffor: January 28th 1696

Samuell Chester
Samuell Rogers."

Thomas Fanning had a Grant of 50 acres of land from the Town of Stonington on the east side of Pawcatuck River, 10 August, 1683.[1]

He also came into possession of 150 acres on the east side of "New London River," which he purchased 31 January, 1694-5, of Samuel Chester.[2]

Thomas Fanning (as well as his brothers Lieut. John and

[1] *Vide* Stonington Records, Town Votes, Book 2, pp. 46 and 47.

[2] New London Deeds, Book 6, p. 50.

Edmund, and their father Edmund) was one of the Volunteers in the Narragansett War and in return for his services received a Grant of land from the Colony of Connecticut. This Grant as afterwards laid out in March, 1706, and relaid out 23 Aprii, 1730, embraced eighty-two acres of land in Voluntown. It was Lot No. 111 of the Volunteer lands, and "the 6th Lot in the 9th tier."

Stonington Town Records (Book 1, p. 130) give the mark of Thomas Fanning as follows:

> "The mark properly belonging to the houfe of Thomas ffaning is a crop on the neer eare and A halfe penney under the off eare. Entered March the 6″, 1688: per me John Stanton Recorder''.

He is mentioned in the Thomas Minor Diary, p. 137: "Aug. 14, 1676, Thomas Fanning was here to mow."

He died at Stonington, 27 April, 1704. The date of his widow's death, however, is not found, nor the burial places of either. No settlement of his estate appears, and these records no doubt were destroyed at the burning of New London, 6 Sept., 1781.

LIEUT. JOHN[2] FANNING (No. 5), AND HIS FORT HILL FARM.

(For Genealogical data concerning him, see page 94.)

Lieut. John Fanning, the third son of Edmund Fanning Senior, the American ancestor, was born on Fishers Island it is supposed about 1657. His parents removed to New London, Conn., previous to 1662, and settled in that part afterward called Groton. Part of the farm was in Stonington. There he grew to manhood. His father dying in 1683, he married and settled on the west bank of the Mystic River.

He purchased a farm there of John Burrows of New London, for £10.–, 26 February, 1683–4. It was a ten-acre lot located one-half mile south of Old Mystic Village, and was originally included in a grant of "ye town of New London unto Robert Isbell." Its location was just south of the old Thomas Welles house (occupied in 1904 by Nathan S. Holloway). The bounds of the farm can easily be traced at the present time: — the brook, still called Spring Brook, the river, the creek, the cold spring and the old cellar hole, and traces of the old cider mill, but no buildings remain. Mr. Holloway, who moved into the Welles house adjoining this farm in 1855, states the Fanning buildings went down before his recollection.

Lieut. Fanning resided on this farm a number of years and sold it 13 March, 1705–6, with all the housing, fencing, buildings, etc., thereon, for £60.–, to Joseph Welles, of Groton, a shipwright, and removed to his other farm on the east side of Fort Hill, where he resided until his decease.

Historic Fort Hill[1] (spelled in olden times "Fourt Hill") lies three miles east of the River Thames in the Town of Groton.[2] On its highest point the Pequot Indians had, previous to 1637, erected their fortress, whence they could communicate by signals with their other stronghold on the neighboring "Pequot Hill," which lies about a mile and a half in a northeasterly direction. From either hill a commanding view of the Sound could be obtained as well as a view of the entire country round about. No better localities for a fortress could be imagined.

In 1636–7 Capt. John Mason and his band of English soldiers conquered the Pequots and drove them from their habitation, burning their fort on Pequot Hill and scattered death and destruction throughout their tribe. Sassacus, their leader, escaped for a time the doom that befell his braves, by fleeing to the western fortress on Fort Hill. Later, however, he too shared the fate of his unfortunate kinsmen, and eventually the entire tribe of Pequots were subjugated and most of them destroyed.

Fort Hill to-day is covered for the most part with woody districts. Many of its forests have been cut down, only to grow again and give little change to the general appearance of the country. Two highways were early laid out, and cross the hill at right angles to each other, the older one being the New London and Mystic road running east and west. Its cross highway is called the Flanders road at its northern part and Fort Hill road or Brook Street at its

[1] The reader will be greatly aided in understanding this description by consulting the map of Fort Hill farm in another part of this work.

[2] The town of Groton received its name from Groton in Suffolk, England where the Winthrops originated.

southern point. One or two less important highways give free access to and from the hill, and numerous paths and cart-ways old and new skirt the woods and fields. Many cellar holes dot the surface here and there and are reminders of the time when Fort Hill was more thickly inhabited and interspersed with farms and houses. These houses have nearly all disappeared.

The northern part of the hill is elongated and forms an extension running due north about a mile and a half.

A number of brooks have their rise in this locality, the largest of which is Noank or Great Brook, as it was called in olden times. This brook skirts the east bounds of the hill and empties into the Sound at Palmer's Cove, the Indian name of which was "Tuskhegonuck" Cove.[1]

Capt. Samuel Fish and Lieut. John Fanning purchased 11 January, 1695, in partnership for £90 a large tract of land on the eastern slope of Fort Hill of Col. John Pynchon of Springfield, Mass.[2] This land was divided 3 March, 1702, Capt. Fish taking the northern part and Lieut. Fanning the southern.[3] The east bounds of both farms was Noank Brook. Both Fish and Fanning settled on their respective portions and resided there until their decease.

The Fish farm, handed down through many generations of the family, finally went into other hands about 1854.

The Fanning farm changed ownership many times from its earliest period until 1877, when it became the William Eccleston Farm, by which name it is known to-day.

Tracing out the original owners of this tract of land, it

---

[1] *Vide* Groton Deeds, Book 8, p. 87.

[2] *Vide* New London Deeds, Book 5, p. 203.

[3] *Vide* Groton Deeds, Book 1, p. 12.

appears on the records that the two hundred acres was first granted to Edward Culver of "Pequit" previous to the year 1655.[1] An unbroken record of deeds traces the land from his ownership down to the time it came into possession of Fish and Fanning.[2] Culver deeded the land to Robert Parke 18 March, 1655–6,[3] and he to James Avery 14 July, 1656, and he to Edward Codner 20 September, 1660,[5] and he to Antipas Newman 25 January, 1661,[6] and he to Amos Richardson 16 October, 1663,[7] and he to Col. John Pynchon of Springfield 25 October,[8] 1665, for £60, and he to Fish and Fanning as before stated. Col. Pynchon also sold them nine acres of salt meadow, on "Six-Penny Island," so called which "had sometime been and now is the improvement of said Fish and Fanning." The division of this two hundred acres is on record at Groton, Book 1, Page 12, of the Land Grants, and is as follows: —

"To all Christian People wherever these presents shall come "Sergeant Samuell ffish and Mr. John ffanning both of the "County of New London in his Majesties Colony or provence "of Connecticut sendeth greeting Know yee that whereas wee "the aforenamed formerly made purchase of a certain tract or "tracts of upland and meadow ground of Collonell John "Pinchon of Springfield Esq. the said purchase being in part- "nership, and in consideration of the full and just sume of "twenty two pounds current silver money lent by the said "Sergeant Samuell ffish unto his loving kinsman Mr. John

---

[1] *Vide* New London Deeds, Book 3, p. 25.

[2] This refutes the statement in the old Lucy Fanning Watson manuscript that Fort Hill was purchased by Edmund Fanning in 1645, etc.

[3] *Vide* New London Deeds, Book 3, p. 25.

[4] *Vide* New London Deeds, Book 3, p. 34.

[5] *Vide* New London Deeds, Book 3, p. 93.

[6] *Vide* New London Deeds, Book 5, p. 203.

[7] *Ibid.* [8] *Ibid.*

"ffanning in order to make payment of the said purchase wee "the aforesaid doe hereby mutually fully clearly & absolutely "agree reciprocally for ourselves our heirs Executors Admin- "istrators & Assigns in order unto the distribution of the "said whole purchase shall be and remain to be the true and "proper divident or stated line betwixt us & our heirs or "assigns forever (viz) Beginning att the brooke which is the "east bounds of the ffarm to a white oake tree marked on "two sides standing by the brooke, And thence west nearest "to a flatt rock with a heape of stones upon itt and thence "upon the same point to the Common It is also agreed and "mutually Consented unto that there shall be a Lane allowed "on the west side of the brooke which is westermost consist- "ing of three Rods wide the Lane to extend down to the In- "dian Rock and to be mutually erected and maintained by "the aforesaid. Sergeant Samuell ffish is to erect & maintain "the west side & Mr. John ffanning is to erect and maintain the "east fence of said lane which is allso to be kept with suitable "and Convenient gates or barrs for the accommodation of the "aforesaid Sergeant Samuell ffish & Mr. John ffanning their "heirs Executors Administrators & Assigns for ever without "any lett hinerance mollestation or by us our heirs executors "or assigns To have and to hold posess & enjoy quietly and "peaceably in Manner and in forme as above agreed & that "freely & clearly acquited & discharged from all former bar- "gain Title Mortgage dower or Incumbrances whatsoever "And in token of all the aforesaid premises mutually agreed "as full and finall Ishue and determination wee bind our- "selves our heirs Executors Administrators & Assigns ffirmly by "these presents, as witness our hands and seals this third day "of March Anno Domini one thousand seven hundred & two

"Signed Sealed and delivered in Samuell ffish
"presence of us John ffanning"
"John Stanton Sen'r
"Thomas V ffanning
his marke

This Fish-Fanning property was added to materially after 1700, and especially the northern part belonging to Capt. Samuel Fish. He purchased land extensively of John Rogers of New London, and later of his son Samuel Rogers of Westerly, R. I., and greatly extended his northern and eastern boundaries. His western boundary, however, remained practically the same through successive generations.

The Fanning farm would contain about one hundred and eighty statute acres at the present time, but was estimated in Lieut. Fanning's inventory in 1738–9 at one hundred and thirty.[1]

By a provision of Lieut. Fanning's will twenty acres of woodland, lying at the south point of his farm and adjoining it, which belonged to his grandsons, John and Thomas Fanning, were made a part of the farm in its distribution, at the time of his death, increasing the farm to two hundred acres.

The west bound of the Fanning farm was a matter of early settlement. Common or sequestered land bounded it at that point until after its acquisition by the Walworths. In 1737 Lieut. Fanning and Thomas Walworth decided upon the division line of their farms. A survey was ordered made by the County Surveyor and a line run south, eight degrees west, from the north line of their farms, two hundred and twelve rods to the highway. This line had mere stones and piles of stones erected every forty rods. A very old wall built at that time locates this bound. The southern termi-

---

[1] This discrepancy can be easily understood, for few farms were accurately measured in those early days. The standard of measurement, too, varied then. The Scotch and Irish acres, which are in use to some extent in those countries to-day, are larger than the statute acre which is the standard to-day in Great Britain and the United States. Forty-eight Scotch acres are equal to sixty-one statute acres, and one hundred Irish acres equal to one hundred and sixty-two statute acres.

nus of the wall was "Indian Rock"[1] so called and referred to many times in the Groton Records.

The south bound of the Fanning farm was Common land until about 1733 when some twenty acres was lotted out by the town to the heirs of John Fanning, Junior.

The east bound was Noank Brook and Packer land.

The common outlet of the Fanning and Fish farms was an old way (never a road, but simply a pent-way), which led south from Capt. Samuel Fish's house, crossing the New London and Mystic road and running down through the plain and by Lieut. Fanning's house, southwesterly and southerly until it reached the Fort Hill road that leads to the head of Palmer's Cove. For a long distance it runs just west of and nearly parallel to Noank Brook. Part of this old way still remains. The old highway running east and west across Fort Hill, and at that time across the southern part of the Fish property, said to have been first used about 1652, was a further outlet for the farms.

This old pent-way, running north and south, passed Lieut. Fanning's house on the north side. On this pent-way (on the southern part of the Fanning farm), John Fanning, Junior, lived, and the old way is frequently referred to in the early Groton Records as "leading down from Lieut. Fanning's to his son John's house."

An old highway was the Fort Hill road running north from the head of Palmer's Cove and joining the New London highway near the Merritt house on top of Fort Hill. It was relaid out in 1733[2] and again in later years. The

[1] Called also "Canopie Rock."

[2] "At a Proprietors meeting held in Groton Oct. 29, 1733, Voated that Ensign W^m^. Morgan, Sr., John Avery and Serg. John Wall-

original road ran close by the southern terminus of the Thomas Walworth farm (see map), but was changed afterward to a more westerly course in order to enable the quarries to be worked that are located there. The old road is very plainly seen to-day. Its southern part is now called Brook Street.

When this highway was relaid out in 1733, the town appropriated an acre from the southwest corner of Lieut. John Fanning's farm. In exchange for this one acre the town gave Lieut. Fanning a deed of three acres out of the Common lands.[1] This three acres was just north of the one acre and was sold by Lieut. Fanning in 1737 to Thomas Walworth, and formed the extreme southern point of the Walworth farm. It had on it a ledge of rocks, and no doubt this was the Indian Rock referred to as the southern terminus of the "lane" which bounded Lieut. Fanning's farm on the west, mentioned in the Fish-Fanning agreement previously referred to.

In the early part of 1700 a strong effort was made to lay out the New London and Mystic highway from the end of the Poquonnock road to Mystic Ferry, running it directly east through Lieut. Fanning's farm, across Noank Brook, through the Burrows and Packer lands to Mystic Ferry. This highway was to pass close to, and just north of, the Fanning house.

---

worth shall be a committee to lay out an open Highway four rods wide from the head of Nawayunk Cove up fourt Hill to the South Contary Road." *Vide* Groton Town Meeting Book, No. 9, p. 6.

[1] "At a Proprietors meeting held in Groton Apr. 26, 1737, Voted that Lieut. Fanning shall have 3 A. in exchange for land taken from him by a Highway Running across the S. W. corner of his land."

Vide Groton Town Meeting Book, No. 9, p. 10.

The Selectmen of Groton 5 July, 1709, passed the following order, laying out the highway from Fort Hill to Mystic River:—

"We whose names are under written being selectmen of said Groton have laid out a Road for people to pass and repafs: begining at the hill usually known by the name of Fourt hill from whense the Countrie Rode is started; from thence eastwardly through Lef^t John fanings land on the north side of his now Dwelling house, over the Brook and so from thence through comon Lands to land now in purfshefson of James Packer and through s^d Packers land by marked trees unto land in possefsion of the Burrows and from thence by marked trees through s^d Burrows land unto Mystick ferry: wee say laid out by us Selectmen, James Morgan, Samuell Fish, John Morgan."

This highway, though laid out by the town, was never built. The nearest there ever came to being a road through there was in 1769, when a "private way" two and a half miles long[1] was laid out on the 9th of January that year, from Pistol Point to the head of Poquonnock road near the Francis E. Merritt house, then the Amos Burrows place.

It ran by "Fanning's Rock" and the old Lieut. John Fanning house on its south side (then owned and occupied by Capt. John Fish), and can still be traced to-day, little changed in its course.

A committee was appointed by the Town of Groton 25 December, 1722, "to relay out" all the open highways and to lay out new highways where necessary.

This committee, consisting of William Morgan, James Avery, Jr., William Latham and Capt. Moses Fish, thereupon relaid out 14 February, 1723, an eight-rod highway in Noank Neck to the salt water, running from the road that was to go past Lieut. Fanning's house by the brook, south-

———

[1] *Vide* Groton Deeds, Book 10, p. 4.

The old farm house of Lieut. John Fanning on Fort Hill, Groton, Conn.
Now known as the Eccleston place. From photograph in 1904.

erly, along the top of the hill to the Sound. This road was to come out where the Noank schoolhouse now stands, and would have joined the present road south of the schoolhouse.

This highway also was never constructed.

Few people, probably, are aware that the original road on top of Fort Hill ran directly north from the present town house building (instead of northeast as now) and joined the New London and Mystic highway fifteen rods west of Charles Morgan's house. The road then crossed the highway and led on up to the old pent-way, which later became the Flanders road. An old stone wall bounds the east side of this very old highway, but otherwise there is no trace of any road there to-day. The Groton Records, however, prove such a way existed in 1737.[1] The highway, as it runs at the present time, from the Town House to the New London and Mystic road, was laid out between 1737 and 1757.

The Poquonnock road at that time ran westerly by Charles Morgan's house (then William Latham's), and on over to Poquonnock Village.

The Flanders highway was laid out 5 November, 1802, and previously to that was only a pent-way. It was a much travelled way, however, and probably dates from quite early times. It is referred to in the Groton Deeds on one occasion in 1765 as a highway, but was not strictly so at that time.

The old Lieut. John Fanning house as it stands today, and known as the William Eccleston house, is a one-and-a-half-story structure with hip-roof and ell and

---

[1] *Vide* Groton Records, Book 4, p. 133.

faces south. (See photogravure.) It is 40 × 29 feet, with interior arrangement similar to other old houses built early in the eighteenth century, having two large front rooms on either side of entrance, and a long, narrow kitchen in the rear, and two bedrooms and two pantries at either end. The usual large chimney is directly in the centre of the house.

The oldest inhabitants say that the house was an old one in their earliest recollection, but that it has been remodelled somewhat and made larger, and the top of the chimney rebuilt.

There is little doubt that the original house was built by Lieut. John Fanning when he located on this property about 1705. The house is referred to in 1709 when the town voted to build the New London and Mystic highway through his farm, and the record reads that the road shall run "easterly on the north side of Lieut. John Fanning's now dwelling house by the brook."

The old well-sweep still in the rear of the house, and the old lane westerly with its sheds on either side, attest their age. The old barn stood on the site of the one recently burned. Traces of the garden referred to in Lieut. Fanning's will can still be seen south of the house, and also the two-acre plot of land he gave to his daughters Prudence and Thankful.

The ancient willow, estimated by some to be fully one hundred and fifty years old, grows by the "brook that runs down by Lieut. John Fanning's house" at a distance of eight rods southeast of the dwelling. Its immense trunk proves its age and takes one back to Lieut. Fanning's time. Part of the tree fell during the summer of 1899.

Fifty rods west of Lieut. Fanning's was the house of

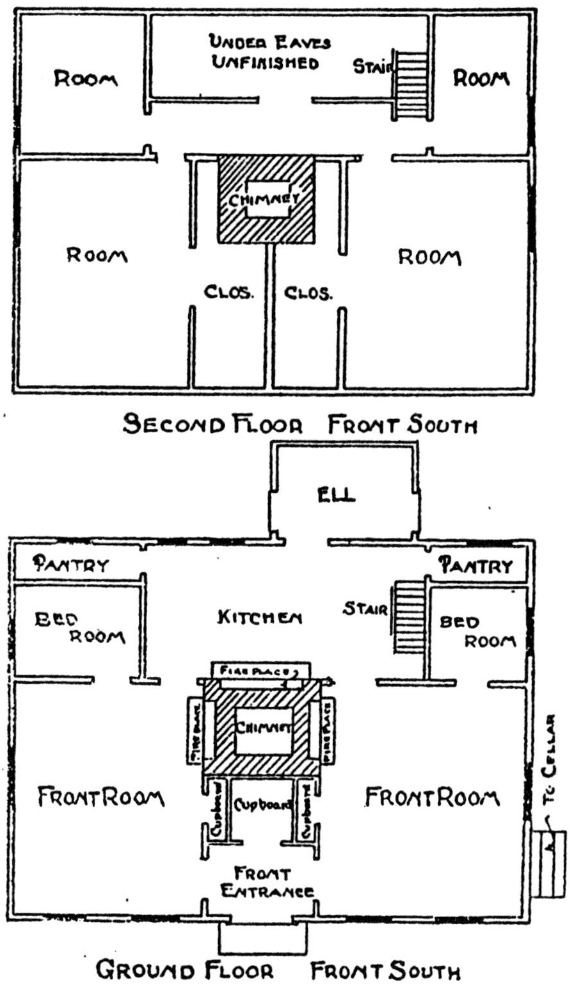

PLAN OF THE LIEUT. JOHN FANNING HOUSE,

FORT HILL, GROTON, CONN., 1902.

Now the William Eccleston Place.

Samuel Fish in 1800. The latter was the grandson of Capt. John Fish. Nothing but a cellar hole remains.

Southerly from Samuel Fish, about forty rods, lived his brother John Fish, who was remembered in his grandfather Capt. John Fish's will in 1795. This old house was removed to Noank, and nothing remains but a lot of stones.

Ten rods farther south, and across a dividing wall, was the Peter Baker place.

Sixty rods north of the Eccleston house recently lived Oren Smith Eccleston, an uncle of William Eccleston. This house, however, is a modern one.

The old schoolhouse, concerning the location of which there is so much doubt, stood on the Fort Hill road, just opposite and north of the Brook Street burying-ground, about five rods back from the highway on a knoll near a stone wall. This was the earliest schoolhouse in the locality, and is mentioned in the Fanning deeds in 1744. It was torn down or removed the early part of the nineteenth century, and rebuilt on the site of the present schoolhouse at Noank, on top of the hill.

The house recently occupied by the widow of Robert Lamb, on the extreme southern part of the Fanning farm, is not an old house, but was built by Thomas and Holloway Latham (grandsons of Joseph Latham) about 1855–60.

Forty-five rods directly north of the Lamb house is a little knoll and evidence that a house stood there at one time. This is supposed to be the location of John Fanning, Junior's, house, and a path led from it up to his father's place, Lieut. John Fanning. John Fanning, Junior, died in 1719.

One of the oldest buildings in this vicinity is the old red house at the head of Palmer's Cove, known as the Palmer house. The date of its erection is not ascertained.

About twenty rods north of the Cove in which Noank Brook empties, on the east side of the highway, stood the old Joseph Latham house during Revolutionary times. The present Thomas Latham house stands opposite the site and was built by his grandfather Joseph about 1791 when the old house was torn down.

Fifty or sixty rods north of Joseph Latham, lived his brother Jasper Latham, on the west side of Noank road, which house was also built about 1791. It is still in a good state of preservation, and now known as the John and Peter Chipman house.

Farther north, up the Noank road, is the Brook Street burying ground, formerly the "Fish burying-ground."

Continuing on up Fort Hill, one comes to the Town Farm on the right. Some twenty rods north of that on the west side of the highway, is an old one-story hip-roof house, formerly the Comfort Brown place, now unoccupied and a part of the Town Farm.

On the brow of the hill, directly opposite the Poquonnock highway, where it turns sharply to the north, is the residence of Francis E. Merritt. This is the old Amos Burrows house, and previously the Thomas Walworth place. The house is a very old one, but has been added to in the present generation. A very old barn and well are near the house — the well referred to in the old records in 1769 as being the "well of Amos Burrows" near his house and near the private way that ran easterly from this point. It is supposed this house dates back to the time Thomas Walworth bought the farm of his brother William in 1732.

The town house is the next building one comes to on the right. This was the old Baptist Church.

Charles L. Morgan's house, a few rods west of the highway, at the point where the New London and Mystic road intercepts the Flanders road, is said to have been built during Revolutionary times, by William Latham. James Latham, residing in Noank in 1899, was born in this house about 1807. His father was William Latham (who married Sabrina Ashby), and grandfather William Latham (who married Eunice Mason).

North of this old Latham house lived the Denisons, Benjamin Burrows (on the site of whose house stands the present Mosher dwelling), Joshua Baker, Zebediah Gates in 1779 (now Peter Crandall), and others. On the east of the Flanders road were Nathan Mix, who lived opposite Benjamin Burrows fifty years ago; Andrew Denison, the Walworths, Deacon Simeon Smith, Richard Williams and others.

The building known as the Middleton house, one mile up the Flanders road, on the east side of the highway, was John Walworth's in 1742, and may have been erected by him about that time. It is not supposed to be as old, however, as the Deacon Simeon Smith house that stood seventy rods south of it. The original house on this Smith site was no doubt the one occupied by the widow Walworth referred to in the Groton Deeds in 1712. Her son William Walworth, Junior, was living there in 1742, and her son John in the Middleton house. The old Simeon Smith house is reported to have burned down during the Revolutionary War and after Deacon Simeon Smith came into possession of it. A new house was immediately erected by Deacon Smith, and this stood the ravages of time until about 1891, when it also was burned. Nothing remains but the cellar hole.

It is difficult to determine the age of the old Fish house, standing east of the chapel on the New London and Mystic highway. It was occupied by James Fish in 1811 (son of

Joseph), and it may have been the residence of Capt. John Fish before 1760. Its antiquity is apparent.

The Daniel Brown house, so called, farther east, was Joseph Fish's in 1799: he was son of Capt. John Fish, and grandfather of the present Thomas B. Fish of Noank, Conn.

The old Prentice house, now owned by the heirs of James Chesebrough, north of Brown, with its long row of red buildings, is without doubt the original house of Capt. Samuel Fish, which he built soon after he bought his farm in 1695. The house has been somewhat remodelled and changed, and new buildings and annexes added. This Fish house and the Lieut. John Fanning house were the first two houses erected in this locality or on Fort Hill.

After Lieut. John Fanning's death in 1738-9, by the provision of his will the northern, or larger part of the farm, with the buildings, descended to his grandson John Fanning, who sold it for £1600 to Lieut. Nathan Smith 23 April, 1744,[1] with all the housing, fencing, etc., thereon.

Lieut. Nathan Smith does not appear to have lived there, however, as he resided at the old Smith homestead near Smith Lake, Poquonnock, all his life of eighty-two years. He had an eldest son Nathan, who married Betsy Denison in 1744, and perhaps he purchased the farm for his sons' occupancy. Nathan, Junior, was the father of Charlotte Smith, born 1763, who married Major Simeon Smith in 1784, son of that Deacon Simeon Smith who married Eunice Walworth and lived on the Walworth Farm north and adjoining the Fish's.

Deacon Nathan Smith sold his Fanning farm 4 November, 1760, to Lieut. John Fish who resided there until his decease in 1796. Thus the bulk of the Fanning farm finally

[1] Groton Deeds, Book 5, p. 7.

became merged into the Fish property. Capt. Fish willed his Fanning farm to his sons, Joseph and Ebenezer, except 40 acres which he gave to his grandsons, Samuel, John and Anthony. Ebenezer received the homestead and resided in the old Fanning house until 22 March, 1825, when he sold his one hundred and twenty-five acres for $1680 to Capt. Silas Beebe, with "dwelling house, barn and corn house." Capt. Beebe did not reside on the farm, however, but rented it for a period of nearly fifty years. His heirs finally sold the farm, which at that time was known as the "Fish Town farm of Capt. Beebe" and contained about two hundred acres, to William Eccleston, 3 August, 1877, who owns and occupies it at the present time.

The southern extremity (forty acres) of Lieut. John Fanning's farm was given by will to his four daughters. He directed his grandson, John Fanning, to give them also twenty acres more which lay south of and adjoining their share. This sixty acres the daughters sold in 1742 to Christopher Stark. He sold it to Nathaniel Palmer in 1758. From the Palmer family it went to Joseph Latham about 1800, and from his grandchildren to Robert Lamb about 1850–60. The widow of Robert Lamb owns the property at the present time.

"Fanning's Pasture," so called, is a tract of land of about twenty or thirty acres, lying east of Noank Brook. At its southern bound lies "Fanning's Rock," which has been used as a landmark many years, and is known to all the older inhabitants. The rock is referred to in the records in 1769 and earlier.

Let us turn to the neighbors of Lieut. John Fanning. On the north was the Fish family, and north of them the Walworths, and north of the Walworths was Aaron Stark in 1721.

It is not a difficult matter to trace at the present day the bounds of the Walworth farm. When William Walworth died in 1721, his homestead farm, adjoining the Fish farm, contained about two hundred and eighty acres, and was nearly in the form of a rectangular parallelogram, two hundred and sixty-two rods in length, and two hundred deep. In its distribution that year William Walworth's widow received as her share of the estate the east end of the farm. It covered an area of about one hundred acres, and ran east and west seventy-five rods, and north and south two hundred rods. To the eldest son, William, was allotted a double share of nearly one hundred acres in the southwest corner of the farm, bounded south by Fish, east by the Widow Walworth, and north by his brother Thomas Walworth. This farm of William Walworth's is to-day known as the Deacon Simeon Smith place.

Thomas' share was a single share lying north of William, and John's a like share lying north of Thomas'. The latter was bounded still farther north by Aaron Stark, which land in 1802 was the Nathaniel Niles farm.

John Walworth appears to have bought out his brother Thomas' interest, for in 1742 John and William both have an equal share of their father's farm, John living on the northern portion and residing in the old house now known as the Middleton house, and William on the southern portion, since called the Deacon Simeon Smith place.

The southern bounds of all this Walworth property was in 1734 a line running east 3½ degrees north, two hundred and sixty-two rods from the highway at the turn of the road near the Peter Crandall House of to-day (known as the Zebediah Gates place).

William Walworth resided on that portion that he inherited

until 1 July, 1765, when he sold his farm to John Kneeland of Boston. John Kneeland's widow Abigail and other heirs in 1777 and 1794 sold the property to Deacon Simeon Smith. It has ever since been known as the Deacon Simeon Smith farm.

The old Walworth burying-ground of about one-half an acre, now grown up with bushes and trees, is in the south-west corner of this farm.

After Deacon Simeon Smith's death, his executor, Rufus Smith, sold his farm of one hundred and twelve acres to Nicholas Chester of Groton, 30 March, 1824. In 1833 it was sold by the Chester heirs to Elisha Rathburn, and in 1853 by Elisha Rathburn to David Nelson Prentice. It was thus merged into the Prentice farm and was sold by his creditors about 1873 with the balance of his farm to Chesebrough and Brown. The latter selling out his interest, it then became the Chesebrough farm, by which name it is known at the present time.

South of the old Walworth property, later known as the Simeon Smith farm just described, and adjoining it, was the farm of Capt. Samuel Fish, who bounded Lieut. John Fanning on the north. The Fish farm was originally, in 1695, only about one hundred acres, but was extensively added to by purchase in later years.

Capt. Samuel Fish deeded to his son, Capt. Moses Fish, 1 July, 1712, the northern part of his farm, and to Samuel, Junior, the southern part. Moses' share was two hundred and fifty acres at that time, and his north line was the south line of the Walworth or Deacon Simeon Smith farm. This line extended, however, farther east than the Smith line, and ran to Noank Brook, which formed the east bound of Moses Fish's property. His southern bound was an east line running from the Flanders road and passing sixty rods south of the Fish dwelling-house and continuing on to the Brook. His west line was the Flanders road.

Samuel Fish, Junior's, portion of his father's farm that was given him 1 July, 1712, consisted of one hundred and forty acres and lay directly south of Moses' share. It crossed the present Mystic highway and lay on both sides of the road. It was bounded on the north by Capt. Moses Fish, on the east by the brook, on the south by Lieut. Fanning, and on the west by Common land. The Daniel Brown house and the old house just east of the chapel on the north side of the New London highway, were both built by descendants of Samuel Fish, Junior. The latter house was owned and occupied some years by Lieut. John Fish, and about 1811 by James Fish. This farm remained in possession of the Fish family until 1854, when Hannah Fish, widow of John Fish, and other heirs sold the property to John D. Williams, and he to Daniel Brown. This whole locality has long been known as "Fish Town."

Capt. Samuel Fish, son of John Fish, the first of the name in Connecticut, died 27 February, 1733, in his seventy-seventh year, and is buried in the Packer burying-ground. Sarah, his wife, died 11 December, 1722, aged about sixty-two years.

On the east of the Fanning farm lay the Packer lands, separated therefrom by Noank Brook. This Packer land was a large tract owned by John Packer of New London and bequeathed by him previous to 1713 to his three sons, James, Benjamin and Joseph. It was bounded at that time on the north by land of John and Samuel Burrows, on the east by the Mystic River, on the south partly with the salt water and partly with Noank Neck, and on the west with land of Lieut. John Fanning. Capt. James Packer bought his brother Joseph's interest in 1713, and resided on the farm until his death 24 April, 1765, in his eighty-fourth year. Capt. Packer married for his second wife Thankful, daughter of Lieut. John Fanning, who survived her husband several years.

Between Lieut. Fanning and the Fort Hill road was the William Walworth farm, afterwards Thomas Walworth's for twenty-five years. It contained 65 acres, and was sold by him 6 December, 1757, to Amos Burrows, and remained in the Burrows family until sold to the present owner, Mr. Merritt.

On this Walworth property was the old Indian Fort of the Pequots about which so much has been said. Authorities differ as to its exact location, but there is evidence and ample proof that it was just north of the Francis E. Merritt house on top of Fort Hill on the east side of the highway. (See map.) Groton Deeds, Book 1, p. 654, records a wood-lot laid out on Fort Hill 30 September, 1721, to William Walworth, and reads as follows: "*begin at the Southwest corner of the Fourt* at Fourt Hill at a heap of stones by the Highway," etc. This wood-lot is shown by dotted lines on the Fort Hill map. It was sold by William Walworth to his brother Thomas Walworth 25 December, 1732, and recorded in Groton Deeds, Book 3, p. 136. A wood-lot just north of this was laid out to Abial Sammons 30 September, 1721, and the bounds of this lot also are described as running from the "*Southwest corner of the old Fourt on Fourt Hill,*" etc. (Groton Deeds, Book 1, p. 654.) From the very clear description given of the bounds of these wood-lots, and an actual survey taken to make their location possible, there seems to be no question as to the locality of the old Indian Fort.

Lieut. John Fanning had a grant of 50 acres of land from the Town of Stonington 4 August, 1683, which he sold to John Parks of New London.[1]

He received also a grant of 50 acres from the Town of Stonington 10 August, 1683,[2] which he sold 24 January, 1718–19, to Philip Palmeter of Westerly, R. I.[3] He came into possession of his brother William Fanning's 50-acre grant, and sold that also to Philip Palmeter at the same time.

He inherited from his father Lot No. 13 of 12 acres which was granted Edmund Fanning, Senior, by the Town of Stonington as a home lot. This land he sold to William Chesebrough 23 January, 1709–10.[4]

Among the town votes at Groton is the following: —

"Proposals made to the town of Groton for dividing of a certain tract of land lying & being in the town of Groton in the county of New London — That all that tract of land lying & being in s^{d} town as above s^{d} comonly know by the name of Nawayunk, bounded northerly with Leut John Faning his land, & westerly by the brook till it comes to the Salt cove near Mr. Ashbe, his dwelling house, and then southerly with the sound till it comes to the turning up to goe up the Salt cove or river comonly called & know by the name of Mistic River, & so bounded with the salt water easterly till it comes to the land now in the possession of James Packer of s^{d} Groton & then with s^{d} Packer's till it comes to s^{d} Faning's land first mentioned; which s^{d} tract of land the Pequit Indians have had a privelege upon; be divided or loted out into equal lots of equal value or worth (as near as may be) that all the proprietors of s^{d} Groton, that have rights therein may draw out each man or person their lots which shall stand good to them, their heirs & assigns forever. Only the Pequit Indians & nevertheless to enjoy their privelege above mentioned

---

[1] *Vide* Stonington Deeds, Book 2, p. 142.

[2] *Vide* Stonington Records, Book II., pp. 46 and 47.

[3] *Vide* Stonington Deeds, Book 4, p. 76.

[4] *Vide* Stonington Deeds, Book 2, p. 513; *vide* also p. 58 of this work.

as it was formerly granted to them by the Town of N. London.
Voated May 22, 1712
Attest Nehemiah Smith Clerk
Samuel Fish Townsman."

(See Map showing distribution of Noank Lots.)

In accordance with the foregoing vote, Lieut. John Fanning had granted him from the Town of Groton, Lot No. 5, first tier, first division, of the Noank Lots when they were first laid out in 1712. He sold this lot 4 July, 1720,[1] to Deacon James Morgan, and it has remained in the Morgan family ever since. The old house now standing on this lot was probably erected by Deacon Morgan soon after his purchase of the land.

The next Noank Lot southerly was No. 4, laid out originally to Samuel Rogers. In 1752 this lot was owned by Lieut. Fanning's grandson, John, who purchased it that year of Samuel Clark. Lieut. Fanning also owned Lot No. 8, first division, second tier. In the second division of Noank Lots, he owned Lot No. 28, second tier.

Lieut. John Fanning was in the Narragansett War, and his name appears among the list of volunteers in that service. (Edmund Fanning, Senior, and his sons Edmund and Thomas, also served therein.)[2]

He received a grant of land from the Connecticut Colony for his services, being Lot No. 19 of 93 acres in Voluntown ("the Volunteer Country"), which was laid out to him 29 March, 1706.[3] This he sold to Samuel Avery, Junior, 30 March, 1709–10.

---

[1] *Vide* Groton Deeds, Book 1, p. 617.

[2] *Vide* Voluntown Records, Book 1, p. 2. Also Bodge's "Soldiers in King Philip's War," 1896, p. 445.

[3] *Vide* Voluntown Records, Book 1, p. 34.

Where he earned his lieutenantcy has not been ascertained. He does not appear other than as a private on the Narragansett rolls, nor do the "Colonial Records" show his appointment as lieutenant. He is recorded, however, time and time again on the Groton Records and elsewhere as "***Lieut.*** John Fanning," and in his Inventory, "***Capt.***" John Fanning. It is supposed, therefore, he must have earned his title in the local militia or "train-band," as it was called, and after his return from the Indian Wars.

Lieut. Fanning was very prominent in town affairs and held many local offices of trust and honor. His name is found recorded in nearly all the town meetings, and he seems to have been a prominent factor in directing its affairs.

In Miss Caulkins' copy of New London Books appears the following:[1] —

> "Town Officers July 11, 1694
> "Collectors of Minister's Rates
> "John Fanning, Samuel Bill east side (of the River)
> "John Richards, Samuel Waller west side (of the River)
>
> "Dec. 30, 1701 Constables:
> "John Fanning east side."

His wife Margaret Fanning was baptized by the Rev. James Noyes in the First Congregational Church at Stonington with her daughter Mary 26 August, 1686, as appears by the records of that church.

No record of his birth, marriage, or death is found at New London, Groton, Stonington, or elsewhere, nor that of his wife or children.

Lieut. John Fanning died in February, 1738–9, and left an estate inventoried at £1846. It comprised one hundred

[1] *Vide* Book 1. p. 142.

80

and thirty acres of land (so inventoried, but equal to one hundred and eighty acres now) in the homestead farm on Fort Hill, valued at £1560. His will, on file at New London, was dated 1 February and probated 13 February, 1738–9. A copy follows. (See also photogravure.)

"LAST WILL AND TESTAMENT OF LEFT. JON FANING, RECEIVED AND RECORDED 13 FEB., 1738-9."

"In The Name of God Amen The first Day of February one thousand seven hundred and thirty eight nine, I John fanning of Grotton in ye County of New london in his Majesties Colony of Connecticut in Newingland being weak of Boad but of perfect mind and memory and Calling to mind ye mortallity of my body I do make and ordain this my laste will and testement that is to say firste and prinsablitey I give my soule unto god that gave it and my body to ye earth to be buread in Decent christian manner at ye Discretion of my Executors hereafter named. and as touching such worldly Estate as it hath pleased god to blesse me with in this life I dispose of in manner and form as following after my juste Debts and funariel charges paid.

Im: firste I give and bequeathe unto my loving wife Margret fanning ye improvement of all my Estate both real and personal after my just Debts and funarail charges are paid During her Natural life.

itim I give unto my loving Dagter mary fox ye fether Bead and Beading and furnuter that I uuse to ly appon after my wifes Decese.

itim I give unto my loving Dagter prudance faning all my house hold Stuf of what Denomination to have after my wifes Decese.

itim Also I give unto my Dagter prudance afore sd ye south room of my house with ye leantoo agioyning with tow acors of land ajoying to said house to improve after her mothers Decese During ye time She is unmarrid or lives singel.

itim my will is that my Dagter Thankfull martin shall live in said house with her sister prudance and improve with her.

itim I give unto my loving grand Dagter Katharin Martin one three year old helfer after my wifes Decese.

itim I give unto my four Dagters (viz.) Mary fox Margret Archcraft prudance fanning and Thankfull Martin all ye reste of my movables after my wifes Decese that is to say tow fifths to prudance and to Mary Margreat and thankfull one fifth apece.

itim also I give unto my foure Dagters above named ye South eand of my farm or home Sted Bounded as followeth begining at a small maple tree now marked on three sid[s] standing in ye low meddow Neare a ploughing path that goes from my house to where my son John fannings house formerly stood from sd maple tree running a North weste line to Thomas Walsworths land all ye land I own to ye south or south weste of said line I give to my four Dagters a fore said after my wifes Decese to them their heirs and assigns forever excepting Margrets Archcraft fourth part of ye sd land which after her ye sd Margret Archcrafts Decese I give it to her sun Daniell Avery to him his heirs and assigns for ever.

itim sd land in ye foregoying paragraft is to be equally Divided between my foure dagters.

itim I give unto my loving Grand Sun John fanning all ye reste of my land or homesstead to ye North of ye a foresd line from sd maple tree Northweste to Thomas Walsworth his land with ye housing and fencing &c after my wifes Decese (excepting ye south eand of my house with tow acors of land ajoying which I have given to my tow Dagters prudance fanning and thankfull Martin During there lives singel. I give it to him sd John faning his heirs and assigns forever, provided he ye said John fanning shall after my wifes Decese give unto his four aunts before named an eaquel lawfull Deed of twenty acors of land lying to ye south of ye land I have given to them his sd four aunts Mary Fox Margret Archcraft prudance faning and Thankfull Martin and in case sd John Faning refuse to give them a Deed as a fore sd. then my wish is that my foure Dagters afore named shall have twenty accors of land adjoying to ye land I have given them on ye North side of sd line from ye maple tree to Walsworth land a for sd.

itim I give unto my grand sun Thomas faning five pounds money to be paid by his brother John faning.

itim My will is that my grand sun John faning shall take up my Bond of fourty pounds which I gave Bannajah Williams and Discharge my Estate from any parte or parcel thereof, and in case ye said John faning refuses to take up said Bond within a yeare after my decese and Discharge my said Estate then my will is that ye south roume above mentioned and ye tow acors of land said to be adjoyning shall be prudance fanings and Thankfull Martins there heirs and assigns forever upon there ye sd prudance faning and thankfull Martin paying sd fourty pounds and in taking up sd Bond and Discharging my said Estate.

itim I constitute make and ordain my loving frinds Capt. James packer and Thomas Eldredg my whole and soule Executors to this my laste will and testement in witness whereof I have hereunto sat my hand and seal ye Day and yeare first above written.

Sinded sealed Declard and pronounsed by ye sd John faning as his last will and testement in presents of us wittensses.

(Signed) John faning (Seal)

Tho. Wallsworth
Ephraim Collver
John Jeffers.

Ephm Colver & John Jeffrey. Sworn in court Recorded in ye 7th Book of wills Page (92) p Jon Curtiss, Clerk."

INVENTORY OF CAPT. JOHN FANING.

(New London Probate Records, Book D, p. 490.)

"Here followeth a true Inventory of y^{e} Eſtate of Capt. John faning late of Grotton Deceſed taken this 8th Day of April 1740 by us y^{e} Subſcribers.

	£ s. d.
To one black coate $3^{£},10^{s}$ to one Drugget Do $2^{£},5^{s}$	5–15–00
To one Drugget Jacket without lining	0–15–00
To 2 pare Drugget Breeches	16–00
To one all woolling Coate $1^{£},5^{s}$ one Jacket ye same 15^{s}	2–00–00
To one Nite Jacket 3^{s} one luſe Coate $1^{£}$	1–09–00
To one flannel ſhurt 15^{s} to one Do 5^{s}	1–00–00
To one holland ſhurt $1^{£}$ to 4 pare of yarn ſtockens 16^{s}	1–16–00
To 2 hankerchiefs 6^{s} to a pare of gloves 2^{s}	08–00
To an old Beaver hat 15^{s} to one ſword $1^{£}$ one gun $2^{£}$	3–15–00
To one pocket Book 2^{s} to one Do 1^{s} to Caſh $4^{£},4^{s},6^{d}$	4–07–06
To one pare of ſhuſe	12–00

	£ s. d.
To one ſether Bead and Bolſter a^{d} 32th	5—00—00
To one black white and yallow Coverled	1—10—00
To one white Bird eyed Do 1£,15^{s} one Dimond Do Ivory color and white	2—05—00
To tow flaniel ſheets	15—00
To one ſheete of check curtains 2£,5^{s} to Beadſted cord and matt	02—15—00
To one ſilk graſs Bead and Bolſter humſpun ticken	2—00—00
To one pare of flaniel ſheats	1—15—00
one check coverlid Bordered on ye edge in ye weaving	1—10—00
one Do black and white check	2—00—00
one yeallow and red check coverlid 2£ one white and red Do 2£	4—00—00
one pare of lining ſheets	1—00—00
To one old under ſether Bead	1—10—00
To one pare of Lining ſheets	1—10—00
To one pare Do	17—06
To 2 table cloths 6^{s} to one pillow Caſe 1/6	07—06
Brot over from ye other side	60—01—00
To an old check Bolſter of ſethers	00—05—00
one large putter plater 7^{s},5^{d} to 2 Do 1£, 16^{s} one Do 14^{s}	2—15—00
To 5 putter plates 15^{s} one warming pan 1£	1—15—00
To one Braſs Kettel 4£, 10^{s} one ſmaler Do 10^{s}	5—00—00
To one Iron pot 1£,5^{s} one ſmaller Do 15^{s}	2—00—00
To 5 Wooden turnd Bools 9^{s} to one quart Baſon 2/6	11-06
To one ſmall Baſon 1^{s} one quart pot 2/6 one Do 2^{s}	05-06
To one Box iron and 2 heaters	15-00
To 2 ſmall wooden bools 2^{s} to 6 wooden trenches 2/6	05-06
To 2 watter pails 5^{s} and one piggain 1^{s}	06—00
To one fire ſhovel and tungues	10—00
To one frying pan 10^{s} one peper box and tunnel 2^{s}	10—00
To 6 putter ſpoons 3^{s} one ſton mug and not Diſh 2^{s}	05—00
To one pare of Sheep ſhears 2/6 one Cheaſt 15^{s}	17—00
To one table 6^{s} to 5 Glaſs bottels 3^{s}	09—00
To 17 chairs 1£,13^{s} and one looking Glaſs 1£	02—13—00
To Worſted and Wooling yarn and raw worſted 14^{lb}	02—02—00
To 3^{lb} of Courſe wool and picyons	04—00
To 4 old hhg 1£, to one old bbl 3^{s} and one churn 7^{s}	01—10—00
To 2 trays 2^{s} one Can 2^{s} one ſaddel and Bridel 2£	02—04—00
one cart and wheels and Iron hoops 2£ one Caſs yoak 8^{s}	02—08—00

	£ s. d.
one ax 8s plow irons ſhere cutter and chiſs plate 1£10s	01–18–00
To one Iron chain 16s one half Buſhiel 3s	19–00
To an old ſcrue-prees for Sider 10s one Cheſe press 5s	15–00
To grinding ſton	15–00
To 36 ſhepe at 20s pr ſhepe	36–00–00
To 3 ſmall ſwine at 40s each	6–00–00
To one old red Cow with a white forehead and calf	8–00–00
brot over	147–08–00
To one Read Cow 10£ one Dupread Cow and Calf 10£,10s	20–08–00
To one Brinddel Cow with a ſtar in her forehead and calf	11–00–00
one Do Browen with a white head and a calf	11–00–00
one Do read with a white ſtar and white taile	11–00–00
one Yallow Brinddel Cow	9–10–00
To 2 read 3 year old heffers 8£ and 8£,10s	16–10–00
To 6 tow year old Cattel at 4£,10s a pece	27–00–00
To one yearling	2–10–00
To one old Bay hors 5£ to a black roan mare 21£	26–00–00
To ye farm gt 130 acors of land with ye houſing orchard and fencing thereon	1560–00–00
To one Iron Cleve and pin 6s	06–00
To one yoake of ſmall oxen 6 year old	23–00–00
	1846–14–00

Ebenezer Avery }
Nathan Smith } Prisers under oath
Thomas Eldridge }

New London County ſd Groton Aprile ye 8th 1740 Cornll Ebenezer Avery Capt. Thomas Eldridge & Mr. Nathan Smith, the above Subſcribers perſonally appearing had the Appriſers oath which is by Law provided administered to them.

Pr Humphrey Avery Just of Peace

June 12th 1740 Capt. James Packer Executor to the Laſt will of sd John Faning of Groton decd made solemn oath that he had made a true presentment to the appriſers of all the Eſtate of the decesd that has come to his hands or knowledge, and that if any thing further conſiderable appears to be his estate he will Cauſe it to be added to this Inventory

Quat Coram John Richards Judge Probate"

EDMUND[3] FANNING (No. 10.)[1]

(For Genealogical data of his family, see page 97.)

Edmund Fanning, the third of the name in direct line, son of Edmund and Margaret (Billings) Fanning, and grandson of Edmund the American ancestor, was born in the town of New London, Colony of Connecticut, in 1682, in that part which was in 1705 set off to form the new town of Groton, and again in 1836 to form the new town of Ledyard.

At his father's death about 1715 he inherited a double portion of the Groton farm that descended from Edmund Fanning, Senior, and which included within its bounds the original grant of 50 acres laid out in 1664. The smaller portion of the farm was allotted to his brother Jonathan.

Edmund and Jonathan agreed upon a dividing line of their farms, which then amounted to nearly 400 acres, 1 July, 1715, Edmund taking the southern part and Jonathan the northern. Edmund's bounds were the Mystic River on the southeast, Jonathan's land on the north, and a brook that runs into Mystic River on the southwest.

Edmund Fanning resided all his life on this farm of his ancestors. He was a thrifty, well-to-do farmer, and his name appears on the Groton Records as well as at Stonington in the transfers of real estate, time and time again.

Of the Noank Lots laid out to the inhabitants of Groton in 1712, he owned the 24th Lot in the first division, first tier,

[1] The reader is referred to the map in another part of this work, giving a complete survey of this farm.

which he inherited from his father. He sold it to Samuel Burrows 25 June, 1715.

He also owned Lot No. 50 of 2½ acres, second division, second tier, which he sold to James Packer 28 December, 1719.

He appears to have been prominent in town affairs and a regular attendant at the Town meetings, on the records of which his name frequently occurs. In the Groton Town Meeting Book, Vol. I, pages 4 and 6, mention is made of him as follows:—

"At a Town Meeting Dec. 22, 1735 Edmond Faning chosen fence viewer."

"Dec. 21, 1738 Edmond Faning chosen Tything man."

As the bulk of the original Fanning farm at Groton descended to him, and his name seems more closely identified with it than perhaps any other descendant, a description of the farm and the oldest houses thereon is given under this article, as follows:—

The oldest house standing to-day on this Groton farm of the Fannings is the Jonathan Fanning house, located a few rods northwest of Alonzo Main's residence, and described in the article under Jonathan Fanning (No. 11). There are traces of an old house, called the "Tenty" (Content) Fish house. It stood four or five rods southeast of the old Fanning burying-ground on or near a small hillock. Nothing remains of it to-day, nor is it known who built the house. It was early occupied by Ambrose and Content Fish. Ambrose died about 1830 and left it and ten acres of land to his grandsons Ambrose and Allen Fish, who sold it to Charles S. Bennett's father the following year, and the house was torn down soon after. An old barn and well were located south of the house and a blacksmith shop southeast, on the road. East of the shop on Mystic Brook was Fish's saw mill, referred to in the deeds in 1777 and 1787.

The house was one story with a straight barn roof, and faced south.

. One hundred and fifty rods a little south of west of the burying-ground is an old cellar hole. This was the house of Samuel Williams 2d, in 1787.

A cellar hole on that portion of the Groton farm owned by David Fanning (No. 33) is still visible. (See page 127.)

In 1777 Capt. Manasseh Short lived a little southwest of David Fanning's house on land that he bought of Fanning in 1765. Only a cellar hole remains there to-day.

The Seth Williams house, so called, now owned and occupied by Stephen Caswell, is known to all the old inhabitants, and stands at the sharp turn of the old highway leading from Mystic to Preston. It was built by Capt. Jacob Gallup for Seth Williams, Senior, and is not a very old house.

Northeast of the Seth Williams house about sixty-five rods, is the Ezra Barnes house (see photogravure). It was recently owned by the Charles S. Bennett heirs, and was bought by him of the Barnes descendants about 1877. This house is next to the oldest one on the old Fanning farm, and was built by Ezra Barnes, grandfather of the present Nathan Barnes of Mystic, soon after 1775. In that year Ezra Barnes bought of George Fanning thirty acres of the old farm with the Fanning mansion house thereon, and which Mr. Barnes tore down, a part of which he used to construct the new house. The old ovens and doors were said by the late Charles S. Bennett to have belonged to the old house. In addition to the dwelling, there are two barns, corn crib, and two old wells on the premises.

81

The old Fanning "mansion" house, so called in the deeds, stood about ten rods southwest of the Barnes house. (See map of the Groton farm.) There is no trace of the old building or cellar hole. There is very little reason for doubting that this oldest Barnes house was the first house built on the Fanning farm at Groton, and was constructed by either Edmund Fanning, Senior or Junior. It is first referred to in the deeds in 1769, and was then spoken of as the "mansion house" of the Fannings, and was old enough then to be in a condition to be torn down within a few years thereafter. Furthermore, it stood on the original fifty-acre grant to Edmund Fanning, Senior, in 1664; and while it may not be proved to a certainty, it probably was the house originally built by him in that year or soon after.

There are three burying-grounds on this Groton farm of the Fannings, viz., the "Williams," "Barnes," and the old "Fanning" burying-ground.

Edmund Fanning died at Groton in March, 1768, aged eighty-six years.

His will, dated 26 July, 1762, recorded at Stonington 5 April, 1768, and on file there, is as follows: —

> "The Last Will and Testament of Mr. Edmund Fanning, late of Groton Decd. was Exhibited in this Court and being proved is approved and ordered to be Recorded.
>
> In The Name of God Amen ye 26th day July A.D., 1762 — I Edmund Fanning of Groton and County of New London &c being weak and Infirm of body but of Perfect mind and memory thanks be given to God, therefore Calling unto mind the mortality of my Body, and knowing that it is appointed for all men once to die, Do make and ordain this my will and Testament, that is to say, Principally and first of all I give and Recommend my Soul into the hands of

God that gave it, and my Body, I Recommend to the Earth to be buryed in decent Christian Burial at the Discretion of my Executors, nothing Doubting but at the General Resurrection, I shall receive the Same again by the Mighty Power of God,
and as Touching such worldly Estate wherewith it hath pleased God to bless me in this Life, I give demise and dispose of the Same in the following manner and form

Imprimis. I give and bequeath to Hopestill, my dearly beloved wife one third part of my Real and personal Estate and the use of my Negro woman Silva, During her Natural Life, but in case She marry, I give her Twenty Pounds Lawfull Money to be paid her by my Executors, out of my Estate, She quiting all her right of Dower and thirds

Item. I give and sequester one half acre of my Land to be laid out conveniently to the burying Place in the north east corner of my Land near mistick River.[1]

Item I give and bequeath to my Two Grand Sons Willm Fanning and James Fanning, all my Lands Lying in Groton or Elsewhere by them and their heirs freely to be possed and enjoyed Sd Lands I order to be Equally Divided for quantity and quality & James to have the first choice, for the consideration of what I shall hereafter order them to pay, I also give my grandson James Fanning two thirds of all my stock and Debts due to me, and all my farming Tools, and my Negro woman Selfa after the Decease of my Widow

Item. I give and bequeath to my beloved Daughter Serviah one fourth part of all my household goods after my wives third are taken out Exclusive of my wearing appearil

Item. I give and bequeath to my beloved daughter Freelove one fourth part of all my household goods after my wives third are taken out, and exclusive of my wearing apparil.

Item. I give and bequeath to my beloved Daughters Fear and Deborah, one fourth part of all my Household

[1] This is the first mention of the old Fanning burying-ground.

goods Each after my wives thirds are taken out Exclusive of my wearing apparil, and a good Cow each

Item I give and bequeath to my Grandson Daniel Harris one Likely young mare worth about Six or Seven pounds Lawfull Money.

Item I give and bequeath to my three grand Daughters (viz.) Hannah, Hopestill and Abigal Harris, Each a good Gold Ring worth twenty Shillings Lawfull Money apiece

I order my Grandson William Fanning to pay one half of my furneral charges and one half of my other just debts, and the three above mentioned gold Rings, to my three Grand Daughters aforesd

I order my Grandson James Fanning to pay one half of my funeral charges and one half of my other just Debts, and two Cows above mentioned to my two Daughters Fear and Deborah aforesd

I also make and ordain my two Grandsons William and James Fanning to be my sole Executors, of this my Last Will and Testament, and Do hereby Disannull all and Every other, and utterly Disallow, all former Testaments, Wills, Legacies and bequeaths and Executors by me Willed and bequeathed Ratifying and Confirming this and no other, to be my last Will and Testament in witness whereof I have hereunto Set my hand and Seal the day and year above written, Signed Sealed Published Pronounced and Declared by the Sd Edmund Fanning, as his last will and Testament in the presence of us the Subscribers.

his
Edmund Q Fanning (seal)
mark

Thos. Alexander.
John Stedman
his
Jonathan + Wood
mark

Recorded from the original
ye 5th day of April 1768
Per Paul Wheeler Clerk.

No record of Edmund Fanning's birth, marriage, or death appears at New London, Groton, or Stonington, nor the death of either wife. Nor are their burial places positively known, but they are supposed to be in the family burying-ground on his Groton farm, and with headstones that are not inscribed, as there are many such stones there.

By his will it will be seen that his grandsons, William and James Fanning, were made executors. James, however, died intestate less than a year afterward, and William executed the trust alone.

Later the court appointed Nathan Niles of Groton administrator of that part of his estate not included in his will, and he served in that capacity.

His estate inventoried 4 April, 1768, £956–10–0. This included his homestead farm of three hundred acres and buildings, valued at £750.[1]

Freeholders were appointed by the Stonington court to set out to the widow Hopestill her interest in the estate, and they made the allotment 21 April, 1769.

Widow Hopestill Fanning died intestate in June, 1772, and Joseph Elliott of Stonington was appointed by the court administrator on the estate 7 July, 1772, but he died before the completion of the trust, and William Fanning was made administrator in 1776.

---

[1] Stonington Probate Records, Book 1, p. 69.

JONATHAN[3] FANNING (No. 11).

(For Genealogical data, see page 101.)

Jonathan Fanning, youngest son of Edmund and Margaret (Billings) Fanning, and grandson of Edmund Fanning, Senior, the ancestor in America, was born in 1684, in the town of New London, in that part afterward named Groton, and now Ledyard.

He came into possession by inheritance of the northern part of the Groton farm that descended from his grandfather, and resided on it during his lifetime. (See map of the Groton farm of Edmund Fanning, Senior.)

Jonathan and his brother Edmund agreed upon a dividing line between their farms 1 July, 1715.[1] Jonathan's bounds were the Mystic River or brook on the east that divides Groton and Stonington towns, his brother Edmund's land on the south, William Williams' land on the west, and Lieut. Joseph Stanton's land and Lantern Hill Pond on the north.

The old house occupied by Jonathan Fanning, built probably by him or his father, is still standing, and is much the oldest appearing house in that locality (see photogravure). It is difficult to determine the year in which it was built, but it has every appearance of having been constructed as early as 1700. It stands on the northeasterly portion of the farm near Mystic Brook and the Lantern Hill road and close to the present residence of Alonzo Main. It has the typical long, sloping roof of early times, with ell, and faces south.

[1] Groton Deeds, Book 1, p. 286.

A light, modern porch has been constructed on the front of the building, but otherwise the structure is little altered. It had an outside cellar a few rods west of the house (mentioned in Jonathan's will in 1757), and this was in a fair state of preservation up to within a few years, but is now covered by a shed or barn that has recently been built. The farm and buildings are now owned by Alonzo Main.

Jonathan Fanning's name occasionally appears on the Groton Records among the land transfers.

In the Hempstead Diary he is frequently mentioned between the years 1713 and 1745.

He married at New London 17 May, 1714, Elizabeth, daughter of Thomas and Ann (Lester) Way, and born 20 April, 1695. The Hempstead Diary gives intentions published 3 January, 1713–14.

Thomas Way was born about 1665 or '70, and died at East Haven, Conn., in 1726. His wife Ann was the daughter of Andrew Lester.

Thomas Way was the son of George and Elizabeth (Smith) Way. George Way was born in England, and died in Saybrook, Conn., about 1690; was one of the colleagues of Roger Williams of Rhode Island, and left Providence after its burning by the Indians. He was there known as Sergeant George Way.

George Way was son of Thomas Way the Puritan born in England (Dorchester, probably) in 1583, emigrated to America in 1630, settled at Dorchester, Mass., where he died in 1667. His wife Elizabeth died there in 1665.

In the distribution of the Indian lands at Noank in 1712 by the town of Groton to its inhabitants, Jonathan Fanning was granted Lot No. 12, first tier, first division. He sold the lot 17 February, 1715–16, to Humphrey Avery.

Jonathan also received Lot No. 59, second tier, second division, which he also sold to Avery, in whose name both lots appear on the Groton Records.

Jonathan appears to have inherited from his father, Edmund Fanning, Junior, Lot No. 97, containing eighty-nine acres, in Voluntown, Conn., which was the fourth lot in the 8th tier of lots laid out to Edmund Fanning in March, 1706, for services in the Narragansett War. This land Jonathan sold to John Butler of Voluntown 9 September, 1742.[1]

Jonathan Fanning died at Groton 28 April, 1761, in the seventy-eighth year of his age. The widow Elizabeth died there 24 July, 1772, in her seventy-eighth year. Both are buried in the Fanning burying-ground on the farm, where their headstones still stand and in a good state of preservation. They are almost the only stones, however, among twenty or thirty there, that are inscribed.

By his will on file at New London, dated 18 August, 1757, he bequeathed the western part of his farm with the house thereon to his son David. The eastern part, with the homestead buildings, he gave to his eldest son Jonathan. His will follows:—

" In ye name of God Amen. August ye 18th 1757
I Jonathan Fanning of Groton in ye County of New London Being aged and Infirm in Body But of a Sound mind and knowing it is appointed for all men once to Die Do make and ordain this my Last will and testament and Principally I Give my Soul to God, and my Body I Recommend to ye Earth to be Buried and my Worldly Estate I Give and Dispose of in manner and Form Following.

Imprimis: I give to my Loving Wife Elizabeth Fanning ye use and Improvement of one Third Part of my Lands During her natural Life also ye use of ye west room in ye House where I dwell with ye chamber over ye same. and a Priviledge in ye

[1] Voluntown Records, Book 2, p. 278.

The old Jonathan Fanning house, Ledyard, Conn. built in the 17th century.
From photograph taken in 1904.

Cellar west of my House and ye Corn Crib During her natural Life I also give her all my House hold Stuff and one Cow and one Riding Beast and ten Sheep and two swine to be to her forEver.

Item. I give to my Eldest son Jonathan Fanning ye East Part of my Homestead Farm in sd Groton, Bounded Beginning at a Button Wood Tree Standing in or near ye South Line of Joseph Stanton's Land thence Southerly to a Black oak staddle marked on Two Sides standing in ye Edge of ye Field near ye Barrs: Thence Easterly to a maple Staddle marked Standing in ye fence on ye Edge of ye Swamp. Thence South to Edmund Fannings Land and so Bounding Southerly on Edmund Fannings Land East on Mystick River and north on Joseph Stanton's Land with all ye Buildings (after my wifes Decease) and appurtenances to be to him his heirs and assigns For Ever he Paying what is hereafter in This Will ordered For him to Pay. I give my sd Son Jonathan, and his heirs ye Libertie of getting Fire wood and Timber For Their own use of from ye west Part of my sd farm. I also give to my sd son Jonathan all my Farming Tools and utensils for Husbandry, and one half of my wearing apparel For Ever.

Item. I give to my Son David Fanning ye west Part of my sd homestead Farm. Bounded on ye East with ye part given to Jonathan on ye South with Edmund Fanning's Land on ye west with William Williams Esqrs Land and on ye north with Joseph Stantons Land with ye Dwelling House There on and ye appurtenances (Excepting ye Libertie above granted to Jonathan to get Wood) To be to him his heirs and assigns For Ever, he Paying what is here after in This Will ordered For him to pay. I also give to my sd Son David ye other half of my wearing apparel For ever.

Item. I give to my grand daughter Dorothy Holdridge Four Pounds Lawful money to be paid her when she arrives to ye age of eighteen years by my two Sons above named. (Provided she lives with my wife Till That Time.)

Item. I give to my Daughter Hannah Fanning Four Pounds Lawful money to be paid her by my Two Sons above named Equally.

Item. All ye remainder of my moveable Estate I give to my Four Daughters (namely) Margaret Mason Anna Clark Mary Brown and Hannah Fanning Equally to be Divided Between Them.

Item. I order my two sons Jonathan and David to Pay all my Debts and funeral Charges &c. — and I do appoint my sd son Jonathan Fanning Executor To This my Will hereby Revoking and making null all Former wills by me made.
Ratifying & Confirming This and no other to be my Last Will and Testament In Witness whereof I hereunto set my hand and seal ye Day First above written.

Signed Sealed Pronounced and Declared by ye sd Jonathan Fanning to be his Last Will in presence of

Simeon Miner
William Gallup
Nathan Gallup

(signed) Jnothan faning" {Seal}

His will was examined and approved at New London by Gurdon Saltonstall, Judge of Probate, 27 May, 1761.

His estate inventoried £456, including the farm and buildings valued at £400.

CAPT. JAMES[3] FANNING (No. 15).

(For Genealogical data concerning him see page 103.)

Capt. James Fanning, son of Thomas and Frances (Ellis) Fanning of Stonington, Conn., was born in that town 30 April, 1695. (*Vide*, Note ‖ on page 93 of this work.)

It is said he was brought up by his uncle Lieut. John Fanning, who lived on Fort Hill, Groton. He removed to and settled on Long Island some time previous to 1718, and was the progenitor of all by the name of Fanning in Suffolk Co., N. Y. He first resided at Smithtown in that County, where he married Hannah, daughter of Justice Richard Smith in 1718. His name first appears on the Long Island records as a witness to the will of Richard Smith in that year.[1]

Mr. Pelletreau states in his "Records of Smithtown" that "Richard Smith's homestead was at Nissequogue, on the "north side of the road, and descended to his son Richard, "and now belongs to the Misses Harries."

Justice Richard Smith was son of Richard Smith, patentee and sole proprietor of Smithtown, L. I. The latter was known as "Bull Richard," and was the ancestor of the family called the "Bull Smiths." These Smiths were not related to Col. William Smith of Long Island, whose descendants were called the "Tangier Smiths." Justice Richard Smith died early in 1720. His will, dated 23 June, 1718, proved 28 March, 1720, recorded in the New York Surrogate's office, mentions among other heirs, daughter Hannah,

---

[1] *Vide* Printed Records of the Town of Smithtown, L. I., by William S. Pelletreau A. M., 1898, p. 41.

to whom he gave one hundred and thirty acres of land in Smithtown, which was laid out to her in the general allotment in 1736. Hannah, wife of James Fanning, had a sister Sarah, who married Nathaniel Woodhull and became the mother of Gen. Nathaniel Woodhull of Revolutionary fame.

Record is found of Capt. James Fanning residing at Smithtown up to April, 1726.[1] Between that date and May, 1734,[2] he settled in Southold town in that part called Aquebogue. The district where he located was at the head of the river and early known as the "River-head," being so called many years previous to Revolutionary times, but was not legally set off from the town of Southold as a new town until 1792. There is no record showing the acquisition of Capt. James Fanning's farm at Riverhead, but there is a deed of sale of part of the farm by his sons Thomas and James in 1753 and 1757.[3] Thomas Fanning's sale of one hundred and thirty acres in April, 1753, soon after the death of his mother would indicate that his possession of it came through her and may have been an estate of inheritance. The Fanning farm went into the hands of the Griffings in 1753. Thomas Fanning sold one hundred and thirty acres of it to John Griffing that year, reserving the burial place thereon, which is the first known burial place in that locality. The plot was where Jetter & Moore's bottling works now are at the southeast corner of Griffing Avenue and Railroad Street. The Griffing House, a large hotel, is situated on the Fanning farm.

Capt. Fanning lived for a time in New York City, where he was residing in 1747. He married for second wife, at

---

[1] *Vide* Voluntown Records, Book IV., p. 247.

[2] *Vide* Stonington Deeds, Book IV., p. 482.

[3] *Vide* Suffolk County Deeds, Vol. B, pp. 320, 322 and 422.

Stonington, Conn., 25 February, 1752, widow Thankful Hinckley Thompson Chesebrough, and went to Stonington to live. He appears on the records there from June, 1752, to November, 1753. In June, 1754, however, he had returned to Southold, L. I. While at Stonington he doubtless occupied his mill property at Wequetequock, which he bought 7 May, 1734, of Samuel Yeoman, Senior, and which he gave in 1754 to his son Gilbert. He owned other property at Stonington which is found mentioned in his will. He probably spent the remaining years of his life at Southold.

Capt. James Fanning was for several years a captain in his Majesty's service, taking an active part in the French and Indian War in 1746–47. In June, 1746, he received a commission to raise a company of infantry for service on an expedition against Canada.[1] In July a company of 100 men were enlisted, 78 from Hempstead and 22 from Jamaica. This company was mustered into the 1st Battalion of Foot, Capt. Fanning's commission dating from the 6th of July, 1746. The term of service of this company expiring on the 25th of November, 1747, Capt. Fanning raised another in Southold and Brookhaven in which his son Phineas was commissioned lieutenant. He served several years under Col. Charles Clinton, during which they formed a friendship which lasted while they lived. Col. Clinton, the ancestor of the Clintons of New York, was born in Longford, Ireland, in 1690, and emigrated to America in 1729, when he settled in Ulster Co., N. Y. Like Capt. Fanning's grandfather, his grandfather was also an adherent of Charles I. and lost his property by confiscation during the Cromwellian régime.

[1] Through Capt. James Fanning's services int he French and Indian War, his descendants are eligible to membership in the Society of Colonial Wars.

It is said Capt. James Fanning owned the mill site at Wading River, was a carpenter by trade, and built the first jail in the town of Riverhead, the Meeting House at Setauket, and owned a farm two miles east of Riverhead, afterwards called the Youngs' farm and later owned by Manasseh Fanning, a descendant. He was connected with the Presbyterian church at Mattituck, L. I., on the records of which church his death is recorded. Capt. Fanning's wife Hannah died on her passage home from England 10 September, 1750, in the forty-eighth year of her age, and was buried in the family burial lot on her farm. Her remains and tombstone were removed in 1861 to the Riverhead Cemetery.

Capt. Fanning died at Southold 15 April, 1779,[1] it is supposed at his son-in-law John Wickham's in Cutchogue. His daughter Hannah wife of John Wickham, had died the November previous. ("Salmon Record" and Mattituck Church Records.) He was buried in the family burying-ground on the Fanning farm at Riverhead, and, it is said, without headstone. In 1849 a large headstone was erected, which was removed together with the remains in 1861 to the Riverhead Cemetery. (See article under "The Riverhead Tombstone.") His will was dated 29 August, 1775, and inventory dated 13 August, 1779. His wife Thankful is not mentioned in his will, and it would appear, therefore, that she died before 1775. Mrs. Henry Stanton of Stonington, Conn., claims Thankful Chesebrough Fanning survived her husband and resided at Stonington many years thereafter.

The following is a copy of a certificate of the University of the State of New York, attesting the service of Capt.

---

[1] *Vide* p. 103 and note thereon.

James Fanning in the Colonial War. (See also photogravure of Capt. James Fanning's muster-roll.)

ALBANY, N. Y., *Dec.* 13, 1898.

This is to certify that on page 68 of a manuscript volume entitled "New York Colonial MSS., vol. 75" in the custody of the Regents of the University of the State of New York in the State Library, is a muster-roll of a company of 100 soldiers raised in Suffolk county, N. Y., for engaging in an expedition against Canada, which company was under the command of Capt. *James Fanning*; and also under the same is a certificate from Robert Robinson and Daniel Smith, Justices, of date July 6, 1746, setting forth the facts above mentioned as to the object of the formation of the company and the fact of its formation and readiness for employment in said expedition.

{SEAL}

Witness the seal of the University of the State of New York.

GEORGE ROGERS HOWELL,
Archivist.

THE WICKHAM FAMILY.

(For Genealogical data of the Wickhams see page 105, No. 47.)

One of the most prominent families connected with the Fannings in this country is that of Wickham. Thomas Wickham, the American ancestor of this family, who emigrated to Wethersfield, Conn., was admitted to the privilege of the franchise on 20 May, 1658. He was probably from Berkshire or Kent, England, and was born about 1620. He died 11 January, 1689, leaving a widow (Sarah), who died 7 January, 1700, and whose will is dated 15 December, 1699, and is recorded in Hartford. The sixth child of this uniqn was Col. Joseph Wickham, born about 1662, who removed to Southampton, L. I., about the year 1697. He married Sarah Satterly about 1684, and among other children had Joseph, who was born 4 June, 1701, married Abigail Parker of Long Island, and died 21 May, 1749, leaving five sons and four daughters, namely: Abigail, Parker, Joseph, Sarah, Thomas, John, Elizabeth, Jerusha, and Daniel Hull. Of the above, three are worthy of special mention. Parker, known as Col. Parker Wickham, was prominent as a loyalist at the time of the American Revolution, and with other members of the family suffered from the political reverses of that period, his estate being confiscated by the government of New York.

Daniel Hull Wickham, a younger brother, was the progenitor of another branch, whose representatives in the third and fourth generations are resident in New York City.

John Wickham, another brother, married Hannah, daughter of James Fanning, and sister of Gen. Edmund Fanning.

John and Hannah (Fanning) Wickham had six children, one of whom, John, was the progenitor of the Virginia and Missouri Wickhams. This son early developed qualities which gave promise of his later distinction and attracted the notice of his uncle Edmund Fanning, who early introduced him into the military service, but on the side of the British. While the war was in progress Fanning wrote to his sister, 16 March, 1778: "If you will send me your son John, I will take the best care of him 'till he is one and twenty years old without expense to his Father." (See Appendix *F*.) Very soon after this date the lad, who was then not quite fifteen years old, having been born 6 June, 1763, was sent to his uncle, as the following letter testifies:—

"CAMP KINGS BRIDGE, *5th April*, 1778.

TO MRS. HANNAH WICKHAM.

My dear sister: —

I yesterday had the pleasure of seeing your Son John. He is grown very fast since I saw him and I think improved in his looks and Education and upon the whole I am very much pleased with him. I have put him under the care of Mr. Humphreys an old Friend and Classmate of mine. Johnny will remain with this Gentleman in New York for three months certainly. You will often hear from him and I hope he will behave & improve himself in such a manner as will make us both happy. You need not send him any article of dress or clothing for none will suit him to wear here that you can get where you live. He shall not want for anything You may depend on it. I thank You, my dear Sister, for your present of some Eggs but I desire You may not send me any more, or anything Else for I do not want anything. We have plenty of everyThing. I desire you will give my tenderest Love & Duty to our good old Father & tell him I will pay him a Visit before next Christmas, if we both live so long. Give my Love to Brother John and to my dear little Girls Abby & Nancy, and tell them if they do not sit up straight & hold up their Heads & look very pretty, that their Uncle will be very much disappointed when he has the Happiness to see them. I have only Time to add that I am

My Dear Sister
Most Affectionately Yours,
EDM. FANNING."

In due time his uncle secured for John Wickham the place of ensign in the celebrated King's American Regiment of Foot, commanded by Col. Edmund Fanning.

He was then sent by his uncle to the Military School at Arras, France; after his return to Virginia, he studied law, and in 1785 began to practice his profession in Williamsburg, Va. In 1790 he removed to Richmond, where he resided until his death 22 January, 1839. He achieved high distinction as an advocate and amassed a large fortune, but was not accorded political honors on account of his course in the Revolution. In 1807 he was one of the counsel for Aaron Burr in his trial for treason. A contemporary says of him: "He was, perhaps, on the whole, the ablest lawyer then practicing at the Richmond bar. He had learning, logic, wit, sarcasm, eloquence, a fine presence, and a persuasive manner. In single endowments he was excelled; but no other man possessed such a variety of talents and resources as Wickham."

He was intimate with and was greatly esteemed by the eccentric John Randolph, of Roanoke, who mentions him in his will as "John Wickham, Esquire, my best of friends . . . and the best and wisest man I ever knew except Mr. Macon"; and bequeaths to him his mare Floyd and his stallion Gascoigne, together with two silver cups and two tankards, desiring that he would have engraved upon them his arms, with the inscriptions: "From John Randolph of Roanoke to John Wickham, Esquire, as a token of the respect and gratitude which he never ceased to feel for his unparalleled kindness, courtesy, and services."

John Wickham numbered many distinguished persons among his friends and acquaintances. Thomas Moore, the poet, and George Ticknor, the author of the "History of Spanish Literature," have both borne testimony to his graces of manner and his scholarly qualities.

Mary Smith Fanning, the first wife of John Wickham, was the daughter of his uncle, the Rev. William Fanning, an Episcopal clergyman of Greensville Co., Va., and granddaughter of James Fanning of Long Island. She was born 25 September, 1775, and was married to John Wickham 24 December, 1791. She died 1 February, 1799. Two sons were born of this marriage: William Fanning Wickham, 23 November, 1793, and Edmund Fanning Wickham, 31 July, 1796. These brothers married sisters, the daughters of Robert Carter of Shirley on the James River and his wife Mary, daughter of General Thomas Nelson of Yorktown, a signer of the Declaration of Independence.

The second wife of John Wickham was Elizabeth Selden McClurg, daughter and sole heir of Dr. James McClurg, of Richmond, a man of eminence in his profession, a staunch supporter of the Federal party, and a member from Virginia of the Convention which framed the Constitution of the United States. The descendants of this marriage are numerous in Virginia, among them being Judge Thomas Ashby Wickham of Henrico County.

William Fanning Wickham, the eldest son of John Wickham, married Anne Carter 9 December, 1819. She was born 27 June, 1797, and died 25 February, 1868. They had two sons: Williams Carter, noticed below, and John, who died without issue.

William Fanning Wickham was a great favorite in Gen. Edmund Fanning's family, and there was always an intimate association, and eventually all the plate engraved with the Fanning arms became the property of his descendants. He specially prized two seals that belonged to Gen. Fanning, — one a carnelian set in gold, the other a silver seal, said to have been brought from Ireland by the first Fanning in America, and which Gen. Fanning prized very highly. William Fanning Wickham died 31 July, 1880.

Williams Carter Wickham, the eldest son of William Fanning Wickham and Anne Carter, was born in Richmond 21, September 1820, and moved with his parents to Hickory Hill in Hanover County in 1827. He was educated at private schools and at the University of Virginia. He studied law and was admitted to the bar in 1842, in Hanover County, but after practicing in a country circuit for a few years he gave up his profession for the life of a Virginia planter. On the 11th of January, 1848, he married Lucy Penn Taylor, daughter of Henry Taylor deceased, granddaughter of John Taylor of Carolina, and great-granddaughter of John Penn, one of the signers of the Declaration of Independence from North Carolina. He was elected to the Virginia House of Delegates in 1849, and was Presiding Justice of the County Court of Hanover County for many years prior to the war. In 1858 he was commissioned Captain in the Virginia Volunteer Cavalry. In 1859 he was elected to the State Senate as a Whig from the district composed of Hanover and Henrico. In 1861 was elected from the County of Henrico to the State Convention as a Union man, and was the only member of that body representing a county of which he was a non-resident. He was opposed to separation and voted against secession. After the ordinance was passed, however, he decided to share the fortunes of his own people, and took his company into active service, participating in the first battle of Manassas and its preliminary engagements. Subsequently he was commissioned Lieutenant-Colonel of the 4th Virginia Cavalry, and on 4 May, 1862, he was desperately wounded at the battle of Williamsburg, and later taken prisoner, but was exchanged by private cartel for Lieutenant-Colonel (subsequently General) Thomas L. Kane of the Pennsylvania Bucktails Regiment and a near kinsman of Mrs. Wickham.

In August, 1862, he was made Colonel of his regiment, and served through the campaign in the battles of Second Manassas, Boonsboro', Sharpsburg, and the cavalry engagements under Gen. Stuart. Col. Wickham was again wounded, but recovered in time to take part in the battle of Fredericksburg on the 12th of December, 1862. The next spring he was active in the conflicts preceding the battle of Chancellorsville, and was posted on the right flank during that battle. Soon after this event he was elected to the Confederate Congress, but did not take his seat, remaining in the field with his regiment.

Col. Wickham was present with his command on the extreme left at the battle of Gettysburg, and aided in covering the retreat. In September, 1863, he was commissioned Brigadier-General and put in command of Wickham's Brigade of Fitz. Lee's Division, and was active in the engagements which ensued until the following February. He was with Stuart in the battle of the Wilderness and in that at Spottsylvania Court House, and was also at Cold Harbor. He served under Early in the Valley campaign during the succeeding fall.

As a cavalry leader in the war he made a reputation second to none in the saddle; he was one of the most skilful and hardest fighters of the cavalry of the South, and led his men in fifty-nine engagements; when the conflict ended he was as much the idol of the Confederate soldier as his highest ambition could have desired.

Gen. Wickham resigned his commission in the Confederate army on the 6th of October, 1864, and took his seat in the Confederate Congress when the session opened. He soon perceived that the end of the Confederacy was drawing near, and he had the hope that reunion could be brought about upon a basis which would in no way tarnish the honor of the armies and people of the South, and would save the lives of thousands of noble men and preserve some of their property from the wreck of war. After the surrender of the armies Gen. Wickham addressed himself to the effort to restore friendly relations between the sections, and to induce his fellow-citizens to accept the situation and throw off the gloom which surrounded them. He stood side by side with his old constituents and shared their fate.

He had been educated as a Whig and a Union man. He regarded the Democratic party as responsible for the war and its results. When the war ended his political faith remained unchanged, and as the Whig party had disappeared he adopted the principles of the Republican party, which he regarded as its legitimate successor. On the 23d of April, 1865, he, in an open letter, allied himself with that party, and by this step estranged many of his old associates from him.

In November, 1865, Gen. Wickham was elected President of the Virginia Central Railroad Company. In November, 1868, he was elected President of the Chesapeake and Ohio Railroad Company in which the Virginia Central had been merged by contract between the States of Virginia and West

Virginia. In 1869 Gen. Wickham found it necessary to bring new men and means into the enterprise, and was made Vice-President of the Company with C. P. Huntington as President, and continued as such until 1875 when he was appointed its receiver, which position he held until July 1, 1878, when upon reorganization of the Company he became its second Vice-President and so continued until his death.

In 1871 Gen. Wickham was elected Chairman of the Board of Supervisors of Hanover County, and was unanimously re-elected as long as he lived.

In 1872 Gen. Wickham was a member of the Electoral College of Virginia and cast the vote of the State for Gen. Grant. In 1880 he was honored by a tender of the then vacant Naval Portfolio by President Hayes, but declined on account of business engagements. He headed the Garfield Electoral ticket in Virginia, and in August, 1881, was tendered the Republican nomination for Governor, but owing to the division in the party on account of the "Mahone Movement," declined. This movement under the name of the "Coalition Readjuster Party" he denounced, and on this issue was again elected to the State Senate, and was Chairman of the Finance Committee of that body until his death, although he occupied an independent position. While not an impassioned speaker he was brave and calm and cool; and he possessed in a remarkable degree the attribute of personal magnetism and the capacity to arouse manifestations of enthusiasm and personal attachment.

On the 23d of July, 1888, he died in his office in Richmond of heart failure, and "the State of Virginia bowed in a profounder sorrow than any that has befallen her since the death of Gen. Lee."

On 5 March, 1890, the General Assembly of Virginia adopted the following —

"Joint Resolution fixing a site on the Capitol Grounds for the statue of General Williams C. Wickham.

"Whereas the City of Richmond, through its council and mayor, has requested the Wickham monument association to present the statue of General Williams C. Wickham to the said City, to be placed by it upon one of the public parks; and whereas the whole State of Virginia is interested in preserving this memorial of one whose devotion to the Commonwealth has rendered his name to the people of Virginia; now, be it

"RESOLVED by the Senate (the House of Delegates concurring) That a site for the said statue, be, and the same is hereby, dedicated by the Commonwealth of Virginia in honor of his memory, upon such portion of the Capitol grounds as may be selected by a committee consisting of the President *pro tempore* of the Senate, the Speaker of the House of Delegates, and the Superintendent of public buildings and grounds; and full power and authority is hereby given said committee in the premises."

On the 29th of October, 1891, there was unveiled in Monroe Park in the City of Richmond, in the presence of a vast assemblage of the people, Valentine's bronze statue of Gen. Wickham, bearing the inscription: —

"Soldier" "Statesman" "Patriot" "Friend"

He is represented in the uniform of a Confederate Brigadier of Cavalry; and the sculptor, himself a Virginian, was successful in both pose and portraiture. "As an artistic achievement it possesses the highest merit." The total height of pedestal and statue is seventeen feet, and the general effect is impressive and realistic. The presence of the Governor of Virginia, the Governor of North Carolina, Supreme Court Judges, Mayor and Council of the City of Richmond, the Veteran organizations of the Confederate Army, the Vol-

WICKHAM
SOLDIER, STATESMAN,
PATRIOT, FRIEND."
CHESAPEAKE AND OHIO
RAILWAY COMPANY

Statue erected 1891 to the memory of
General Williams Carter Wickham.

unteer Soldiery of the State and the various associations of organized labor (with which he was always in the closest touch), gave dignity to the occasion, while Gen. Fitzhugh Lee, the former Governor of the State (more recently Consul-General in Cuba and Brigadier-General, U. S. A.), delivered the oration, which was alike worthy of the soldier speaker and the soldier subject.

Henry Taylor Wickham, son of Williams Carter and Lucy (Taylor) Wickham, was born at Hickory Hill in the County of Hanover, Virginia, 17 December, 1849. He was prepared for college at home schools, and in 1864 was sent to Washington College at Lexington, Va. (now Washington and Lee University). He was an inmate of the family of the late Gen. W. N. Pendleton, and had the advantage of resuming his studies under the supervision of Gen. Robert E. Lee, who after the war was made President of the college. The influence of Gen. Lee and the desire to win his approval at all times exercised a very marked influence upon the young men of his day.

After completing his course there he studied law at the University of Virginia under Professor John B. Minor, graduating in 1870, and immediately began the practice of his profession in the city of Richmond, Va.

In 1874 he was appointed Assistant Counsel for the Chesapeake and Ohio Railroad Company.

In 1879 he was elected to the House of Delegates of Virginia from the County of Hanover as a "Debt-payer," served one term, and declined re-election in favor of Hon. R. H. Cardwell, now a member of the Supreme Court of Appeals of Virginia, whom he warmly supported.

In 1886 he was made General Solicitor of the Chesapeake

and Ohio Railway Company and still holds this position.

In 1888 he was elected to the Senate of Virginia to fill the vacancy occasioned by the death of his father, Gen. Williams Carter Wickham, whose statue stands in Monroe Park as an evidence of the love and admiration of his fellow Virginians.

When Mr. Wickham first entered the Senate the State of Virginia was being harassed by the "Debt question," and from the first he took an active part in the settlement of the debt, being a member of the Finance Committee, and the mover of the resolutions for the appointment of the "Debt Commission."

For several years after, as a member of the Commission, by his industry in investigating the problems which came up for solution, the financial friends which he had made in his business, and his active work, he did his full part in accomplishing the settlement of the question to the mutual satisfaction of the creditors and his State.

In 1891 he was re-elected to the Senate of Virginia, and again in 1895 without opposition, when he became Chairman of the Finance Committee, and was also Chairman of the Democratic Conference of the Senate.

In 1897 he was made the President *pro tem* of the Senate, and still holds the positions named, being again elected to the Senate of Virginia without opposition.

In 1885 Mr. Wickham married Miss Elise W. Barksdale of Richmond City, Va., and has two sons, Williams Carter and George Barksdale Wickham.

He resides at Hickory Hill in the "Slashes" of Hanover, where he has extensive farming interests, to which he is delighted to give all the time that can be spared from his professional and public duties.

DIAGRAM

showing Henry Taylor Wickham's line of descent through two sources from Capt. James Fanning.

CAPT. JAMES FANNING

had issue

Rev. William Fanning, who m. Mary Tazewell
had issue

Hannah Fanning, who m. John Wickham
had issue

Mary Smith Fanning, who m. John Wickham Junior,
had issue

William Fanning Wickham
had issue

Gen. Williams Carter Wickham
had issue

Henry Taylor Wickham.

JOHN[3] FANNING (No. 18).

(For Genealogical data concerning him, see page 113.)

John Fanning, Junior, eldest son of Lieut. John and Margaret (Culver) Fanning, of Groton, Conn., and grandson of Edmund Fanning, Senior, the ancestor in America, was born about 1688 in the town of New London, Conn., in that part which was in 1705 set off to form the new town of Groton.

His father resided at that time on the west bank of Mystic River, one-half mile below the present village of Old Mystic, but afterward removed to his Fort Hill farm, where John Fanning, Junior, was brought up.

He was admitted an inhabitant of Groton 22 May, 1712. He married about the year 1716, Deborah, daughter of William and Hannah (Frink) Parke, of Preston, Conn., and had issue two sons, John and Thomas. His residence, at the time of his death, cannot now be determined, but it was probably on his father's farm at Fort Hill. There is mention in his father's will in 1738–9 of a path that leads to "where my son John Fanning's house formerly stood." This path is still used to-day, and near by are the cellar holes of two or three old houses, one of which, no doubt, was the residence of John Fanning, Junior.

In 1712 the town of Groton distributed to its inhabitants the reservation of the Pequot Indians at Noank. The Indians had been removed in 1667 to Mashantucket. In this distribution of lands John Fanning, Junior, received as a grant from the town, Lot No. 45, second tier, second division. This he sold on the 10th of January, 1714–15, to Edward Yeomans, and bought of the latter Lots No. 64

and 66 in the first tier, second division of same. The lots were the eighth and ninth lots south of the highway that was to run east and west over Fort Hill by Lieut. John Fanning's house, which highway was laid out by the town of Groton, but was never built. John Fanning also owned Lot No. 33, first division, first tier, which lot was originally laid out to him by the town 7 May, 1712. It was the second lot from the most northerly one in that tier, and was probably sold before his death, as it was not included in the inventory of his estate.

John Fanning died intestate, early in life, from the cutting of an artery in his leg, and the widow Deborah was appointed by the Court administratrix upon his estate, and took oath 7 April, 1719, which administration is recorded at New London, Probate Journal No. 2, p. 45. His inventory was taken 15 December, 1718, a copy of which is found on the New London Probate Records, Book B, p. 457. (Originally recorded 14 April, 1722, in the fourth book of Wills, folio 210, which book was among those destroyed by fire 6 September, 1781, when the town of New London was burned.) Inventory, £126-2*s*-11*d*. It mentions "debt due frome an Indian sold to Mr. Nehemiah Smith, £06-07*s*-00*d*.," and also mentions "2 great loots of Land In Nawaunck Neck containing 5 acres the two," valued at £8-0-0. The estate was divided 18 July, 1722, when the widow received one-third and the children, John and Thomas, their portion, — a double one to the eldest son John, and a single one to Thomas. Lieut. John Fanning, the grandfather, was appointed by the Court guardian over John, and William Parke of Preston, Conn., was appointed guardian over Thomas Fanning, 25 July, 1722.

The Inventory is as follows: —

"An Inventory of the Eſtate of John ffaning Junr Late of Groton	
Deceased Taken Dec. 15, 1718	£ s d
To his Wareing Aparill vallued at	12-00-00
To a horſe 7$^{£}$a mare 5$^{£}$	12-00-00
To 5 Cowes at 4$^{£}$ each	20-00-00
To 4 do & vantages, 2 ſtears & 2 hefers	11-00-00
To 3 yeare & vantage cattle at	4-00-00
To a Yoake of oxen at 11$^{£}$ to 4 Laſt Spring Calfes 13^{s} each	13-12-00
To 20 ſheep at 7$^{£}$-15^{s}; To 4 young ſwine at 8^{s} each	9-02-00
To 2 Greate loots of Land In Nawaunck Neck Containing 5 acres the two	8-00-00
To a ſadle & Bridle 25^{s}	1-05-00
To a feather Bed Bolſter and one Pillo	5-00-00
To a ſet of Curtins & Vallins at 2$^{£}$-15^{s}	2-15-00
To Coverlits 40^{s} & 2 Blankitts 36^{s}	3-16-00
To two ſheets 16^{s}-8^{d} one Braſs Kitle 40^{s}	2-16-08
To an Iron poot 12^{s}	12-00
To an Iron Kitle 11^{s} & 4 trays at 12^{d} pr	15-00
To 2 pailes 2^{s}-6^{d} A Pigan 12^{d}	03-06
To 2 Pewter Platers at 9^{s} each & 3 leſor dito at 6^{s} & 4^{d} each	1-17-00
To A Pewter Quart Poot 4^{s}-6^{d} and 6 potingers	10-06
To 2 Pewter Plates at 2^{s} pr & 2 Dito at 18^{d}	07-00
To a Pewter Baſson at 2^{s} to 2 Earthen Plats at 2^{s} each one at 14^{d}	07-02
To fire tongues & ſhovels at 4^{s}-6^{d}, a paire Plow Irons 23^{s} a draught-chaine 12^{s}	01-19-06
To an ax 7^{s} an old ax 3^{s} to a chest 8^{s} a ſmall Table 8^{s}	01-06-00
To a frying pann 4^{s} a Braſs ſkillet 4^{s}	08-00
To 4 ſmal chairs at 2^{s} each	08-00
To a ſpining Wollen Whell & a lining whell	07-06
To a Cheſe Preſs 8^{s} to an old hhds 3^{s}	11-00
To 2 Barrills 6^{s}, 2 old Do 2^{d}	08-00
To a Bible 9^{s} to a ſeine 20^{d} to a Candleſtick 15^{d}	11-11
To a Tunnel 8^{d} To ye $\frac{1}{2}$ of a Grindſtone 4^{s} a paire of Sheep ſhears 2^{s}-6^{d}	00-07-02

	£ s d
To one ſmall 4 year old Hyfer 3£-10s	03-10-00
To a Debt due frome an Indian ſold to Mr Nehemiah Smith	06-07-00
	115-06-10

The within & above Inventory taken pr. us

Saml[ll] Avery
James Packer"

"Capt. Samuel Avery & Mr. James Packer made oath that they had apprized the Estate Contained in this Inventory According to the best of their Judgment, New London Aprill 7th 1719 before me Richard Christopher Judge of Probate

Deborah Fanning administratrix of the Eſtate of her deceaſed huſband John Fanning Junr late of Groton made oath in a Court of Probate held in New London Aprill ye 7th 1719 that she gave unto the apprizers a true account of the Eſtate of her ſd Deceaſed huſband according to the beſt of her knowledge and if any thing further appear to be his Eſtate that is Conſiderable she will add it to this Inventory.

	£ s d
Brought from ye other ſid	115-06-10
on this ſide	10-16-01
	126-02-11

Recorded In the fourth Book of Wills fol 210 Aprill 14, 1722.

Test C. CHRISTOPHER *Clerk*"

GENERAL EDMUND[4] FANNING, LL.D. (No. 46).[1]

(For Genealogical data concerning him, see page 165.)

Edmund Fanning, son of Capt. James Fanning, and great-grandson of Edmund Fanning, the first settler of the name in Connecticut, was born in Suffolk Co., L. I., 24 April, 1739. He was educated at Yale College where he became a Berkeleian scholar and graduated with distinction in 1757, receiving the degree of Bachelor of Arts. He soon after removed to North Carolina, where he studied law with Attorney-General Jones of that province, was admitted to the bar in 1762 and settled at Hillsboro, Orange County.

At that time William Tryon was governor of North Carolina. Tryon was trained to arms, yet was well versed in all the arts of diplomacy; knew when to flatter and when to threaten. He was cool and calculating — devoid of all religious principles, but free from all religious intolerance. His administration was disturbed by the agitation caused on account of the excessive taxes imposed on the people, as well as by the knavery and venality of many of the civil officers.

The learning and ability of Edmund Fanning attracted the attention of Gov. Tryon with whom he soon became a great favorite. In 1765 the Governor appointed him Clerk of the Supreme Court, and afterwards Recorder of Deeds and Colonel of Militia for Orange County, which county he also represented in the General Assembly for several years. For various reasons Fanning was the most unpopular officer in

---

[1] *Vide* Appendix *G* for Biographical statement written by General Fanning.

North Carolina in 1766, and it is stated that his conduct more than anything else caused the insurrection of the Regulators of Orange County.

In April, 1768, the inhabitants of that county banded together under the name of Regulators and resolved to pay only such taxes and fees as were imposed by the General Assembly. At the September term of the Court during the same year Fanning was indicted on six several counts of which he was found guilty; but being protected by the power of Gov. Tryon, he was fined only one penny in each case. Three Regulators whom he had arrested and brought to trial before the same Court were each sentenced to pay a fine of £50 or to be imprisoned for six months in case the fine was not paid.

During the March term of the Court in 1770 the Regulators prevented the Judge and lawyers from attending the Supreme Court at Hillsboro, so that the session was adjourned to the September term. When the people learned that the Court had adjourned they proceeded to wreak vengeance on those whom they considered their enemies. At an inquiry held on the 9th of October, 1770, relating to the outrages committed on this occasion, Ralph McNair, one of the witnesses, deposed that on the 24th of April he saw the Regulators at Hillsboro armed with cudgels and cowhide whips. He saw them beating and pursuing Col. Fanning until he took refuge in a store which they assaulted with brickbats. On the 25th of April his house was torn down and all the rich furniture which he had imported from England destroyed.

The same year the Regulators resisted the tax collectors, and beat and otherwise maltreated many of the sheriff's officers. Col. Fanning, as the chief official of the county, raising a clamor against the odiousness of rebellion, called out the militia of Orange County, but not more than one hundred and twenty men responded. Gov. Tryon, as the King's representative, empowered Fanning to call out the militia of eight counties besides Orange.

On the 24th of April, 1771, the Governor marched from Newbern at the head of a military force for the purpose of suppressing the Regulators and overawing the people. On the 9th of May he encamped near Hillsboro, where he was joined by Col. Fanning with a force of militia. Soon after the combined forces attacked the Regulators at Allamance Creek, where after a conflict of two hours the Regulators were completely defeated. After this battle Tryon and Fanning resumed their march, forcing all the men on their route to take the oath of allegiance to the King.

When Gov. Tryon was transferred to New York in 1771, Edmund Fanning accompanied him as private secretary. Gov. Martin, who succeeded Gov. Tryon in North Carolina, presented Fanning's losses to the General Assembly; but that body refused to even consider the petition, and rebuked the Governor for thus interfering with the business of the House. In 1779 all of Fanning's property in North Carolina was confiscated to the State.

It is not improbable that Edmund Fanning's unpopularity while in North Carolina was greater than his offences deserved. Party spirit ran high at the time, and neither the members of the Assembly nor the people at large were in a frame of mind to do justice to opponents. Some contemporary historians describe him as haughty and supercilious, and his conduct as an officer overbearing and extortionary; loading the estates of Orange County with doubt as to their titles, and demanding new and seemingly unnecessary deeds.

There can be no doubt but he was of a haughty, stern and unyielding disposition; but he was very highly talented and well educated, and is described by his political opponents as courteous and gentlemanly at all times. In 1771 a pamphlet was published in Boston entitled, "A Fan for Fanning and a Torch for Tryon," in which both were unmercifully excoriated.

Soon after the arrival of Col. Fanning in New York in 1771 he was appointed Surrogate-General of the Province of New York, and in 1774 to the lucrative position of Surveyor-General by letters patent from the King as a recompense for the losses he had sustained in North Carolina, still retaining the position of private secretary to the Governor. In the latter part of 1775 Gov. Tryon, Col. Fanning, and several other royalists were forced to leave New York City. The Governor and Col. Fanning remained on board the ship *Duchess of Gordon* until the following summer, under the protection of His Majesty's ships *Asia* and *Phoenix*.

In December, 1776, Col. Fanning received a warrant from Gen. Howe to raise a regiment of loyalists for the King's service. In furtherance of this object New York contributed £2,000, Staten Island £500, King's County £310, and Jamaica £219. This corps was completed and mustered into service 8 June, 1777, under the name of the King's American Regiment of Foot or Associated Refugees. The regiment was in active service during the war, during which Col. Fanning was twice wounded.

At the close of the War of the Revolution Col. Fanning sailed for Nova Scotia, of which colony he was appointed Lieutenant-Governor on the 24th of February, 1783, with a salary of £500 a year — no salary having previously been attached to that office. In explaining to the British House of Commons the increase in the estimates for Nova Scotia for the year, Lord North stated that "it arose from the circumstance that Col. Fanning was appointed Lieutenant-Governor of the Colony at a salary of £500 a year, the propriety of which appointment he believed no man would call in question when he considered the merits of that gentleman, his sufferings in the cause of this country, and his unshaken loyalty and attachment to his Sovereign throughout the whole of the American War."

Commissioners having been appointed by Act of Parliament to inquire into the losses and services "of all such persons who have suffered in their rights, properties and possessions during the late unhappy dissensions in America in consequence of their loyalty to His Majesty's government," Col. Fanning presented his claim for compensation to them. With regard to his extensive and valuable properties in New York and Vermont, the Commissioners refused to take these claims into consideration, as no proof of confiscation and sale could be obtained. In reference to the North Carolina property, he received the following letter from his agent in London: —

LONDON, *June* 27, 1784.

Sir, —

I have at last got your North Carolina schedule before the Commissioners, and was examined before the same on the 24th inst. You have here enclosed the amount as stated in the Schedule in Virginia currency, which when reduced to Sterling amounts to £21,273.

I am, Sir,
Your obedient servant
JOHN MCLELLAN.

To Gov. Fanning,
Halifax, N. S.

Mr. McLellan was a resident of Hillsboro, N. C., from 1770 to 1777, and for several years acted under William

Johnson who was attorney in that province for Col. Fanning, and as such had the management of his lands and the receipt of the rents thereof after Fanning went to New York. The Board of Commissioners closed its proceedings in 1789: the amount of compensation finally awarded to Col. Fanning for the losses he had sustained in North Carolina cannot at present be ascertained.

Col. Fanning resided at Point Pleasant near Halifax while Lieutenant-Governor of Nova Scotia. There on the 30th of November, 1785, he was married to Miss Phebe Maria Burns by the Rev. Joshua Wingate Weeks, rector of St. Paul's Church, Halifax. Several historians state that Fanning married a daughter of Gov. Tryon, but there is not a particle of evidence to sustain the statement. The fact is that Gov. Tryon had no daughter, at least none of marriageable age, during his administration of affairs in America.

By a despatch from Lord Viscount Sydney, Secretary of State, dated at Whitehall 30th of June, 1786, Col. Fanning was empowered to administer the government of the Island of St. John (now Prince Edward Island) during the absence of its first governor, Walter Patterson, who was recalled to answer charges of mal-administration. Fanning arrived in Charlottetown 4 November, 1786, but Patterson refused to surrender to him the control of the government, alleging that the season was too far advanced to enable him to repair to England. On the 5th of April, 1787, a despatch was addressed by Lord Sydney to Patterson, dismissing him from office for disobedience of His Majesty's orders, and another was sent to Fanning confirming him in the office of Governor of the Island of St. John. This position he held until 5 July, 1805, when owing to failing health he resigned.

During Gov. Fanning's administration in the Island two provincial corps were raised by order of His Majesty; the barracks were rebuilt in Charlottetown by order of the Duke of Kent, then Commander-in-chief of the forces at Halifax; three troops of volunteer horse were also organized, and in 1799 the name of the Island was changed to Prince Edward Island in compliment to the Duke of Kent. In recognition of his long and faithful services His Majesty granted Gov. Fanning a pension of £500 sterling per annum during the remainder of his life, to commence from the time of his delivering up the government to his successor, Col. J. F. W. DesBarres. He embarked for England 6 August, 1805, but returned to Prince Edward Island 27 November, 1807. He took his final departure from the Island on the 23d of November, 1813. In 1816 he closed his accounts at the Audit Office, London, when His Majesty's ministers, to mark their approval of his administration, deviated from their usual course and granted an increase in his salary from the period of his appointment in 1786 to the time of his resignation in 1805.

In October, 1793, Gov. Fanning was promoted to the rank of Major-General in the British army; in June, 1799, he was further advanced to the rank of Lieutenant-General; and on the 25th of April, 1803, he attained the rank of General. In 1764 he received the honorary degree of A.M. from Harvard College, and in 1772 a similar degree from King's (now Columbia) College and Yale also. He was given the degree of D.C.L. by Oxford University in 1774. The honorary degree of LL.D. was conferred on him by both Yale and Dartmouth Colleges in 1803, on the strength of an application which he made in 1802 to his classmate Burroughs, from which the following is an extract: —

"It is with the most sincere and heartfelt satisfaction that I can say, in the time of impending ruin and meditated conflagration, she (Yale College) owed her salvation and present existence to the mediatorial and supplicating influence of one of her sons who has, as well as her own honors, had the honor to receive a Degree of Master of Arts at Cambridge College or University, and also at King's College or Columbian University at New York; was president of the College, now University in North Carolina, and Doctor of Laws at the University of Oxford. Has been many years Governor, first of the province of Nova Scotia, and now of Prince Edward Island, and also a Lieutenant-General in the service of the King of Great Britain or Emperor of the British Isles; and is now desirous of having his name appear with suitable distinction in the Catalogue, and receiving from them a proper testimonial of such his civil, military, and literary honors."

As regards the claim here made that Yale College owed her salvation to Fanning at the time of the British invasion of New Haven in July, 1779, it seems probable that the college authorities in 1803 thought that it was not without foundation. We only know that Gov. Tryon was in command of the British on that occasion and that Edmund Fanning was his trusted friend and secretary. The claim of Fanning to the presidency of a college in North Carolina has reference to Queen's College at Charlotte of which the act of incorporation in January, 1771, names him first in the Board of Fellows or Trustees.[1]

Gen. Fanning's only son, Frederick Augustus, a captain in the 22d regiment of British infantry, died unmarried 22 September, 1812, shortly after returning from the East Indies. The General never fully recovered from the loss of his son. He died at 7 Upper Seymour Street, Kensington, London, on the 28th of February, 1818, at the age of sev-

[1] *Vide* references to Edmund Fanning in "Literary Diary of Ezra Stiles, D.D., LL.D., edited by Franklin Bowditch Dexter, A.M.," 3 vols., published by Scribner, 1901; Vol. I., p. 114; Vol. II., pp. 357, 397.

enty-nine years, and was buried in the vault under the chancel of Kensington Church. The *Gentleman's Magazine* of the time published the following notice of his death:—

"General Edmund Fanning died in London at an advanced age. The world contained no better man in all the relations of life as a friend, landlord and master. He lost a large property by raising a regiment in the Revolution. He was Lieutenant-Governor of Nova Scotia. Next he was Governor of Prince Edward Island nineteen years. He resigned from ill health and to attend to his private affairs to the grief of all. He left a widow and three accomplished daughters."

A mural tablet to his memory is placed in Kensington Church, and another adorns the walls of St. Paul's Episcopal Church, Charlottetown, Prince Edward Island, of which the following is a copy:—

(See photogravure.)

"SACRED to the beloved and honored memory of
GENERAL EDMUND FANNING L. L. D.
Formerly Lieu^t. Governor of the Province of Nova Scotia
and late of this Island:
who universally esteemed and most deeply lamented
died, in England on the 28 February 1818 aged 79 years.
Alike distinguished for his loyalty and zeal,
with fidelity and honor he discharged the duties
of the several military and civil situations which he filled
During a long and honorable life
passed in the service of his King and Country,
in this Colony,
over which he presided as Lieu^t. Governor for nearly nineteen years,
he will long be remembered.
Ever actuated by the warmest zeal for its interests,
the benefactor of the indigent and the friend of the distressed,
it was his unwearied and successful endeavor to contribute
to the prosperity and happiness of the people he governed."

Mural Tablet to the memory of
Genl. Edmund Fanning LL.D. in St. Paul's Episcopal Church.

ALSO

"To the memory of his beloved and only son
FREDERICK AUGUSTUS FANNING
Captain in His Majesty's 22nd Foot, a most promising young Officer,
who to the deep regret of the Reg' and all who knew him,
departed this life on the 22nd of September 1812, Aged 23 years,
and lies interred with his father,
In the vault under the Chancel of Kensington Church.
The afflicted and disconsolate family,
who are left to mourn their double loss,
as the last tribute of their unceasing affection
and regret
have caused this monument to be erected."

Copy of epitaphs on two stone mural tablets, in the Church of "St. Mary Abbots," Kensington, London, *W.*: —

"Sacred to the Memory of General Edmund Fanning who departed this life on the 28th of February 1818 Aged 79 years and whose Remains are deposited near those of his only son in the Vault under the Chancel of this Church.

"This amiable and truly estimable man, exhibited through a long and honourable life, a model of superior excellence as a public character. Distinguished both in the Civil and Military service of his country, he ever manifested the warmest zeal for its interest, and in all the relations of private life was not to be surpassed in the uniform practice of every social and domestic virtue.

"To perpetuate his beloved and revered memory, this Monument is erected by his once happy but now afflicted and disconsolate family."

"Within the Vault under the Chancel of this Church, are deposited the Remains of Captain Frederick Augustus Fanning, of His Majesty's 22nd Regiment of Foot, who died in this Town on the 22nd September 1812, aged 23 years.

"He was the only son of General Edmund Fanning and was returning to his family in British North America after an absence of nearly eight years in the East Indies, when a fatal disease, contracted on service in its unhealthy climate, terminated a life short in duration but distinguished in its course by all that could do him honour as a Soldier, a Brother, and a Son. His afflicted parents and three sisters are left to mourn in his untimely fate the early wreck of their fondest hopes, and to find in the recollections of his many virtues, with the humble confidence of a re-union in a better world, the only consolation for their irreparable loss in this.

"As a small tribute to his exemplary filial worth, and as a memorial of the sincerest parental affection, this monument is raised and inscribed by his bereaved Father."

Copy of letters from Edward, Duke of Kent, father of Queen Victoria, to Gen. Edmund Fanning, L.L.D.: —

KENSINGTON PALACE, *March* 2^d^, 1810.

"*My dear General:*

I do myself the pleasure to acknowledge the receipt of your letter of the 12th Decr last, with its inclosures, and feel satisfied from the whole tenor of my conduct towards you from our first acquaintance, that you must be convinced that I could have no greater gratification than in serving you as far as lays in my power. Under these circumstances I have the less hesitation in giving you my candid opinion respecting your Son's promotion, which is that, according to the existing rules at the Horse Guards, he has no chance of getting a Company after 5 years service, unless by Regimental Seniority, without his pretensions are founded upon your just claims to such a favor in consideration of your long and faithful services both civil and military. I have not therefore stirred in the business from a conviction that the little influence I possess at the Horse Guards cannot render you any service in it, and would advise you suspending any further application on that head until your return to England, as you propose in the Spring, will enable you to make a direct one to Sir David Dundas in person, which can hardly fail of success.

I remain with sincere regard,

My dear General,

ever your's faithfully,

EDWARD.

L^T^ GENL. FANNING."

KENSINGTON PALACE, *March 19th*, 1810.

"*My dear General:*

I have great satisfaction in informing you that, since I last wrote to you, it has been in my power to recommend your Son for a Company in the 4th Ceylon Regi'mt (as you will perceive from the annexed extract of a letter which I have rec'd on that subject from Lt. Col. Torrens, Mil. Lieut' to the Commander in Chief). He has since been gazetted for it accordingly, and I am now endeavoring to obtain for him an exchange into a Regimt. stationed in North America.

Your long and faithful services fully entitle you to that small favor and I feel the greatest satisfaction in having been instrumental in bringing forward your pretentions upon the present occasion.

I remain with sentiments of the most friendly regard,
my dear General,
ever Your's faithfully,

EDWARD.

L[T] GEN[L] FANNING."
&c &c

Copy of Will of Gen. Edmund Fanning, L.L.D.:—

"In the name of God, Amen. I Edmund Fanning, L.L.D. and General in the army, at present resident in Prince Edward Island, but being about to embark for the Kingdom of Great Britain, and being of sound mind and memory, blessed be God, therefore do make this, my last Will and Testament, in manner following that is to say: First I give and recommend my Soul into the hands of Almighty God that gave it and my body to the earth to be buried in a decent manner, and as touching such worldly estate wherewith it has pleased God to bless me, I give, devise and bequeath the same in manner and form following: In the first place I desire that all my just debts be paid and satisfied, and after payment thereof I do hereby give, bequeath and devise to my beloved wife Phoebe Maria Fanning her Heirs and Assigns forever, the three farms lately conveyed to her with the stock and farming utensils thereon, and every other Horse, Cattle, and other thing usually called hers. Item I give and bequeath to my said beloved wife, an annuity or clear yearly Rent Charge, of Two hundred Dollars to become payable out of and chargeable upon the Rents issuing out of my lands, houses and tenements on my half of Lot or Township Number (65) Sixty-five, so long as she shall remain my widow, and in case of her intermarriage, then and thereafter an annuity of one hundred dollars chargeable in like manner, during the term of her natural life which said annuity together with the provision hereafter made by me for her support I do hereby declare to be in lieu and full satisfaction of her right of Dower, and all other claims whatsoever, and I do direct that my plate, Horses, Carriages, household furniture and other effects whatsoever, not otherwise disposed of by me, be sold and disposed of by public auction within six months after my decease and that a credit of twelve months be allowed to the purchasers for any sum exceeding five pounds on their giving security to the satisfaction of my Executrices, hereafter named, that of the money arising from such sale, one thousand dollars be paid to my said beloved wife Phoebe Maria Fanning and that the residue therof be equally divided amongst my three daughters, Louisa Augusta Fanning, Maria Susannah Matilda Fanning, Margaret William Tryon Fanning, and the survivors of them share and share alike, reserving nevertheless to my said wife or any of my said children such horses, Cattle or other stock as are or have been reputed to belong to either of them as their property, to their own use or disposal. And I do hereby give, bequeath and devise to my said beloved daughter Louisa Augusta Fanning My Farm, called the Hermitage now under lease, to Mr. Robert Pike, consisting of Pasture Lots, Nos. 238, 197, 237, 191, 189, and part of Nos. 246 and 247, containing in the whole about eighty acres little more or less, also My Town Lots Nos. 14 and 15, in the Second Hundred called the office, also Lots Nos. 76 and 77 in the second hundred and Nos. 13 and 14 in the third hundred leased to Fade Goff Esq. with houses and appurtenances thereunto belonging to her and the heirs of her body, lawfully begotten and in default of such Heirs, then to her and her Heirs and Assigns forever, and I do hereby give and bequeath to my said beloved Daughter Maria Susannah Matilda Fanning my Farm and Lands at the head of Hillsborough River, containing Five hundred acres and my Town Lot adjoining Howel's, and Lot No. 50, in the second hundred in Charlotte Town, together with the Houses, Buildings and Appurtenances, thereunto belonging to her and the Heirs Male of her body lawfully begotten and in default of such Heirs then to her and her Heirs and Assigns forever. And I do hereby give, bequeath and devise to my said beloved daughter Margaret William Tryon Fanning My Farm called Fullarton's Marsh, now leased to Angus McInnes, containing Two hundred and Sixty-six Acres, also my Town Lots Nos. 93, 94, 95 and 96 in the first hundred and Nos. 36, 37, 38 39 and 40 in the second hundred, together with the Houses, Buildings and Appurtenances thereunto belonging to her and the Heirs Male of her body lawfully begotten and in default of such Heirs, then to her and her Heirs and Assigns forever. And I do hereby give bequeath and devise to my Relation Edmund Frederick Augustus Fanning, a minor son of Captain Edmund Fanning Grandson of my deceased affectionate brother, Colonel Phineas Fanning of Long Island in New York, North America, Ten thousand acres of land, situated on Lot or Township Number Sixty-seven (67) in this Island, and also Pasture Lots in the Royalty of Charlotte Town Nos. 34, 364, 374, 393, 411, 342, 363, 373, and 410, containing twelve acres each also Town Lots Nos. 77 and 78, in the fourth hundred with the Houses, Buildings, and Appurtenances, thereunto belonging to him and to the Heirs Male of his body lawfully begotten and in default of such Heirs then to him and his Heirs and Assigns forever. I also give, bequeath and devise to my said relation Edmund Frederick Augustus Fanning my five thousand acres of land, adjoining the land of his Father, in the State of Vermont, to him and the Heirs Male of his body lawfully begotten and in default of such Heirs to him and his Heirs and Assigns forever. And I also give, bequeath and devise to my said relation Edmund Frederick Augustus Fanning My Island, called Oak Island or Fanning's Island, and my Lots Nos. 17, 18, 19, 20, 59, 60, 61, and 62, in the Town of Fanningsburg to him and his Heirs Male of his body lawfully begotten, and in default of such Heirs then to revert to me and my Heirs and their Heirs and Assigns forever. And I do hereby give, bequeath and devise to my said daughter Louisa Augusta Fanning and Maria Susannah Matilda Fanning all my lands on Lot or Township No. 50 in this Island with the houses, buildings and appurtenances, and all Rents, Issues and Profits issuing out of and arising from said lands to them and their Heirs and Assigns forever, and I do hereby give, bequeath and devise to my said three dutiful and affectionate daughters, Louisa Augusta Fanning, Maria Susannah Matilda Fanning and Margaret William Tryon Fanning, my half of Lot or Township Number (65) Sixty-five with the houses and Buildings thereon and the Lands called the Warren Farm and appurtenances and all Rents issues and profits issuing out of and arising from said lands, subject however to the payment of the annuity hereinbefore granted to my beloved Wife Phoebe Maria Fanning, to them and their Heirs and Assigns forever. Item I do also hereby give, bequeath and devise, to my said affectionate three daughters all my lands on Lot or Township Number Sixty Seven, not herein-before devised, with the houses, Buildings and Appurtenances, and the Rents, issues and Profits thereof, to them and their Heirs and Assigns forever. Item and lastly I do hereby give, bequeath and devise to my said three affectionate daughters all my Estate, Real, Personal and Mixed of what nature or kind soever, or where soever situated in the King's dominions and in the United States of America or elsewhere, not herein otherwise disposed of to them and their Heirs and Assigns forever and I do hereby nominate, constitute and appoint my said beloved wife and three daughters Executrixes of this my last Will and Testament and I do hereby revoke, and make annul all other and former will or wills by me made and I do hereby empower and it is my request that my said Executrixes hereinbefore named, and mentioned do amicably in convenient time after my decease, get the Lands, Tenements and Estate fairly and equitably divided among them according to their several and respective shares and proportions in as fair and equal a manner as may be and without contention or dispute. In witness whereof I have to this my last Will and Testament subscribed my hand and seal, at Charlotte Town in the Island Prince Edward this Tenth day of November in the year of our Lord one thousand eight hundred and thirteen.

(Sig'd.) EDMUND FANNING [L. S.].

"Signed, Sealed, Published and declared by the above named Testator in the presence of us, who at his request have subscribed our names as witnesses thereto.

(Signed), ANN KELLY, JAMES MCDONNELL, JNO. LOBBAN.

"I General Edmund Fanning of No. 7 Upper Seymour Street Portman Square in the County of Middlesex do hereby make and declare this to be a Codicil and to be annexed to and considered as part of my last Will and Testament. Inprimis, in case of my death in this Country, I desire to be privately buried, without parade or expense. Item I do hereby give, and bequeath unto each of my three daughters mentioned in my will, in addition to what I have therein specifically given and bequeathed to each of them, Two thousand guineas each, to them and their heirs, I should wish the said sums to be in the Five per cent Navy Fund, as the half yearly memento on these bequests, I also give and bequeath my said three daughters, Two hundred and fifty pounds each, to them and their heirs that sum being secured for my life as may be seen, by referring to the Policy of Insurance. In witness whereof I have to this my Codicil set my hand and seal, the Twenty fourth day of February, in the Year of our Lord One thousand eight hundred and eighteen.

(Signed) EDMUND FANNING [L. S.].

"Signed, Sealed, published and declared as a Codicil to my last Will and Testament in the presence of

(Sig'd) JNO. BINDON."

"Charles by Divine Providence Archbishop of Canterbury Primate of all England and Metropolitan do by these presents make known to all men that on the Twenty first day of April in the year of our Lord one thousand eight hundred and Eighteen at London before the Worshipful Jesse Adams Doctor of Laws Surrogate of the Right Honorable Sir John Nicholl Knight, Doctor of Laws Master Keeper or Commissary of our Prerogative Court of Canterbury lawfully constituted the last Will and Testament with a Codicil of Edmund Fanning late Governor of Prince Edward Island in North America and of Upper Seymour Street Portman Square in the County of Middlesex Doctor of Laws and a general in his Majesty's Army. Deceased hereunto annexed was proved approved and registered the said deceased having whilst living and at the time of his death Goods Chattels or Credits in divers Dioceses or Jurisdictions by reason whereof the proving and registering the said Will and the granting administration of all and singular the said goods chattels and credits and also the auditing allowing and final discharging the acount thereof are well known to appertain only and wholly to us and not to any Inferior Judge; and that administration of all and singular the Goods Chattels and Credits of the said Deceased and anyway concerning his Will was granted to Phebe Maria Fanning widow the relict and Louisa Augusta Fanning and Maria Susannah Matilda Fanning spinsters the daughters of the said Deceased, three of the Executors named in the said Will they having been already sworn well and faithfully to administer the same, and to make a true and perfect Inventory of all and singular the said Goods Chattels and Credits and to exhibit the same into the Registry of our said Court on or before the last day of October next ensuing and also to render a just and true account thereof. Power reserved of making the like grant to Margaret William Tryon Fanning spinster the daughter also the other executrix when she shall apply for the same. Given at the time and place above written and in the fourteenth year of our translation.

(Signed) GEO. GOSTLING, NATH GOSTLING, R. C. CRESSWELL — Deputy Registrers.

"The above Written Probate was duly registered the 26th day of September 1818 (Sgd.) Robert Gray Judge of Probate."

The Seal of the Prerogative Court of the Archbishop of Canterbury.

THE CONTENTION OF GEN. EDMUND FANNING'S WILL.[1]

Gen. Edmund Fanning's brother, Phineas Fanning, of Long Island, had a son Barclay, a lieutenant in the King's American Regiment in 1777. He afterwards attained the rank of captain and was retired on half pay. He married in Nantucket and died, it is believed, in London. This Capt. Barclay Fanning had a son Edmund, who was born in Nantucket in 1785 and who followed the sea. He visited Prince Edward Island, and stayed with his grand-uncle, the General, for considerable spaces of time. During these visits Gen. Fanning often remarked to him that if he had a son born to him and named him after his (the General's) son, he would remember him in his will. Edmund Fanning, the sea captain, had for his first child a son born at Nantucket 28 December, 1808, whom he named Edmund Frederick Augustus, who like his father followed the sea.

The General by his will devised entail male to his relation, Edmund Frederick Augustus Fanning, whom he therein describes as "a minor son of Capt. Edmund Fanning,

[1] From information furnished by Hon. George Alley, Charlottetown, P. E. I.

Grandson of his deceased affectionate brother, Col. Phineas Fanning, of Long Island," 10,000 acres of land in Township No. 67, two town lots in Charlottetown, and nine pasture lots containing twelve acres each in Charlottetown Royalty, all in Prince Edward Island; also 5,000 acres of land adjoining the land of his father in the State of Vermont; and the Island called Oak Island or Fanning's Island (containing about 1,000 acres) and eight lots in the Town of Fanningsburg (now Wallace) in Nova Scotia. Township No. 67 is one of the sixty-seven townships into which Prince Edward Island was laid off when originally granted by the Crown. It contained in all 28,480 acres, and on May 26, 1829, the boundaries of that portion of it devised to Edmund F. A. Fanning were defined under an agreement entered into between him and the three daughters and co-heiresses of Gen. Fanning.

By deeds of lease and release dated 24th and 25th of September, 1830, and in consideration of $1,200 Edmund F. A. Fanning granted and conveyed to the General's three daughters all the land so devised to him in Prince Edward Island, without barring the entail therein.

In 1844 he commenced legal proceedings to repossess himself of the property he had sold on the plea of his nonage at the time of the sale and conveyance. He employed the late Jonathan Shore of Boston, Mass., to conduct these proceedings, who retained the Hon. James H. Peters, then Solicitor-General of Prince Edward Island, to bring an action of ejectment for the two town lots in order to test the question. With Mr. Peters were associated as counsel the Attorney-General Hon. Robert Hodgson (afterwards Sir Robert Hodgson, Kt.) and Hon. Alexander Stewart, an eminent counsel of Nova Scotia, and afterwards Master of

87

the Rolls of that province. The defendants were represented by Edward Palmer (afterwards Chief Justice of Prince Edward Island) and Hon. James W. Johnston, the Attorney-General and subsequently Equity Judge of Nova Scotia. The grounds of defence were: —

(1) That Fanning had, by various acts after attaining his majority, confirmed the deeds of conveyance.

(2) That he was an alien, and hence not entitled to recover.

A very large outlay was incurred in counsel fees and in obtaining evidence in England and the United States by commissions issued for that purpose and in otherwise preparing for the trial. For various reasons the trial was delayed from term to term until the first of January, 1848, when Fanning died at Oak Island, Nova Scotia, leaving three minor sons surviving him: another son was born after his death. On the 29th of September, 1848, Mr. Peters was raised to the Bench. The conduct of the suit was then transferred to Attorney-General Hodgson and afterwards to Charles Palmer as attorney for the plaintiffs. Mr. Palmer obtained leave to amend the declaration by adding counts in the names of the infant heirs, which in some degree altered the features of the plaintiff's title and of the defence. Attorney-General Sir William Young of Nova Scotia (subsequently Chief Justice Sir William Young of that province) was retained to assist Mr. Palmer.

The appointment of Attorney-General Hodgson as Chief Justice in 1853 operated as an additional barrier to the suit, as the Bench of the Supreme Court was now entirely composed of two of the former counsel for the plaintiff. Added to this Mrs. Fanning, after her husband's death, removed with her young children to Richmond, Ind., and their helpless ages and distant residence as well as her want of pecuniary means tended further to delay the trial. Owing to these reasons proceedings were suffered to lapse for a number of years.

In 1871 proceedings were renewed to recover the property in question at the instance of the sons of Edmund Frederick Augustus Fanning, the youngest of whom had then attained full age. They retained Messrs. Alley and Davies, a firm of leading attorneys in Charlottetown, who took active and energetic measures to enforce the claims of the plaintiffs. Two ejectment suits were at once commenced, one against Lady Wood and Miss Fanning for the recovery of the two town lots in Charlottetown, and the other against John Henry Gates for the recovery of certain pasture lots in Charlottetown Royalty, which he held under a title derived from the General's daughters.

In bringing the former suits it was assumed that Edmund F. A. Fanning was born on the 28th of December, *1809*, but on careful investigation by Messrs. Alley and Davies it was found that the date of his birth was the 28th of December, *1808*, as recorded in the family Bible, and that he was of full age when he executed the conveyances of the lands in question. (See note on page 353.) The following are the grounds upon which the claims of the sons were based: —

(1) That Edmund F. A. Fanning was of age when he executed the lease and release to Lady Wood and the Misses Fanning in 1830, and being tenant in tail, his life interest only passed under the deed, as the entail had never been barred.

(2) That the right of his sons to make an entry or bring an action to recover the lands first accrued at the time of his death on the first of January, 1848; and that as they were all at that time under the disability of infancy, the

Statute of Limitation would not bar their claim until the expiration of ten years after the removal of such disability. That the eldest son, John B. Fanning, was born on the 14th of January, 1842, and became of age on the 13th of January, 1863, and consequently would not be barred from bringing his action until January, 1873.

The surviving daughters of Gen. Fanning, Lady Wood and Miss Fanning, were represented in these suits by Edward Jarvis Hodgson, afterwards one of the Judges of the Supreme Court of Prince Edward Island. The suits were brought to issue and notices of trial were given therein for June, 1871, when the trials were postponed at the instance of the defendants on the ground of the absence of material witnesses. Notice of trial was then immediately renewed in each suit for the next term of the Supreme Court held in January, 1872, and active steps were taken to bring them then peremptorily to trial. Witnesses were brought at great expense from Indiana, Rhode Island and Nova Scotia, but the trials were again postponed owing to the illness of Edward J. Hodgson, the counsel for defendants.

Before this last postponement negotiations were commenced between the attorneys on both sides with a view to compromise. These negotiations led to a settlement being effected, shortly after the sitting of the Court, on the following terms: —

(1) The defendants to give up to the plaintiffs the two town lots immediately.

(2) The defendants to give up, after the death of Lady Wood, so much of the 10,000 acres as was then in their possession. A few hundred acres, it was said, had been disposed of.

(3) No claim for mesne profits to be made.

(4) No claim to be made by the plaintiffs on purchasers of pasture lots, and Lady Wood's title to be confirmed.

(5) Plaintiffs and defendants to pay their own costs.

An agreement embodying these terms was signed by the attorneys on both sides on the 11th of April, 1872. On the following day news was received of the death of Lady Wood who expired on the 19th of March previously. It appeared by later intelligence that under her will, dated 5th of May, 1870, she had devised the lands in litigation as well as all her other lands in Prince Edward Island to the Chief Justice and Attorney-General of said Island, the Rev. Charles Lloyd, B. A., of Englishcombe near Bath, and Edward Jarvis Hodgson, her attorney, in trust, to sell the same except the two town lots and to pay the interest of the proceeds to her sister, Miss Fanning, for life, and after her death, out of one-half the proceeds of such sale to institute an asylum for deaf and dumb persons born in Prince Edward Island, and to apply the other half for the benefit of the Micmac Indians frequenting the said Island; and that the trustees should hold the town lots after the death of Miss Fanning to build thereon the said asylum for the deaf and dumb.

This state of affairs gave rise to new complications in the carrying out of the agreement previously made, and necessitated proceedings in Chancery against Miss Fanning and the trustees of Lady Wood's will for specific performance of its terms. A suit was accordingly brought to which no defence was entered, and a decree was made vesting in the heirs of Edmund F. A. Fanning all the estate of Lady Wood and Miss Fanning in the lands embraced in the agreement, and directing that the trustees under Lady Wood's will should be the trustees of the said land and should hold the same for the claimants pursuant to the terms of the agreement. After the particular farms in Township No. 67 were set off for the Fanning heirs under the direction of the Court, in order to make up the 10,000 acres, there still remained subject to Lady Wood's will 2,889 acres in the Township as well as a number of town and pasture lots held by her at the time of her death. The 10,000 acres awarded to the Fanning brothers were sold by them to the government of Prince Edward Island for $25,250 on the 5th of January, 1877. The two town lots were sold at auction and realized $6,000.

With regard to the remainder of Lady Wood's lands in Prince Edward Island as herein stated the trusts of the will are up to the present time unexecuted. Rev. Charles Lloyd expressly renounced the trusteeship, and the other trustees have not actively assumed the duties devolving on them.

Of the sons of Edmund Frederick Augustus Fanning, John B., the eldest, died intestate and without issue, during the pendency of the litigation. The fund derived from the sale of the Prince Edward Island lands was therefore divided between his surviving brothers, William W., Sylvester H., and Edmund F. A. Fanning.

THE MEMBERS OF GEN. EDMUND FANNING'S FAMILY WHO SURVIVED HIM.

The widow of Gen. Fanning died at Bath, England, on the 7th of May, 1853. Her remains were interred at Lansdown, Somersetshire.

In 1849 the house in which Gen. Fanning and his family resided in Charlottetown, Prince Edward Island, was destroyed by fire. Among the few articles saved was the fly-leaf of the family Bible, the only unburned portion thereof. The entries on this fly-leaf were in the handwriting of Gen. Fanning, and contained the records of his marriage and the baptism of his eldest child: —

"This is to certify that Colonel Fanning, Lieutenant Governor of Nova Scotia, was married to Miss Phebe Maria Burns on the 30th day of November 1785 by him who is with great Respect and Esteem his most faithful and very humble servant,

J. W. WEEKS.

A true copy verbatim & literatim.
Attest — EDMD. FANNING.

"This is to certify to whomsoever it may concern that Louisa Augusta Fanning daughter of his Excellency Lieut. Governor Fanning & Phebe Maria Fanning his Wife was baptised by me at Point Pleasant on Sunday 22nd October 1786 in the Parish of St. Pauls and Province of Nova Scotia.

J. W. WEEKS, Minister
of sd Parish &c.

A true copy literatim.
Attest — EDMD. FANNING."

The paper containing these memoranda remained successively in the possession of Mrs. Fanning and her daughters until their deaths, when, with other family papers, it passed into the hands of relatives. Copies of these papers are on file in the High Court of Justice, Chancery Division, London, England.

Louisa Augusta, the eldest child of Gen. Fanning, married Sir Gabriel Wood, a Commissary in the British Army. He died without issue at Bath, England, on the 29th of October, 1845, and was buried at Lansdown. In accordance with the provisions of his will the Sir Gabriel Wood's Mariners' Asylum of Greenock, Scotland, was founded by his widow, Lady Wood, and his sister, Miss Frances Ann Wood of Greenock, as a harbor of refuge for aged seamen.

These estimable ladies retained a potential voice in the administration of the asylum during their lives, always exercising their powers with much zeal and discrimination, besides generously contributing to the endowment of the institution.

Lady Wood died at Bath on Tuesday, the 19th of March, 1872, in the eighty-sixth year of her age, and was buried at Lansdown on the 26th of March. In the obituary notice of her the *Bath Express* said: — "By the death of Lady Wood the poor of this city and elsewhere have lost an ever kind and liberal friend and many charitable institutions an uniform supporter." When apprised of her death the trustees of the Sir Gabriel Wood Asylum ordered hour flags to be displayed on the institution. The same ceremony was performed at the Mid Church by order of the magistrates, and the ships in the harbor of Greenock showed their flags at halfmast until after the hour fixed for her interment.

Lady Wood's will, which is very lengthy, contains a number of charitable bequests; all her property in Prince Edward Island being devised (after the death of her sister Maria) to founding a deaf and dumb asylum in that island and aiding the Micmac Indians.

Mariah Susanna Matilda, the third child of Gen. Fanning, resided at Bath after her father's death, where she died unmarried on the 6th of February, 1879, in the eighty-eighth year of her age, and was buried at Lansdown. (See pp. 167 and 168.)

The following is a copy of her last will and testament: —

"This is the last will and testament of me Maria Susanna Matilda Fanning formerly of No. 3 the Circus, Bath, in the County of Somerset but now of No. 4 Royal Crescent, Bath aforesaid, spinster, and I hereby revoke all other wills by me heretofore made and appointing my dear sister Margaret William Tryon

Cumberland wife of Lt. Col. Bentinck Harry Cumberland of Enham Lodge, Leamington, Warwickshire and William Ford Esquire of South Square, Grays Inn, London, Solicitor, to be Executors of this my last will.

"Firstly I direct that all my just debts shall be paid as soon as they conveniently may be after my decease. To each of my Executors above named I give respectively the sum of £150 each. To my Brother-in-law Lt. Col. Bentinck Harry Cumberland I give and bequeath the sum of £500 for his life, and at his decease the same sum to be conveyed to my God Son Robert Bruce Walsand third son of the late Rev. Theodore Augustus Walsand of Lee in the County of Kent, absolutely. I also give and bequeath to my cousin William Fanning Wickham, of Hanover Court House, Hanover County, near Richmond, Virginia, in the United States of America, the sum of £500 absolutely and eventually all my plate engraved with the arms of Fanning. I give and bequeath to my sister Margaret William Tryon Cumberland all my trinkets, wardrobe and personal property of every kind. As to the personal property of my sister the late Dame Louisa Augusta Wood omitted to be disposed of by her said will which may have devolved upon me and my sister Mrs. Cumberland as next of kin to the said Dame Louisa Augusta Wood, I give and bequeath my share of the same and upon the decease of my sister Mrs. Cumberland the same to be conveyed to the Trustees for the time being of the Asylum or Institution established by the said Dame Louisa Augusta Wood and the late Miss Frances Ann Wood near Greenock called Sir Gabriel Woods Mariners Asylum to be held by their heirs, survivors and assigns upon and for the like trusts and purposes as are declared in and by a Deed of Constitution dated the 23rd day of May 1854 and a Deed of Alteration dated the 15th day of January 1858. The amount of the general Bequests and expenses contingent on the execution of this my last will and testament to be defrayed out of my Russian Bonds of 1862 and the amount awarded me by the Land Commissioners under the Land Purchase Act of Prince Edward Island in 1875. The balance I bequeath to my sister Mrs. Cumberland for her lifetime and at her decease to be conveyed to the Trustees of the Institution of the deaf and dumb in Prince Edward Island, British North America. Lastly I revoke all former or other wills or testamentary dispositions by me made at any time heretofore and declare this to be my last will and testament.

"In Witness whereof I have hereunto set my hand this 24th day of March 1879.

MARIA SUSANNA MATILDA FANNING."

" Witness. CHARLES COWARD CLARK
70 Miles Building, Bath.
LUCY ANDERTON LOYDS Maid
4 Royal Crescent."

"In Faith and Testimony whereof these letters Testimonial are issued.

"Given at London as to the time of the aforesaid search and the sealing of these Presents this 14th day of October 1879.

"This exemplification was filed and registered on 3rd September 1880.

CHARLES YOUNG
Judge of Probate."

Margaret William Tryon, the fourth and youngest child of Gen. Fanning, was married to Capt. Bentinck Harry Cumberland of the 96th Regiment of Infantry in the British army, on the 23d of November, 1833, in All Saints' Church, Parish of Marylebone, London, England. Shortly after the marriage they went to Prince Edward Island, where Capt. Cumberland was commandant of the garrison at Charlottetown. By the marriage the Captain acquired Township No. 65, a tract of about 20,000 acres of land near Charlottetown which was let to tenants on long leases. Capt. Cumberland and his wife lived on a fine farm at the entrance to Charlottetown harbor known as Warren Farm. Here they resided until 1858, when they returned to England, where Capt. Cumberland attained the rank of Lieutenant-Colonel. He died at his residence, Enham Lodge, Leamington, Warwickshire, on the 30th of June, 1880, without issue.

The Hon. George Alley, at present a County Judge of Prince Edward Island, gives the following account of Capt. Cumberland: — "I knew Capt. Cumberland and his wife very well. The Captain was a very tall, handsome, and well-proportioned man of striking appearance. He had two pronounced characteristics — stammering and swearing. He was also professedly a very devout man, and he obliged all his farm servants to attend family prayers conducted by him night and morning. I have understood that after his return to England his fine appearance and soldierlike bearing attracted the attention of the Duke of Cambridge, the Commander-in-chief, at a military review which the Captain attended as a spectator. Through the Duke's influence he was reinstated in the army with a lieutenant-colonel's commission."

By his will dated the first of February, 1876, Lieut.-Col. Cumberland bequeathed all his lands and personal estate to the use of his dear wife, Margaret William Tryon Cumberland, and his nephews Col. Charles Edward Cumberland, R. E., and the Rev. Henry Cumberland Stuart, upon trust, to sell with his wife's consent all such estate as shall not consist of money. He left to his niece, Adela Russell Cumberland, the income arising from his Prince Edward property. By a codicil dated the 3d of April, 1879, he directed that the sum of £1,000, in lieu of the Prince Edward property, which he had sold, should be held in trust, the income arising therefrom to be applied to the use of his niece, Adela Russell Cumberland, during her life, and the said sum to be thereafter divided among her children in such manner as she may by her last will direct.

The will with the codicil was proved at London on the 17th of November, 1881, by Margaret William Tryon, the widow, and the Rev. Henry Cumberland Stuart, two of the executors to whom letters of administration were granted.

Mrs. Margaret William Tryon Cumberland, the last descendant of Gen. Edmund Fanning, died at Enham Lodge in April, 1887. (See Appendix *H*.)

JOHN[4] FANNING (No. 59).

(For Genealogical data, see p. 113.)

John Fanning, eldest son of John and Deborah (Parke) Fanning, was born in Groton, Conn., in 1717 or 1718. His father died while he was an infant, and his grandfather, Lieut. John Fanning, with whom he resided on Fort Hill until maturity, was appointed his guardian. He inherited from his grandfather at his death in 1738–9 the greater part of the Fort Hill farm, estimated at 114½ acres, the southern part of the farm being left to the Lieutenant's four daughters. John Fanning sold his share with the homestead buildings thereon, for £1600 to Deacon Nathan Smith, 23 April, 1744.

On the 5th of March, 1745–6, he bought of John Dunbar a fifty-acre farm in Groton with dwelling-house and sawmill at Burnett's Corners (now so called).[1] The sawmill was later known as the Crary sawmill, and was afterwards used as a gun shop and is now a machine shop owned by Minor Bacon. It is on the road leading north from Burnett's Corners, about a quarter of a mile from the centre of the village.

The dwelling-house was located where Minor Bacon's house now stands, but was torn down previous to 1806, the year of the erection of the present building. A few rods east of this is the Jabez Watrous house, built in 1829.

On the 27th of Aug., 1746, John Fanning bought of Thomas Chipman 57 acres more adjoining his farm in two tracts, one of 20 and the other of 37 acres,[2] thus increasing his farm to 107 acres. His purchase had a grist-mill, fulling-

[1] *Vide* Groton Deeds, Book 5, p. 87.

[2] *Vide* Groton Deeds, Book 5, p. 88.

mill and "mansion" house on it. The grist-mill has since been made into a ropewalk, and is now owned by Dr. Leander Barber. The fulling-mill was east of the grist-mill on Mill Brook, and was afterwards made into a sash and blind factory, but was long ago torn down.

The mansion house purchased with this tract was on the south side of the road to Old Mystic, directly opposite the house now owned and occupied by Miss Lucy Houch, but was torn down many years ago. The old well remains and the site of the building is easily discernible. He purchased 23 Dec., 1749, of Peter Crary, Junior, thirteen acres of land for £265.[1] This land adjoined his other property on the south side of the post-road, and was easterly of it, extending to the brook. In his deed, Crary reserved a spot four rods square, where "the Bodyes of some persons Lyes Interred for the use of a bureing place." John Fanning operated this mill property only a few years, however. The fifty acres he sold to Daniel Fish 10 Nov., 1749, for £1250.[2] Forty acres, which included the thirteen acres purchased of Peter Crary and part of the land purchased of Thomas Chipman, he sold 8 Oct., 1750, to Henry Williams for £2450.[3] Sixteen acres had previously been sold 10 Nov., 1746, to Peter Crary for £139.[4] In the forty-acre tract is located the Crary burying-ground just south of the post-road. The west line of the entire property south of the post-road extended from the "Corners" south by Mystic highway about eighty rods, thence east, and thence north eighty rods, to Mill Brook, thence down the brook, joining the thirteen acres bought of

[1] *Vide* Groton Deeds, Book 4, p. 205.
[2] *Vide* Groton Deeds, Book 5, p. 95.
[3] *Vide* Groton Deeds, Book 5, p. 105.
[4] *Vide* Groton Deeds, Book 5, p. 119.

Peter Crary. The south bound of the farm was Mill Brook. A brook also formed the east bound of that portion south of the post-road.

After selling his property at Burnett's Corners, John Fanning purchased a house lot with building thereon, at Noank. It was the 4th lot in the first tier, first division of lots laid out to the inhabitants of Groton in 1712, and originally granted to Samuel Rogers. Fanning bought it of Samuel Clark 22 Dec., 1752, and resided thereon a few years.[1]

There his daughter, Lucy Fanning Watson, was born in 1755. In March, 1756, he sold the property for £100 to Deacon James Morgan, who[2] owned the lot adjoining northerly (No. 5) having bought it in 1720 of Lieut. John Fanning.

After disposing of his Noank lot, he removed to Stonington village, and, preferring commerce to agriculture, entered into mercantile business, and became the owner of several vessels.

He eventually failed, and, selling out, he left Stonington with his family, intending to establish himself on Otter Creek, Vt., but owing to the difficulties of travelling in those days, advanced no further than Walpole, N. H.,[3] where he settled. After a few years' residence in New Hampshire, becoming discontented, he descended the Connecticut River with his family, and located at Little Egg Harbor, N. J.

While residing there the war of the Revolution broke out.

---

[1] Mayflower Descendant, page 105. Extract from Diary of Jabez Fitch, Junior, March, 1757: "ye 14th I went to Noanck With Brother to Se Jno Fanens Child that was Scolt, then to Sam^{ll} Burrowss to John Lathams Thos Walworths then Home With Him. Trimd Some Peech trees, at Night a Company of ye Nabors was there Thos. Eldridge & His wife & Jos^{h} Burrows Staid all Night Singing Anough we Had."

[2] *Vide* Groton Deeds, Book 4, p. 213.

[3] *Vide* History of Walpole, N. H., by George Aldrich, published at Claremont, N. H., 1880., pp. 37 to 40.

Imbued with the patriotic fervor which animated his family, he immediately embarked in the cause of the struggling colonies. He built and fitted out a privateer, but had commanded her only a few days when he was captured by a British cruiser and transferred to the Stromboli prison ship in New York Harbor, where he died in 1781. His three sons, who were officers in the American Navy, also met untimely deaths. His widow, Abigail, died at Little Egg Harbor, N. J., 27 Sept., 1777, of the "dead palsey."

The Stromboli prison ship, on which John Fanning died, was an old transport changed into a floating prison for captured American seamen and anchored near Paulus Hook. The sufferings of these prisoners were almost indescribable. Their food consisted of an insufficient supply of mouldy biscuit, sour flour and meal, damaged peas, and condemned beef and pork which was boiled in a large copper kettle. They were imprisoned in the hold, which reeked with filth and vermin, the prisoners being allowed no opportunity to clean it. Every morning the harsh command came below, "Rebels, turn out your dead." The dead were selected, each sewn in his blanket, if he had one, and thus conveyed in a boat to the shore by his companions under a guard, and hastily buried. Every morning the prisoners brought their bedding on deck to be aired. After washing the decks, they were allowed to remain above until sunset, when they were ordered below with the savage command, "Down, Rebels, down," and the hatches closed. In the latter years of the war the Stromboli was used as an hospital ship.

Captain William Watson, the husband of John Fanning's youngest daughter Lucy, was imprisoned on board this ship for some time. On the 10th of November, 1781, his house at Burlington, N. J., was set on fire and himself taken prisoner by the infamous refugee, Joe Mulliner, who carried him to the New York provost, by whom he was lodged in prison: but becoming sick from ill treatment, he was transferred to the Stromboli hospital ship, in which he was detained until exchanged on the 10th of March following. Joe Mulliner was afterwards hanged at Burlington for his numerous crimes.

The name of Abigail, wife of John Fanning, appears on the church records at Groton, Conn., where she was received into full communion 8 Nov., 1743.

CAPTAIN THOMAS[4] FANNING (No. 60).

(For Genealogical data, see page 182.)

Captain Thomas Fanning was born in Groton, Conn., in 1719. The same year his father, John Fanning, Junior, prematurely died from the severing of an artery in his leg, leaving Thomas and an elder brother, John, both mere infants. Thomas was placed under the guardianship of his grandfather, William Park, of Preston, by the Probate Court at New London, 25 July, 1722, and John under that of his grandfather, Lieut. John Fanning, of Groton.

When of a suitable age, Thomas was apprenticed to the carpentry trade, which he successfully followed for several years. On the death of his grandfather Fanning in 1739, he received a legacy of five pounds sterling; the homestead property on Fort Hill and all its appurtenances being left to his elder brother John. Thomas inherited, however, from his grandfather, William Park, half of his farm of 190 acres, that lay partly in Preston, partly in Groton, and partly in Stonington, and which now forms part of the Appleton Main farm.

After marrying Elizabeth, daughter of Walter and Hope (Whipple) Capron, in 1744, Thomas purchased of Deacon Jonathan Brewster of Preston 24 January, 1746–7, for £1600 a farm of one hundred acres "with a new barn thereon," situated in the northern part of Groton (now Ledyard) near the Preston line, at a place now called Shewville. This one hundred acres was part of Captain Joseph Latham's two hundred acre grant, that he sold to Deacon Brewster in 1739.[1] It is seven miles southeast of Norwich, and adjoins the lo-

[1] *Vide* Groton Deeds, Book 4, p. 71.

cality known as Preston Plains. He no doubt built during that year the house now standing on this property, which may therefore rightly be called one of the oldest Fanning houses remaining. It is on the northeasterly side of the road, right in the middle of this little hamlet or factory village. In fact, this is about the only farmhouse there, the remaining buildings being the Post Office, sawmill, and buildings attached to them, and a dozen small houses connected with the mill property. Pine trees stand in front of the farmhouse; and the entrance, which was in early times at the southeast end, is now on the southwest side, facing the road which runs southeast and northwest. The old stone chimney, which originally occupied the centre of the building, was removed some years ago for need of room, and in its place a modern chimney erected. Otherwise the house is little changed from its early appearance.

Thomas built a sawmill on Poquetanuck River, which ran through the farm near his dwelling-house. This sawmill was known for many years as Fanning's Sawmill. It remained a sawmill until after Elisha Ayer, Senior's, ownership, when at his death in 1853, other mills were added to the property. A shingle-mill and grist-mill were constructed, as well as a woollen-mill and blacksmith shop, and buildings for carding machinery, clothiers' work, and wagon-making.

In 1762 Thomas Fanning added to his farm fifty-four acres, which he bought of Ebenezer Avery, but in 1770 he disposed of thirty acres to John Avery, leaving his farm in extent about one hundred and twenty acres.

Thomas Fanning was prominent in town affairs, his name appearing on the Groton records at nearly all the meetings. He held many offices of trust and honor. In 1752 he was chosen Surveyor of Highways, which position he filled for

The old Homestead of Capt. Thomas and Elizabeth (Capron) Fanning,
Shewville, Conn. as it appeared in 1898.

fourteen years. He was Selectman in 1775 and 1776, during the troublesome times of the Revolutionary War. On the 10th of October, 1765, the General Assembly of the Colony of Connecticut appointed him 1st Lieutenant of the 5th Company or "Trainband" in the town of Groton, and in October, 1771, he was appointed Captain.

At the outbreak of the Revolution he espoused with heart and soul the cause of his native land, and opened the first recruiting office in the State of Connecticut, afterward appointed by the Government. Being too old for active service, the Government continued him in the recruiting department. He was, however, well represented in the field, as five of his six sons, inflamed by the enthusiasm of their father, took up arms in defence of American liberty; the sixth being too young to bear arms, as he was only ten years of age and an invalid. Of the five sons who did enlist, Frederick was only seventeen, Elkanah nineteen, and Thomas twenty-two years of age at the time.

At Captain Thomas Fanning's death in December, 1787, the widow Elizabeth was appointed administratrix by the Probate Court at Stonington, but she declined to serve, and upon her suggestion letters of administration were granted to her son, Captain Charles Fanning, of Preston, 24 December, 1787, who executed the trust.

The homestead farm passed from the heirs to Frederick Fanning, he buying out the rights of his brothers in 1789, and occupying the premises. Captain Thomas' son, Elisha, daughters Hope and Prudence and the Widow Elizabeth, retained their equity in the property. On the 25th April, 1793, Frederick Fanning sold the farm of 136 acres, excepting above equity, to Elisha Ayer, Senior, who married his sister Hope. The house was not occupied, however, by him, but by his sons, Elisha, Junior, and Frederick Ayer. By will of Elisha Ayer, Senior, who died 20 June, 1853, the Fanning farm with the exception of four acres, including the Mill, which he ordered to be sold, descended to his grandchildren, James, Frederick, and Lovisa Ayer, children of Frederick. The two former gave their share to their sister Lovisa, who married Arden Moffitt, and who thereupon occupied the homestead. Elisha and Frederick Ayer lived at the Fanning homestead until the latter's death in 1821. Elisha then moved to Northampton, Mass. Later the farm was sold to Philip Karoli, who occupies it at the present time, 1904. (See photogravure of house.) Captain Charles Fanning, as administrator of Captain Thomas Fanning's estate, sold the sawmill and privileges attached to same and also eighteen acres of land on Poquetanuck Brook to Captain Frederick Fanning, his brother, 15 April, 1790. Frederick sold the sawmill and dam privileges to Joseph Latham of Groton for £50. Latham died about, or previous to, 1799, and willed the mill and privileges to his sons Jonas, Cyrus, and William Latham, who disposed of it in 1806 and 1808, to William Witter of Preston. Witter sold it to Thomas Hallet of Groton, 24 May, 1809, and Hallet to Elisha Ayer, Senior, of Groton, 16 February, 1814.

Elisha Ayer also bought one-fourth of an acre of land with dwelling-house adjoining the mill property on the west side of the brook. He owned and operated the mills until his death in 1853. The mill property was then sold to Ebenezer Stoddard. From him it passed to the Brown Brothers, and they sold it to A. P. Sturtevant of New York (proprietor of the well-known hotel, the Sturtevant House), and from whose son-in-law, Mr. Shew, the factory village received its name, "Shewville." The Sturtevant heirs have since that time sold their interest in the property it is stated.

Captain Thomas Fanning died intestate at Groton on the 15th of December, 1787, in the 68th year of his age, and was buried in the Preston Plains Cemetery, where his gravestone still stands (1904).

The distribution of his property is found on the Stonington Probate Records.

The inventory of his estate, taken 30 January, 1788, filed 5 February following, amounted to £815–16*s*.–5*d*., of which amount £562–10*s*.–0*d*. represented the farm with dwelling-house, "sawmill and Irons" and all other buildings.

After Captain Thomas Fanning's decease, his widow, Elizabeth (Capron) Fanning, continued to reside at the old homestead, which was aptly spoken of in 1803 as being "at the head of Groton." Her sons Thomas and Elisha, and Thomas' wife, Susannah Faulkner, resided with her (with the exception of two or three years) until her decease, which occurred 27 April, 1810. She was buried beside her husband in the family plot, in the old Avery Pond burying-ground, better known as the Preston Plains Cemetery. Her gravestone still remains.

Her will, dated 20 February, 1810, proved 7 August, 1810, is on file at Stonington, a copy of which follows;[1]

"In the name of God Amen, I Elizabeth Fanning of Groton in the County of New London although Labouring at Present under some Indisposition of body yet being of sound and disposing mind memory and understanding through the mercy of God do make and ordain this my last will and Testament in manner and form following. First and Principally I Resign my soul with the utmost humility into the hands of almighty god my creator humbly hoping for a Blessed immortality through the merits and mediation of my Blessed Saviour and Redeemer Jesus Christ

[1] *Vide* Stonington Probate Records, Book 8, p. 155.

and my body I desire may be decently buried at the discretion of my executor as near as conveniently may be to my late dear husband and as for such temporal estate as the lord in his great goodness and mercy hath entrusted me to be steward of I give and dispose of as follows

"I give and bequeath to my daughter Prudence Tracy one dark chintz gound two pair sheets, one pare pillow cases Likewise my chintz Loose gound and camblet riding hood.

"I give to my daughter hopey Ayer one large table cloth.

"I give to my daughter in Law Susannah Fanning wife of Thomas Fanning one bed, bedstead underbed & cord, a pr Pillows & Cases two pr sheets one Callico bed quilt and bed curtains Also one high case of drawers and Table likewise all my chairs.

"I give to my two grandsons Benjamin Fanning the son of Walter Faning and Alphred Fanning the son of Thomas Fanning all my notes and dues of whatsoever kind nature name Likewise all the moneys that I may be Posesed of (after deducting my honest debts and funeral expenses) to be equally divided between them.

"I give to my grand Daughter Catherine Clark daughter of Walter Fanning my gold Neck lace and black cambrick gown likewise three diaper napkins.

"I give to my Grand daughter Elizabeth Fanning daughter of Walter Fanning my side saddle Likewise one pr Sheets one pr Pillow Cases and three Diaper napkins.

"I give to my grand daughter Polly Fanning daughter of said Thomas Fanning my best bed bedstead under bed & Cord one pr Pillow Cases one paire sheets and Brown bed quilt.

"I give to my grand daughter Fanny Ayer one of my large pewter Platters and three puter plates.

"I give to my grand daughter hopey Ayer my other Large puter Platter and three Pewter plates one large Pewter Bason also one Large Flower[d] delph platter, and one two Quart glass and my Silver Sizers Chain

"All the Rest and residue of my estate whatsoever and wheresoever I give devise and bequeath to my said daughter in Law Susannah Fanning and I declare this to be my only last will & testament and do appoint my Friend Thomas Hallet Executor thereof In witness whereof I have hereunto set my hand and seal this 20 day of February 1810

Signed Sealed published and Delivered by the said Testator as and for her last will and Testament

JONAH WITTER
SAMUEL HALLET

her
ELIZABETH X FANNING"
mark

CODICIL TO WILL OF ELIZABETH FANNING.

"Since it has Pleased almighty God to deprive my dear child Elisha Fanning of natural mental abilities sufficient to take care of himself and when deprived of my parental care It is my earnest desire and Request and my only legacy to him that he may be taken care of by my Daughter in Law Susannah Fanning.

her
ELIZABETH X FANNING."
mark

In presence of
JONAH WITTER
SAM'LL HALLET

New London County ss. Groton May 14,1810 Personally appeared Jonah Witter Esq & Samuel Hallet both of Lawfull Age & testified under solemn oath that they were present & saw Elizabeth Fanning the foregoing testator to this will sign seal & execute the foregoing will & that they heard her declare & Pronounce the same to be her Last will & testament that they then Looked upon her to be of sound mind & memory that she desired them to set to their hands as witnesses & that they did Set to their hands at that time as witnesses in Presence of the testator & in presence of each other

"Sworn before me Isaac Avery Justice of peace."

DR. JAMES COOK AYER,

Grandson of Elisha and Hope (Fanning) Ayer (No. 161).

(For Genealogical data, see page 190.)

James Cook Ayer, M.D., was born in that part of Groton, Conn., which is now the town of Ledyard, on the 5th of May, 1819. He was one of five children of Frederick and Persis (Cook) Ayer, and his early years were passed at what was known as Ayer's Mills, on the Poquetanuck River, where his father operated the works in various lines of industry which had been established two generations before, and since maintained in the family. Frederick Ayer died in 1825, leaving his widow with four children. Lowell, Mass., was where the subject of this sketch received the foundation of his education in the grammar and high schools of that place, and at Westford Academy. Desirous of obtaining a liberal education, he pursued the study of Latin and Greek and other required branches under tuition with the intention of entering Harvard University, but circumstances prevented the full carrying-out of his plans, and he finally relinquished them to take up the study of chemistry and medicine, in which he was directed by Drs. Dana and Graves, well-known Lowell physicians of that period. In the meantime he entered the apothecary shop of Jacob Robbins as an apprentice, and this establishment he purchased three years later, in 1841. He took his medical degree at the University of Pennsylvania.

In order to establish himself in business he was obliged to borrow the sum of $2,500, but this venture was the beginning of his later prosperity. He was one of the first in this country to enter into the compounding and sale of proprietary medicines on a large scale, and he was also an

J. C. Ayer

innovator in his methods and proportions of advertising, often borrowing, it is said, large sums of money to be expended in this way, which returned him marvellous results. The suggestion to engage in this enterprise came through the demand for specifics from emigrants who were about to settle in the West and other remote places where the services of a physician could not be obtained; and in response to this call Dr. Ayer prepared from certain formulas of his own the preparations widely known as Cherry Pectoral, Sarsaparilla, Ague Cure, Ayer's Pills, etc., the immediate success of which induced him to devote his energies and time almost wholly for a period to their manufacture. He established and maintained the extensive laboratory in Lowell which increased in proportions until three hundred persons were employed. His Almanac, published in several languages to advertise his medicines, reached in some years a circulation of fifteen millions of copies.

His enterprise and clear judgment were not, however, exhibited in this direction alone, for he engaged in many other undertakings, the uniform success of which proved his business acumen, foresight and originality. In 1861 he purchased several plantations at Hilton Head in Georgia, and engaged in the raising of sea island cotton, employing black labor on the wage system, and this was a revelation to the Southern people, for he produced larger crops with free labor than the masters had been able to force from their slaves.

In 1865 Dr. Ayer invented methods for disintegrating and desulphurizing rock by liquid applied while incandescent, by which means the ore could readily be extracted. The patents he sold for large sums.

Later he was interested in supplying the city of Rochester, N. Y., with water from Hemlock Lake, and afterwards was connected with the project of a ship canal at Lake Superior, opening a route by which over one hundred miles of dangerous navigation was saved, and this great enterprise was mainly suggested by him. He became a large owner in the Lake Superior Ship Canal and Iron Co., which built the canal. He also acquired large interest in the Tremont and Suffolk Mills in Lowell, and operated them with success after they had become bankrupt and idle under former management. In addition he assumed various other responsibilities, most of which resulted to his benefit.

In 1874 Dr. Ayer received the Republican nomination for Congress from the Lowell District, but failed of election as did several other Republicans that year, a Democratic tidal wave passing over the country.

Dr. Ayer's benefactions to Lowell and to the town named in his honor were notable, a fine town hall in Ayer commemorating his generosity.

Although he devoted his life in so large a measure to business and to the accumulation of wealth, Dr. Ayer did not neglect self-culture and mental improvement. He had great love for science, literature and art, and he was a scholar of uncommon attainments. He was familiar with several languages, and at the age of fifty learned Portuguese. He spoke French fluently, and was a student of the classics. He collected a large and valuable library. He died on the 3d of July, 1878, at the early age of fifty-nine, his life being undoubtedly shortened by his strenuous endeavor and unresting application to the many and diverse interests and responsibilities with which he was connected. He left a fortune aggregating many millions.

LIEUTENANT NATHANIEL[6] FANNING (No. 110).

(For Genealogical data see page 249.)

Nathaniel Fanning, eldest son of Gilbert and Huldah (Palmer) Fanning, was born at Stonington, Conn., 31 May, 1755. Early imbued with the idea that the independence of the American Colonies would redound to the advantage of the people, he took an active and decided part in favor of his native land.

After having made two successful cruises against the British, he embarked on the third at Boston as prizemaster of the brig Angelica on the 26th of May, 1778. The Angelica was a new vessel, mounting sixteen guns and carrying a crew of ninety-eight officers, men and boys, under command of Captain William Denison. On the 31st of May the Angelica was captured by the British man-of-war Andromeda on board of which was General Howe on a return voyage to England. By orders of Howe the captured crew were treated with great cruelty as rebels. They were deprived of their baggage, stripped of their clothes, and being furnished with frocks and trousers, imprisoned in the hold. The Angelica was then set on fire and blown up.

The sufferings of the imprisoned crew from heat and foul air, while confined in the hold of the Andromeda, was almost unbearable. So intense was the heat that they were obliged to go stark naked. Orders were issued by General Howe that they be given only sufficient food to keep them alive and a half-pint of water per day for each man.

The day succeeding their capture a plan was set on foot by the surgeon of the Angelica by which they hoped to make themselves masters of the frigate. The plan was to be put into execution on the 3d of June at 11.30 P.M. Many of the crew of the Andromeda were dissatisfied with their officers. The surgeon had frequent conversations with forecastlemen and sentinels, who agreed to join him in his daring scheme. Arms and cutlasses were secretly conveyed to the prisoners, and all was in readiness when the plot was discovered. At 9 P.M. on the 3d of June one Spencer, Captain Denison's clerk, stole on deck and informed General Howe of the intended attack. The marines and sailors were instantly called to arms, the lower hatches barred down, and the sentinels doubled.

The condition of the prisoners would have been unbearable had they not discovered that they were lodged over the water casks. From this source they obtained an abundant supply by a proof glass. Soon after they discovered that only a plank partition separated them from General Howe's storeroom. They soon made a breach in this partition and obtained food and wine every night, on which they lived during the remainder of the voyage.

On the 30th of June they arrived at Portsmouth, where the prisoners were examined by Commissioners of the Admiralty, by whom they were committed to Forton prison, near Gosport, on charges of piracy and high treason. Here they were watched by peasants with dogs, who received a reward of £5 for the capture of an escaping American, but only half a guinea for the capture of a French prisoner of war. In this prison the Americans were treated with extreme rigor and cruelty. On the 2d of July, 1779, it was the good fortune of Nathaniel Fanning to be included in an exchange of prisoners. On the 6th one hundred and twenty of the four hundred and eighty American prisoners at Forton were marched to Gosport, preceded by a fife and drum band, playing Yankee Doodle, and embarked on a cartel which arrived at Nantes on the 12th. From Nantes Nathaniel Fanning proceeded to L'Orient, where he took service under John Paul Jones as midshipman and private secretary. On the 14th of August, 1779, Jones sailed from L'Orient on the Bon Homme Richard, mounting forty guns, and carrying a crew of four hundred and fifteen officers, men and boys. On the 16th the Richard took as prize a large English ship laden with bales of silk and other valuable merchandise, which was sent to France in charge of a prize crew. On the 21st Jones captured eleven English vessels. One, being valuable, was sent to France: the others were sunk. On the 22d he captured a letter of marque of 22 guns without resistance. The companion ship, Alliance, Captain Landais, captured a letter of marque of 24 guns the same day. Both were sent to France. Jones next cruised around the Orkney Islands, where he burned and otherwise destroyed sixteen vessels. He next directed his course to the southeast coast of Scotland, where he burned four large vessels laden with coal.

At noon of the 23d of September, while cruising off Flamborough Head, the Bon Homme Richard, having in company the Alliance and Pallas frigates, sighted a fleet of forty-two sail which proved to be merchantmen under the convoy of the British ship Serapis of fifty guns, commanded by Captain Pearson, and the frigate Countess of Scarborough, twenty-two guns, commanded by Captain Percy. On sighting Captain Jones' ships, orders were signalled to the merchant vessels to disperse and make for port. At 4 P.M., after sighting the enemy's ships, signals were immediately displayed on the Richard, as the Commodore's ship, for a general chase. The officers were assigned to their duties;

Richard Dale, the first lieutenant, being assigned to duty on the second, or middle, gundeck, where he nobly distinguished himself during the ensuing fight by his coolness and bravery. Nathaniel Fanning, who had received command of the maintop from Jones, was ordered on the quarterdeck, as were the captains of the fore and mizzen tops, both very young midshipmen, neither of them being above seventeen years. Here they received orders from Jones in person to the effect that at first and until the enemy's tops were silenced they should direct their fire from the Richard's tops to the enemy's tops with musketry, blunderbusses, cowhorns and swivels. Having received their orders, they mounted to their stations, fifteen marines and four sailors being assigned to Fanning as captain of the maintop, ten marines and three sailors to the captain of the foretop, and six marines and two sailors to the captain of the mizzentop.

The following account of the noted and bloody battle between the Bon Homme Richard under the command of John Paul Jones, and the British ship Serapis, commanded by Captain Pearson, is from the pen of Nathaniel Fanning, who served as captain of the maintop during the engagement on the 23d of September, 1779:—

"A few minutes before 8 P.M. we had nearly closed within hailing distance of the enemy which now plainly showed her double row of teeth. Orders were given by the Commodore (Jones) to haul up our courses and clew up the topgallant sails; at the same time directing by signal for the Alliance to support us.

"At first she kept aloof out of gun-shot, and afterwards, when she came up, she so badly performed as to do us more hurt than she did the enemy.

"The Pallais was also directed to attack the small ship. The enemy now hailed thus: 'What ship is that?' The answer from Captain Jones was: 'Come a little nearer and I'll tell you!' The enemy instantly commenced the fight by a broadside from her upper tier, we returning it with ours, as well as musquetry, etc. In a few minutes we were convinced that the ship we had engaged was a two-decker, and more than our match as we had by this time received several of her eighteen-pound shot, through and through our ship; and to add to our hard fortune, the first time three of our eighteens were discharged, they burst killing the most of the men that were stationed at them. In consequence of this, Captain Jones sent orders to the lieutenant of this division not to discharge another of the eighteen pounders, but to promptly abandon them.

"The wind being now very light, and the enemy finding that she could outsail us, made use of this advantage and ran under our stern, raked us fore and aft, killed the main part of the marines that were stationed on the poop, and obliged the colonel that commanded them, with the surviving ones, to abandon it, besides doing much damage in the other parts of the ship.

"From this she ran athwart our fore-foot, (after discharging her broadside, and giving us an opportunity of returning the same), raked us a second time, and killed a number of our men; in fine, she galled us in this manner so confoundedly that orders were given to lay her aboard; accordingly, as she passed our fore-foot, we ran our jib-boom between her mizzen shrouds and starboard mizzen whang. Captain Jones at the same time in an audible voice, said, 'That's well, my lads! — we've got her now!' The enemy, finding that they were foul of us endeavored to get clear, by letting go an anchor, but the wind dying away she swung round upon us, and carried away our ensign-staff and ensign, both falling into the sea, with her jib-boom; her jib-stay being now cut away aloft, fell in upon our poop, which Captain Jones, and the sailing master made fast to our mizzenmast. The firing had not ceased during these manoeuvres except the cannon *a-mid-ships*, which now could not be worked or managed *on board either ship*. Several attempts were now made to board the enemy, but they did not succeed. The enemy also endeavored to board us, and actually came on board, but were beaten back, and our men pursued them on board their ship and were again repulsed in their turn; for we both lay so near together that it was an easy matter to step from one ship on board the other.

"It now fell entirely calm, and the enemy having an anchor

down, we both rode to it with the current, we being then about a league from Flamborough Head.

"The action had now been commenced about three hours and a quarter, when the enemy's tops were silenced, and we now directed our fire upon their decks with much success; about this time the enemy's light sails got on fire, this communicated to her rigging and from thence to ours. Thus were both ships on fire at one and the same time; therefore, the firing on both sides ceased till it was extinguished by the contending parties. The action then began anew, and was continued sharply on both sides, when our carpenter went and told the gunner that our ship had four feet of water in her hold, that Captain Jones was killed, and all the rest of the officers that ranked above him, and that the only way for them to save their lives would be to go upon deck — call for quarters, and haul down our colours. Upon this the gunner and carpenter made haste to get on deck, and were joined on their way thither by the master-at-arms. As soon as they had got upon the quarter deck, they cried, 'Quarters! Quarters! for God's sake, quarters! — our ship is sinking.' From this they mounted the poop with a design of hauling down the ensign, but finding them missing they descended to the pendant halyards, where they were met by Captain Jones, he being upon the forecastle when they first came upon deck; hearing these fellows halloo for quarters, he cried out thus: 'What cowardly rascals are these? Shoot 'em, kill 'em!' Having met with them, his pistols having been previously discharged, he sent them with all his force at these poltroons, who immediately knew Jones and fled below. Two of them were badly wounded in the head with Jones' pistols. Both ships now took fire again, and on board of ours it had communicated to the main top, so that we were in the greatest consternation imaginable for some time, and it was not without some difficulty we quenched it.

"The enemy now cried, 'If you ask quarters, why don't you strike your pendant!' — 'Aye, aye,' said our commodore, 'we'll do it when we can fight no longer, but expect to see you strike first.'

"Having now begun the action afresh, it was continued with redoubled vigor on both sides. The two ships now lay alongside each other with their yards locked and, having cleared the enemy's tops of their men, this gallant officer, in daring bravery, now led his men under his command, across on the ship's yards and into the Serapis' top and then directing their fire, with hand grenades and other missiles, down on her decks, causing so much slaughter, as that in half an hour they could not perceive a single man of the enemy above deck. They, however, kept playing four of their starboard bow guns into us, which still annoyed us, and which induced us in our main-top gang, to redouble our activity in the further able and effective acts which succeeded in driving their men from their stations at those before-mentioned guns, on their gun deck, in spite of their officers, and which acts were admitted as prominent in obtaining the victory.

"Thus, at length one of our hand grenades being thrown by us, from the top, fell upon the enemy's upper gun-deck — from this it rebounded, and fell between decks, where it set fire to some powder which lay scattered upon the enemy's lower gun-deck, and blew up (as we subsequently learned) about seventeen of them. This threw them into confusion, and as they were upon the point of crying for quarters — the Alliance unexpectedly made her appearance, and began a heavy fire upon us, as well as on the enemy, which at first, made some of our officers as well as men imagine she was an English ship of war.

"The signal of reconnoissance was now ordered to be made on board of our ship, which was three lanthorns placed in a horizontal line upon the fore, main, and mizzen shrouds, to undeceive the Alliance; as she had by this time killed eleven of our men and wounded several others, by raking us; notwithstanding, we did at the first hail her, and told them that she was firing on the wrong ship. A few minutes after this accident (although most of the officers of the Good Man Richard and some belonging to the Alliance think it was done designedly)[1] and about a quarter past twelve, we were pleased with the crying out of 'Quarters! Quarters!' by our enemy.

"We immediately boarded the enemy's ship. Thus ended this long and bloody fight, we having lost on our part one hundred and sixty men killed, mortally wounded, and missing. On the part of the enemy, one hundred and thirty-eight men were killed and died of their wounds — which were the number of lives lost in both ships, and those exclusive also of the wounded that re-

[1] Landais, the captain of the Alliance (a Frenchman) and Captain Jones were bitter enemies, and it is thought that Landais took this opportunity of avenging himself on his mortal enemy.

covered. Our prize proved to be the Serapis, commanded by Captain Pearson, who, after he had surrendered to us, with his lieutenant and other officers, came on board of our ship and inquired for Captain Jones, for it seems he had been informed who commanded our ship. When they met, Captain Pearson accosted his antagonist thus, presenting him his sword, ''Tis not without the greatest reluctance that I resign to you this, for of all men upon the face of the globe, 'tis you that I hate the worst.' Jones took his sword, saying, 'You have fought like a hero, and I make no doubt your sovereign will reward you in a most ample manner for it.' Captain Pearson then asked our Commodore of what his crew consisted, mostly Frenchmen or Americans? 'Americans,' said the latter. 'Well,' said the former, 'then it has been diamond cut diamond with us — a desperate family fight — brother against brother, for,' said he, 'I must own, that I think the Americans equally as brave as the English.' The Serapis had lost her main and mizzenmasts during the engagement, the former having been cut almost entirely off, by our shot, on a level with her gangway, and having fallen overboard, as we swung from alongside of her. We were now alarmed in having two enemies to encounter, almost as formidable as the one we had just conquered, viz. fire and water; we could not keep our ship free with all the pumps, and as many hands as could go to and work at them, but she kept gaining upon us every minute, which was no great cause of surprise, we having received several shot between wind and water (and some of these breaches could not be come at). The fire had also communicated itself to several parts of the ship, where it being dry and rotten it was found impracticable to extinguish it. In the dilemma, our Commodore ordered the signal of distress to be made and the Alliance, Pallais, and Vengeance brig, sent their boats to our assistance, when the Commodore embarked with Captain Pearson, in one of them and went on board the Serapis, leaving orders with the narrator and another midshipman, to get all the powder up out of the magazine, and see that it was sent on board of the other ships of the squadron, together with all the wounded men, prisoners, etc., and after having executed these orders, to abandon the Good Man Richard.

"The fire had now communicated itself to several parts, and burned with amazing rapidity within one foot of the magazine. Having got the powder and wounded men sent off, the prisoners (to the number of about fifty) made an attempt to take the ship from us, there being then on board but about twenty of our crew.

The action between the Serapis and Bon Homme Richard, Sept. 23, 1779.

They had made themselves master of our quarter-deck and forecastle, braced round the yards, and got her before the wind, with a design to run her ashore. In consequence of this another battle ensued, but having the greater part of the arms in our possession (suitable for a close fight) we soon got to be masters of the ship again, after killing two of them and wounding several others.

"When the boats came alongside again, we caused these desperate fellows to be by them conducted on board the Pallais. After the action had ceased, it was not thought advisable to despatch either of the squadron after the fleet of merchantmen in sight, whose convoy we had captured, as the situation of the Good Man Richard *then* needed the assistance of the *whole* of our squadron.

"Having now executed the orders of the Commodore, left with us, we thought of leaving the poor Good Man Richard to the mercy of the waves.

"However, before doing so, I went down into the gun room with some men, to see to the embarkation of the officers' trunks, which had been deposited here, but, alas, what havoc! not a piece of one of them could be found as large as a continental dollar bill; it is true, several shirts, coats, etc., were found, but so shockingly were they pierced and cut in pieces with the enemy's shot, that they were not worth carrying off. There was such a breach from one side of the gun room to the other, that (in the common way of speaking) a coach and six could have passed through it.

"The number and bulk of splinters were prodigious, many of them as fine as carpenters' chips. After this, and taking a survey of the dead bodies that were scattered about the decks, I could not help shuddering at the horrid sight. The blood which had issued from them covered the decks in such a manner that it was over shoe in several places. This dreadful sight I must confess sickened the hearts with feelings against ever battling again with our fellow-men to such bloody destruction of human life. Upon the whole, I think this slaughtering fight may with propriety be said to have been a scene of carnage on *both sides*.

"During the action, the enemy had thrown into our gun room a number of loose cannon cartridges, in order, as they afterwards owned, to blow us up. With the destruction of the officers' trunks, the narrator lost all his wearing apparel; and those remaining on his back at the close of the battle, were partly burned in the act of extinguishing the several fires, especially those of the tops and rigging.

"We thought of nothing now but abandoning the Good Man Richard, that was soon to serve so many as a sea coffin, and embarked accordingly in the boats, and soon after arrived alongside of the Serapis. Here Captain Jones ordered me not to get out of the boat, but to receive two or three additional men and to promptly return back on board of the Good Man Richard, 'for,' said he, 'in such a part of my cabin you'll find such and such papers — go and bring them and make no tarry.' These orders I went to carry into effect if possible; the Good Man Richard was then lying head to the wind with top-sails aback. I shot up with my boat under her stern, and was just a-going to lay her alongside, when I perceived the water run in and out of her lower ports. This somewhat staggered and brought me to a stand, but very soon, finding our situation dangerous, I ordered the men to use their oars in backing off from her. We thus had got, I judged, about three rods from her, when she fetched a heavy pitch and disappeared instantaneously; but although we were now under brisk sternway gaining fast some further rods from her, yet the agitation of the sea and its waves, with the whirlpool was such, that we came near sharing the same fate and going down with her. Thus, sinking head downwards, went to the bottom the Good Man Richard, about four hours after her crew had taken possession of her prize, and it was a thankful relief to us, to safely step on the Serapis' deck on our return to her.

"We now went to work, and in a very short time we had got jury masts erected, and sail enough spread to shape our course for the Texel in Holland, the wind being *contrary* to steer for France. On the 3rd of October we arrived with our little squadron and prizes at the Texel. Just as we came to anchor, we discovered in the offing an English sixty-four gun ship and three frigates; these had, as we subsequently learned, been despatched in pursuit of us, as soon as the English had got intelligence of our squadron being upon their coast."

In a proper time after the action Commodore Jones, in presence of his officers, mentioned, as highly praiseworthy those daring and brave acts of the command of the Good Man Richard's maintop; and subsequently handed to this brave officer the following certificate to the American Congress:

CERTIFICATE TO CONGRESS.

"I do hereby certify, that Nathaniel Fanning, of Stonington, State of Connecticut, has sailed with me in the station of midshipman eighteen months, while I commanded the Good Man Richard, until she was lost in the action with the Serapis, and in the Alliance, and Ariel frigates.

"His bravery on board the first-mentioned ship in the action with the Serapis, a King's ship of fifty guns, off Flamborough Head while he had command of the maintop will, I hope, recommend him to the notice of Congress in the line of promotion, with his other merits.

JOHN PAUL JONES.

L'Orient, (in France) December 17th, 1780."

The Bon Homme Richard was an old line-of-battle ship cut down to a razee. On her lower gundeck she carried six eighteen-pounders; on her gundeck twenty-eight twelve and nine pounders; and on the quarter and spar decks six six-pounders. On entering this engagement she had a crew of about 380 officers, men and boys, the original number with which she sailed from L'Orient being diminished by the absence of prize crews and by desertions.

The Serapis was a new ship, having on the lower gundeck twenty eighteen-pounders: on the upper gundeck twenty nine-pounders; and on the quarterdeck and forecastle ten sixteen-pounders. She carried a crew of 308 officers, men and boys.

On the 16th of October Jones transferred his crew to the

Alliance frigate, and French officers and crews took possession of the Serapis and Countess of Scarborough.

On the 28th of December Captain Jones left the Texel on a cruise and captured two prizes off the coast of Spain, after which he sailed for the port of L'Orient. While in this port the Alliance was transferred to his enemy Captain Landais, with whom many of his officers and crew embarked to the United States, as they were dissatisfied with John Paul Jones for withholding their wages and prize money.

On the 7th of October, 1780, Nathaniel Fanning again sailed under the command of Paul Jones on the frigate Ariel, twenty-four guns, having under convoy fourteen American vessels, including three letters of marque. They were forced to return to L'Orient by stress of weather after cutting away the masts. During their stay in France the officers became disgusted with the conduct of Jones, and when the Ariel again sailed on the 15th of December, Fanning, as well as others, refused to accompany him. While staying at L'Orient, Fanning made the acquaintance of a merchant named Bellimont, who was then fitting out a privateer at Morlaix. He was proffered the command of this vessel, which was a lugger mounting fourteen three-pounders and called the Count de Guichen; but as the officers were commissioned by the King of France, the principal command was given to Captain Anthon, a capable French officer, and Fanning appointed to the second position. Most of the crew being Americans, Fanning was virtually the commander. On the 23d of March, 1781, the lugger sailed from Morlaix for the south coast of Ireland, where she arrived two days after. Here on the 27th she took four prizes, which were ransomed for twelve hundred guineas. On the 28th she captured an English letter of marque of four hundred tons, mounting twenty-six guns, bound from Bristol to the West Indies with a cargo of dry-goods valued at £30,000. This capture was effected after a running action of an hour, during which the English vessel lost three officers, four seamen and a boy killed, and eleven wounded, and the lugger five slightly wounded. The prize was afterwards separated from the privateer in a storm and fell into the hands of the English. The Count de Guichen then sailed for Brest, where she refitted. She again sailed for the coast of Ireland on the 7th of April, where she arrived on the 10th. On the 1st of May she took three sloops, two of which were ransomed and one sunk. By 2 P.M. of the same day had eleven vessels brought to, and at 5 P.M. had them all ransomed. At 8 P.M. on the same day took two large ships and a brig which were ransomed, the ships for 3200 guineas and the brig for 500 guineas. The lugger then sailed for Morlaix, having in the captain's possession ransom bills amounting to 10,450 guineas, and eleven men on board as hostages until the ransoms were paid. During the return trip she fell in with the Aurora frigate of twenty-eight guns, was captured on the 4th of May, and taken to Mount's Bay. Being searched for ransom bills the captain delivered two parcels of bogus bills made up during the chase, the genuine ones being secreted in his trousers. These bills were afterwards sent to France by a safe conveyance and the amounts collected.

On the 7th of May the prisoners were landed, being treated with every mark of consideration by Captain Collins of the frigate. Next day the officers went to the Mayor of Falmouth for the purpose of being paroled. Captain Anthon, being accused of having broken his parole a few months previously, was committed to prison. Being asked if he desired parole, Nathaniel Fanning said that if his captain went to prison he thought it his duty to accompany him. The same night they were lodged in a prison about two miles from Falmouth. Fanning describes this prison as the dirtiest and most loathsome he ever saw. On the 15th they got permission to walk outside the prison yard every day provided they promised to return at sunset, and that they would travel no further than a mile and a half from the prison. After six weeks' imprisonment they were exchanged. Fanning then went to Morlaix, where he engaged passage on a letter of marque for the West Indies. Having made a settlement with the owners of the privateer Count de Guichen and received about a thousand dollars in cash he invested this sum in wines and drygoods, which he placed on board the letter of marque and sailed from Morlaix on the 12th of July, 1781. On the 14th they were driven on shore by a violent gale, when the brigantine and cargo were entirely lost, the crew and passengers barely escaping alive. By this disaster Nathaniel Fanning lost every cent of money and property he had in the world. In this condition he came to the determination of not crossing the Atlantic until the war in America had ceased, considering that it made but little difference whether he fought under the French or American flag so long as he fought against the English, the French at the time being the friends and allies of the Americans.

On the 3rd of December the Eclipse cutter under command of Captain Anthon sailed from Ostend on a six weeks' cruise, Fanning being second in command. On the 10th she captured two prizes, one of which was ransomed for four hundred and seventy guineas and the other sent to France. On the 14th the Eclipse fell in with a large English letter of marque, mounting eighteen guns, which surrendered after a fierce fight of three-quarters of an hour. The weather, which had been heavy, now lightened and showed an English frigate nearly within gunshot, which caused her to abandon her prize. The frigate gave chase, but in about an hour it was found that the Eclipse could easily outsail her. The Eclipse next sailed for Land's End, where on the 15th of December she took two large sloops, which were ransomed. The same day she captured a large brigantine richly laden, which she sent to France in charge of a prize crew. On the 16th she put into Cherbourg, where she refitted. On the 23d she left Cherbourg and fell in with an English frigate which chased her for six hours, during which she sprung a leak and was forced to put into Cherbourg. After two days she again sailed towards Land's End and was chased every day until the 1st of January, 1782, when she fell in with a letter of marque, carrying twelve guns, bound from Plymouth to the West Indies. The letter of marque surrendered after four of her crew had been killed and seven wounded, the Eclipse having two slightly wounded. This prize, being richly laden, was sent to France. On the 13th of January a brig laden with coal was captured and sent to France. On the 14th the Eclipse put into Morlaix to refit and recruit the crew. She then sailed towards the coast of England, and on the 6th of March, captured a large ship off Dover and carried her to Dunkirk. There the Eclipse was disarmed and the men paid off.

The owners offered Fanning the command for the next cruise, which he readily accepted, having some time before been naturalized as a French subject. Men were immediately employed in refitting the Eclipse for another cruise.

During these preparations Fanning took a trip to London with letters of credit for fifteen hunred guineas. It seems he was engaged at this time to undertake this trip for the purpose of ascertaining the trend of public opinion in London regarding the continuance of the American war, and that it was undertaken under the auspices of some gentlemen high in authority connected with the French government. He remained in London about three weeks, and after securing the desired information, he returned to Dunkirk, on the 8th of April, where he reported the result of his mission to certain gentlemen in the town hall. He was then sent to London with letters from the Court of France to Lords Shelburne, Stormont, Keppel and others, the purport of which was proposals of peace and proposals to the English Court for the liberation of Captains Ryan and McCarter, two Irishmen, who had commanded privateers in the French service and had captured a great number of English vessels before they were taken by the British. They were confined in Newgate prison under sentence of death on account of having been taken under French colors. The French government interested itself in saving the lives of these men, because they were both lieutenants in the French navy and had rendered important service to France. Fanning left Dunkirk on the 9th of April, arrived in Dover at 5 o'clock the next morning, and four hours later was in London, where he delivered his letters. By his expedition on the journey he was the means of saving the lives of Ryan and McCarter, who were reprieved and soon after set at liberty. He remained in the city incognito under a protection signed by Lord Stormont, and afterwards appeared in public. After being in London about four weeks he departed for Dunkirk. On the 12th of May, 1782, he was invested with the command of the Eclipse cutter newly refitted, mounting eighteen six-pounders, and carrying a crew of one hundred and ten officers and boys, fifty-five of whom were American and the remainder of various nationality.

On the 6th of June the Eclipse sailed for the coast of Scotland, and on the 10th captured a brigantine laden with coal which was sent to Dunkirk, after which she ran a large sloop on shore near Scarborough and set fire to her. The next day two large sloops were sunk after their crews had been taken aboard the Eclipse. On the 15th Fanning captured a large ship with a valuable cargo, off the coast of Buchan-Ness, on board of which he put a prize crew with orders to steer for France. He next steered for the Orkney Islands, where in Hope's Bay he captured seven vessels which he set on fire. On the 27th, finding two frigates in his vicinity, he effected his escape from Hope's Bay. On the 28th he captured two sloops which he sent to France, and on the following night he took four sloops. Three of these he sunk: on board the third he placed his prisoners with liberty to go where they pleased after they had signed a writing that they had been captured by the cutter Eclipse under French colors, Capt. N. Fanning commanding. This certificate placed the English government under the obligation of releasing an equal number of French prisoners. On the 29th he sunk two sloops. On the 30th he was chased for twelve hours by two British frigates, during which he suffered much from the shot of the enemy, several of his men being wounded, but none killed. Night coming on he escaped. On the 1st of July he encountered a letter of marque off Sline Head on the west coast of Ireland. She surrendered after being boarded. During the action she lost a mate, boatswain, six sailors and two boys killed and eleven wounded. The Eclipse lost two killed and seven wounded. She was found to be the Lively Lass of Nevis with twelve guns a side, laden with West India produce. She was sent to France with a prize crew. Next day he took another prize laden with provisions from Galway to Portsmouth and sent her to France. On the 3d he shaped his course to L'Orient for the purpose of refitting, and arrived on the 7th.

On the 24th of July he left L'Orient and sailed for the coast of Ireland. On the 27th he captured a galliot laden with sugar and coffee, and a sloop laden with broadcloth, linen, etc., and sent both to France. On the 29th fell in with a British privateer, mounting twenty-six guns. After an action of thirty-one minutes, she surrendered. Besides her crew she had on board one hundred and twenty-seven British officers and soldiers destined for America. She had fourteen killed on board besides others killed who had been thrown overboard during the battle. The Eclipse had three killed and seven wounded. This prize was sent to France.

Fanning next directed his course towards Land's End, where on the 9th of August he took two prizes which he sent to France. He next took a brig and sloop near Falmouth. The brig, being richly laden, was sent to France: the sloop was given to the prisoners (then amounting to one hundred and ninety-five officers and men) after they had signed the certificate of their capture.

On the 11th of August the Eclipse was chased by three frigates and a cutter in the English Channel. Having disabled the cutter which lay in her path, she soon outsailed the other vessels, except the Jupiter, a fifty-gun ship and reputed the fastest vessel in the British navy. At 3 P.M. the Eclipse reached within three leagues of the Channel Fleet ahead, drawn up in a line extending nine miles south from the eastern end of the Isle of Wight. Captain Fanning now ordered the French colors hauled down and the English colors raised. All of the crew who could not speak English were sent below deck, and the Eclipse boldly entered the centre of the line, passing between two three-deckers. Being hailed from both ships with the question, "What cutter is that?" Captain Fanning answered, "His Majesty's cutter Surprise," at the same time dropping the peak and dousing the colors, but not shortening an inch of sail. The Eclipse had nearly got beyond hailing distance when she was ordered to bring to. Fanning answered, "Ay, ay," but kept on his course. The ships of the line in the centre then fired several shots which passed over the Eclipse without doing any injury. Finding she did not bring to, three frigates, a sloop of war, and a cutter gave chase. The fifty gun ship Jupiter at the same time passed through the fleet and continued the chase. The cutter seemed to outsail the other vessels: in fact, she outsailed the Eclipse. Perceiving this, Captain Fanning ordered the drag overboard to retard the speed of his own vessel. When the English cutter was within musket shot she began firing. Fanning gave her two broadsides which cut away some of her rigging, after which she did not attempt to follow. This was in the dusk of the evening, at which time the other ships gave up the chase, except the Jupiter. Towards midnight, when Fanning thought that ship had also given up the chase, he went below for much needed rest, and the crew, shortening sail, busied themselves making some necessary repairs. In this situation they were hailed from the Jupiter (who had run under the stern of the Eclipse) with the words, "Strike, you d——d Irish rascal — drop the peak of your mainsail — hoist out your boat and come on board His Majesty's ship!" Captain Fanning, who had come promptly on deck when apprised of the Jupiter's proximity, answered that his boat was so full of shot holes she would not float. It was now 4 o'clock in the morning with no moon, and pretty dark. They replied from the Jupiter that they would hoist out their own boat, and ordered Fanning to hoist a lighted lantern at the peak, which was done. At this time the Jupiter had her light sails taken in ready for action with head to southward. The Eclipse pointed in an opposite direction. By Captain Fanning's orders his ship was gradually got under way while the Jupiter's boat was being lowered and manned. Perceiving this, the boat returned, and a fire was directed on the Eclipse from every part of the Jupiter. Fanning, himself taking the helm, had in the meantime ordered his crew to lie flat on the deck. The Jupiter wore ship, crowded sail, and while chasing continued firing. Captain Fanning received flesh wounds in the leg and forehead from splinters by which he was stunned momentarily, but still keeping to the helm, he gained gradually, and at daylight was four leagues to leeward of the Jupiter, which then gave up the chase, during which the Eclipse had thirteen slightly wounded but none killed.

At 10 A.M. Fanning captured a brig which he sent to Dunkirk. He also took a sloop in ballast, on board of which he placed his prisoners (ninety-four in number) after they had signed the usual certificate.

The next day he encountered a large ship which proved to be the Lord Howe, six hundred tons, mounting twenty-four six-pounders besides swivels, etc., and commanded by a lieutenant of the British navy with a crew of eighty-seven sailors of the navy. She had also on board one hundred

Lieut. Nathaniel Fanning
of Stonington, Conn.
1755 — 1805

and ten officers and soldiers, and was bound from Cork for the Downs. During the engagement she lost of the military one major, one lieutenant, and twenty-one of the soldiers, and of the crew a master's mate, boatswain, seventeen seamen and three boys killed, and thirty-eight wounded. The Eclipse lost a quartermaster, gunner's mate, boatswain's mate, ten seamen, five marines and two boys killed, and twenty-two wounded out of a crew of seventy-two. Captain Fanning was wounded in the left leg by a musket ball.

Scarcely had the Lord Howe surrendered and the prisoners secured on board the Eclipse when Fanning was obliged to abandon his prize in consequence of a British frigate heaving in sight. Having carried off the colors and spiked the guns of the Lord Howe, he sailed for Dunkirk, where he arrived on the 14th of August and was received with enthusiasm by the inhabitants. Here he was confined to his room for three weeks in consequence of his wounds, and during that time was treated with every mark of kindness. In October he received a commission as lieutenant of the French navy.

On the 23d of October he sailed from Dunkirk in command of the privateer Ranger of forty tons, having on board a gunner, a boatswain, a lieutenant and twenty seamen, to each of whom he had advanced ten guineas for a fifteen days' cruise. He shaped his course to the Downs, and at daylight next morning found himself in the midst of a fleet of sixty vessels not far from Dover, all appearing to be westward bound. Captain Fanning deemed it prudent to sail along in the same direction, and kept company with the fleet (which was under convoy of a frigate and three privateers) for three days and two nights. On the third night he boarded and captured one of the ships, named the Maria, a letter of marque, mounting eight six-pounders, with a crew of thirty-five men and three passengers, laden with supplies for the fleet at Portsmouth. This vessel he sent to France. He next took a large brigantine, which made no resistance on which he also placed a prize crew with orders to sail for France. He now left the fleet, having as crew on board the Ranger with him only two Irish lads whom he had shipped as Americans at Dunkirk, and sailed for France. At 2 P.M. he was overhauled and captured by an English cutter, from which he was unable to escape in consequence of being shorthanded. At 10 A.M. of the second day after the capture they arrived at Dover, where Fanning was stoned and otherwise maltreated until he was placed under an escort of over a hundred soldiers. He and his lads were taken to the fort for examination. The youths were found to be Irish. They were sent to the guardship and afterwards hanged. Captain Fanning was imprisoned at Deal. Ten days after he was exchanged, and returned to Dunkirk, where he arrived on the 9th of November, the seventeenth day after he had sailed on a cruise by which he made over a thousand guineas.

After returning to Dunkirk he purchased a lugger of twenty-five tons, mounting six three-pounders, on which he shipped a crew of twenty-one officers and men. On the 14th of November he departed on a cruise. On the second day out he was captured by the British frigate Belle Poole of twenty-eight guns. Captain Fanning was placed in irons, and while so was abused and kicked by members of the crew. While cruising off the Isle of Wight the frigate was captured by the French and Fanning released.

Fanning did duty as lieutenant on board the French flagship for some time. After the cruise she put into Brest, where it was then rumored that a general peace would be proclaimed in two months. Although offered a position in the French navy, he declined to accept it, and departed for Dunkirk, where he was offered the command of a brig then being fitted out as a privateer. This offer Fanning accepted. The brig was ready to sail on the 30th of December, but the signing of the preliminary articles of peace prevented further privateering. On the 26th of July, 1783, he left Dunkirk for Paris, where he arrived on the 9th of August and waited on Dr. Franklin, who gave him a passport to L'Orient. Next day he waited on Mr. Barclay, the U. S. Consul-General at Paris, who had power of attorney to collect money due him by merchants of Dunkirk and other places in France. After completing his business with Mr. Barclay, he set out for L'Orient, where he engaged a passage for New York in a French ship which sailed on the 30th of September and on which he arrived in New York Harbor the following November, at a time when the British were making final preparations for leaving that city.

After the close of the war and his return from Europe, Nathaniel Fanning resided at New York City for some time, later removing to Stonington, Conn. He was living in New York in 1792, '95 and '96. In 1798 he held the office of Fire Warden of the Seventh Ward in that city. He was residing in Stonington in 1797, '98 and 1802, and lived in his father, Gilbert Fanning's, house.[1]

---

[1] A wrong impression seems to have gained ground that Nathaniel Fanning's home in Stonington was the little house just west of the pumping station at the Mistuxet Water Works. A photograph of this house was published in the New York Mail and Express Supplement of Saturday, July 30, 1898, and a statement that he resided "many years in this house" and that "after the war he came back to the house where he lived to a good old age," etc. There is no evidence to substantiate this. The Connecticut

On the 5th of December, 1804, he was commissioned lieutenant in the United States Navy, and received appointment to the command of a gunboat. While on active duty in command of the Naval Station at Charleston, S. C., he died of yellow fever on the 30th of September, 1805.

Nathaniel Fanning is described by those who knew him intimately as a man of fine personal appearance, inclined to display in dress, rarely being seen on the street without dress tights, silk stockings, and buckles; much disposed to talk of his adventures, and somewhat vainglorious (although a man who had fought on the Bon Homme Richard and had Paul Jones' indorsement of his bravery may be pardoned some boasting).

While residing in France he was a great favorite, and learned to speak the French language fluently. He wrote a very interesting book of Memoirs, which was published in New York in 1808.[1]

---

records show that Deacon William Morgan bought this property on both sides of Mistuxet Brook from Elisha Gallup in 1777 and on it was the house in which Mr. Gallup then lived and now known as the old "Palmer" house (with gambrel roof). Elisha Gallup's father, Capt. Joseph Gallup, died in 1760, and bequeathed the farm to Elisha, who was living there at the time. Joseph obtained it from his grandfather, Capt. John Gallup. So it seems to have been Gallup's land from very early times.

Nathaniel Fanning lived at Stonington, Long Point, and in New York City for a time, and died in Charleston, S. C., at the early age of fifty. He was born at Wequetequock, the first residence of his father, Gilbert Fanning, in the town of Stonington.

[1] *Vide* Memoirs by Nathaniel Fanning, New York, 1808.

CAPTAIN EDMUND[6] FANNING (No. 117).

(For Genealogical data, see page 255.)

Captain Edmund Fanning, son of Gilbert and Huldah (Palmer) Fanning of Stonington, Conn., was born in that town 16 July, 1769. At an early age he embraced a seafaring life, making his first voyage as a cabin boy at the age of fourteen years. From this position he rose through the regular grades of seaman, second mate, first mate and captain, until he attained an exalted rank among the most famous and successful navigators of that century.

After performing three voyages from his native port to the West Indies in the capacity of first mate he determined to sail from New York as there were no prospects at Stonington of a career suitable to his ambitious views. After a short sojourn in New York he was engaged on board a brig belonging to Messrs. Murray, Mumford and Bowen, commanded by Captain Miller, for a six months' voyage to Hispaniola. Upon the arrival of the brig at Aux Cayes, both mates being discharged, Fanning was appointed first mate, in which capacity he performed duty during the remainder of the voyage. Fanning next engaged in the employ of Elias Nexsen, a New York merchant, in whose vessels he made several voyages to Curacoa as first mate.

In May, 1792, Mr. Nexsen fitted out the brig Betsy for a voyage to the South Seas for sealskins, in which Mr. Fanning was engaged as first mate. Unfortunately for the success of the expedition, an incompetent captain, named Steele, was given the command, who knew nothing of seals or seal-fishing. By great exertion a full cargo of sealskins was procured at the Falkland Islands by the month of January,

1793. The captain manifesting no haste to return, Fanning, who was loath to spend his time in needless idleness, accepted the offer of a passage to New York made by an old acquaintance and arrived there the following March. The Betsy arrived in June when Captain Steele was peremptorily discharged. Mr. Nexsen also directed that Fanning be given his full proportion of shares.

Mr. Fanning was next employed as first mate of the ship Portland, Captain Robinson commanding. The Portland sailed from New York for Norfolk in May, 1793, where she received a cargo of flour and cleared for Havre, France. When off the Scilly Islands she was seized by a British frigate and sent to Falmouth Harbor. There the cargo was seized and the flour stored in the government storehouse. The next day the officers underwent the customary examination by the mayor, who, learning that Mr. Fanning was a relative of Gen. Edmund Fanning, Governor of Prince Edward Island, to whom he was greatly indebted, granted them their freedom. Soon afterward Fanning and all the crew but two (Captain Robinson being absent in London) were impressed into the service of a British frigate, which arrived at Falmouth, but by the intercession of the mayor, they were liberated the following day. After the return of Captain Robinson from London the Portland sailed for New York.

Fanning was next appointed to the command of a new schooner, the Dolly, belonging to Snell, Stagg & Co., merchants engaged in the Curacoa trade. On the return voyage, when off Sandy Hook, the Dolly was seized as a prize by a British frigate on the pretext of sailing from a blockaded port (which Curacoa then was), but when the captain, however, learned that Fanning was a nephew of General

Edmund Fanning, he promptly released him and his vessel.

In 1797 Captain Fanning originated the project of fitting out suitable vessels which should proceed to the South Seas to procure cargoes of sealskins, thence cross the Pacific Ocean to Canton, where such merchandise was ascertained to be in great demand and at prices which would furnish a handsome profit. He consulted Mr. Elias Nexsen on the project, who approved of Fanning's plans and placed the brig Betsy at his disposal. The Betsy was a Charleston packet of one hundred tons' burden. After the necessary stores were put on board together with an invoice of goods suitable for trading with the natives of the islands, the Betsy, having shipped part of her crew, proceeded to Stonington, where the remainder joined her. On the 13th of June, 1797, she sailed from Stonington for the South Seas with a crew of twenty-seven. By the 2d of April, 1798, she had secured a full cargo of sealskins, and sailed from the island of Massafuero for Canton, China. During this voyage Captain Fanning performed the unprecedented achievement of placing standing rigging on his vessel while at sea.

On the 11th of June, 1798, Captain Fanning discovered three uninhabited islands in latitude 3° 51′ 30″ N., longitude 159° 12′ 30″ W., situated in the form of a triangle, the northern and southern ones being each nine miles long and the eastern one six miles long. To these islands his crew gave the name of Fanning's Islands. At noon on the 12th of June he discovered another uninhabited island in latitude 4° 45′ N., longitude 160° 8′ W., to which was given the name of Washington Island.

On the 13th of August, 1798, the Betsy arrived in the harbor of Macoa, China, and on the 24th reached Canton. After disposing of his cargo and obtaining in return one of teas, silks, china ware, etc., Captain Fanning sailed from Canton 30 October on his return voyage. He arrived at New York 26 April, 1799, after a passage of one hundred and seventy-eight days. The expedition was a great success, netting to the owners the sum of $52,300 after all charges had been deducted. Captain Fanning received well-merited praise from the American and European press for the ability with which he conducted the undertaking. To him may be awarded (by this and subsequent voyages) the credit of setting in motion the great commercial enterprises which built up the mercantile navy of the United States and opened up new places of trade in every quarter of the world.

In January, 1800, the corvette Aspasia, twenty-two guns, just from the stocks, was purchased, provisioned and armed by a company of New York merchants for an exploring and sealing expedition to the South Seas under command of Captain Fanning. She was commissioned as a letter of marque by the President of the United States. On the 11th of May the Aspasia sailed from New York for the sealing fisheries of South Georgia and New South Shetland Islands. On the 8th of February, 1801, she commenced her voyage to Canton, having on board fifty-seven thousand sealskins. Arriving there her cargo was sold and a return cargo received on board, and Captain Fanning sailed for New York, where he arrived 4 March, 1802.

In 1803 the brig Union, Captain Pendleton commanding, was fitted out for the South Sea seal-fishery and Canton trade by Captain Fanning, acting as agent for a company of New York merchants. After collecting fourteen thousand sealskins at Border's Island, Captain Pendleton sailed for Sydney, New South Wales, where he placed the skins in storage, and then made a voyage to the Fiji Islands to procure a cargo of sandal-wood for the Canton market. After landing on the Island of Tongatabu 1 October, 1804, Captain Pendleton and his boat's crew were massacred by the natives. Mr. Wright, the first officer, deemed it prudent to return to Sydney in order to replace the number of the crew destroyed. This being accomplished, the Union again sailed for the Fiji Islands. On arriving near the islands, the brig encountered a heavy squall by which she was cast upon a reef and wrecked. Every person on board was either drowned or massacred by the natives.

Captain Edmund Fanning, as agent, next fitted out the ship Catherine in 1804 with everything requisite for a two and a half years' voyage. She was placed under command of his brother, Captain Henry Fanning, who rediscovered the Crozet Islands off the coast of Australia. There a cargo of sealskins was procured and exchanged in Canton for such goods as suited the New York market. A very handsome profit was netted for the owners by this voyage.

On the 31st of August, 1806, under the directive agency of Captain Edmund Fanning, the ship Hope, belonging to the firm of E. & H. Fanning & W. Coles, sailed from New York under the command of Captain Brumley. At the Fiji Islands she took on board a cargo of sandal-wood, and, having completed all preparations, sailed for Canton 6 September, 1807. On the 3d of October, Captain Brumley discovered a hitherto unknown island in latitude 5° 15′ N., longitude 165° 17′ E. of London, which he named Hope's Island. After exchanging the cargo of sandal-wood for teas and other Chinese goods, the Hope commenced her return voyage on the 27th of December and arrived at New York on the 3d of May, 1808.

On the 1st of March, 1807, the keel of a new vessel was

laid in the ship-yards of Adam and Noah Brown in New York for the firm of Edmund & Henry Fanning & William Coles. She was launched in the following May and called the Tonquin, and was three hundred tons' burden, double flush decked, carrying twenty-two guns, and of great speed. On the 26th of May she sailed from New York for China in command of Captain Fanning, and returned on the 6th of March, 1808, after a profitable voyage. Thus the Tonquin was built, coppered, rigged and launched, and performed a voyage to China and back in the unprecedentedly short time of twelve months and five days.

On the 15th of June, 1808, the Tonquin sailed for a cargo of sandal-wood to the Fiji Islands, Captain Brumley commanding. He discovered 5 April, 1809, a previously unknown island in latitude 11° 52′ S., longitude 169° 44′ E. of London, to which he gave the name of Tonquin Island. Having exchanged the sandal-wood for a cargo of Chinese goods, the Tonquin sailed for New York, where she arrived after a very prosperous voyage. After the return of the Tonquin, she was sold by Fanning & Coles to John Jacob Astor, by whom she was employed in the fur trade of the Northwest American Coast under Captain Thorn. While anchored in Newatee Bay, Vancouver's Island, a dispute arose between the Indians and Captain Thorn, when he unceremoniously expelled the natives from his ship. They departed with threats of vengeance. The next day the Indians visited the ship in an apparently friendly manner for the purpose of renewing the trade. Having gained the deck in large numbers, they drew their concealed weapons and attacked the crew, who were all slain but four seamen. The captain, though mortally wounded, gained the cabin. Here he and the four surviving sailors cleared the deck of the savages with their firearms. The next day the Indians visited the Tonquin in vast numbers and crowded on board. The captain, who was still alive, crawled to the magazine, blew up the ship and all on board perished.

In the spring of 1812 Captain Edmund Fanning received a commission from President Madison as commander of a discovery expedition to consist of the ships Volunteer and Hope, intended for exploring the seas of the southern hemisphere, and circumnavigating the world. Accompanying the commission were letters of recommendation procured by James Munroe, Secretary of State, from the ambassadors of the different nations of Europe accredited to the United States. The expedition was in preparation and nearly on the point of sailing, when it was suspended and finally given up in consequence of the breaking out of war between the United States and Great Britain.

On the 5th of June, 1815, the ship Volunteer, under the command of Captain Fanning, with a crew of thirty officers and seamen (among whom William A. Fanning, the captain's son, ranked as purser), sailed from New York for the South Seas. He visited the Falkland Islands and doubled Cape Horn, and, after obtaining some sealskins at the Island of Mas-a-fuera, finally arrived at Coquimbo, Chili. After a short detention there, he cruised among the Galapagos Islands, where he secured 25,000 sealskins and reached New York 13 April, 1817. Owing to representations of Captain Fanning to the government on his return from this voyage, United States war-ships were stationed on the Pacific Coast for the purpose of protecting American commerce.

On the 4th of September, 1817, Captain Fanning sailed from New York for the South Seas in command of the Sea Fox. He procured a cargo of oil and sealskins at the Falkland Islands and arrived in New York 27 April, 1818.

In July, 1819, William A. Fanning, Captain Fanning's son, sailed as supercargo on the brig Hersilia from Stonington, Captain Sheffield commanding, on an exploring and sealing voyage. They rediscovered many of the south Shetland Islands, and after procuring several thousand sealskins, returned to Stonington where they realized a handsome profit on the sale of the vessel and cargo.

In 1829 the brigs Seraph (built by Captain Edmund Fanning at Stonington) and Annawan under command of Captains Benjamin Pendleton and Nathaniel B. Palmer, respectively, were fitted out under the directive agency of Captain Fanning for a trading and exploring expedition to the southern hemisphere. A report of the expedition in 1829 and 1830 was made by Captain Pendleton to Captain Fanning, who submitted it to Congress, by whom it was ordered printed:[1] —

Having for a long time been imbued with the idea that great benefits would result to the commerce of the United States from a National Exploring Expedition to the South Seas under Government management, Captain Fanning sent the following memorial to Congress: —

"To the Honourable the Senate and House of Representatives of the United States, in Congress assembled: —

"Your petitioner, Edmund Fanning, having obtained satisfactory evidence, by the trial and result, that any private exploring expedition cannot ever produce, or obtain, the desired and wished-for national benefit to navigation, commercial trade, the whale and seal fishery, science, &c.; therefore, under a full acquired

[1] *Vide* full report of expedition in "Voyages Round the World," etc. by Edmund Fanning, New York, 1833, pp. 478, et seq.

belief of its national importance, impressed as your memorialist is, by personal experience, in the necessity of a governmental exploring expedition to those parts of our globe, doth, in his national feeling and zeal, and in all humble deference, most respectfully recommend and pray, that Congress, in its wisdom, will be pleased to grant an appropriation, with power for a competent National Exploring and Discovery Expedition to the South Seas, Pacific, &c. In aid and support of which recommendation, your memorialist has heretofore made sundry discoveries in those seas, and had long and much experience relating to the subject. And your memorialist, as in duty bound, will ever pray.

EDMUND FANNING.

New York, November 7th, 1831."

This petition was referred by Congress to the Committee on Naval Affairs and ordered to be printed.

In 1833 Captain Fanning again petitioned Congress on the same subject in the following memorial, which was referred to the Committee on Naval Affairs and ordered to be printed: —

MEMORIAL
OF
EDMUND FANNING.

"To illustrate the views in a petition presented to Congress, praying that a National Discovery and Exploring Expedition be sent out to the South Seas, &c.

"To the Honourable the Senate and House of Representatives of the United States, in Congress assembled: —

"Your petitioner, Edmund Fanning, respectfully asketh leave to submit the following explanations, reasons, &c., to illustrate his views of the national advantages and benefits prayed for, in his petition before Congress, and on file with your honourable committee, that a national discovery and exploring expedition be sent out to the South Seas, &c., &c.; and does also farther respectfully request, that the said explanations, remarks, &c., with his former petetion, and papers attached thereto, on file with your honourable naval committee, may be again printed. Your petetioner, in all deference, requests leave to observe, that, at the early date of 1792, he entered and engaged on those South

Sea voyages, with a view to obtain information on the seal fishery, commercial trade, pecuniary profit, &c., that which at this time was thought might be obtained from those foreign ports and unexplored regions.

"In 1797, your memorialist sailed on his voyage, in the capacity of commander, supercargo, and director, to prosecute this commercial trade and seal fishery, to the South Seas, Pacific Ocean, China, and around the world. This new and enterprising voyage opened the gate to his fellow-citizens to this South Pacific and China commercial trade; by which, and thereafter, under his command or agency, were taken from these regions to China, on American account, the first cargoes of sandal-wood, seals, fur, beach-la-mer, bird's nest, mother of pearl, pearls, shark's fins, turtle shell, &c., being the productions of the land, seas, in those South Seas, and Pacific regions; which, on being exchanged in Canton, for China goods, and those brought home into our ports of the United States, not only enriched his brother citizens, the adventurers, but poured streams, by duties on the same, of hundreds of thousands, ay, millions of dollars into the public treasury, thus enriching our country in the aggregate; and which, in the course of some few years, therefore, caused this commercial traffic and fishery to increase to upwards of twenty sail per annum, out of the ports of the United States, and which has now got dwindled down to a very limited number. In your petitioner's next voyage to the South Seas, the Pacific, China, and around the world, he was honoured in the command of a superb new corvette ship, of 22 guns, commissioned by the President of the United States, with a complement of five lieutenants, a master, a surgeon, eight midshipmen, with a competent number of petty officers and men, which voyage was also safely performed around the world, without any unpleasant occurrence, or difficulty, but in good discipline, harmony, &c. And having, during his voyages in the command and directing agency had the fortune to discover the group of Fanning's Islands, Palmyrie Island, Washington Island (so named on its discovery by the subscriber, a beautiful green Island that stands recorded on the charts in use, by this name of the father of our country), Border's Island, as also, the continent of Palmer's Land, and rediscovered the group of Crozett's Islands, the South-Antipode's Island, were the first Americans at the Feejee Islands, and to the new South Shetland Islands: — from all of which there has been produced much wealth to our beloved country, as well as to its national treasury; — were the first from among our enterprising fellow-citizens, that took from those regions and seas, on American account to China those products of sandal-wood, &c., &c., which then, as before-mentioned, being exchanged in Canton for silks, nankins, teas, &c., &c. (China goods), not only produced large profits to the adventurers, but also enriched the national treasury. And in the utmost respect the subscriber hereunto would remark: — Do not these discoveries and their effects, with the millions of wealth which this trade and fishery have heretofore brought into our country, by its enterprising citizens, and also to its national treasury, have a parental claim on government for a competent exploring and discovery expedition, to endeavour now to revive it again!

"And to revive this commercial trade, fishery, &c., as well as to obtain other important national benefits, I do now most respectfully and earnestly petition and pray Congress for this discovery and exploring expedition to be sent out, to explore and search out new resources, or places, to obtain those products, articles, &c., which places, it is confidently conceived and believed, are yet numerous to be found, and thereby the said products will be again obtained in plenty, when those contemplated new places of resort, &c., are discovered and marked down on the chart, by this exploring, *with proper vessels*, on such national service.

"Presuming your petitioner's information, by such lengthy experience to be equal to that of any other, and that your pettitioner has had the fortune to do as much, if not more, thna any other citizen, in searching out and bringing forward those national advantages and benefits, touching on the before-mentioned business of commercial trade, &c., to the South Seas, Pacific, and China, as well as by first opening the gate-way to the prosecuting this valuable fishery and commercial trade, which has so enriched the national treasury, and brought such wealth to his fellow-citizens, which your petitioner conceives, in all due deference, entitles him to, and gives to him the firm ground of confidence, and of claim to respectfully ask, by his said petition, of our nation's Congress, the granting it, by the authorizing the prosecution of this national project.

"But laying aside, this Pacific and China commercial trade, your memorialist would observe, adverting to the subject, that the whale and seal fishery to the South Seas, of late years, has increased in the number of vessels beyond that of any former time, from out of the ports of the United States, and are still on the increase: — therefore the more urgency there is now of this national exploration, in the immediate need to its support: — Also in further illustration, as touching on the seal and whale fisheries, history gives to us the fact, that the British Greenland Whale and Seal Fishery at their old fishing ground, had got reduced in their fleet engaged in this business, by the scarcity of the whales and seals, from upwards of eight sail, down to a very limited number; — when the exploring and discovery voyages sent out by their government, under captains Ross Parry, having discovered new fishing grounds, never before having been disturbed, up Davis' Straits, Baffin's Bay, &c., where the whales and seals were plenty, or numerous, revived again this fishery to such a degree, that they now have, annually, a fleet of between ninety and a hundred sail employed again in it, (which revival would undoubtedly have been lost to that nation, had not those exploring and discovery voyages been performed) with renewed advantages, not only in bringing wealth to the nation, but in also establishing an additional nursery for seamen, which, it is well known, is the main spring of a navy.

"And your memorialist is now in possession of the fact, that losing voyages by our American vessels have already, and lately been made, owing to the scarcity of fishes and animals at their old grounds, or places of resort, for their requisite, natural, and annual wants of feed, propagation, &c.; particularly the latter, *the seals*; which ill success and hard fortune will still prevail, and in an increased measure, if not to a total abandonment in a few years, if this national exploring and research are not soon entered upon and effected, by discovering, marking down, and promulgating new resorts, grounds, and places, where those amphibious animals and fishes are to be again found in plenty, as they are still met with, numerous, on their travels, in those seas.

"The vessels now employed in this whaling and sealing business to the South Seas, Pacific Ocean, &c., on taking their departure from our ports, proceed direct for the old grounds and places of resort of those fishes and animals where they are now found and met with, so scattering and wild as to protract their voyages, often to such a length as to frequently exhaust their provisions, which were laid in for the voyage; and, of course, obliged them to recruit in a foreign port, or force them to return home with a losing voyage, and which, it is confidently believed, such an exploration would prevent, and cause a more sure, prompt, and successful voyage and return, by its discovery and marking down of new grounds and places of their resorts: — which expedition would also make more sure and safe the life of the mariner, by placing in their true situation the many dangers, &c., and thereby aiding and benefitting navigation as well as science, &c.

"Further, your petitioner and his associates, in their arduous enterprising and persevering endeavours for many years past, to the general national good, and to promote this fishery, and commercial trade, and in discoveries, have had the fortune to discover a new continent, or extensive lands, in the southern hemisphere: — which, by the generous act, as due to American enterprise, of a talented circumnavigator,[1] belonging to a powerful and magnanimous nation, has received the name of Palmer's Land, and which, it is earnestly desired, may be explored and surveyed by this prayed-for national expedition, for the general public good of our nation; as it is yet uncertain what valuable sources of rich furs, oils, &c., it may contain and supply to our hardy, adventurous South Sea mariners.

"Now, therefore, your petitioner doth humbly pray, that this much required government expedition be sent out to endeavour to obtain those national benefits herein set forth, and which cannot, as in evidence by trial, be done or performed by any private means.

"As your memorialist is of opinion such a national discovery and exploring expedition would, in a very weighty degree, accomplish those before-mentioned benefits to navigation, commerce, the fisheries, science, &c., your petitioner is likewise strongly in the belief that said expedition, in traversing those unfrequented seas, would make new discoveries of lands and islands, which would likely tend to advance our commercial trade, &c.

"Also, further, that they would search out, discover, and mark down at inhabited as well as at uninhabited *lands* and islands, as also at the sea-banks and coral reefs, new depots, sources, &c., where those products could be again procured in abundance, viz. of sandal-wood, bird's nest, beach-la-mer, pearls, turtle shell, &c., which would much revive again this commercial trade to China, &c.

[1] The commander of the Russian Discovery Ships.

"Furthermore, your petitioner feels confident that this expedition would discover, and do an act of great humanity in their routes, by falling in with and returning again to their homes, some of those now missing ship's crews of American citizens thus long absent from their country, families, friends, and civil society, and which, perhaps, are now dragging out a lonesome and suffering life, after being cast away upon some uninhabited island, or in slavery to some cannibal chief on an inhabited one; which pains the heart in deep distress of feeling in the suffering thought of those most unfortunate missing fellow-citizens and voyagers: — And, to relieve even a single ship's crew of them by such an expedition, what a parental act of government this! And yet further, your petitioner feels sure that they would greatly benefit and improve navigation by exploration and survey, and in correcting the situation, and placing them true on the charts, to be in use, of many islands and dangers, and thereby make the now dangerous hazard much less to the mariner, in our whale, seal, and trading ships and vessels, when traversing those oceans and seas.

"Finally, all will admit that such an expedition would add much to the history, science, &c., and your memorialist is sincere in the belief, that, if land is not discovered in the way, they may reach a very high south lattitude, if not in the vicinity of the south pole. The noted voyager, Captain Weddell, who obtained to the S. lattitude of 74° 15′ states, in this lattitude the sea was then free of ice, and that he had fine mild weather. And should the American expedition discover land in their way on proceeding south on its examination, who knows but what it may afford or produce in valuable and rich furs, oils, &c., in addition to a new discovery?

"And your petitioner would here respectfully remark, with a view to show the rate and length of time his mind has been engaged intent on this exploring subject, and requests, in all deference, permission to state in illustration, that, while engaged in the command and agency in prosecuting those South Sea, Pacific, and China voyages, he has for upwards of thirty years past, had before his mind's eye the evidences of the advantages and benefits of such an exploring expedition to his nation, with the constant increasing surmises and evidences coming up before him in observation, touching and relating to the most *proper kind of vessels*, with their fitments, &c., to enable and give the most sanguine promise to such an expedition, to obtain the greatest favorable and brilliant result; which, if this petition be granted, he is freely willing to communicate for the national benefit.

"Also, personal experience has taught the subscriber that situations will occur on such voyages of exploration, both in high and low lattitudes, which would be fatal to the large and heavy ship, when the small and lighter vessel would escape.

"The writer of this has wintered in his ship in a high lattitude, in the icy regions towards the south pole, and personally observed the formation, and make, and movements of the ice islands, bergs, &c., on the break up of the winter, and of its frozen massive barriers, causing a terrific, thundering roar, like that of ten thousand cannon, seemingly making terra-firma tremble to its foundations; and been with his ship in very trying and painful situations in the mountainous swell of rolling billows or turgid seas, in calms and currents, in the equatorial lattitudes among the coral reefs, when at the same time beset and surrounded by the savages, which would have been fatal, beyond possibility of human means, to extricate her, if a heavy ship, but having a lighter vessel he escapes from this awaiting dreadful fate; but which happened to be the lot of our first ship, and all on board of her which was sent to the Feejee Islands after sandal-wood, &c.: — she being a full built, heavy vessel, was wrecked by drifting, and being hove by the billowed sea, in a calm and current on the coral reef, and every soul on board of her, save the Tonga native pilot, perished, or were massacred by the savages, as each individual obtained, through the breakers and surf, a foothold on the rocks.

"A similar situation and case was no doubt the fate and destruction of the much lamented and unfortunate La Perouse, his frigates and their crews, which, with more proper and lighter vessels would perhaps have been avoided.

"Also, as an additional evidence of weight of advantage such an exploring has been to his mind, he would respectfully mention a fact, viz.: That an expedition of two ships was prepared, and nearly ready for sea in their departure on this service, in the spring of 1812, under his command, and a commission was granted by the President of the United States, to your petitioner, in the command of the same, when the sudden declaration of war by Congress put a stop to its sailing, and finally caused it to be abandoned.

"Your petitioner also respectfully begs, it will be here noted, that since that date the additional weighty call, or necessity, that such a national expedition should be sent out, is, that the important discovery of the continent of *Palmer's Land* has been made by Americans; which will also show in evidence, that in our South Sea mariner's and voyager's minds, at least, this exploring project petitioned for is not a visionary idea, but for real and important national benefits that are much needed.

"All which is most respectfully submitted.

EDMUND FANNING.

December 7th, 1833."

Largely through the efforts of Captain Fanning, who paid frequent visits to Washington in furtherance of the project, the South Sea Exploring Expedition was authorized by act of Congress on the 14th of May, 1836. In answer to a letter sent to the Secretary of the Navy a short time thereafter Captain Fanning received the following reply: —

"NAVY DEPARTMENT, 15*th June*, 1836.

"If Congress had authorized such Exploring Expedition to be conducted by citizens and not by officers of the navy, your claim to command the expedition would be a strong one, — but Congress have made it an affair of the navy, — and I find you renounce all desire to sail in the expedition, as you believe the officers of the navy equal in all respects to the task.

"Your zeal in procuring a law for an explorer's expedition is well known.

I am, with great respect, your ob'd't servant,

M. DICKERSON.

CAPTAIN E. FANNING,
New York.

Commodore Thomas Ap Catesby Jones was appointed to the command of the expedition, but was forced to resign, owing to ill health, in November, 1837. The command was then given to Commodore Charles Wilkes, and the expedition, composed of five vessels and a store-ship, sailed from Norfolk, Va., 18 August, 1838. The history of the four years' cruise was written by Commodore Wilkes under the title of a "Narrative of the U.S. Exploring Expedition of 1838, 1839, 1840 and 1842" and published in Philadelphia in 1845.

There can be no doubt but Captain Fanning felt keenly the disappointment of not being employed in the fitting out of this expedition for the authorization of which he had labored so long and arduously, and in the organization of which he considered his aid and counsel (founded on long experience) would be of the greatest importance.

In January, 1840, he again petitioned Congress, soliciting on this occasion a government loan of $150,000 which he would supplement with $100,000 from his own resources, the whole sum of $250,000 to be expended in fitting out suitable vessels for trade and explorations in the South Seas. This petition was ordered printed by the Committee on Naval Affairs, but no further action taken.

On the 19th of April, 1841, his wife died at his residence 163 Hudson Street, New York City, in the seventy-second year of her age. Four days after, Friday the 23d of April, 1841, Captain Edmund Fanning died of grief (according to the records of vital statistics) at the same place. Both were buried in the family burying-ground at Stonington, Conn.

From his voyage as first mate of the Betsy in 1792, Captain Edmund Fanning commanded or acted as directive agent for upwards of seventy expeditions to the South Seas and China. Besides the ships already mentioned which were built for him in New York, he built the following at Stonington: the ship Hydaspy in 1822; ship Almyra, which was sold in New York; brigs Seraph, Othello, and Bogartar.

As an inducement to him to enter into the Naval service of the United States, he was tendered the command of either of two new frigates by President Jefferson, as the following certificate will show: —

"NEW YORK, *January 19th*, 1837.

"This certifies that I was personally known to Mr. George Warner, on his return from Washington, having brought from President Jefferson an invitation and tender to Captain Edmund Fanning to the command of either of the new United States frigates, the New York or the Adams, as an inducement for him to enter into the naval service of the government; his commission to take date the day the frigate was launched. This was, as my memory serves, between the years 1801 and 1803.

W. E. NEXSEN.

Attest, JOHN R. BLEECKER.

This flattering offer was declined, as Captain Fanning was at that time actively engaged in fitting out expeditions for the South Seas.

Captain Edmund Fanning published two books of voyages: the first, entitled "Fanning's Voyages Round the World," appeared in 1833; and the second, "Voyages to the South Seas, Indian and Pacific Oceans, China Sea, etc.," in 1838.

Captain Edmund Fanning's residence at Stonington, Long Point, was on the corner of Water (formerly called West Main Street) and Trumbull Streets. (See photogravure.) The land was originally Denison land, and this corner lot of thirty-two rods was sold by Joseph Denison 2d to Andrew Brown 20 January, 1775. The dwelling-house and other buildings on it were built by Mr. Brown previous to that date (as is proved by Stonington Deeds, Book 9, p. 479). Brown sold the property to Robert Sheffield 22 March, 1781.[1] On the 13th May, 1806, Robert Sheffield Junior, for his father, deeded the property to Nathaniel M. Pendleton. It then contained, in addition to the large dwelling-house, a black-

[1] *Vide* Stonington Deeds, Book 10, p. 288.

smith's shop.[1] Mr. Pendleton sold it 23 July, 1819, to Nancy Pendleton of New York,[2] and she 4 August, 1851, to Francis Pendleton of Stonington for $800.[3] It was bequeathed by will in 1875 by Francis Pendleton to his son Albert, and now belongs to his widow, Ada Pendleton. In the will the house is spoken of as the "Fanning House."[4] Captain Edmund Fanning never owned this property according to the Stonington Records, but there is no doubt of his residence there, which fact is confirmed by the older inhabitants. Captain Fanning owned a house and lot on the north corner of Water and Harmony Streets. The house has now been taken down and a new one erected by Dr. C. O. Main. It is not known, however, that Captain Fanning resided there, and it is thought not. He also owned a house and lot on Harmony Street, next east of his corner lot, which was the old Acors Sheffield place bought about 1770. This Sheffield property soon went to his son, Captain William A. Fanning, who sold it to Benjamin Pendleton 22 May, 1821. He also owned at times other property in Stonington.

His ship-yard was on the water's edge west of his house and just south of the present Attwood Morrison Machine Shop, and the breakwater.

[1] *Vide* Stonington Deeds, Book 15, p. 251.
[2] *Vide* Stonington Deeds, Book 17, p. 205.
[3] *Vide* Stonington Deeds, Book 25, p. 232.
[4] *Vide* Stonington Probate Records, Book 18, p. 75.

CAPTAIN CHARLES[6] FANNING (No. 158).

(For Genealogical data, see page 291.)

Captain Charles Fanning, son of Captain Thomas and Elizabeth (Capron) Fanning, was born at Groton, Conn., 16 December, 1749. Early in life he moved to Preston — North Society — in that part which was afterwards the town of Griswold and the village of Jewett City. There on the 31st of March, 1774, he married Anne Brewster, daughter of Simon and Anne (Andrus) Brewster, and had by her eleven children.

Charles Fanning was among the first who entered into service in the American army on the call for troops in April, 1775, and was an actor in some of the most prominent scenes of the war. He was in the Battle of Long Island and at Monmouth. He shared the sufferings of that hard winter at Valley Forge, and was at Yorktown at the surrender of Lord Cornwallis. He was one of the few who served the full quota of time, seven years and eight months. He was mustered in on the 8th of May, 1775, as Sergeant in Captain Tyler's Company of Preston, in the 6th Regiment commanded by Colonel Samuel H. Parsons of New London. This Regiment was recruited from New London, Hartford, and the present County of Middlesex. Two companies at once marched to Boston: the others (including Tyler's) remained on duty in New London until the 17th of June, when they were ordered to the Boston Camp, where they were posted at Roxbury until the expiration of their term of service on the 10th of December, 1775.

On the 20th of June, 1776, Charles Fanning received his commission as Ensign from Jonathan Trumbull, Captain-

General and Commander-in-chief of the Continental forces of Connecticut, and served under Captain Joshua Huntington in the 4th Battalion of Wadsworth's Brigade, commanded by Colonel Selden. This Battalion was raised to reinforce General Washington at New York. It served there and on Long Island. During the retreat of the American forces from New York City it suffered much loss. Colonel Selden was taken prisoner and incarcerated in the city, where he died on the 11th of October, 1776. The term of service of the Battalion expired on the 25th of December following.

Charles Fanning re-entered the service on the 1st of January, 1777, as Second Lieutenant in Captain Abner Bacon's Company of the 4th Regiment of the Connecticut Line, commanded by Colonel John Durkee. On the 15th of March, 1779, he received a commission as First Lieutenant to rank from the 15th of November, 1778,[1] and on the 1st of May, 1779, he was appointed paymaster. This Regiment, like the others of the line, was raised for service during the continuance of the war. It went into camp at Peekskill in the spring of 1777, and in September was ordered to join Washington's forces in Pennsylvania. It was engaged at the battle of Germantown, on the 4th of October, 1777. The Regiment being afterwards assigned to Varnum's Brigade, a detachment of it took part in the brave defence of Fort Mifflin on the Delaware, November 12–16. It wintered at Valley Forge in 1777–1778, and on the 26th of June following was engaged at the battle of Monmouth, Colonel Durkee commanding the Brigade.

After this battle the Regiment was encamped with the

[1] *Vide* Conn. His. Society Collections, Vol. VIII, Revolutionary Rolls and Lists, 1775–1783, p. 47.

main army at White Plains until ordered into winter quarters at Reading, where it was assigned to the 1st Connecticut Brigade under General Parsons. In the campaign of 1779 it was engaged in the movements on the east side of the Hudson River and took part in the storming of Stony Point on the 15th of July. During the following winter it was encamped with the Connecticut Division on the outposts at Morristown. In 1780 it was with the main army on both sides of the Hudson and wintered opposite West Point. The Regiment took an active part in all the succeeding events of the war until the surrender of the British at Yorktown. At the close of the war in 1783 it was mustered out of service, when Charles Fanning received the brevet rank of Captain.

His original commission as Ensign, signed by Jonathan Trumbull at Hartford, 20 June, 1776, and his commission as Second Lieutenant "by order of Congress" signed in the bold hand of John Hancock, President, 7 January, 1777, are still preserved as precious heirlooms by his descendants.

After the close of the war he returned to the duties of a citizen. In early manhood he engaged in mercantile business near Griswold Paper Mill, better remembered as the site of "Glasgo's Iron Works." Afterwards he carried on business in Jewett City, where he was one of the pioneer merchants. His store was situated just east of his house, and was a one-story building painted red and with gambrel-roof. It had half-doors, so called, and the counter in the store had a hole or slit in it through which pennies could be dropped, a common custom in those times.

On the Fourth of July, 1786, he was enrolled as one of the original members of the Society of the Cincinnati, the certificate of membership being dated at Mount Vernon, and signed by George Washington as President and John Knox as Secretary. (See photogravure.)

In 1788 he was chosen as Selectman, and was a Justice of the Peace in 1810 and for many subsequent years, from which office he received the appellation of "Squire Fanning," by which he was designated in his latter years. He was chosen a Representative to the Legislature in 1792, 1794, 1796, 1803, 1804, 1806, 1807, 1811, and 1814, being the candidate of both parties when any matter of special interest to the town was at stake.

In 1814 Charles Fanning was instrumental in establishing the Fanning Manufacturing Company at Jewett City for the manufacture of cotton yarn and cotton cloth. The Company consisted of four partners: Charles Fanning, Christopher Avery, Joseph Stanton and Joseph C. Tyler.

When General Lafayette visited the United States in 1824, on his journey from New York to Boston, he visited Charles Fanning at his house in Jewett City and embraced him after the French manner, exclaiming, "God bless you, Comrade Fanning!"

Squire Fanning has been described by those who recollect him as a delightful gentleman, greatly respected and beloved by all who knew him. He was a fine looking man, always well dressed, wearing silver-buckled shoes, silk stockings, knee-breeches, and coat in the fashion of the period, and always carrying a cane.

His dwelling-house in Jewett City, a large, square, two-story white house and one of the most substantial built residences in the town, stood on the northwest side of the Main Street near the Quinebaug River where the Rev. Mr. Shipman's house now stands, under the shadow of venerable oaks. Here he died on the 22d of March, 1837, at the age of eighty-seven years, three months, and six days. His second wife, Hepzibah Bull, whom he married at Hartford on the 30th of August, 1814, survived him. She died on the 31st of March, 1843, without issue, aged seventy-four years. The house in which Squire Fanning lived was occupied by his daughter Betsy and son Franklin after his death. Some years after her decease it was removed to another part of the village opposite the Railroad Station, where it was remodelled and was known as the Jewett City Hotel. This was burned to the ground on the morning of July 5, 1878.

Squire Fanning was a prominent member of the Church and took a leading part in every religious movement. He united with the Congregational Church at Jewett City soon after its organization, under the ministry of its first pastor, Rev. Seth Bliss. During his residence in Jewett City, until his last illness, his attendance at the house of worship on Sundays was so punctual that the other villagers were wont to exclaim on seeing him pass by, "Come, it is time to go to church. There goes Squire Fanning." His life was never more replete with usefulness than during the last fifteen years; — though the oldest man in town, he was still active and sound both in body and mind. His society, his example and his charities were such as caused his death long to be remembered and mourned.

Fanning Island, in an expansion of the Quinebaug River on the Lisbon side of Jewett City, was named after Squire Charles Fanning.

THOMAS[5] FANNING (No. 160).

(For Genealogical data, see page 297.)

Thomas Fanning, son of Captain Thomas and Elizabeth (Capron) Fanning of Groton, Conn., was born on the 22d of May, 1755, was a farmer and resided at Groton, and later at Norwich. In his youth he learned the trade of ship-carpenter, and followed that occupation for several years at Groton, Mystic, Stonington, Conn., and New York City.

When the Revolutionary War broke out, Thomas, then twenty years of age, was early imbued with the spirit of '76 under the influence and active guidance of his paternal parent, Captain Thomas Fanning. His father was captain of the 5th Company or "Trainband" of Groton and took an active interest in the war, opening a recruiting office and sending five of his six sons, all of whom went through the service and two of whom were wounded. His sixth, and youngest son, was only a lad of ten years.

On the 18th of March, 1777, Thomas enlisted for the war as a private, and was appointed Corporal same day, in Captain Amos Stanton's Company (whose sister Prudence Stanton married Captain Roger Fanning (No. 68)) of Colonel Henry Sherburne's Regiment.[1] Three of the six companies

[1] Thomas Fanning's Pension Papers in possession of the compiler furnish this evidence.

Connecticut Revolutionary Rolls, page 255, however, say "he enlisted in Stanton's Company 18 March, 1777, and was transferred to Col. Samuel B. Webb's Company 1 May, 1780, appointed Corporal 1 August, 1780."

On his Pension Papers he appears as private only.

A letter from the Pension Department, Washington, D. C., dated 4 January, 1897, says "he received a pension for six years actual service as a Private in the Connecticut Troops Revolutionary War."

Capt. Amos Stanton's original Muster Roll is in possession of Mrs.

of this regiment were raised in Connecticut by Lieutenant-Colonel Jonathan Meigs of Middletown; the others by Colonel Sherburne in Rhode Island. On the 1st of May, 1780, the regiment was disbanded: most of the officers retired from active service and the enlisted men were distributed among other commands.

The record of the regiment is identical with that of Colonel Samuel B. Webb's, with which it was brigaded; the record of which regiment is as follows: — (Taken from "Connecticut Revolutionary Rolls.")

"Col. Samuel B. Webb's Regiment 1777–81 — One of the sixteen additional regiments of Infantry raised at large for the 'Continental Line' of '77 to continue through the War, recruited mainly in Hartford County and eastern part of State.

"Went into Camp at Peekskill in Spring of '77 and served in Parson's Brigade under Putnam during movements of the following Summer and Fall. On advance of the enemy and the loss of Forts Clinton and Montgomery October, 1777, it crossed to west side of Hudson and served under Governor Clinton of New York for a time. On December 10, the Regiment engaged with other troops in an expedition against Long Island, which met with accidents leaving Col. Webb and other officers prisoners in the enemy's hands. Regiment wintered with Parson's Brigade at West Point and assisted in construction of permanent works there. Redoubt Webb doubtless named after the 'Colonel.' In Summer of 1778, it was attached to Varnum's Brigade and marched to Rhode Island engaging in the battle there of August 29, 1778, and commended for its conduct. Wintered in Rhode Island 1778–'79 and remaining there till Fall of 1779, marched to winter quarters Morristown, New York, 1779–'80; assigned to Stark's Brigade, Lieut. Col. Huntington, commanding. Present at Battle of Springfield, New Jersey, June 23, 1780, and during following Summer served with main army on the Hudson. It was designated the 9th Regiment and went into Winter quar-

Christopher Morgan, Mystic, Conn. In it are the names of "Corporal Thomas Fanning, appointed 18 March, 1777," enlisted for the war. Also David Fanning (No. 79), private, 23 March, 1777, enlisted for 3 years.

ters 1780–'81 with the Division at camp 'Connecticut Village' above the Robinson House. There it was re-organized for formation of 1781–'83."

Thomas Fanning also served in Captain William Clift's Company in Colonel John Durkee's Regiment, Connecticut Line, and in Colonel Ebenezer Huntington's Regiment. He served until the close of the war, June, 1783.

He was wounded during service, a ball plowing through the scalp on the top of his head, leaving a scar which in after years he was wont to show to his grandsons, saying:— "Boys, put your finger in that furrow — that was made by a d——n Redcoat's bullet."

By an Act of Congress passed on the 18th of March, 1818, he became a United States pensioner for six years actual service in the Army of the Revolution and for wounds and disabilities received, at the rate of eight dollars per month. His pension certificate, No. 7298, was dated 6th of March, 1819, and signed by John C. Calhoun, Secretary of War. After his death his widow, by Act of Congress 7th of July, 1838, drew half pension of $48 a year.

After the war Thomas Fanning returned to Groton, where in 1785 he married Susannah, daughter of John and Susannah (Willson) Faulkner of Groton.

A few years previous to 1800 they removed to New York City. His name appears in the City Directory there in the year 1798 as "Thomas Fanning, 33 Bancker St." There on the 22d of September, 1800, their infant son Thomas died of yellow fever, whereupon they immediately returned to Groton to live. In 1803 his name again appears in the New York Directory as living at 156 Harmon Street, but it is doubtful if his family lived there at that time. It is more probable that he went to New York simply to work at his trade, that of ship-carpenter. He afterward returned to Groton where he received his share of his brother Frederick's legacy. On the 19th of April, 1815, he purchased a dwelling-house, shop, barn, and twenty-one acres of land in Norwich from Thomas Smith, in that part of the town now called East Great Plain (Gifford Street). Thither he removed with his wife, daughter Fanny Maria, daughter Mary, son Alfred, and his brother Elisha. On the 30th of March, 1820, he deeded this Norwich property to his daughter Fanny Maria Fanning. At her death in 1876 her sons Charles H. and Frederick L. Gardner inherited the property. The former buying out Frederick's interest, resided on the farm until his death in 1896. Charles' widow Ellen then continued to live there until 1898 when she sold the property to Stephen N. Yerrington.

Thomas Fanning has been described as a man of large frame, tall and portly, and of a very frank and kindly disposition. He and his wife were generous and hospitable. They kept open house at Norwich, where their friends and relations were welcomed at all times. He died 15 April, 1828, in his seventy-third year. His widow, Susannah Faulkner Fanning, died 4 March, 1841, aged eighty-two years. She was small of stature and very straight, exceedingly active and energetic even in the last years of her life. Both are buried in the old Norwich City Cemetery in the family lot.

This lot is in the old part of the cemetery near the Elm Street entrance. The old headstones having disappeared, a monument was erected in 1903 by David H. Fanning, of Worcester, Mass., a grandson, to the memory of those buried there, *i.e.*, Thomas, Susannah, Alfred and Elisha Fanning.

Susannah Faulkner, born in Groton in 1758, was seven-

The Gardner Farm, East Great Plain, Norwich, Conn. 1896.

teen years old at the breaking out of the war. When the traitor Arnold burned New London at the time of the Massacre of Fort Griswold, 6th of September, 1781, she helped to carry water and supplies to the patriot soldiers.

In her old age she enjoyed relating to her grandchildren the incidents of her early life during the stirring period of the Revolutionary War. She was a great friend of old Mother Bailey. Both were born in the same year, went to the same school, and were intimately associated during their youth. This friendship was further cemented by the same feeling of patriotism which swayed their hearts.

At one time, not long before her death, Mrs. Fanning, while visiting her son Henry at Jewett City, requested her eldest grandson Henry, as he was going to New London on some business, to call on old Mother Bailey over at Groton. "Tell her you are Susan Faulkner's grandson," she said. Henry, not daring to disobey his grandmother's command, knowing that he would be held to a strict accounting, reluctantly performed the required duty. He crossed over to Groton after transacting his business at New London, and, arriving at old Mother Bailey's house, knocked long and loudly for admission. He was finally confronted by the old lady herself, who upon opening the door cried out, "Why on earth don't you come in and not stand there knocking like a darned fool! Don't you know this is a public house? Who the devil are you anyway?" "I am Susan Faulkner's grandson," tremblingly ejaculated the youth. "Oh!" cried Mrs. Bailey, and thereupon she softened her tone and welcomed him in. She showed him all over the house, and among other things pictures of Daniel Webster and Henry Clay "hung up by the heels" as she expressed it (upside down), for she hated all Whigs, the new anti-Jackson party.

Old Mother Bailey was a remarkable character in her day. Her maiden name was Anna Warner. Her parents dying in her youth, she was adopted by her uncle Edward Mills, who was one of the victims of the Fort Griswold Massacre. She exhibited great heroism at this trying time and during the whole Revolutionary period, being animated by the most fervid patriotism. After peace was established, she married Elijah Bailey of Groton. During the War of 1812, Decatur and his little fleet of three vessels were closely blockaded by the British squadron under Commodore Hardy, then in full view in Fishers Island Sound. Marauding parties were landed from time to time and the inhabitants feared a general landing of the enemy. In this situation the garrison of the fort at New London was found to be deficient in flannel for cartridges. An appeal for flannel was made to Mrs. Bailey as she was crossing the street to visit a neighbor. Like the other inhabitants she had sent her blankets with her other goods inland for safety; but quick as thought she passed her hand under her skirt, unloosed the band of her flannel petticoat, dropped it at her feet and then handed it to the officer with the remark that she hoped their "aim might be true and the execution on the Englishman thorough." The garment was conveyed to the fort and the story repeated to the garrison. With loud huzzas for Mother Bailey it was raised on a pikestaff with the remark that no better banner was needed to stimulate the men to deeds of heroism. The "Martial Petticoat" incident was lauded through the land and was the theme of prose and poetry, of song and story. When President Jackson visited Mother Bailey long afterward he presented her with a gold snuff-box, having a locket at the reverse side containing a lock of his hair. This locket she was very proud of and loved to exhibit to her friends and visitors, but would only open it a trifle for fear that the lock of hair, which was very small, owing to the President's scanty growth of that article, would fall out.

The old Willson-Fanning Family Bible, printed in 1712, is known to have been in the possession of Thomas Fanning and his wife Susannah Faulkner, and came into their hands from Susan's grandparents John Willson and his wife Mary Cunningham, who were married on the 3d of September, 1730, according to the first entry in the Bible. From Thomas Fanning it passed to his daughter Fanny Maria Gardner, who lived and died in the old Fanning homestead at Norwich. Mrs. Gardner presented it to her niece Lucy Fanning Hawkins, who previous to her death in 1892, presented it to her nephew, Walter F. Brooks, of Worcester, Mass., in whose possession it now is.

CAPTAIN RUFUS[6] FANNING (No. 171).

(For Genealogical data, see page 306.)

Captain Rufus Fanning, son of Asher and Priscilla (Kinne) Fanning, was born at Groton, Conn., in April, 1775.

He early evinced a fondness for the sea, and before he was fifteen years of age he had made several voyages.

An account of a voyage and its accompanying hardships which he made to Demerara in the year 1790, in the form of a letter to his Uncle Phineas Fanning of Groton, is preserved by his descendants and gives a good idea of a sailor's misfortunes.

Nothing daunted, however, by his ill luck on that memorable voyage in 1790, he continued to follow the sea until before many years he became a captain and was in command of his own vessel. He followed this occupation the greater part of his life. He was captain of the vessel "Criterion," which it is said was captured in the War of 1812.

He resided in the northeast part of Groton near the Stonington line. The house, now known as the Ira Main Place, is located at the foot of Lantern Hill; on the west side of the highway.

Capt. Rufus Fanning was a member of the order of Masons, having joined Charity Lodge No. 68 F. & A. M., 25 Oct., 1825.

Late in life he removed to the West, and married a second time and had issue. He died at Bath, Summit Co., O., 20 December, 1845.

HENRY WILLSON[6] FANNING (No. 350).

(For Genealogical data, see page 408.)

Henry Willson Fanning, son of Thomas and Susannah (Faulkner) Fanning, was born at Groton, Conn., 8 February, 1786, and was named after his grandmother Willson. He was brought up on his grandfather Captain Thomas Fanning's farm at Groton, afterward occupied by his father, which locality is now known by the name of Shewville.

He early learned the trade of a blacksmith of Joshua Barstow of Preston City, which trade he continued to follow during his lifetime. Possessed of natural ingenuity he became very skillful at it, and had the reputation of being one of the most ingenious men in his line.

Soon after his apprenticeship he located in Marlboro, Conn., where he followed his trade and where he married, in the fall of 1811, Sarah, daughter of David Hale of Glastonbury. She was a school teacher and taught in Marlboro, living with her Uncle Foote. They resided there until 1816, during which period three children were born to them. Being urged by his father to remove to Norwich and set up business there, he did so in June of that year, and located on the farm at East Great Plain, which his father had bought the year previous. He built a blacksmith shop on the premises and commenced work, but did not stay there long, removing within a year and a half to Jewett City. He then built him a blacksmith shop near what was the "Woolen Factory." Later this was torn down, and he constructed another across the Quinebaug River on the Lisbon side. It was on the northwest side of the highway and directly opposite Captain Charles Fanning's house.

His first residence in Jewett City was in the southeastern part of the village. In 1834 he moved into a new house which he built on the Main Street in the northeast part of the village, on land bought of Enoch Baker. This land adjoined the meeting-house lot in the Second Ecclesiastical Society of Griswold. Neither he nor his wife lived, however, to long enjoy their new abode, as they both died within two years.

Henry served a short time in the War of 1812. He was Corporal in Enos H. Buell's Company of Connecticut Militia, and served about two months, marching from Marlboro, where he was then living, to New London and Groton at the time they were threatened by the British. His period of service, according to the Connecticut Rolls, dates from 18 July, 1813, to 16 September, 1813. It is said he was unable to continue in the army on account of his being very deaf, and a tradition exists in the family that he narrowly escaped being shot, through his inability on an occasion to hear his name called for the third time at muster roll, or while on duty.

Henry Willson Fanning was of medium height, stout built, and resembled very much his eldest son Henry Williams Fanning, of Newton Upper Falls, Mass.

He died at Jewett City, Sunday afternoon, 3 July, 1836, at the early age of fifty, his wife dying in less than a year afterward, 10 June, 1837, aged forty-nine years.

DAVID HALE[7] FANNING (No. 697).

(For Genealogical data, see page 528.)

The subject of this sketch is a self-made man. In a genealogical consideration of the Fanning family, this feature of his career is worthy of mention, as it indicates the staunchness of the parent stock.

David Hale Fanning was born 4 August, 1830, in Jewett City, a village in the town of Griswold, New London County, Conn. He was the son of Henry Willson and Sarah (Hale) Fanning, and the youngest of nine children. His father, a native of Groton, Conn., was born 8 February, 1786. His mother, a daughter of David and Ruth (Hale) Hale, was born in Glastonbury, Conn., 19 July, 1788.

When David was seven years of age, his parents died, and he remained in the care of an older brother until he reached the age of sixteen. Meanwhile he received such education as the district schools of the neighborhood afforded. The exacting discipline of his brother, the narrowness of his own life, the hopelessness of any development, and the inborn craving to be somebody and to do something, made David ambitious to see the world and make his own way. This characteristic had to assert itself, and has ever been a conspicuous part of his make-up. So, with his few possessions, among which was a Testament given him by his mother (which he has always faithfully kept), and a cash capital of $2.50, he left his native place on foot to seek his fortune. After a twenty-mile walk, David reached Danielsonville, Conn., at the end of his first day, there obtaining supper, lodging and breakfast, for which he paid sixteen cents. He then made direct for Worcester, at that time a town of some 10,000 inhabitants. There he hoped to find employment, but not succeeding, went on to Clinton, then a part of Lancaster, where he found employment in a factory. It is worthy of record that his first business experience was in a counterpane mill at sixteen years of age.

He remained in this position two years, and by attention to work, was promoted. By economy, he saved sufficient money to give him a start in life. Coming to Worcester in 1848, he served a short apprenticeship at the machinist trade.

In 1853 he was proprietor of a country store in Groton Junction, now the city of Ayer, Mass. Disposing of this business later, he went West, remaining in Cleveland two years, returning to Worcester again in 1857. During the next four years he was employed as a salesman. In 1859 he married Rosamond Hopkins Dawless, of Sterling, Mass., by whom he had issue, a son who died in infancy; Agnes Maria and Helen Josephine. Mrs. Fanning died 14 December, 1901.

In the year 1861 Mr. Fanning engaged in manufacturing hoop-skirts, under the name of the Worcester Skirt Co. Two or three years later he added the making of corsets to his business, and as the hoop-skirt gradually passed into disuse, corset-making became the principal feature of the business, the title of which was changed to that of the Worcester Corset Co. It was conducted as a private business until 1888, when it was incorporated as a stock company.

The same painstaking, diligent attention to business that had characterized Mr. Fanning's entire life, soon brought his manufactures into universal prominence, and in 1901 another change in the business was made, and its name became the Royal Worcester Corset Co. Mr. Fanning began his business in a small way at the corner of Main and

David H. Fanning

Front Streets, and as it expanded, occupied quarters respectively in Franklin Square and Hermon Street, finally moving to the extensive and complete factory on Wyman Street, erected by the company for its business, where it is at present located. From a very modest beginning, by persistence and faith in the country and its resources, and untiring diligence, Mr. Fanning has developed the great industrial institution known throughout the world, the Royal Worcester Corset Co., with its magnificent plant, and branch offices in all the large cities of the country, and business connections in every civilized country on the globe.

Notable among Mr. Fanning's personal characteristics is his intense patriotism. He springs from men who fought in all wars in which our country has been engaged, even back to the French and Indian Wars. In politics Mr. Fanning is a Republican. He is a man of pronounced opinions, and once he knows he is right, whether it be a business or a personal proposition which confronts him, he goes ahead, and nothing stands in the way of his accomplishing his end. In business Mr. Fanning is a disciplinarian. His influence is felt everywhere in his great factory. Cleanliness, deportment, order, system and attention, which are so much in evidence about him, are the results of his constant care and training. In spite of an active business life, Mr. Fanning has found time to study men and things; conditions historical and geographical; keeps thoroughly in touch with all the contemporaneous news of the time, and will stand in commercial history as a forceful illustration of what a man may be if he will.

JUDGE ADELBERT CANEDY[8] FANNING (No. 735).

(For Genealogical data, see page 535.)

Adelbert Canedy Fanning was born in Springfield, Penn., 25 July, 1851. His father, David Grace Fanning, was one of the pioneers of Bradford County, and for fifty-nine years was a Methodist class leader. He died 15 March, 1903. His wife, Antis Brown, daughter of Alexander and Catharine (Brown) Canedy, of Halifax, Vt., was born 28 April, 1815, and died at Wetona, Penn., 11 September, 1870.

Of the six children of David Grace and Antis Brown Fanning, Adelbert Canedy was the youngest. He was reared on the farm in Springfield Township, where he received his first school privileges. He was graduated from the Mansfield State Normal School in 1872 and from the Law Department of the Michigan University at Ann Arbor in 1874. In September of that year he was admitted to the bar, and at once took high rank in his profession. He began practice at Athens, Penn., but after a few months removed to Troy in that State. He was District Attorney for three years of Bradford County, and in September, 1899, was appointed by Governor Stone President Judge of the Forty-second Judicial District of Pennsylvania to succeed the late Hon. Benjamin M. Peck. In January, 1900, Judge Fanning entered upon the ten-year term to which he had been elected the preceding fall.

Bradford County, being a large county, forms one district, and upon the Judge falls the entire burden of trying all cases that come into the courts, — civil, criminal, and equity cases. Appeals from this court in matters not involving over fifteen hundred dollars are taken to the Su-

perior Court, and in excess of that amount to the Supreme Court of the State. As the duties also comprise the disposition of license applications, the position of the Judge is an arduous one. There are four regular terms of the Court at Towanda, usually of three weeks' duration each; four Grand Jury and Argument Courts of one week each; two terms of Court at Troy, the half-shire town, of two weeks each; besides an Argument Court the first Monday of each month, and frequent adjourned Argument and Jury Courts. The late Chief Justice of the Supreme Court of Pennsylvania was once the President Judge of Bradford County, as was David Wilmot, of "Wilmot Proviso" fame.

Judge Fanning is actively interested in educational matters, and was for twelve years a member of the Board of Education of Troy. In religion he is a Methodist, and for seven years was superintendent of the Troy Sunday school, and later filled the same place at Towanda. He is a Free Mason, a member of Trojan Lodge, No. 306, Troy Chapter, No. 261, Northern Commandery, No. 16, and has filled the highest positions in the Order. Is a member of Towanda Lodge of Perfection, Hayden Council, Princes of Jerusalem Calvary Chapter Rose Croix of Towanda, Penn., Williamsport Consistory 32 and Irene Temple A. A. O. N. M. S., Wilkesbarre, Penn.

He is a member of the Bradford County Bar Association, Trustee of the Mansfield, Penn., State Normal School, Trustee of Robert Packer Hospital at Sayre, Penn., and a member of a number of Historical Societies.

He is a Republican, and for years has advocated the cause of that party on the stump: he is popular as an orator, and is in frequent demand on public occasions.

WALTER FREDERIC BROOKS.

SON OF CHARLES EDWIN AND ELIZABETH (FANNING) BROOKS (No. 694).

(For Genealogical data, see pages 410, 411.)

Walter Frederic Brooks, son of Charles Edwin and Elizabeth Capron (Fanning) Brooks, was born at Worcester, Mass., 13 January, 1859. He was educated in the public schools of that city, graduating from the High School in 1877 and fitted for Harvard College, but preferring a mercantile life, he entered the office of the Crompton Loom Works the same year, where he remained about two years. In July, 1879, he entered the banking-house of William H. Morse with whom he was associated eleven years. In 1891 he severed his connection with Mr. Morse and took a lease in partnership with James F. Rock, of the Worcester Theatre, then newly built, they purchasing and assuming the interest of the old lessees Rich, Harris and Rock of Boston. The new lessees successfully operated the house for three years, but relinquished their lease in February, 1894, owing to the excessively high rental and during the Cleveland administration.

In December, 1895, Mr. Brooks was elected treasurer of the Worcester Corset Company, of which company his uncle, David H. Fanning, is President, General Manager and principal owner. The company was re-incorporated in 1901 as the Royal Worcester Corset Company. Mr. Brooks is still connected with the new company in that capacity.

In politics he is a staunch Republican. He is a life member of Montacute Lodge A.F. and A. M., Eureka Royal Arch Chapter, Hiram Council R. & S. M., Worcester County

Commandery Knights Templar, Worcester Society of Antiquity, New England Historic Genealogical Society, Boston, New London County Historical Society, Conn., and Suffolk County Historical Society of New York. He is also member of the Worcester Club, Tatnuck Country Club, Worcester Board of Trade, Home Market Club, Boston, and other societies.

He is author and compiler of this "History of the Fanning Family."

He is unmarried and resides at Worcester, Mass.

THE RIVERHEAD TOMBSTONE.

(See Photogravure.)

On a gravestone in the Cemetery at Riverhead, Long Island, is the following inscription: —

"Capt. JAMES FANNING,
died 1776, in the 93 year of
his age.

"He was the great grandson of DOMINICUS FANNING, who was Mayor of a City in IRELAND, (under CHARLES 1st) was taken prisoner at the Battle of DROGHEDA 1649, all the Garrison, except himself put to the sword. he was beheaded by CROMWELL his head stuck upon a pole at the principal gate of the City, his property confiscated, because when CHARLES 1st made proclamation of peace, as a member of the Irish Council, he advised not to accept unless the British Government would secure to the Irish their religion, their property and their lives:
O'Conners History.

His son EDMUND was born in KILKENNY, IRELAND, married CATHERINE daughter of HUGH HAYS Earl of CONNOUGHT and Emigrated to this country with his family, Consisting of his wife CATHARINE, two Sons, THOMAS and WILLIAM, and two Servants, LAHORNE and ORNA, Settled in STONINGTON C^t: WILLIAM in a Battle with the Indians was killed by King WILLIAM who split his head open with a Tomahawk. THOMAS had a daughter CATHARINE PAGE, and one Son JAMES: this Capt. JAMES FANNING Served under Great Britain which government was at war with FRANCE, Married HANNAH SMITH of SMITHTOWN, had five Sons and four Daughters, Viz. PHINEAS, THOMAS, GILBERT, EDMUND, JAMES, CATHERINE, BETHIA, SALLY, and NANCY. PHINEAS had a Son, PHINEAS who graduated at Yale College 1768, two of whose Sons are now living 1850, Viz. WILLIAM FANNING in New York City, and P. W. FANNING in WILMINGTON, N. C. His wife HANNAH, Son THOMAS, & daughter CATHARINE buried beside their father. GILBERT settled in STONINGTON Ct. EDMUND became Leut. Governor of NOVA-SCOTIA where

Tombstone of Capt. James Fanning
at Riverhead, L. I.

he held large estates, JAMES settled on Long Island, had two Sons JOHN, and JAMES, the latter was a merchant many years, residing three miles east of RIVER-HEAD, had five Sons, four of whom are now living: the Elder, JAMES, died at MORICHES in his 72 year 1848. NATHANIEL resides in Town of SOUTHAMPTON, two MANNASSEH and ISRAEL reside in RIVER-HEAD Town, and the fifth Son, JOSHUA FANNING Physician in Greenport, SOUTHOLD Town. SALLY FANNING married Capt. JOSIAH LUPTON, CATHARINE married a MUMFORD, BETHIA married a TERRY, and NANCY married Maj. JOHN WICKHAM. L. S. Hill Sculptor."

The gravestone was originally erected in the year 1849 on the Griffing farm, formerly belonging to the Fannings, but was removed to the Riverhead Cemetery in 1861, together with other headstones of the Fannings buried there.

The old plot on the Griffing or Fanning farm was located about where Jetter and Moore's bottling works stand, at the southeast corner of Griffing Avenue and Railroad Street, and was the old burial-place of the Fannings. Interred there were the remains of Captain James Fanning (No. 15) and his wife Hannah, daughter Katharine, son Richard, and brother Thomas Fanning (No. 38), all having headstones. There were other unmarked graves in the old plot.

The removal of the remains and headstones was made by George Hill, father and predecessor of the present firm of Frank H. Hill & Bro., Marble Workers and Undertakers, of Riverhead, who died in 1888, and brother of Lester S. Hill, who cut the inscription on the Fanning tombstone. Israel Fanning (No. 206) made the contract and furnished the inscription, and Peter Fanning (No. 210), it is said, bought or donated the cemetery plot. O. T. Fanning of Port Jefferson, L. I. (No. 484), procured the funds for cleaning up the stones and plot.

The tombstone contains many errors of statement. Captain James Fanning died 15 April, 1779 (not in 1776), as is proved by the "Salmon Record" and the Mattituck, L. I., church records. In a letter written by General Edmund Fanning, his son, to his sister, Mrs. Hannah Wickham, 16 March, 1778, which is still preserved by his descendants, he sent his "best regards" to his "aged father."[1] Other letters also in existence prove he was living in 1777. So he could not have died in 1776, as stated on the tombstone.

Nor was he ninety-three years old, for he was born either in 1694 or 1695, as is evident from the town and church records of Stonington, Conn.[2] He was consequently eighty-four or eighty-five years old at time of decease.

In regard to Edmund Fanning, the elder, and the contention that he was son of Dominick Fanning, there is not the slightest evidence that Dominick had such a son. This matter is treated fully in another part of this work.[3]

Dominick Fanning was a resident of Limerick, Ireland, and mayor and alderman of that city. He was not in the Battle of Drogheda, nor taken prisoner there in 1649. On the contrary, he was beheaded at the fall of Limerick in 1651 by General Ireton, being one of twenty-one prisoners exempted from pardon.[4]

The statement that Edmund Fanning married Catharine Hays, daughter of the Earl of Connaught, is ridiculous. No person of the name of Hugh Hays ever bore the title of Earl of Connaught, nor was there any Earl of Connaught in existence in the 17th century, when the marriage of Edmund Fanning took place. Edmund's wife was named Ellen and not Catharine, as proved by the Connecticut records.

[1] *Vide* copy of letter in Appendix F.
[2] *Vide* page 93 of this work and Note ‖ thereon.
[3] *Vide* pages 29–40 of this work, — also Introduction.
[4] *Vide* Ferrar's *History of Limerick*.

THE OLD FANNING BURYING-GROUND.

The Fanning burying-ground is located on the old Groton farm of Edmund Fanning, about twenty rods west of Mystic River or Brook, and one hundred rods south of Alonzo Main's dwelling-house. It is in extent from one-half to three-quarters of an acre, and is now thickly grown up with bushes and trees. It is first mentioned in the year 1762, in the will of Edmund Fanning (No. 10), who reserved the burying-ground as follows: —

"I give and sequester one half acre of my land to be laid out "conveniently to the burying place in the northeast corner of "my Land near Mistick River."

His grandson William Fanning (No. 65), who inherited the farm, also reserved the burying-ground "containing ¾ of an acre," in his deed of the land to Samuel Williams, 3d, 15 March, 1777, and the latter made like reservation in his deed to Ambrose Fish, 6 August, 1777. In the subsequent deeds, however, no mention is made of the burial plot.

In the burial place are some fifteen or twenty gravestones, only three of which are legibly inscribed. Two of these are the headstones of Jonathan Fanning (No. 11) and his wife Elizabeth, both in a good state of preservation. The inscriptions read as follows :—

In Memory of
Mr. Jonathan Faning
who died April ye
28, 1761, in ye 78th
year of his age.

In Memory of
Mrs. Elisabeth ye wife
of Mr. Jonathan Faning
who died July 24th
1772 in ye 78th year
of her age.

The third stone is marked: —

P × M
1753

but it cannot be learned who was buried there. Lieutenant John Fanning had daughters, Mary and Prudence, who married Samuel Fox and Jacob Parke, respectively. Both husbands died in 1752, but the dates of decease of Mary and Prudence are not ascertained. If both died the following year, the interpretation of the inscription may possibly be "Prudence and Mary, 1753," but this is mere conjecture.

The burying-ground lies on both sides of a dividing stone wall, and the north portion seems older than the south. In the latter part are several headstones in a good state of preservation, among them "Zerviah Niles" (No. 23). North of the wall the oldest stones appear, most of them being rough and unshaped rocks placed at the head and foot of the graves.

There is little or no doubt that the majority of the first three generations of the Fannings were interred there, though with unmarked headstones, and an effort is now being made to redeem the old burying-ground and form an Association to take care of it, and erect a suitable monument to the memory of Edmund Fanning the Elder, and those of his descendants who are buried there.

UNIDENTIFIED FANNINGS AT GROTON, STONINGTON, AND NORWICH, CONN.

ESTHER FANNING, born about 1760, a poor child, put out to serve until she was eighteen years old as an apprentice to Caleb Lamb of Groton, 25 April, 1763, by Joseph Morgan, Nathan Niles, Jonathan Latham, Selectmen and Overseers of the Poor, and with consent of Christopher Avery, a Justice of the Peace for County of New London.

JORDAN FANNING'S name appears in the Probate Records of Stonington or Groton in 1781 or 1782.

There was a Jordan Fanning of South Brimfield, Mass., who served in the Continental Army, 1778–1780, but no evidence to show who he was.

HENRY C. FANNING, Norwich, Conn., in Civil War; died 28 Oct., 1862, of wounds received at Sharpsburg, Md., aged eighteen years. (*Vide*, Caulkin's "History of Norwich," p. 683.)

SOLOMON FANNING, Norwich, Conn. It is said his name was Buddington and that he changed it to Fanning. He resided in the family of Thomas Fanning (No. 160) when a young man. He lived in New York City for a number of years, but returned to Norwich, where he died about 1890. Was a portrait painter. Had issue: *William D.*, *Theodore A.*, *Michael Angelo*, *Charles Tracy*, and three daughters, *Inez*, *Emma*, and *Belle*.

LISTS OF SOLDIERS.

The Fanning family, noted for its patriotism and zeal, has borne more than its share in the wars of the country. The following lists of soldiers are compiled from the records at hand, but it is doubtless incomplete, owing to the lack of data obtainable from members of the family. Furthermore, the collection of Revolutionary War Records at the Pension Office, Washington, D. C., is far from complete. The absence, therefore, of a name from any of the following lists should not be accepted as conclusive evidence that the person did not serve in that war.

SOLDIERS OF KING PHILIP'S WAR, 1675–'76.

	PAGE
Private Edmund[1] Fanning, Senior (No. 1)	85
Private Edmund[2] Fanning, Junior (No. 2)	91
Private Thomas[2] Fanning (No. 4)	92
Lieutenant John[2] Fanning (No. 5)	94

OTHER EARLY INDIAN WARS.

—— William[2] Fanning (No. 6) killed by Indians between 1704 and 1718	85

FRENCH AND INDIAN WARS.

Captain James[3] Fanning (No. 15), 1746–'47	103
Private David[4] Fanning (No. 33), 1759–'62	127

REVOLUTIONARY WAR.

Seaman Thomas Fanning (No. —?), perhaps No. 160	129
Private Nathan[5] Fanning (No. 80), also marine	129
Captain Thomas[4] Fanning (No. 38)	138
Colonel Phineas[4] Fanning (No. 39)	144
Commissary Gilbert[4] Fanning (No. 44)	154
Captain Gilbert[5] Fanning (No. 111)	157

WAR OF 1812.

TWO SEMINOLE INDIAN WARS.

MEXICAN WAR.

CIVIL WAR.

SPANISH-AMERICAN WAR, 1898.

OTHER WARS.

APPENDICES

APPENDIX A.

(Refer to pages 29 and 30.)

Will of Symon Fanning of Limerick, Alderman.* (1636)

"In the name of God Amen: I Symon ffanninge of Limerick, Alderman, being att this p.sent bound for Dublin, And for Divers other consideracons me thereunto movinge. Doe make this my last will & Testam^t in manner and fourme followinge, ffirst I bequeath my soule to Almighty God, my Creator and Redeemer, And to the blessed virgin Mary, And my bodie to be buried to my friends discretion, when I shall happen to dye.

Item I leave and bequeath unto my well beloved wife Jouan ffanninge ats Arthur my now dwelling Stone house in St Marie's p.ish in Limerick aforesaid, meared wth ffrancis ffannings stone house on the east, John Stritch' his stone house on the west, Edmond ffanninges lands on the south, and Creaghes land on the north, (except the house wherein christian ffox and margarett Russell[1] sometymes dwelt and the sell^{rs} lyinge under those rooms wth all ye members yards kitchens shambles & other appurtenances, unto my said wife for and during her natural life And from and after her decease I leave and bequeath the same rents unto my sonne and heire Dominicke ffanninge and the heires males of his boddie lawfullie begotten and to be begotten And for want of such heires males of ye boddie of ye said Dominick ffanninge the said stone house to come to my second sonne John ffanninge, and the heires males of his boddie lawfullie begotten or to be begotten; And for want of such issue, To my third sonne Bartholemewe ffanninge And the heires males of his boddie lawfullie begotten or to be begotten; and for lacke of such issue to my ffourth sonne

[1] This name Margaret Russell and also the names John Stritch and Christian Fox appear in the Connaught Certificates of persons transplanted 1653-54.

Richard ffanninge and the heires males of his boddie lawfullie to be begotten And for lacke of such issue to my ffith sonne James ffanninge And the heires males of his boddie lawfullie to be begotten; And for want of such issue to the heires males of myne own bodie lawfullie to be begotten hereafter, And for want of such issue to my nephew Nicholas ffanninge fitz Edward and the heires males of his boddie lawfully to be begotten And for lacke of such issue the said stone house to come unto the right heires of the said Symon ffanninge for ever.

Item I leave and bequeath unto my said wife Jouan Arthur all that and those my sheep cowes and Garrans in Garranynealane, Rathbane, Ballyneknocke, and all the corne and graines above ground, her lynnen cloath togither also wth all her Jewells now in specie, three silver braceletts onely excepted:

Item I leave and bequeath unto my said wife a batrie brewing panne contayninge a hoggsett or thereabouts, The best crocke for distilling of Aquavitæ, And a brass Kettle contayninge a barrellfull, togither also wth all my small brass boyling pannes.

Item I leave and bequeath unto my nephew Nicholas ffanninge the q^rter fishinge I have in Castleroy now in the occupation of Rorie o carroll for & during fortie yeares to come, iff he live soe longe, paying thereout his ma^ties rent And after his disease I bequeath and leave the same to my ffourth sonne Richard ffanninge and his heires males forever.

Item I leave and bequeath unto the said Richard ffanninge and my wife Jouan Arthur ioyntly & equally Gortdirabohan, Rahenenergonlebegge, and Rathgrellane in mortgage of Three score pounds ster.[1]

Item I leave & bequeath unto my Son John ffanninge the house or lower rooms wherein Christian ffox and Margarett Russell sometymes dwelte under my dwelling stone house and the seller under the said roomes for the tearme & space of ffour Score & nyneteen yeares wth free ingresse & regresse into the land under my said house during the saide tearme paying thereout to my grandchild Patrick ffanninge five shillings ster. p. anm duringe the tearme aforesaid.

---

[1] The best authorities rate a pound sterling in the reign of Charles I at nearly ten times its present value.

Item I leave & bequeath unto my sonne Bartholomew ffanninge the shoppe lyinge in the front of John Roche's stone house in S[t] Nicholas his p. ishe and his heires males forever.

Item I leave & bequeath unto my ffourth sonne Richard ffanninge the sume of sixteene thousand Reales w[h] Edemont ffanninge rec[d] from Stephen England in Spaine, or as much thereof as shall be had of him.

Item I leave and bequeath unto my sonne Richard my garden plott w[th]out S[t]. John's gate w[h] I purchased of Nicholas harrold.

Item I leave and bequeath unto the said Richard ffanninge the Tenement w[h] I purchased of Robert Waring in S[t] John's p. ishe and contayninge one hundred & fortie five foote longe, And the said Richard shall give & bestowe uppon the poor sixe pence ster. almes in bread or candles every Sunday from Mich. as till S[t] Patricks every yeare for ever out of the said house and garden.

Item I leave and bequeath unto my sonne James ffanninge the Tenem[t] w[ch] I have in S[t] Nicholas his p. ish now in the tenure of Daniel Arthur. I leave and bequeath unto Nicholas o Riurdane carpenter my pte of the Tythes of Donoghmore he paying foure pence ster. every Saterday in the yeare to the poore prisoners besides the rent due to the parson of Donoghmore aforesaid during my lease therein.

Item I leave and bequeath two hundred full & lawfull hydes to be paid to Madam Jana a widowe in S[t] Maloes or her assignes if I owe her any reckoninge.

Item I leave & bequeath unto my ffourth sonne Richard ffanninge the halfe plowe Land or quarter of Killincully lying in the countie of Clare w[h] is in mortgage unto me from Sir John McNamara for one hundred pounds and odd moneys w[h] is in the occupacon off Moghowne m[c]Conoughour the said Richard ffanninge paying unto the said Moghowne or his assigns five & twentie poundes ster. in consideracon thereof, wch the said Symon ffanninge oweth by bond unto the said mohoune.

Item I leave & bequeath to my son Richard ffanninge the revercon of the Lysense of sellinge Aquavitæ in the countie of Lymericke and ye countie of ye citie of Lymericke w[h] goes in his own name according to the patent payinge the yearly rent w[h] is tenne pounds ster. p. annum.

Item I leave & bequeath to ye said Richard ffanninge the stone house and garden lying at Inish in the p. ish of Dromcleasse in ye countie of Clare w[h] I hold by lease from my lord of Thomond, the shoppe lyinge in the front thereof onely excepted, w[h] I leave to my servant Michaell Stritch during my said lease therein, he paying ffive shillings ster. yearly rent thereout unto my said sonne Richard ffanninge.

Item I leave & bequeath unto my sonne John ffanninge the mortgadge off the halfe plough land of Ballymeknocke in the p. ish of Killnemoney w[h] I have from fflan o Neallane, immediately after the decease of my said wife.

Item I leave & bequeath to my said sonne John ffanninge the halfe ploughland of Carhineneblow in the p. ish of Kil Kidy in the countie of Limerick aforesaid after the decease of my said wife, which I purchased in the said John's name.

Item I doe bequeath and give unto my sonne Richard ffanninge the whole stocke and goods which he hath uppon his landes betwixt I and him to his owne use for ever of w[h] I hereby acquitt & discharge him for ever.

Item I leave & bequeath unto my coozin Patrick Arthur fitz Piers the sume of ffour score pounds ster. to be leavied and taken from my sonnes John ffanninge and James ffanninge concerninge the stocke & goods w[h] they have the one halfe thereof belongeth unto me to be distributed and defrayed for and towards ye paveinge of monesalluffe.

Item I leave and bequeath unto the said Patrick Arthur my p.te of the stocke and goods betwixt me and Michaell Stritch and Symon Daniel (being the one halfe of such stocke belonginge unto) to be distributed & defraied by him the said Patricke for and towards ye buildinge & erectinge off a poor house in S[t]. John's p.ish lyinge between the house of Geo: ffox on the north and the Tenem[t] of John Rice on ye south.

Item I will and soe I desire that the summe of ffortie poundes ster. shall be taken out of my goodes after payinge my debts by Nicholas ffanninge Alderman And James Stritch fitz William, gent. to be distributed by them for and towards the paveing or making of a bridge where they think best in the countie of Clare.

Item I doe make constitute nominate and appoint my sonne Richard ffanninge and my Sonne in lawe James Stritch fitz William executo[r] of this my last will and Testam[t]

And Nicholas ffanninge of Limericke Alderman and David Nihill of the same Burgesse Tuto[s] and overscers over them. In witness whereof I the said Symon ffanninge have to this my last will and testam[t] sett my hand and seale dated the xxi day of October Anno Dm. 1636.

Being p.sent also at the signeing & sealing hereof as alsoe when the said Symon ffanninge acknowledged ye same to be his last will & Testtam[t] Wee whose names ensue,
JAMES DANIEL
WILLIAM ROCHE
JOHN ARTHUR.

SYMON FFANNINGE

(SEAL)

AN INVENTORIE OF SYMON FFANNINGE OF LIMERICKE ALDERMAN HIS GOODES & CHATTELLS AS HEREAFTER FOLLOWETH.

Imprimis I have in my seller seaventeene Dickers off salted cowe hides w[h] Stephen whyte hath as an assurance for ffortie poundes ster. from May last, w[h] said 17 Dickers of hydes I leave to my servant Michael Stritch the revercon thereof after paying the sum of ffortie poundes ster. aforesaid.

Item I have in Michaell Stritch his seller elleaven dickers of salted cowe & oxe hydes w[h] I gave as an assurance to Will[m] Stritch fitz william for the pay[mt] of Thirty pounds ster. the last of May.

Item I have in mine owne seller elleaven hoggsetts of salted salmon w[h] I gage as an assurance of ffortie pounds ster. to Michaell Stritch for the payment of Dominicke Creagh and Nicholas oge Bourke w[h] I am indebted unto.

Item I have in cashell a hundred & Sixtie salted cowe & oxe hydes w[ch] I owe for them tenn pounds ster. to Symon Saule of Cashell m.chant, the revercon whereof I leave to the said Michaell Stritch after payment made of the some of tenn pounds aforseaid, in consideracon he came bound for me for the payment of Thirtie poundes ster.

Item I charge & appointe my said servant Michaell Stritch to pay over to James Stritch fitz John the sum of seaven poundes two shillings & six pence ster. of an arreare of Twentie pounds & two shillinge & six pence ster. for hoggsetts of Gassquine wyne w^{h} I was to pay to the said James att his owne adventure in ffraunce off w^{h} said sume of Twentie pounds ster. the said James Stritch and his son have received the sume of Thirteene pounds ster. both in Dublin and Lymericke.

Item I charge and appointe the said Michael Stritch to pay to James Stritch fitz John aforesaide the sume of eight pounds ster. of an arreare off neynteene dickers of hides w^{h} was to be paide to the said James his father John Stritch by appointment of Mussier Menetie off St Maloes, Burgesse.

A Note of all the debts that is due unto me.

Imprimis theres due unto me uppon Loughlin oge o Hehir high sherriffe in the countie of Clare the sume of seaventeene pounds ster. or thereabouts; w^{h} he was to pay the same uppon All Sts Day Last was twelvemonth w^{h} bond lyeth in the office off Thomond.

Item mohowne m^{c}Conoughour Roe off Thounogh in the countie off Clare, gent. and Conoughour Reatten of the same, gent. doe owe unto me by bond the sum of seaventeene poundes ster. wch they were to paie me the last yeare.

Item Donogh Oge Cunnowe of Killinbog in the Barronie of Inchequin w^{in} the countie off Clare gent. oweth me Twentie poundes ster. by bills w^{h} I had Judgem^{t} against him about June last, wch said bills lyeth in the office.

Item there is due unto me upon John m^{c}Brouddine and the rest of his sureties by bill the sume of sixe pound ster. wch bill lyeth in the office.

Item there is due unto me upon Meanus o Davoirin the sume of eight poundes & tenne shillings ster. as appeares by his lease: besides the halfe proffitt for selling of wyne & aquavitæ in the Barronie of Corcumroe.

Item Donell o Griffa, Teige oGriffa and Peirs Walsh oweth me the sume off Twentie poundes ster. wch was adiudged unto me att the court of Common pleas and att the court of Councell table in Thomond as app^{eth} by their bills besides the use thereof of w^{h} sume I received of Peirs Walch a plough garran in ffortie shillings ster.

All wch said debts I leave to my said executors Richard ffanninge and James Stritch to be disposed of by them towards the paym^t^ of my debts and my servants wages.

Item I leave and bequeath to my sonne & heire Dominicke ffanninge and Richard ffanninge equally between them the halfe of corquinroe wch I hold from the corporacon.

Item I leave & bequeath unto the said Dominicke & Richard the sum of Twentie pounds ster. for and towards the ffencing and bancking of the said lande to come unto them *for* and out of the orchard & tenemente rents wch I hold from the corporacon in mongreate land.

Item I leave & bequeath unto ye said Dominicke & Richard the sume of ffoure & thirtie shillings ster. being an arreare of rent that fell due to me uppon Cornelius Thunkoir for selling of wyne & aquavite in six mile bridge at may last.

Item I leave & bequeath unto the saide Dominicke & Richard the Sume of ffortie shillings ster. wch was due uppon the said Cornelius for the last gales rent being Michaelmas last.

Item I bequeath to legacie and leave unto my sonne Richard ffanninge the lysence of selling off wine & aquavitæ in the Barronie of Ilandes in ye countie of Clare wch I hold from his ma^tie^ by Patent in my Son John ffanninge's name. I bequeath and Leave unto the said Richard ffanninge the Lysense of sellinge off wine & aquavite in the Barronie of Tullagh.

Item I bequeath, legacie & leave unto my welbeloved wife the lysense of sellinge of wine & aquavita in the Baronie of Bunratty in ye countie of Clare, payinge his ma^ties^ rent 40^s^ ster. p. anm and after her discase the revercon thereof to come to my said sonne John ffanninge.

Item I bequeath & leave unto my said son John ffanninge the lysense of selling of wine & aquatvitæ in the Barronie of Clounderlaw and ye barronie of Ibrican payinge his ma^ties^ rent due thereout being ffoure pounds ster.

Item I leave & bequeath unto my sonne Bartholomew ffanninge the lysense of sellinge wine & aquavitæ in the baronie of corcumRoe in the countie off Clare, my whole interest therein wch goeth in John ffanninges name to my use, ye said Bartholomew paying his ma^ties^ rent due thereout.

Item I leave & bequeath unto my son James ffanninge ye lysense of sellinge of wine & aquavitæ in ye Barronie of Burrine in ye countie of Clare he payinge his ma^ties^ rent due thereout.

Item I leave & bequeath unto Patricke ffanninge my grandchild the lysense of sellinge wine & aquavitæ in the Barronie of Inishcoyn excepting onely the towne of Killinboy wch I leave to Michaell Stritch he ye said Michaell Stritch payinge rent to the said Patricke three poundes ster. p. anm and the said Patricke paying his ma^ties^ rent due thereout. Provided hereby that iff annie controversie shall att annie tyme hereafter arise betweene my wife, children & Michael Stritch concerning annie matter or legacie herein made I hereby nominate authorise and appointe Nicholas ffanninge David Nihill and James Stritch fitz William to decide determine & finally end annie such matter or cause of controversie to happen betweene them or annie of them. In witness whereof I the said Symon ffanninge have to this my Inventorie of Goods sett my hand & seale, dated the xxi day of October A° D.ni 1636

Beinge p.sent at ye signinge
& sealing hereof whose
names ensue.
JAMES DANNIELL,
WILLM ROCHE,
JOHN ARTHUR.

Probate 23 November 1637.

APPENDIX B.

(Refer to page 33.)

ABSTRACT OF WILL OF DAVID COMYN OF LIMERICK, ALDERMAN, 24 FEB., 1637. PROVc. 1637.

In the name of Jesus commends soul to Almighty God, hoping for salvation by intercession of Blessed Virgin, Blessed St. Francis, and of all the blessed "quires of Sts and angells of heaven," etc.

Wife, Katherine Arthur.

Son[1] and heir, Nicholas Comyn, to whom mansion house, etc.

[1] Given in this order in will.

Second son, Thomas, fourth son, John, fifth son, Lawrence, first son, Francis, third son, Stephen.

Daughters: Anne (£15 annuity) and Phillis, £100: if marries with consent, £400.

Brother, Robert Comyn,

"Cozen Wm Comyn and his brother Geo: Cozen John Comyn."

Patrick Comyn of Limerick, trustee.

Son Stephen studying beyond seas, £20 a year.

John Arthur, Patrick Arthur, Thomas Comyns, and many other names mentioned.

House commonly called Jenkins mills in par. of B. V. M. Limk. Comyn's castle, etc.

Witnesses Thomas Neilan, Jane Roche, Lawrence Comyn.

APPENDIX C.

(Refer to page 86.)

Copy of Deed of James[2] Fanning of Stonington (Edmund[1]) to Lieut. James Avery of New London—60 Acres, 19 January, 169⅔[1]

"Know All men ℘ These presents That I James ffaning of stonington in the Collony of Conecticott Have for Divers good Causes And valluable Considerations in hand Received And off & from Lew^t James Averie of New London: and of the Collony Above syd: to witt the sum of twentie four pounds in money with which I Acknowledg myselfe fully sattisfied Content & payed: for A house orchard and fencing And halfe the Land within the fence; joyning to the orchard: as it is now devided between me & my Brother Thomas ffaning; with the one halfe of All the Land without the fence belonging to the same farm which was my fathers Edmund ffanings Deceased, lying in the bounds of stonington: say I doe by These presents sell Allienate tranffer and make over to the sayd James Avery the house orchard and farm with the land Above mentioned, itt being the one halfe of A hundred & twentie Acres, as it was layd out by the surveighors of stonington bounded as in the Records in stonington, the house orchard Land & fencing with All the Commonage, Comonages, preveledges and Appurtenances that thereunto belongeth; and I the sayd James ffaning doe for my selfe my Heirs executors Administrators Covenant p.mise and Agree to & with the sayd

[1] *Vide* Stonington Records, Book II., p. 212.

Averie his Heirs Adminiſtrators & Aſſignes ſshall and may quietly & peaceably uſe poſſeſs improve, and dispose of the ſyd houſe orchard land and fencing without Any Lett hinderance trouble molleſtation or objection of me the ſayd ffaning or of Any of my Heirs executors Adminiſtrators or from Any other perſon, or perſons whatſoever—In Confirmation of the Above Premiſes I doe hereunto ſett my hand & seale in New London this 19th day of januarie $169\frac{1}{2}$

signed sealed & Deli:
in preſence of us

JAMES FANNING (SEAL)

JAMES MORGAN JUNIO^r:
MATHEW DUNN.

Januarie 19th: $169\frac{1}{2}$: James ffaning Appeared And did Acknowledge the Above written inſtrument to be his Act & Deed before me James Averie, Commish^r.

Entred in stonington Januarie the 26th day Anno Dom: $169\frac{1}{2}$:
℔ me JOHN STANTON Record^r

APPENDIX D.

(Refer to page 120.)

The estate of James Fanning No. 64, as distributed by the Freeholders 2 May, 1769, to his heirs, comprised very nearly all of the original grant of fifty acres to Edmund Fanning, the elder, in 1664.

APPENDIX E.

(Refer to page 152.)

An abstract of the Will of the Rev. William Fanning is given on page 151, to which the reader is referred. The full copy of will is omitted here for lack of space.

APPENDIX F.

(Refer to page 657.)

CAMP KINGS BRIDGE, 16 March, 1778.

My dear Sister:

I have received your two letters. They were both opened before I got them, pray do not write to me again by any Body, but by the Bearer Sergeant Smith, who will deliver it to me with his own hands. I love you, and your Husband, and children, most sincerely; and You may at all times depend on my best endeavors to make you all as happy as possible. If you will send me your son John, I will take the best care of him 'till he is one and Twenty years old without any expense to his Father. I wish he would come up with the Bearer, if not he must write to me. I desire my love to Brother John and all your children, and am, Your most affectionate and loving Brother,

EDM[D] FANNING.

To Mrs Hannah Wickham,

N.B. Pray give my duty and best regards to our Aged Father.

E. F.

APPENDIX G.

AUTOBIOGRAPHICAL STATEMENT OF GENERAL EDMUND FANNING, (NO. 46).

(Refer to page 672.)

I was born in the Province of New York. My Father was several years a Captain in His Majesty's service. My Mother was the daughter of Colonel Smith of Smith Town and sole Proprietor thereof. In the ninth year of my age, I was, by my father, who then lived in the city of New York, sent to a Grammar School on Long Island and some years after I was removed to the University of New Haven in Connecticut, where after four years residence I was admitted to the Degree of Bachelor of Arts. From thence I went to Harvard University at Cambridge near Boston, where I also had conferred on me the degree of Master of Arts. I was afterwards honored with the like degree at Kings College New York and Queen's College at Mecklenburg, since greatly endowed and styled Washington University in North Carolina. I have since in the year 1774 been honored with the Degree of Dr of Civil Law in the University of Oxford, England.

In the time of his Majesty's civil Government, in the year 1760, I was elected a trustee and commissioner of the incorporated Town of Hillsborough, N. Carolina, and one of the two Representatives of the County of Orange in the General Assembly. In 1762 I was admitted to the Bar as a Lawyer and also appointed by Gov[r] Dobbs, Registrar of the County of Orange. In 1765 I was appointed by Gov[r] Tryon one of the Judges of the Supreme Court of Justice in North Carolina, in the room of

Mr Justice Moore, who was dismissed from office on suspicion of his favoring the public commotions at that time existing in the Provinces and throughout America on account of what was called the "Stamp Act." This office I accepted at that perilous period of Riot and Popular discontent from a principle of Loyalty to my king and just zeal for the support of His Majesty's Government, and resigned it again to the Governor immediately after the public Ferment had subsided by the repeal of the said Act.

In 1771 Govr Tryon being removed from North Carolina to the Government of New York, he requested me to accompany him thither and immediately appointed me his Private Secretary, and Surrogate General of the Province. In 1774 I was appointed by commission from the King, Surveyor General of His Majesty's Lands in the same province. This office was given me by Lord North in consequence of my losses, sufferings, and services during the insurrection in North Carolina.

In 1759 The Indians making incursions upon the Frontier of North Carolina, the Militia of Orange County was embodied by law and the command given to me, and in this command I continued till the peace in 1763. In running the Boundary line between the Cherokee Indians and the Inhabitants of North Carolina I was employed to raise a corps of Provincials for the protection of that service with the work and pay of Colonel. In 1768 I again raised a corps of 800 Provincials to oppose the violence and threatened attempts of a large body of Insurgents styling themselves "Regulators" to resist the execution of the laws, stop the Courts of Justice and to rescue some of their principal leaders who had been apprehended and bound over to take their trial. This service performed the corps was sometime after paid off and disbanded. In that year I received the Public Thanks of Gov[r] Tryon in Council and House of Assembly for my conduct and behavior in support of the laws and Civil Government of the Province.

In 1771 I again raised and embodied a corps of Provincials to oppose and suppress the Insurrection in North Carolina and on the 16th of May commanded the left wing, of the first line in the Battle of Allamance in which action after a long and obstinate resistance from vastly superior force, the Insurgents were defeated and totally routed. Gov[r] Tryon on the Field of Battle after the action, publicly thanked me in the presence of the different Regiments saying that my King and my Country could never sufficiently reward me for my distinguished Bravery and Gallant services in the compleat and signal victory of that day.

In 1776 By Warrant from the commander in chief in America General Sir William Howe I raised the Kings American Regt. of which I was Colonel and with which I served during the Revolutionary War. In 1782 the Regiment was placed on the British Establishment and disbanded at the Peace in 1783.

MEMO. ADDED BY MRS M. W. T. CUMBERLAND, HIS DAUGHTER.

Appointed Lt. Governor of Nova Scotia 24th of February 1783.
Lieut. Governor of Prince Edward Island 26th July 1786.
Major General in the Army 12th Oct. 1793.
Lieut. General 26th June 1799.
General the 25th of April 1803.
Retired from the Gov^{rt} of Prince E. Island 1805.
Returned finally to England in 1813.
Died in London 28th of February 1818.

In a letter dated Hanover County, Va., 23 July, 1869, William Fanning Wickham wrote as follows: —

"The foregoing sketch of Gen. Edmund Fanning's family, education, services &c is from a copy sent to me by his daughters Lady Louisa Wood & Miss Maria M. Fanning in Oct. 1866 — The dates of his appointments &c subjoined are in the handwriting of one of them. They have lived many years as they still do in the City of Bath, England, where I visited them in 1852. Gen. Fanning was 79 years old at the time of his death when he was carried off by a short illness. Until then he enjoyed good health and did not suffer from the infirmities of age. He was six feet two inches in height; with a finely proportioned form, and was remarkable for his strength and activity. A portrait of him half length was taken a few years before his death in the scarlet uniform of a British General which I saw in Bath and of which my cousins sent me an excellent miniature copy."

APPENDIX H.

(Refer to page 699.)

ENHAM LODGE,
LEAMINGTON, (ENGLAND)
June 23rd 1880

My Dear Cousin;

On Saturday last, the 19th inst, I sent to Mr and Mrs Emmons, an American family residing here, and who are about revisiting your part of the world, a small Box, which they have kindly consented to take charge of as far as "New York," but as they propose remaining there only long enough to pass their luggage through the Custom House, my box must be left there unless some Person is on the spot to take charge of it. To ensure this I wrote about a fortnight since to your nephew, Mr Chapman Leigh, requesting he would be good enough to be on the lookout for the arrival of the "Britannia" Steamer in which vessel Mr and Mrs Emmons leave "Liverpool" on the 24th inst. I trust Mr Leigh's arrangements will admit of his doing me this favour. My parcel is addressed to you in *the first instance* and then to the care of Messrs Leigh & Fry in case one of them shall be absent at the time, as I am very anxious (that to me) such valued articles, shall reach you safely uninjured. The Box contains only miniatures of my dear Relations and self. That of my late dear Father in the double case is a copy taken from a large oil Painting which, you may perhaps recollect to have seen at "3 Circus Bath" and for which he sat a year or two only, before his death. The one of him in the *dark frame* is that from which the engraving I enclose was copied. My dear Brother's is from a *sketch* taken by a Brother officer at home in "India," and who, after his death, superintended the miniature in the case with my Fathers. He (my brother) died in India in 1812 aged 23 a Captain in the 22^d^ Regt.

My Father died in 1818, aged 79. The one in *green velvet* I sat for two or three years after my marriage. The last I have to mention is that of your cousin Louisa (Lady Wood) at 18 which she had painted and sent to our Brother in "India" and which he held in his hand when he died in this Country without the comfort and happiness of having one of us near him. I extremely regret not being able to send you one of my dear Sister Maria, as she would not consent to sit for her likeness now, for it would have been a beautiful Picture. She retained her sweet expression of countenance until her death. Pray excuse an abrupt conclusion as I have no time to loose in getting this posted to-day, and have to write a business letter by the same Post to an Agent in "Prince Edwd Island" in reply to one from him recd last evening. Accept and say everything that is kind to yourself and family. Hastily from your

Very affectionate cousin,

M. W. T. CUMBERLAND.

My husbands very kind regards.

To Mr. William Fanning Wickham.

APPENDIX I.

Colonel David Fanning, the Tory and notorious outlaw of North Carolina, born about 1754, was not a descendant of Edmund Fanning of Connecticut.

In his "Narrative," written by himself,[1] he refers in a schedule of property to his being "*heir to an Estate of my "father of* 550 *acres in Amelia County, Va., with dwelling "house, etc.*" A careful research of the records in that county discloses a family of Fannins who, in 1748, resided in Nottaway Parish, Amelia County (now Nottaway County since 1789). A Patent of 280 acres in Amelia County was granted by George II. to Bryan Fannin 20 July, 1748,[2] and a Patent of 308 acres in Halifax County by George III. to William, Thomas and Achilles Fannin, 15 June, 1773.[3] Elizabeth, Laughlin and John Fannin are also mentioned in the records — the latter living in Sussex County, in 1785 — but no record is found of a David Fanning. The inference, however, is he was connected with these Virginia Fannins.

[1] *Vide*, Narrative of Colonel David Fanning, giving an account of his adventures in North Carolina from 1775 to 1783, as written by himself; published Richmond, Va., 1861.

[2] *Vide*, Book 26, p. 484. [3] *Vide*, Book 42, p. 277.

APPENDIX J.

The Fannin Family of the South.

This family spells its name "Fannin," and traces its ancestry back to James Fannin, who married Elizabeth Saffold 13 October, 1767.

James Fannin was born 28 November, 1739, and died 4 November, 1803.

Elizabeth Saffold was born 12 November, 1748, and died 30 March, 1814.

They resided in Greene County, Ga., and were the progenitors of a large family of descendants, well and prominently known throughout the South.

It is common tradition among the "Fannins" that they are related to the northern "Fannings," some members claiming that James Fannin, born 1739, was a brother of General Edmund Fanning of Long Island (No. 46), but there is not a particle of evidence to sustain the claim. A long and painstaking research has not revealed any relationship. It is claimed by the Fannins that the letter "g" was dropped from their name by their earliest progenitor on account of the loyalist tendencies of some members of the family during Revolutionary times. This may be the correct explanation of their dropping the letter "g," but it does not furnish any evidence of a relationship of the Fannins to the northern family of Fannings recorded in this work,[1] and if any connection exists it has not yet been made evi-

[1] Much data of the descendants of this James Fannin, who married Elizabeth Saffold, has been collected by the author with a view of inserting it in this work, but the relationship not being proved, the genealogical data is therefore omitted. The reader is referred, however, to the very admirable record of the Fannins, recently published by Kate Haynes Fort, entitled "Memoirs of the Fort and Fannin Families," Chattanooga, Tenn., 1903.

dent. It is the opinion of the author and compiler that James Fannin of Georgia was a first settler and not related to the northern Fannings.

James and Elizabeth (Saffold) Fannin had issue: —

i. ANN, b. 18 Sept., 1769: m. 21 July, 1786, Littleton Mapp.

ii. SARAH, b. 15 Oct., 1771: m. 4 Sept., 1794, James Allison.

iii. WILLIAM Y., b. 22 Oct., 1773: m. 19 Jan., 1807, C. Martin.

iv. JOSEPH DECKER, b. 1 Jan., 1776: m. 18 March, 1802, Betsey Low.

v. ISHAM SAFFOLD, b. 17 April, 1778: m. 29 Aug., 1809, Margaret Porter.

vi. JOHN H., b. 14 May, 1780: m. 3 Feb., 1820, Mary Wright.

vii. JAMES W., b. 29 April, 1782: m. 11 Feb., 1817, Ann P. Fletcher.

viii. JEPTHAH, b. 17 Feb., 1785: m. 10 April, 1814, Kate Porter.

ix. ELIZA, b. 29 June, 1787: m. 9 April, 1811, Stephen Bishop.

x. ABRAHAM BALDWIN, b. 19 Nov., 1789: m. 15 Nov., 1821, Jane P. Williamson.

The hero of the Goliad Massacre, Colonel James W. Fannin, was related to the Southern Fannins, and a worthy member of that family. The story of his bravery and tragic death is too well known to need a lengthy account here.

He was born in Georgia about January 1, 1804, and was sent to West Point Military Academy for a short time, but did not graduate. He married in Hancock County, Ga., Miss Minerva Fort, and by her had issue, two daughters, one of whom was born two months after his death. He became a captain in the Texas service in 1835. By order of General Austin, Commander-in-Chief of the Texan forces, Captain Fannin and Captain Bowie marched at the head of ninety men to Bexar, where they defeated a superior Mexican force, 28 October, 1835. Captain Fannin was soon afterward made Colonel-of-Artillery and Inspector-General by General Houston. In January, 1836, he was sent to reinforce Dr. James Grant, who was on an expedition to Matamoras, but hearing of his defeat Fannin fell back to Goliad, which he put in a state of defense. On the 19th of March, with a force of less than four hundred men, he was attacked by the enemy in vastly superior numbers, under General Urrea, on the Coleta River, but after a desperate fight was compelled to capitulate on the 20th. It was agreed that the Texans should be treated as prisoners of war and sent back to the United States. They were then taken to Goliad, where, by orders of Santa Anna, on March 27th at dawn, three hundred and fifty-seven of the prisoners were shot, only twenty-seven escaping. Fannin was killed last.

The State of Texas honored him by naming a County after him, as did also the State of Georgia.

APPENDIX K.

James Fanning, Founder of the James Fanning Charitable Institution, Waterford, Ireland.[1]

The family of James Fanning consisted at one time of wealthy and influential landowners in the County Kilkenny,

[1] Abridged from the Report of the James Fanning Charitable Institution for 1852

who lost their estates by the Cromwellian and Williamite confiscations. His grandfather was a farmer in easy circumstances at Rochestown in the barony of Knocktopher. He had two sons, Sylvester and William. William, the younger, engaged in business in the City of Waterford, where his son James (the subject of this sketch) was born and educated.

Early in life James Fanning went to Spain and entered into business as a general merchant at Cadiz. Having realized about four thousand pounds sterling, he retired from business and returned to his native city in 1763. In December of that year he married Frances Butler, only daughter and heiress of Richard Butler, Esquire of Luffany, County Kilkenny. By this marriage he became possessed of a large personal property and considerable landed estates in the barony of Iverk, County Kilkenny.

Owing to the rigorous enforcement of the penal laws, Mr. Fanning was compelled to dispose of his landed property. In 1775 he retired to France with his wife and two children. Here he purchased the estate of LaRoche Talbot in 1777. In 1778 his wife died, and four years after his son and daughter, both unmarried.

On the outbreak of the French Revolution, James Fanning became involved in the general proscription of the nobility; and upon his flight in 1791, his property was confiscated. During the short peace of 1802, he returned to France to claim the restoration of his estates, but was unsuccessful. In 1804 he made a will in which he bequeathed one-third of his estate to his relative, Lieutenant Januarius Fanning of the Royal Italian Regiment at Naples, which Januarius, he specifies, was son to his cousin, Captain Richard Fanning, the son of his uncle Sylvester. Another third

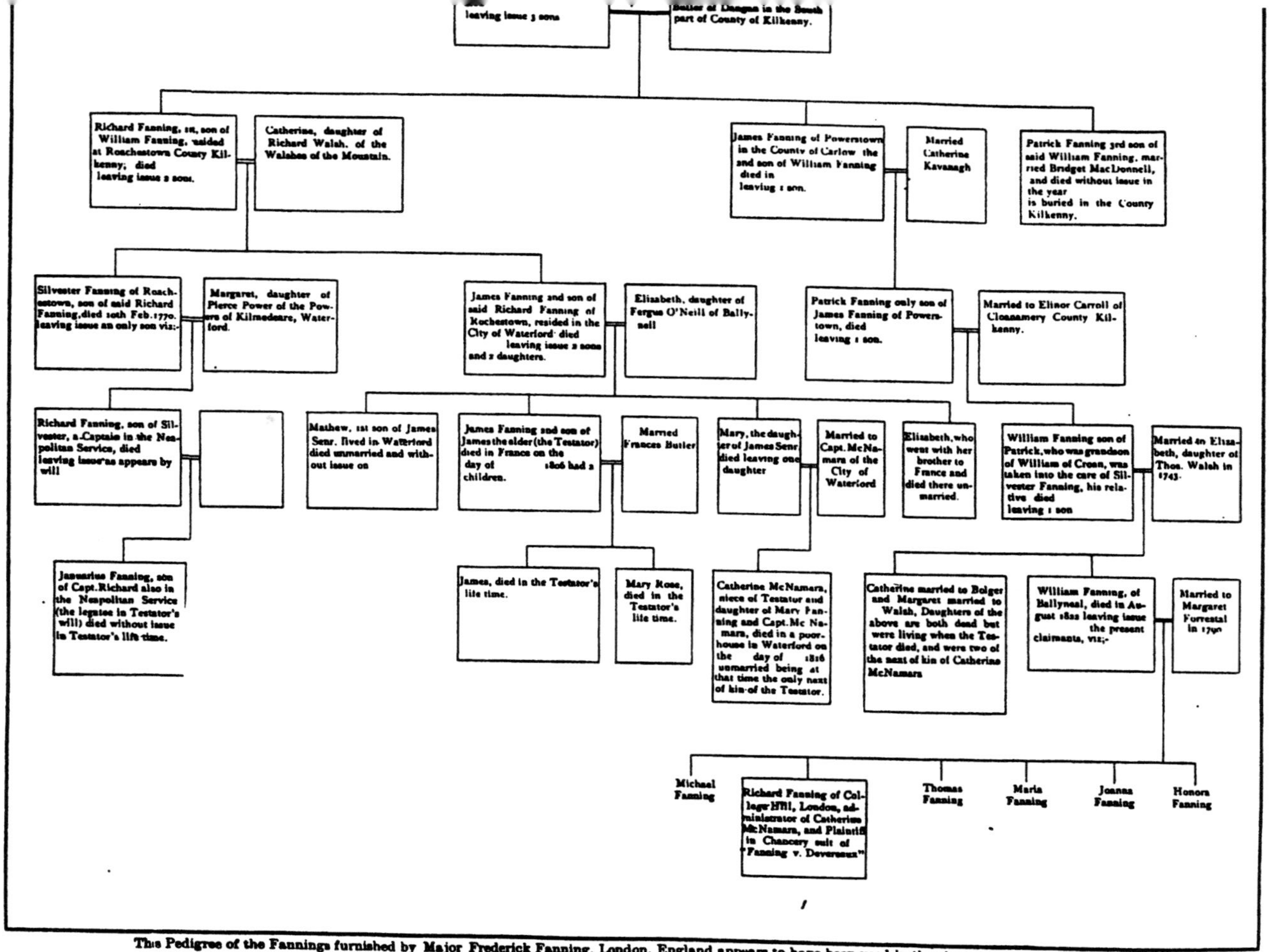

This Pedigree of the Fannings furnished by Major Frederick Fanning, London, England appears to have been used in the chancery suit of "Fanning vs Devereaux" and pertains to the Family of James Fanning of Waterford. It is printed just as received by the author and without verification.

he bequeathed to his cousin, James Edward Devereaux, and the remaining third to the poor of Waterford City. Of the four thousand acres of land, in the State of Georgia, which had been granted to him and his lately deceased brother, Mathew, by King George III., previous to the American Revolution, he bequeathed two thousand acres to James Edward Devereaux, one thousand acres to his friend, Edward Christian of London, and one thousand acres to the Baron of Beauford. Mr. Fanning died in Paris in 1806, but the will was inoperative until the peace of 1814.

Under the Convention of 1815 between Great Britain and France, a commission was constituted for the purpose of adjudicating the claims of British subjects for losses sustained during the Revolution. To this tribunal the Fanning executors submitted their claims. In 1820 an award of 760,577 francs was made in full of all their claims.

In 1821 the Board of Charitable Donations and Bequests for Ireland took measures to secure the legacy bequeathed to the poor of Waterford. Owing to various claims set up by the next of kin of Mr. and Mrs. Fanning, a tedious litigation ensued. In 1841 the matter was decided in favor of the Board of Charitable Donations and Bequests, when the Court of Chancery ordered the payment to said Board of £31,514–10*s*. in three per cent consols producing an annual income of £945–7–8.

When the order of Chancery was issued it was determined by the Corporation of Waterford to found an institution for the aged and infirm of both sexes who had seen better days and were accustomed to some of the comforts of life, but who, through no fault of their own, were unable to procure the means necessary for their support. This institution — called the James Fanning Charitable Institution — in memory of the testator, was opened in the spring of 1843, when thirty-four men and forty-three women were admitted. Since then its income has been largely increased by bequests and donations, and the aid extended to the deserving poor has been in proportion to the increase of income.

APPENDIX L.

(COPY OF LETTER RECEIVED FROM THE ULSTER KING OF ARMS, DUBLIN, IRELAND.)

1 March, 1897.

Fanning.

Dear Sir:

I have received yours of 17 Feb. and in reply beg to say that the first Registration of Arms is for "James Fanning of the City of Cadiz, merchant, lineally descended from Simon Fanning of Fanningstown Co Limerick Esquire," 10 Dec., 1759.

There being a mistake in the genealogy, it was cancelled and re-registered 22 April, 1775, for "James Fanning of Stonehouse Co Waterford Esquire, lineally descended from John Fanning of Ballingary in the County of Tipperary Esquire."

On comparing these Pedigrees, James Fanning of Cadiz (1759) and James Fanning of Stonehouse (1775) appear to be the same person.

The Arms in each case are the same. No Fanning Arms appear to have been recorded here earlier than 1759. What is the nature of the Document which gives the date 1673? Is it a Certificate, or Grant, issued by Ulster King of Arms, and how does the date appear? If you can give these particulars, I may be able to find out something further.

You have not incurred any further fees by this enquiry.

Yours faithfully,

(Signed) ARTHUR VICARS, Ulster.

W. F. BROOKS, ESQR.,
54 Queen St.,
Worcester, Mass.,
U. S. A.

(COPIES OF LETTERS RECEIVED FROM JOHN O'HART, THE EMINENT AUTHORITY AND ANTIQUARIAN, OF IRELAND.)

1, WOODSIDE, VERNON AVE.,
CLONTARF, IRELAND.
26, February, 1898.

WALTER F. BROOKS, ESQ.,
Worcester, Mass., U. S. A.,

My dear Sir:

Your letter of the 12th instant has reached me. In reply, I feel pleasure in sending you the enclosed *Memoranda* which I have found among my Papers since I received your letter — bearing on the "Fanning" family; whose pedigree I give in p. 202, Vol. II., of the two-volume edition of my *Irish Pedigrees*. For the greater reference' sake I mark them A. B. C., etc., and in chronological order.

It strikes me that Mem. (C) will give you the information you desire. I am unable to give you any additional information. . . .

I may observe that this family name has been variously spelled: *Fanan*, *Faning*, *Fanning*, and *Fanninge* (with an *e* final).

The Notes from which I compiled my "Pedigrees" were unfortunately destroyed when, in 1889, on the death of my only son (in his fortieth year of age, and unmarried) I left Ringsend, and went to live at the sea-side in Kilkee, County Clare, where, in my grief, I meant to spend the remainder of my life! For family reasons, however, as well as to be near my last resting-place with my dear son in Glasnevin Cemetery, I returned to Dublin in 1892.

In my present old age my dear wife feared that my health could not stand the strain of the labour and fatigue which any further genealogical research should entail. Submitting to her entreaties, I then assented to destroy all my Genealogical Notes from which, as above mentioned, my "Pedigrees" were compiled. But fortunately the Notes mentioned in the enclosed *Memoranda* were not in the portfolio then destroyed.

Before I found these *Memoranda* on yesterday I had written to a gentleman of the "Fanning" family, requesting any information on the subject of your letter which he might be able to give me. But I am satisfied that the gentleman (if he reply to my letter) cannot give me more definite information *re Edward or Edmund Fanning* who, in 1653, emigrated to America and settled in Connecticut, than I give in said Mem. (C).

If I hear from the gentleman here alluded to, I shall let you know.

I may here mention that Vol. I., of the People's Edition of my *Irish Pedigrees* is in the hands of Mr. P. J. Kenedy, Book Publisher, 5 Barclay Street, New York City, who tells me the work wll be ready for delivery this spring. My two-volume Edition of the "Pedigrees" was considered too voluminous and necessarily too expensive to meet the means of legions of our countrymen in the New World, who would be glad to learn the origin of their respective families. Vol. II., of the People's Edition of the "Pedigrees" will follow, whenever called for by Mr. Kenedy.

My kindest regards.

Very sincerely yours

(Signed) JOHN O'HART.

(Memo. referred to in above letter.)

(A.) Nicholas Fanning was in 1641 the Proprietor of Lower Englandstown, in the Parish of Askeaton, Barony of Connello, and County of Limerick, whose forfeited lands were conveyed to Brook Bridges.

(B.) Thomas Fanning was one of the A.D. 1649 Officers, who served Charles II. in the Wars of Ireland, before the 5th day of June, 1649.

(C.) Simon Fanning, Mayor of Limerick, who died 7th March, 1636, and who is (see p. 202, Vol. II., of the two-volume Edition of my *Irish Pedigree*) No. 4 on the "Fanning" of Ballingarry and Fanningstown, Co. Tipperary, pedigree, had a brother named Francis, whose name appears in the "Connaught Certificates," 1653–1654. This Francis had a son *Edward* or *Edmond*, who, in the then unhappy state of Ireland under the Commonwealth Rule, emigrated in 1653 to America and settled in Connecticut.

(D.) John, eldest brother of Dominick, who is No. 5 on the "Fanning" pedigree, was enrolled among the "Decrees of Innocents," under the Cromwellian Rule in Ireland.

(E.) Geoffrey Fanning of Ballingarry forfeited in the reign of Charles II., under the Act of Settlement, A.D. 1661.

(F.) Richard, a younger brother of Dominick Fanning, who is No. 5 on the "Fanning" pedigree, served in 1663 as "Capitan Don Ricardo Fanan," in the Spanish Netherlands.

(G.) Jeffrey Fanning, of Fanningstown, Co. Tipperary, married Gyles, daughter of Thomas Power (d. 1637), son of James, son of Thomas of Cullefin, Co. Waterford, son of Richard, Lord Power. This Jeffrey's name appears among the "Names of Persons in the Grants," under the Act of Settlement, A.D. 1661.

(Signed) JOHN O'HART.

Clontarf, Ireland,
26 February, 1898.

1, WOODSIDE,
VERNON AVENUE, CLONTARF,
DUBLIN, 28-3-98.

WALTER BROOKS, ESQ.,
Worcester, Mass., U. S. A.

My dear Sir:

In reply to your letter of the 14th instant I regret to have to say that, so far, the only information I can give you bearing on the "Fanning" family — outside of what is given in the family pedigree, in p. 202, Vol. II., of the two-volume Edition of my *Irish Pedigrees* — is contained in the *Memoranda* I lately sent you. Since I sent you that information, I have, I assure you, looked up every available source, but, so far, with no success. I shall continue the research, with God's help; and I shall in the Public Record Office, Four Courts, Dublin, look up the Will of *Francis Fanning* — if he left one — and, if he did, I shall send you the contents thereof.

Unfortunately I cannot recall where I got this or that information contained in my Books; but I am satisfied that, when I noted any information for insertion in my works, the sources of my information were reliable and authentic!

After the death of my good son I retired from Ringsend, Dublin, and went to live in my grief to Kilkee, Co. Clare, where I meant to spend the remainder of my life. On leaving Ringsend I sold my Library; and, at the request of my dear wife (who, on account of my health and old age, entreated me to destroy all the papers which I employed in the compilation of my Books, so as to publish no further Editions of my works) I assented to destroy most of my Notes — those contained in one of my portfolios. Now I keenly feel the loss of those papers; for, from family reasons, I found it advisable to come back to Dublin, in 1892; and have since condensed each of the two large volumes of my *Irish Pedigrees*, for publication in America. The first of these two condensed volumes is now in the hands (as I think I already told you) of Mr. P. J. Kenedy, Publisher, 5 Barclay Street, New York, who, in November last, wrote me that said Vol. I of the People's Edition would be ready for delivery in this Spring.

In the "copy" of Vol. II. of the People's Edition of the *Irish Pedigrees*, which I have ready for Mr. Kenedy whenever he calls for it, after Vol. I. is published, I have, in continuation of the narrative under Simon, No. 4, on the "Fanning" pedigree, added the following:—

"This Simon Fanning had a brother named Francis, whose name appears in the 'Connaught Certificates,' in 1653-1654, and whose son Edward or Edmond, in the then unhappy state of Ireland under the Cromwellian Rule, emigrated to America in 1653, and settled in Connecticut."

My kindest regards.

Very faithfully yours,

(Signed) JOHN O'HART.

APPENDIX M.

FISHERS ISLAND.[1]

John Winthrop, Junior, obtained from the General Court of Massachusetts on the 7th of October, 1640, a grant of Fishers Island, which was confirmed to him by the Connecticut Court, 9 April, 1641. The Island had been regarded as belonging to Connecticut, but in 1664 it was included in the patent of New York, and Winthrop obtained from Governor Nichols of that colony a patent dated 28 March, 1668, which confirmed to him the possession of the Island.[2] It is probable that he began building and planting

[1] "It is said the oldest deed in America, probably, is in the possession of Major Leland of New York. It antedates the landing of the Pilgrims one hundred and ten years, and was written eighteen years after the discovery of the new world by Columbus. It is a deed of Fishers Island, near the mouth of Long Island Sound, by certain Indian chiefs to John Cabot, the celebrated navigator, and bears his signature."

[2] *Vide*, History of New London, Conn., by Frances M. Caulkins, last edition, p. 40.

there in the spring of 1644 and his house is said to have been the first English residence in the Pequot country.[1] Gov. Winthrop died 5 April, 1676, and his real estate including Fishers Island, descended to his two sons Fitz John and Wait Still and was possessed by them jointly during their lives. Fitz John having no male issue, it descended to John, only son of Wait Still.[2] Miss Caulkins, in her "History of New London," states that William Walworth was lessee of Fishers Island under Fitz John Winthrop about 1690, coming over from England at the invitation of the owner who wished to introduce English methods of farming, and later his son, John Walworth, leased it for a long term of years.[3] Joshua Hempstead of New London, on page 89 of his Diary, makes mention of the houses on Fishers Island under date of June, 1719: "I was at Fishers Island all day (except ye going over) we Rode a(bout) West End to See ye Island & Deer &c." . . . "wee Rode fr ( ) End where wee Lodged to the East-house & there wee dined & came away." This would signify that there were two houses on the Island at this time — one at the west, and the other at the east end.

In April, 1727, "Ms. Havens moved off Fishers Island & al her Children & servts."[4] and Charles Dickinson, Senior, hired it the next two years[5] and probably until 1731 as Hempstead at that time, together with Justice Richmond and Mr. Mumford, went over to receive the stock of him,

[1] *Vide*, History of New London, Conn., etc., supra, p. 41.
[2] *Ibid.* p. 189.
[3] *Ibid.* p. 345.
[4] *Vide*, Diary of Joshua Hempstead of New London, etc., 1901, p. 183.
[5] *Ibid.* p. 200.

and speaks of viewing the house at the east end.[1] In the spring of 1735-6, Captain George Mumford leased Fishers Island.[2] In 1738 Mumford was still on the Island, as Hempstead tells in his Diary that he, with some others, had set sail for Sag Harbor in November and the wind and sea, being too great, "wee got Safe into fishers Island Hay harbour about 9 Clock & After about 2 hours Stay went up to the House where wee Stayed al night & Mr. Mumford Entertained us very courteously & would take nothing of me or mine."[3]

From the foregoing it would seem that Mr. Mumford lived in the house at the west end near Hay Harbor. In October, 1739, Hempstead with Madam Winthrop, Mr. Saltonstall, and several others went over to the Island with George Mumford in his boat. He says, "wee all Rid Down to the East End & back & Lodged at Mr. Mumfords again." . . . "wee all hands Rid out to the west End Med. & Woods aftern We went a hunting Deer."[4] John Winthrop died in London in 1747,[5] and his son John Still came into possession of the Island. In August, 1752, he, with Hempstead, went over to the Island and Hempstead writes in his Diary "wee measured the Length of the Island almost. wee began att the west point & Measured Six mile towards the East End & made heaps of Stones att the End of Each Mile & also measured the Distance from ye house to ye West point & also to ye East End."[6]

[1] *Vide*, Diary of Joshua Hempstead of New London, etc., 1901, p. 233.
[2] *Ibid.* p 300.
[3] *Ibid.* p. 342.
[4] *Ibid.* p. 356.
[5] *Ibid.* p. 490.
[6] *Ibid.* p 594.

Mumford continued to lease the Island until 1756, when Winthrop rented it to Benjamin Brown, of Rhode Island, for £500 per annum.[1] On the 7th of May that year Mr. Winthrop, with Justice Perkins, Captain Mathew Griswold, and Mr. Hempstead, went over to the Island to receive the stock of Mumford and delivered it to Brown, the new tenant, who was already there with his family.[2]

Brown was still on the Island in 1777. Miss Caulkins, in her "History of New London," says that the British ships on the 5th and 6th of May, 1775, took 1,100 sheep, besides cattle and other provisions from Fishers Island,[3] and on the 14th of March, 1777, the British fleet seized and nearly swept the Island clean of supplies of all kinds as they had the previous year, for all of which they made reasonable compensation to Mr. Brown.[4] On the death of John Still Winthrop in 1776,[5] Fishers Island descended to his son John, who in his will, proved 5 October, 1784, gave it to his brother Francis Bayard Winthrop.[6] Francis Bayard Winthrop, at his death left it to his son, William H., who in his will, proved 11 September, 1860,[7] ordered it to be sold. The sale of the Island was made 2 December, 1863, by Jane P. Chester and Mary T. Pratt (daughters of William H. Winthrop) to Robert R. Fox[8] for $55,000. The heirs of Robert Fox sold it 19 July, 1889, to Edmund

[1] *Vide*, Diary of Joshua Hempstead of New London, etc., 1901, p. 665

[2] *Ibid.* p. 668.

[3] *Vide*, History of New London, Conn., by Frances M. Caulkins, last edition, p. 517.

[4] *Ibid.* p. 525.

[5] *Vide*, New London Records, Book I, p. 510.

[6] *Ibid.* Book I, p. 125.

[7] *Ibid.* Book XIII, p. 369

[8] *Vide*, Suffolk County Records Book 124, p. 162.

M. Ferguson of Pittsburg, Pa. (one of the present owners), for $250,000.[1]

The Fergusons sold a small area of it in 1898 and in 1901 to the United States for the purposes of a fortification and fort, and it is said received $167,000 for it.

M. G. Goodell was the resident manager at the east end of the Island in 1902.

[1] *Vide*, Suffolk County Records, Book 321, p. 185.

ADDENDA.

PAGE 66. The "Diary of Joshua Hempstead," published since the early pages of this work went to press proves that the original Edmund[1] Fanning (No. 1) house at Stonington, Conn., referred to on page 66 of this work was torn down, 25 May, 1722, by William Denison, "in presence of Jo, Denison, Gershom Holdridge, and Edmund Fanning" (grandson of Edmund Fanning, Senior).[1] For this act, Hempstead, who owned the farm and house, recovered damages of Denison in a suit at law.

In December, 1742, Hempstead leased the Fanning farm to Daniel and William Bennett for £20 per annum for three years, they to build a house on it and leave it for him.[2] The house was evidently constructed soon afterward, for Hempstead wrote in his diary 1 May, 1750, "Chris Eldredge is got on ye upper most in the house "william Bennet & Danll Built. Wm is Still there."[3] Hempstead wrote, 30 March, 1750-51: "Ichabod Wick-"wire & Jonat Hamilton came from Paugwonk to buy "my upper farm (Fanning farm) and offered £700."[4] Hempstead evidently did not sell as Christopher Eldredge was living there at the time of Hempstead's death in 1758.

There is evidence of but one cellar-hole and the house built about 1743 was probably constructed on the site of the original house of Edmund Fanning, and presumably is the one, a plan of which is shown on page 66, and was torn down in 1842 by Clark N. Whitford.

PAGE 91. The widow of Edmund[2] Fanning (No. 2) was living in 1720, and was the "widow Fanning" referred to in the "Diary of Joshua Hempstead," 20 Dec., 1720, page 104.

PAGE 93. Catherine[3] Fanning (No. 14). The will of Katharine Page of Stonington is on record at New London,[5] dated 2 June, 1763, proved 2 Aug., 1763, and mentions grand-

[1] *Vide*, "Diary of Joshua Hempstead of New London. Conn." pub., 1901, p. 121.

[2] *Ibid*, p. 403.

[3] *Ibid*, p. 548.

[4] *Ibid*, p. 567.

[5] Probate Records, Book H., p. 282.

daughter Hannah Page, brother James Fanning, daughter Katharine, and Richard Fanning (Executor). Inventory completed 8 Aug., 1763, by Oliver Grant and Joshua Grant.

PAGE 98. Zerviah^{4} Niles (No. 23) joined the Baptist Church at Groton, Conn., 3 Nov., 1770.[1]

PAGE 99. "Those who have joined (the Church) since 1769, "Oct. 26, — Fear^{4} Stanton." (No. 26.)[2]

PAGE 100. Twenty-seventh line: "XII. DEBORAH HALEY," etc. Mrs. Henry Stanton, Stonington, Conn., says: "I know from old people that Elihu Hancox' wife was John Haley's daughter and that they lived near the Road Church District. . . . Elihu Hancox (sometimes called Elisha) was a son of Edward and Lucy (Chesebrough) Hancox, m. 1741. The name of Elihu or Elisha gives him away as to his mother's parentage. My mother often said this old ditty:

> "Joseph Cutler lives at the Mill
> Elisha Haley lives on the Hill,
> Blind Dewey lives at the Rocks,
> Wheedle-te-cut, old Johny Hancocks!"

These people lived below the old Dr. Grey place on an old Road that led to the village of Stonington.

PAGE 101. The Diary of Joshua Hempstead furnishes further data about Jonathan^{3} Fanning (No. 11): "Jonathan Fan-"ning and Elizabeth Way published January 3, 17$\frac{13}{14}$

"Child baptised, Elizabeth, June 24, 1716.

"Child baptised, Jonathan, Oct. 27, 1717.

"Child baptised, Thomas, Apr. 23, 1721."

PAGE 103. Last four lines: The Mattituck, L. I., Church Records give date of death of James^{3} Fanning (No. 15), 15 April, 1779, which agrees with the "Salmon" Record, and is no doubt the correct date.

PAGE 110. Katharine^{4} Fanning (No. 49). The Mattituck, L.I., Church Records (Presbyterian) state "David Mulford of "Brookhaven and Catharine Fanning of Aquebogue were "married 23 July, 1775. Issue:

"JAMES FANNING MULFORD, baptised May 17, 1778.

"DAVID MULFORD, baptised May 17, 1778."

---

[1] *Vide*, Groton Baptist Church Records at Old Mystic, Conn.

[2] *Ibid.*

PAGE 114. William[3] Fanning (No. 22) may have had a second wife, Joanna Bellows, born 24 March, 1711, daughter of Nathaniel and Dorcas (Rose) Bellows of Groton, Conn.[1] The will of Nathaniel Bellows of Groton recorded at New London, Book H. p. 158, dated 17 May, 1762, proved 10 August following, mentions son Ithamar, grandson John, daughters Damaris, Joanna, Margaret, and Dorcas. He gave to his daughters Joanna and Margaret ". . . meet "recompense for their extraordinary care of him since his "wife's death."

PAGE 127. David[4] Fanning (No. 33). The will of Mary Fish of Stonington, is recorded at New London, Book H, p. 295. It is dated 21 June, 1763, proved 15 August following and mentions daughter Abigail Fanning of Groton, wife of David Fanning, eldest granddaughter (but gives no name), granddaughter Wealthie Fanning, daughters-in-law Lucretia Fish and Jemima Fish, and appoints David Fanning of Groton, her executor. Estate inventoried 14 Aug., 1763, £31–19–01.

PAGE 129. Last line of text: Thomas Fanning was probably No. 160 in this work.

PAGE 138. Thomas[4] Fanning (No. 38). Thomas Fanning and Jonathan Havens were Town Assessors of Shelter Island in 1754. Thomas Fanning and Thomas Conklin were Overseers of the Poor of Shelter Island in 1757.[2]

PAGE 154. Gilbert[4] Fanning (No. 44). Capt. Nathaniel Fanning then "of Stonington," on the 12th of Nov., 1801, gave a life lease of the house and lot formerly owned by his brother William, to his parents, Gilbert and Huldah Fanning, who were living there at the time. Gilbert died[3] in this house 18 December, 1801. The lot was a 16-rod house-lot on Union Street — the first lot west of the new Baptist Church, corner of Main and Union Streets.

[1] *Vide*, Groton Deeds, Book VI., p. 220, which deed refers to "our cousin Nathaniel Bellows of Groton, a minor child," etc., in 1768, and is signed by William and Joanna Fanning of Stonington. Also *Vide*, "Bellows Genealogy," by Thomas Bellows Peck, Keene, N. H., 1898, pp. 621, 622.

[2] *Vide*, "Shelter Island and its Presbyterian Church," by Rev. Jacob E. Mallmann, N. Y., 1899.

[3] *Vide*, Stonington Deeds, Book XIV., p. 273; also p. 489.

Nathaniel, still "of Stonington," sold the above property to Benjamin Smith, 30 Sept., 1802.

The widow Huldah was residing in this house at that time, but removed and possibly went to live with her son, Captain Henry Fanning at New Rochelle, N. Y., where she died in December, 1813.[1]

PAGE 163. Phineas[5] Fanning (No. 120). He was not Phineas Fanning of Norwich, N. Y., in 1804, as the latter was no doubt No. 73 on page 203 of this work.

PAGE 171. Richard[4] Fanning (No. 55). His wife Hannah was born in 1706.

PAGE 172. In second line after the words "Preston Centre" insert: "He was born in Stonington, Conn., was a soldier in the Revolutionary War and died at Preston Centre, Chenango Co., N. Y., 20 Aug., 1848, aged 86 years. Buried in the family burying-ground in a corner of the Eccleston farm. The headstone, however, with others has been recently removed and stands against a stone wall, and the ground over the graves is now in a state of cultivation.

---

[1] It is to be regretted that so many errors have crept into print about the homesteads and residences of the Fannings at Stonington. Miss Grace D. Wheeler, in her "Homes of our Ancestors in Stonington, Conn.," published 1903, gives illustrations or descriptions of three Fanning houses and localities, every one of which is erroneous.

On page 57 she gives an illustration of "*The Fanning House, built by Gilbert Fanning about 1750.*" There is no evidence whatever that the author can find to show Gilbert Fanning (or his son Nathaniel) ever owned or occupied this house. He resided at Stonington Long Point. (*Vide*, footnote, p. 737.)

Page 128 gives an illustration of the "*Capt. Edmund Fanning House.*" This was never the *Edmund* Fanning house but was the *Gilbert* Fanning house. The *Captain Edmund Fanning* house was on the corner of Water and Trumbull Streets.

On page 270 Miss Wheeler states "*The First Fanning house was situated southwest of the home of Miss Emma A. Smith, on the Stanton land.*" This is entirely wrong, as no Fanning ever built on this Stanton farm. The first house of the Fannings was north of Hempstead Plains, near the Everard Whitford house, three miles from the old cellar hole on the Smith farm referred to.

PAGE 299. After twenty-sixth line insert: "Frederick Lester Gardner died at Norwich, Conn., 31 January, 1905, and was buried in Yantic Cemetery."

PAGE 306. After thirteenth line insert: "Mary Brown was a widow Barber when Capt. Rufus Fanning married her, and a relative of old John Brown of Kansas fame."

PAGE 412. After last line on page insert: Gurdon McClarahan Fanning, died at Norwich, Conn., 25 May, 1904.

ERRATA.

PAGE 135. Last line: Read "in 1716," instead of "about 1700."
PAGE 159. Third and fourth lines: Read "£348-0-7," instead of "£346-0-7."[1]
PAGE 162. Twenty-third line: Read "Thomas Edmund[5], b. at Stonington," etc., instead of "Thomas[5], b. at Stonington."
PAGE 171. Last paragraph of sketch, "He died at Preston, N.Y., about 1825 and his widow about 1835." Read: "He died at Preston, N. Y., 23 July, 1809, aged 73 years. She died at Preston, N. Y., 3 May, 1826, aged 90 years. Buried on their farm at Preston Centre, N. Y.
PAGE 176. Twenty-second line: Read "Strombolo," instead of "Stromboli."
PAGE 260. Last line: Read "Frederick Deveau[6]," instead of "Frederick DeVeau.[6]"
PAGE 266. Third line from last: Read "in his 75th year," instead of "in her 75th year."
PAGE 298. Eighth line: Read "Henry Willson[6]," instead of "Henry Wilson[6]."
PAGE 324. Fourth line from bottom: Read "Simeon Benjamin[7], born at Franklinville, L. I., 31 Dec., 1827," instead of "1828."
PAGE 415. Fifth line from bottom: Read "James Madison Bromley," instead of "James L. Bromley."
PAGE 427. Fourteenth line: Read "Elisha Philander[8]," instead of "Elisha Philip[8]."
PAGE 435. Fourth line from bottom of page: Read "Henry Canoll," instead of "Henry Carroll."
PAGE 480. Second line from bottom: Read "Los Angeles," instead of "Los Ageles."
PAGE 517. Twelfth line: Read "29 Sept., 1849," instead of "30 Sept., 1849."
PAGE 629. Eighteenth line: Read "Roswell Brown," instead of "Daniel Brown."
PAGE 703. Fifth, tenth, and twenty-eighth lines: Read "Strombolo," instead of "Stromboli."
PAGE 704. Fourth line, *ibid.*

Wherever the wills of the Long Island Fannings read "on file at Riverhead," read "recorded at Riverhead."

[1] *Vide*, Stonington Probate Records, Book IV., p. 95.

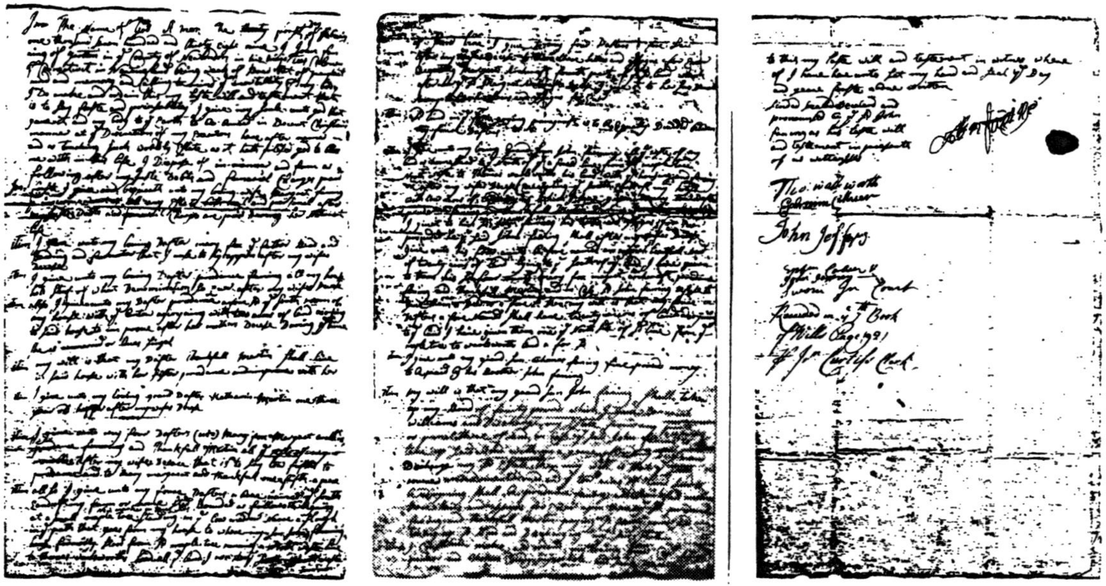

Will of Lieut John Fanning Groton Conn
February 1st 1738 9

INDEX TO FANNING NAMES

INDEX TO NAMES OTHER THAN FANNING

[Intermarriages and descendants]

MISCELLANEOUS INDEX